DATE DUE

1-7-18			
GAYLORD			PRINTED IN U.S.A.

CRITICAL READINGS OF
JOHN 6

BIBLICAL INTERPRETATION SERIES

VOLUME 22

CRITICAL READINGS OF JOHN 6

EDITED BY

R. ALAN CULPEPPER

R. Alan Culpepper, Ph. D. (1974), Duke
University, is Dean of the Mercer School
of Theology. His recent publications
include *John, the Son of Zebedee: The Life
of a Legend* (1994) and *"Luke" in the New
Interpreter's Bible, Vol. 9* (1995).

BRILL
LEIDEN · NEW YORK · KÖLN
1997

This book is printed on acid-free paper.

ISSN 0928-0731
ISBN 90 04 10579 4

CONTENTS

vi   CONTENTS

PREFACE

A collection of essays by an impressive array of international scholars offers readers a distinctive resource. It focuses attention on the importance of the topic under discussion, in this case the interpretation of John 6. It also simulates a seminar or conference in which papers are presented and discussed, and indeed the present volume began as a collection of papers presented at the Johannine Writings Seminar of the Studiorum Novi Testamenti Societas between 1991 and 1993. This core of papers was supplemented by others that extend the discussion of John 6 into additional areas. The chief value of a collection of essays such as this one, however, lies in the opportunity it affords the reader to view a complex subject from a variety of perspectives and to consider a series of alternative theses.

In this collection the reader will find essays on John 6 that use various methods and approaches to interpretation, and essays that treat various parts of this chapter. Rather than a survey of the Gospel that treats broad topics in a more cursory fashion, this collection allows the reader to explore the strength of prevailing theories regarding the origin and composition of the Gospel of John as they are applied to one of the Gospel's central chapters. John 6 has been the focus in recent scholarship of theories regarding the composition history of the Gospel, the history of the Johannine community, the relationship between sign and discourse material in the Gospel, the tension between free will and determinism in Johannine theology, the role of the Eucharist in John, the function of Johannine metaphors, the Gospel's use of motifs drawn from the Jewish Wisdom tradition, and many other important and enticing issues. The montage of different perspectives in this volume further sensitizes the reader to the richness of the Gospel, the multiple layers of its historical, literary, and theological elements, and the challenges it poses for contemporary interpreters. By the time readers reach the end of the collection they will be able to draw interesting conclusions regarding areas of agreement and divergence in the interpretation of this chapter and the Gospel of John as a whole. They will also be able to focus questions for further discussion. The essays, therefore, represent an ongoing conversation, and they are offered as an invitation and stimulus for further fruitful conversation about the intriguing complexity of the Fourth Gospel and the interpretations it has spawned in contemporary Johannine scholarship.

Because this volume is a collaborative effort, thanks are due to many people who have participated in its development and publication. We thank the authors who have contributed their creative work freely, exchanging ideas, responding to one another, and inviting readers to join in the interpretive dialogue with the text. The SNTS, and its Johannine seminar in particular, has served New Testament scholarship well as a forum for international and multi-lingual discussion. Several of the essays in this collection, originally submitted as papers for the seminar, were subsequently published elsewhere and are reproduced here by permission. Johannes Beutler's essay was originally published in German under the title, "Zur Struktur von John 6," in *Studien zum Neuen Testament und seiner Umwelt* 16 (1991), 89-104. Peder Borgen's "John 6: Tradition, Interpretation and Composition," was published in Martinus C. de Boer, ed., *From Jesus to John: Essays on Jesus and New Testament Christology in Honour of Marinus de Jonge*, JSNTS 84 (Sheffield: Sheffield Academic Press, 1993). Maarten J. J. Menken's essay, "John 6:51c-58: Eucharist or Christology," originally appeared in *Biblica* 74 (1993), 1-26. John Painter's "Jesus and the Quest for Eternal Life" is based on a short main paper presented at the Cambridge SNTS meeting in 1988 that was published under the title, "Tradition and Interpretation in John 6," in *New Testament Studies* 35 (1989), 421-50. It has appeared in more developed forms in *The Quest for the Messiah* (Edinburgh: T. & T. Clark, 1991 and 1993). Ludger Schenke's contribution to the present volume was first published in German as "Das johanneische Schisma und die 'Zwölf' (Johannes 6.60-71)," *New Testament Studies* 38 (1992), 105-21. David E. Orton, who has encouraged and contributed to this volume in many other ways also, kindly prepared the English translation of Schenke's essay. Robert Baker did some of the early editing of these essays, and Mrs. Cynthia Cobb ably assisted in preparing the final draft of camera ready copy.

Finally, I wish to express my gratitude to the contemporary "Johannine School"—that group of New Testament scholars whose vocation is the interpretation of this intriguing Gospel. Their intelligence and creativity, ably represented in this volume, is truly remarkable. One suspects that their civility and collegiality even in the midst of sharply conflicting points of view—which could be a model for scholars in many other disciplines—is probably born of their perennial brooding over the depths of the Gospel of John.

R. Alan Culpepper

CONTRIBUTORS

Prof. Paul N. Anderson
George Fox College
Newberg, OR 97132

Prof. Johannes Beutler, SJ
Hochschule Sankt Georgen
Offenbacher Landstr. 224
D-60599 Frankfurt a.M.
Germany

Prof. Peder Borgen
Department of Religious Studies
University of Trondheim
7055 Dragvoll-Trondheim
Norway

Dr. R. Alan Culpepper
McAfee School of Theology
Mercer University
3001 Mercer University Drive
Atlanta, GA 30341-4415

Dr. Robert Kysar
Candler School of Theology
Emory University
Atlanta, GA 30322

Prof. Maarten Menken
Oude Arnhemseweg 315
3705 BG Zeist
The Netherlands

Prof. Francis J. Moloney
Salesian Theological College
Bosco Street
Chadstone
Vic 3148
Australia

Prof. Gail R. O'Day
Candler School of Theology
Emory University
Atlanta, GA 30030

Prof. John Painter
Religious Studies
La Trobe University
Bundoora
Victoria 3083
Australia

Prof. Dr. Ludger Schenke
Mainzer Weg 6
6501 Klein Winternheim
Germany

Dr. Marianne Meye Thompson
Fuller Theological Seminary
Box O
Pasadena, CA 91182

ABBREVIATIONS

ACEBAC	Association Catholique des Études Bibliques au Canada
AAR	American Academy of Religion
AB	Anchor Bible
ANRW	*Aufstieg und Niedergang der römischen Welt*
AusBR	*Australian Biblical Review*
BAGD	W. Bauer, W. F. Arndt, F. W. Gingrich, and F. W. Danker, *Greek-English Lexicon of the NT*
BETL	Bibliotheca ephemeridum theologicarum lovaniensium
BEVT	Beiträge zur evangelischen Theologie
Bib	*Biblica*
BibSciRel	Biblioteca di scienze religiose
BLE	*Bulletin de la littérature ecclésiastique*
BN	*Biblische Notizen*
BTB	*Biblical Theology Bulletin*
BU	Biblische Untersuchungen
BZ	*Biblische Zeitschrift*
Conc	Concilium
ConNT	Coniectanea neotestamentica

ABBREVIATIONS

CBQ	*Catholic Biblical Quarterly*
Drev	*Downside Review*
EB	Echter Bibel
ExpTim	*Expository Times*
EWNT	*Exegetisches Wörterbuch zum Neuen Testament*
FRLANT	Forschungen zur Religion und Literatur des Alten und Neuen Testaments
HKNT	Handkommentar zum Neuen Testament
HTKNT	Herders theologischer Kommentar zum Neuen Testament
HNT	Handbuch zum Neuen Testament
HTCNT	Herder's Theological Commentary on the New Testament
ICC	International Critical Commentary
JBL	*Journal of Biblical Literature*
JJS	*Journal of Jewish Studies*
JSNT	*Journal for the Study of the New Testament*
JSNTSup	Journal for the Study of the New Testament Supplement Series
JSOT	*Journal for the Study of the Old Testament*
JTS	*Journal of Theological Studies*
LQ	*Lutheran Quarterly*

LSJ	Liddell-Scott-Jones, *Greek-English Lexicon*
LTP	*Laval théologique et philosophique*
MDB	Le monde de la Bible
MeyerK	H. A. W. Meyer, Kritisch-exegetischer Kommentar über das Neue Testament
NCB	New Century Bible
NedTTS	*Nederlands theologisch tijdschrift*
NIB	New Interpreter's Bible
NovT	*Novum Testamentum*
NovTSup	Novum Testamentum, Supplements
NTAbh	Neutestamentliche Abhandlungen
NTD	Das Neue Testament Deutsch
NTOA	Novum Testamentum et Orbis Antiquus
NTS	*New Testament Studies*
ÖTKNT	Ökumenischer Taschenbuchkommentar zum Neuen Testament
RB	*Revue Biblique*
RHE	*Revue d'histoire ecclésiastique*
RSR	*Recherches de science religieuse*
SBB	Stuttgarter biblische Beiträge

ABBREVIATIONS

SBL	Society of Biblical Literature
SBLDS	SBL Dissertation Series
SBLSBS	SBL Sources for Biblical Studies
SBS	Stuttgarter Bibelstudien
SJLA	Studies in Judaism and Late Antiquity
SJT	*Scottish Journal of Theology*
SNTU	Studien zum Neuen Testament und seiner Umwelt
SNTSMS	Society for New Testament Studies Monograph Series
Str.B.	[H. Strack and] P. Billerbeck, *Kommentar zum Neuen Testament*
TRE	*Theologische Realenzyklopädie*
TRu	*Theologische Rundschau*
TTZ	*Trierer theologische Zeitschrift*
TWNT	*Theologisches Wörterbuch zum Neuen Testament*
WBC	Word Biblical Commentary
WUNT	Wissenschaftliche Untersuchungen zum Neuen Testament
ZKT	*Zeitschrift für katholische Theologie*
ZNW	*Zeitschrift für die neutestamentliche Wissenschaft*
ZTK	*Zeitschrift für Theologie und Kirche*

THE *SITZ IM LEBEN* OF THE JOHANNINE BREAD OF LIFE DISCOURSE AND ITS EVOLVING CONTEXT

Paul N. Anderson

John 6 may well be called "the Grand Central Station of Johannine critical issues." In no other place does the same confluence of historical, literary, and theological debates come to the fore as they relate to the Gospel of John. From comparison/contrasts with Synoptic corollaries—to inferences of narrative and discourse sources—to redaction analyses—to christology, semeiology and sacramentology debates—to text disruption and rearrangement theories—to form-critical midrashic analysis—to reader-response approaches (just to mention some of the obvious critical issues), John 6 has time and again provided the *locus argumenti* for scholars wishing to make a definitive contribution to Johannine studies.

What one also finds when doing a "field test" in John 6 is that one hypothesis will affect and be affected by other kinds of hypotheses. For instance, one's view of the evangelist's christology will affect one's assessment of the literary origin of the signs material (vv. 1-24), "I am" sayings (vv. 35ff.) and the so-called "eucharistic interpolation" (vv. 51c-58) in John 6. Indeed, the most far-reaching and enduring approaches to Johannine interpretation are ones that address several of these key issues effectively, and there are few better contexts within which to test them critically than John 6.[1]

One approach which takes into consideration a variety of these issues is a form-critical analysis of the "Bread of Life Discourse" in John 6. The recent works of P. Borgen, R. E. Brown, B. Lindars and others[2] have

---

[1] Exceptions in terms of John and Synoptic comparison/contrasts would of course include the Passion narrative, the Temple-cleansing and various Synoptic-like allusions in John; but none of these sections has a combination of miracle stories, "I AM" sayings, apparent redactional interpolations, homilies and misunderstanding dialogues all within the same context. Likewise, other discourses and signs narratives in John are worthy of investigation, but their parallels in the Synoptics are not as clear as those found in John 6. For these and other reasons one can understand why there has been such an intense interest in John 6—for instance, why the SNTS "Johannine Literature Seminar" has spent three years now discussing John 6, as well as why there has been such a large volume of recent articles and monographs produced on John 6 (see Bibliography II, "John VI" in Paul N. Anderson, *The Christology of the Fourth Gospel; Its Unity and Disunity in the Light of John 6*, WUNT II 78 (Tübingen: J. C. B. Mohr [Paul Siebeck], 1995).

[2] P. Borgen, *Bread From Heaven* [Leiden: E. J. Brill, 1965), believes John 6:31-58 constitutes a unitive homiletical exploration of the Christian meaning of the manna motif in Exodus 16:4. R. E. Brown, *The Gospel According to John* Vol. I (Garden City: Doubleday, 1966), believes the Bread of Life Discourse in John 6 actually reflects two delivered homilies within Johannine Christianity—vv. 35-50, which are sapiential, and vv. 51-58 which are a later eucharistic doublet. B. Lindars, *The Gospel of John* (Grand Rapids: Eerdmans, 1972), follows Brown's division of verses, but he argues that the entire section had been formed and

demonstrated that the Johannine Bread of Life Discourse is indeed a written record of early Christian homily (or homilies) expanding on the meaning of the feeding for later audiences. One's analysis of its dialogues and discourses will thus lend valuable insights into the dialectical situation of the Johannine audience. In other words, if the *Sitz im Leben* and literary form of the material within this chapter is assessed correctly, something of its origin, meaning and implications of its content may be more adequately inferred.

The thesis of this study is that because the Johannine Bread of Life Discourse reflects an exhortative homiletical unit, connecting the ministry of Jesus with ongoing crises affecting the Johannine community of faith, an investigation into the rhetorical thrust of its message will illumine—and be illumined by—one's understanding of the Johannine situation and its evolving context. More specifically, as the central exhortative thrust of the discourse is "Work not for food that is death-producing, but for the food that is life-producing—eternally, which the Son of Man shall give you" (v. 27), the misunderstanding dialogues between Jesus and four groups of discussants actually betray four distinctive crises within the history of Johannine Christianity. These crises are also suggested by the Johannine Epistles, the writings of Ignatius and other historical markers in the contemporary situation. Before launching into such an exploration, however, one's findings regarding critical literary, historical and theological issues should be stated.

A. FINDINGS AS BEGINNINGS

While space will not allow a full discussion of the critical issues mentioned above in the first paragraph,[3] condensed ones are offered as preliminary conclusions, whence further investigations have their departures. In that

---

used previously within the Johannine eucharistic setting and that it is used sapiently by the evangelist on the Gospel-writing level. Whatever theory of composition one espouses, two levels of history accompany the interpretation of John 6: first, the level of the events themselves (and their transmission through traditional and other means); and second, the level of the contemporary audience to whom the message was originally addressed. The latter level of history is the main focus of this study.

[3] These can be reviewed more fully in the aforementioned book (Anderson, *Christology*). In it the judgment is made that while Johannine studies have indeed advanced significantly over the last half-century, studies which do not come to full grips with Bultmann's magisterial contribution (R. Bultmann, *The Gospel of John*, trans. by G. R. Beasley-Murray, R. W. N. Hoare and J. K. Riches [Philadelphia: Westminster Press, 1971]) often fail to understand the rationale and the theological implications of his provocative—though at times unconvincing—judgments, to their peril. For this reason, four of my ten chapters deal specifically with Bultmann's treatment of John 6: "The Stylistic Unity and Disunity of John 6" (Ch.4); "The Relationship Between Sign and Discourse in John 6" (Ch.5); "The 'Eucharistic Interpolation'" (Ch.6); and "The Dialectical Character of John 6" (Ch.7). While these findings cannot be argued here in detail, they must be summarized lest the informed reader be inclined to disallow the grounds upon which new constructs are built.

sense, critical findings become the sources of new analytical beginnings. These findings are as follows:

1. *The style of John 6 is basically unitive.*

Upon reviewing Bultmann's literary criteria for distinguishing the *semeia* source, when those measures of style[4] are applied throughout John 6, they fail the test of statistical significance. Nearly two thirds of all the sentences in John 6 begin with the main verb (within 3% points of the inferred *semeia* source). All the rest of the sentences in John 6 *except two* begin with simple connections such as δέ and οὖν. And, every time μαθηταί occurs in John 6 it is accompanied by αὐτοῦ. Bultmann has indeed identified the style of the Johannine narrative as representing "Semitising Greek," but so is all of John 6, as is the rest of the Gospel as well.[5]

Regarding the style of the *Offenbarungsreden* source and the supposed contribution of the redactor in John 6, Bultmann confesses that the former is written in "Hellenized Aramaic" and is indistinguishable from the style of the evangelist, while the latter has obviously imitated the style of the evangelist.[6] Precisely how "Semitising Greek" may be antiseptically

---

[4] Bultmann's view, of course, is that the style of the *semeia* source is "clearly distinguishable from the language of the Evangelist or of the discourse-source..." (*The Gospel of John*, p. 113). Says Bultmann about John 6:

> Stylistically the source shows the same characteristics as the sections which we have already attributed to the σημεῖα-source. The style is a "Semitising" Greek, but it does not seem possible to discern in the story a transition from a literary Semitic source. The passage is characterised by the placing of the verb at the beginning of the sentence; also by the lack (in vv. 7, 8, 10 where K pl have δέ) or very simple form of connection between the sentences (δέ and οὖν). Ποιήσατε (in Greek we would expect κελεύσατε . . . ἀναπεσεῖν v. 10 corresponds to the Semitic causative (see Rev. 13.13 and Schl.). The constantly repeated αὐτοῦ is not Greek (it corresponds to the Semitic suffix) after the different forms of μαθηταί vv. 3, 8, 12, 16 . . . (p. 211, n. 1).

[5] Bultmann confesses elsewhere that the style of the evangelist is also "Semitising," as is to a lesser degree that of the *Offenbarungsreden* (p. 204, n. 1).

[6] "The editor clearly models himself on the Evangelist's technique; but it is easy to see that it is an imitation. " (Bultmann, p. 235, n. 4; see also p. 243, n. 4)

In order to identify the presence of *Offenbarungsreden* material in John 6 and its "correct" (original) order, Bultmann identifies strophic/metric couplets that deal with revelation themes and rearranges them into an acceptable progression (see Anderson, *Christology*, Table 5). In doing so, however, he omits vv. 26b, 29b, 32, 37a, 38-40, 46, 50f., 53-58, and 63 etc. One wonders why. One also questions the statistical likelihood that the earlier edition of John 6 could have been disordered ten times (albeit for "external" reasons) precisely between sentences of uneven length (with a mean average of 80 characters per sentence) within the middle of a book. The statistical probability of such an occurrence is 1:80 to the 10th power; or slightly less than 1:10 quintillion!

Bultmann's detection of the style and contribution of the evangelist *is* convincing, however (see Anderson, *Christology*, *Table 6*: "Bultmann's Identification of the Evangelist's 'Connective Prose' in John 6"). The question is whether these facts are at all suggestive of multiple sources. Synchronic and diachronic scholars alike all believe that the evangelist

distinguished from "Hellenized Aramaic" is difficult to understand, let alone to do. One may just as easily, and certainly with greater statistical success, amass typical linguistic and stylistic characteristics of Johannine action narrative as well as typical linguistic and stylistic characteristics of Johannine theological discourse, and upon applying such "criteria" throughout the Gospel discover that the former correlates significantly with John's *semeia* accounts and that the latter correlates significantly with the "I am" (and other) sayings of Jesus in John. The question is whether this would be at all suggestive of stylistic disunity within John, enough to infer anything about the presence of more than one basic literary source in John.[7]

2. *"Aporias" are not necessarily indicative of editorial seams in John 6.*

Lest it be concluded that the stylistic unity of John 6 "proves" anything about the evangelist's use or non-use of sources, Bultmann has been quick to point out that contextual and theological kinds of evidence also corroborate his diachronic judgments.[8] This being the case, Bultmann believes that contextual oddities in transition may reflect "editorial seams" suggesting the evangelist has taken over a source and added to it his own contribution.[9] The two primary examples of this in John 6 are Jesus' abrupt

---

employed a historicizing style of narration and that he added interpretive asides throughout the story line. This kind of data, however, belabors the obvious. John was organized by a narrator of miracle stories, discourses, and events which have special theological implications for a late first-century audience. That much is clear; alien origins of the material is not.

[7] This is not to say that diachronic scholars who have sought to improve on Bultmann's work have always followed such procedures (Although, see V. S. Poythress, "Testing for Johannine Authorship by Examining the Use of Conjunctions," *Westminster Journal of Theology* 46 (1984), 350-69, for a compelling demonstration that the organizing of stylistic data categories by recent Johannine source critics since Bultmann tends to be more demonstrative of typical Johannine narrative versus typical Johannine discourse and narratological connectives—not exactly significant source-critical data!). Nor is it to claim that John did not use sources (Although, see the most extensive evaluation of the Semeia source hypothesis yet in Gilbert van Belle's *The Signs Source in the Fourth Gospel; Historical Survey and Critical Evaluation of the Semeia Hypothesis* [Leuven: Leuven University Press, 1994], who after considering nearly everything written on the most plausible source thought to underlie John, comes to a negative conclusion, pp. 376f.). It is to say that convincing stylistic evidence for written, non-Johannine sources underlying the Fourth Gospel is still lacking, and those who believe in them must do so on some basis other than empirical data (possibly working backwards from the rejection/acceptance of implications). To *de-Johannify* a gospel narrative in order to *re-Marcanize* it, despite arranging it into an albeit clever sequence with other cropped units, does not a *semeia* source make.

[8] D. Moody Smith articulates well this interplay between stylistic, contextual and ideological evidence in Bultmann's diachronic constructs, *The Composition and Order of the Fourth Gospel* (New Haven: Yale University Press, 1964), pp. 9ff., as does R. Fortna, *The Gospel of Signs* (Cambridge: Cambridge University Press, 1970), pp. 15-22.

[9] Fortna believes these are the most objective of the three "criteria" for inferring alien sources in John (*The Gospel of Signs*, pp. 19ff.), but not all "aporias" in John are equally problematic. For instance, while the abrupt ending of ch.14, the apparent first conclusion of the Gospel at 20:31 (with its reformulation at 21:24f.) and the seeming continuity between the

answer to the crowd in v. 26 and the redundant request of the crowd for another sign in vv. 30f.[10] What Bultmann has missed is the unitive motif of *testing* throughout this section and the entire chapter, and also the evangelist's employment of local and sustained irony in narrating the events. Indeed, the function of irony is to disturb and dis-locate the focus of the reader in order to re-locate his or her attention along another path. Throughout vv. 6-15 and vv. 25-40 the crowd is tested as to whether it will see beyond the bread which Jesus gives to the "Bread" which Jesus is. In v. 26 Jesus discerns their real question (which would have been obvious to the first-century audience): "When did you arrive . . . and *when's lunch?*" Jesus is portrayed as understanding full well their hidden question, which is still with them in their failure to understand the kind of food Jesus really offers (obviated by their misunderstanding comments: vv. 28, 30f., 34; and declared explicitly by the narrator: vv. 14f., 36). John 6:25-30 does not betray insoluble aporias requiring a diachronic rescue; rather, the passage reflects the evangelist's use of sustained irony in depicting the failure of the crowd to pass the test of bread versus "Bread."

3. *The "eucharistic interpolation" in John 6 is neither.*

The primary theological tension in John 6, calling for consideration of vv. 51c-58 being the redactor's interpolation, is the fact that the purely christocentric soteriology of the evangelist is absolutely incompatible with instrumentalistic sacramentology, and worse yet, with pagan theophagy. On this point, Bultmann deserves a fresh audience. Recent tendencies to soften Bultmann's penetrating insight here fail to take seriously the profound radicality of Johannine spirituality. Bultmann is absolutely correct to challenge the notion that a saving, pistic response to God's revelation in Jesus can ever be measured or effected on external levels alone.[11] It can

---

events in chs.5 and 7 *do* call for a diachronic theory of composition, many of the aporias cited by Bultmann and others are not always as problematic as the sharp relief into which they are cast.

[10] In response to the question, "Rabbi, when did you get here?" Jesus responds, "You seek me not because you saw the signs, but because you ate the loaves and were satisfied." And, it seems odd that the same crowd that had just witnessed a sign the day before now poses the request, "What sign will you do then, that we may see and believe you? What will you do?" Bultmann's method of identifying these "seams," however, is self-contradictory. Between verses 25 and 26 the transition is too rough to assume a unitive source, while between verses 28f. and 30f. the connection is too smooth (implying the crowd understood Jesus' exhortation in v. 27). Either way, Bultmann is happy to solve these "aporias" by offering a diachronic solution (pp. 218-24).

[11] See Anderson, *Christology*, Bibliography III, "The Sacraments in John;" and the excursus, "What is Meant by 'Sacrament'?" A growing tendency is to assume that while the member of the Johannine audience is expected to "come to" and believe fully in Jesus, the way this is to be exercised is through cultic participation in the eucharist (see P. Borgen, *Bread from Heaven* [Leiden: E.J. Brill, 1965], ad. loc.; G. Burge, *The Anointed Community* [Grand Rapids: Eerdmans, 1987], pp. 178-89; D. Rensberger, *Johannine Faith and Liberating*

only be appropriated existentially by an authentic "yes" to the divine
initiative, eschatologically spoken though the Word made flesh. In that
sense, the incarnation scandalizes not only the religion of "the Jews," but all
religious constructs of human origin (including developing Christian, and
certainly Jewish or Hellenistic, expressions), and the Johannine Christian is
called to attend the present leadership of the resurrected Lord which is
effected through the comforting/convicting/guiding work of the *Parakletos*.
To insist upon any externalization of such inward trust (ritual or otherwise),
other than the command to love, is to fail to understand the core of
Johannine soteriology, which is so radically christocentric. Thus, if vv. 51c-
58 really advocated the indispensability of the eucharist for salvation, they
would have to be deemed an interpolation. The fact, however, is that they
do not.

There is a broad difference between saying one must participate in a
eucharistic rite in order to receive eternal life and *using eucharistic imagery
to appeal for solidarity with Jesus and his community in the face of
persecution*. John 6:51c is not an introductory sentence, but a concluding
clause. The bread which Jesus will offer finally is his *sarx*, given for the life
of the world. This is a blunt reference to the cross, and it bespeaks the
paradoxical cost of discipleship for Jesus' followers. To hope to share with
Christ in his resurrection is to be willing to participate in his suffering and
death. No wonder the disciples were scandalized (v. 60)! They are
portrayed as understanding full well what it means to "ingest" the flesh and
blood of Jesus: the willingness to go to the cross. This Bultmann has
recognized clearly, as he includes vv. 60-71 in the section entitled "The
Way of the Cross" (pp. 443-451). He wrongly, however, places it after John

---

Community [Philadelphia: Westminster Press, 1988], pp. 64-86; and L. Schenke, *Die
wunderbare Brotvermehrung* [Würzburg, 1983]). Such a view, however, has several problems
to it which make it unacceptable:

a.) It is *anachronistic*. While Johannine Christianity must have had some sort of
fellowship meal (within which the feeding narrative and Bread of Life discourses were
probably recounted), this is not to say that it had become a symbolic ritual meal such as is
reflected in the transition between 1 Cor. 10 and 11, even by the time of the writing of John 6.

b.) The total lack of sacramental ordinances and institutionalization of sacraments in
John suggests *a critical view of rising institutionalism* within the late first-century church on
the part of the evangelist. He may have tolerated some sacramental innovation, but he
believed the essence of faith was radically christocentric—an affront to the instrumentality of
all religious practice—preliminarily helpful though it might be to the believer. Its origin is
human, not divine, and thus can never replace an abiding response of faith to the divine
initiative. On this matter, Bultmann is correct.

c.) For the evangelist, the final sacrament is the *incarnation*, and the sacramental *topos*
where the human/divine encounter happens most fully is the gathered community of faith.
This is the sacramental reality in which true believers (at the time of the writing of John 6) are
called to participate, and toward the facilitating of which eucharistic imagery is co-opted. But
in the face of escalating Roman hostility under Domitian in Asia Minor, such allegiances
undoubtedly involved embracing the cross. *That* was the difficult and scandalizing message
for the Johannine audience contemporary with the final production of John 6.

12:36 and fails to see it as the direct implication of John 6:51c-58. Viewed from this perspective, the passage is powerfully unitive, having the provocative sort of message that would have challenged the contemporary audience with absolute clarity.

While Bultmann is also wrong to assume that vv. 51c-58 reflect the influence of theophagic Mystery Religions (also wrongly claimed to be represented by Ignatius' "medicine of immortality" motif), his allusion to the Ignatian situation indeed sheds light on the Johannine. Both Ignatius and the Fourth Evangelist are challenged to keep their Christian communities together in the face of Roman persecution. In doing so, Ignatius raises the value of adhering to the singular bishop (and thus to Christ), while the Fourth Evangelist raises the value of adhering to the community of faith (and thus to Christ). Neither, however, advocates sacramental instrumentalism as such, or pagan theophagic religion.[12] Thus, the main theological objection to the chapter's disunity fails to convince, as well.

4. *John 6 must be considered a basically unitive composition, and it was probably added to a later edition of the Gospel's composition.*

Of the theories of composition analyzed, the most attractive is that of B. Lindars.[13] The most convincing justification of the need for reordering the chapters into a 4, 6, 5, 7 sequence is not the connection of water (ch. 4) to bread (ch. 6—the living bread/living water sequence between 6:27-58 and 7:37-39 works perfectly well), but the fact that the Jerusalem debate with

---

[12] The emphasis of Ignatius' φάρμακον ἀθανασίας (*Eph.* 20:2) is not upon the salvific effect of ingesting the eucharistic loaf, but upon the salutary result of breaking *only one loaf* (instead of breaking off and holding sectarian cultic meals). The final goal of each is communal unity—the indispensability of solidarity with Christ and his community in the face of suffering—not the indispensability of a eucharistic ritual, proper. The failure to notice this theological and ecclesiological distinction has been an unnecessary source of division and pain within the church and beyond.

[13] See Anderson, *Christology*, Ch.2, "A Survey of Recent Commentaries." B. Lindars' commentary, *The Gospel of John* (Grand Rapids: Eerdmans, 1972), pp. 46-54, is most attractive because it addresses most of the genuinely problematic aporias in John within a fairly straightforward and believable history of text composition. Rather than resorting to speculative displacement/rearrangement moves, Lindars addresses many of the same problems with a theory of multiple (at least two) editions. Quite credibly, Lindars selects such units as John 1:1-18; ch.6 (Lazarus material? 11:1-46; 12:9-11); chs.15-17 and ch.21, as well as a few comments by the redactor (the eye-witness and Beloved Disciple motifs, for instance) and suggests that these comprise "supplementary material" that has been added (not necessarily all at once) to an earlier rendition of the Gospel. The interpretive implication for the present study is that the acute situation addressed by the evangelist at the time of finally composing John 6 may have been commensurate with the situation represented by the rhetorical concerns implied by the other supplementary material. The debate with the Synagogue has probably cooled, and the community is now facing a docetizing threat in the face of Roman harassment and persecution, as well as the intramural threat of rising institutionalism within the mainstream church. These will be explored later.

the Jews over the Sabbath in 5:16-47 appears to continue in 7:15-52 and seems interrupted by the Galilean narrative. If the original sequence was something like chs. 4, 5 and 7, there would have been no geographical flip-flop (between Jerusalem and Galilee), and John 6 may be understood as having been inserted where it is as a means of following the ending of ch. 5, "If you would have believed Moses you would have believed me; for Moses wrote of me."[14] The implication is that given the stylistic, contextual and theological unity of John 6, it may rightly be considered a basic unity which was added to an earlier edition of the Gospel.

5. John 6 represents a tradition parallel to, and yet independent from, Mark 6 and 8.

While C. K. Barrett and T. Brodie[15] (among others) believe that John drew at least from Mark, and perhaps from other gospel traditions, the majority of scholars have been more and more impressed with the radical independence of John's tradition. Stemming from the 1938 contribution of P. Gardner-Smith (*Saint John and the Synoptic Gospels*; Cambridge: Cambridge University Press), a majority of scholars have been been coming to what D. Moody Smith feels is an impressive agreement regarding John's

---

[14] This is certainly Lindars' view (1972, pp. 234ff.), and Professor Borgen has illuminated the connectedness between John 5 and 6 all the more clearly by showing the ways such themes as Jesus' works, the Father and the Scriptures bear witness to Jesus in John 6 (SNTS paper, 1992, "The Works, the Father, and the Scriptures Bear Witness; Themes from John 5:36-40 being illustrated in John 6"). One is not certain, however, that the clear connections between John 5:36-40 and John 6 imply that any of John 6 was composed as a conscious development of those themes. They certainly are found in much of John's other material as well. The least one must admit is that John 6 follows John 5 extremely well, and if it were added later, either as an excursus related to John 5:46f. or as a narratological following of the second healing miracle (6:2), complex rearrangement theories become unwarranted, as well as unlikely.

[15] Professor Barrett, *The Gospel According to St. John*, 2nd edition (Philadelphia: Westminster, 1978), pp. 42-54, acknowledges that he represents an older position among Gospel critics, agreeing, for instance with B. H. Streeter that the similarities between John and Mark make it easier to suppose John's familiarity with Mark than non-familiarity (p. 42). In doing so, Barrett outlines ten sequential similarities of events between John and Mark (p. 43), at least twelve verbal similarities (pp. 44f.), and several other similarities of detail and theological perspective (pp. 45-54).

T. Brodie's new book, *The Quest for the Origin of John's Gospel* (New York: Oxford University Press, 1993), unhesitatingly explores connections between John and the Synoptics (especially Mark), the Pentateuch, and Ephesians, assuming that nearly all similarities imply Johannine dependence on other sources. Indeed, the Fourth Evangelist probably was an encyclopedic type of a writer (pp. 30ff.), but some connections Brodie over-accentuates, and he fails to account for the possibility that some of the influence may have flowed the other way as well. Given the high degree of orality versus scripturality of first-century Christian traditions, one wonders whether any of John's sources were used as written ones and read by the evangelist before his writing, other than some scripture citations, of course.

being parallel to—yet independent from—the Synoptics.[16] Even Bultmann, for instance, was forced to infer a Passion source underlying John 18–20 (while at the same time admitting that it did not differ from the contribution of the evangelist stylistically, contextually or theologically, pp. 632ff.) simply because John's Passion narrative was so strikingly independent from those of the Synoptics. The independence of John 6 from Mark 6 and 8 is even more compelling.

One of the astounding things discovered when analyzing the parallels between John 6 and Mark 6 and 8 is that we really do have three independent accounts (although in Mark 6 and 8 the interpreted significance of the feeding is similar—Jesus has power over nature to perform miracles if he chooses) representing individuated traditions with their own independent histories. Whereas P. Gardner-Smith discussed four major differences between John 6 and Mark 6, one can actually identify at least *24 similarities and differences* between John 6 and Mark 6, and *21 similarities and differences* between John 6 and Mark 8.[17] Despite having some connectedness to Marcan detail, there is *never* a time among forty-five similarities that John aligns with the Marcan tradition verbatim for more than a word or two at a time, and every single convergence is also significantly different! The implications of this fact are hard to overstate. While some connection must have existed between Marcan and Johannine

---

16 In his book, *John Among the Gospels* (Minneapolis: Fortress, 1992), D. Moody Smith identifies an impressive movement from the view that John was dependent upon the Synoptics (esp. Mark) earlier in the century, and that following the work of P. Gardner-Smith the independence of John rose to the fore as the prominent view. However, within the last decade or two, the tendency has shifted once more toward a Synoptic-dependent view of John, and this movement has undoubtedly been influenced significantly by the 1990 Leuven Colloquium on the study of John and the Synoptics (the essays have been compiled in *John and the Synoptics*, ed. by A. Denaux [Leuven: Leuven University Press, 1992]). Building on the earlier work of F. Neirynck, M. Sabbe, and others, one detects a clear resurgence of the view that John either used the Synoptic tradition or at least had some contact with it. After considering the thirty-eight articles in that volume, however, one remains unconvinced that John had access to and/or used any of the written Synoptic Gospels. There are *no* identical contacts between John and the Synoptics, and none that are explained better on the basis of written dependence than on the basis of contact during the oral stages of the traditions. In that sense, Gardner-Smith's hypothesis should be modified somewhat by accentuating the contacts between an independent Johannine tradition and the oral stages of the Synoptic ones, but it does not appear to be overturned.

17 See Anderson, *Christology*, Tables 7 and 8. What is significant is that while these lists account for nearly all the connections between John 6 and the Marcan tradition (to which John is indeed closest in terms of inclusion and detail), in *0 out of 45* cases is John's tradition ever identical to Mark's. This is highly significant, not only as it relates to John's composition, but as it relates to the historical development and character of gospel traditions, themselves. Could it be that there was *never* a time in which there was one, singular rendition of Jesus' ministry, but that from the early traditional stages there may have been differing views of the significance and implications of Jesus' ambiguous words and deeds? This is especially suggested by a detailed comparison/contrast between the sea-crossing narratives in John and Mark (see Anderson, *Christology*, Ch.8, "Not an Attesting Miracle . . . But a 'Testing' Sign: An Exegesis of John 6:1-24").

traditions, these must have occurred during the oral stages of their development, as such details as the plentiful grass, two hundred denarii, twenty-five or thirty furlongs, δύο ὀψάρια, etc. would likely have been the sort of detail remembered from an oral rendering. It is also highly significant that when one considers Matthew's and Luke's redactions of Mark 6 and 8, the kind of detail they leave out is precisely the sort of detail most prolific in Mark and John. *Non-symbolic, graphic and illustrative detail* (Luke and Matthew often omit names of people and illustrative detail) and *theological asides* are precisely the sort of things Luke and Matthew *omit* from their written source, Mark. John, on the other hand, has even more of this sort of material than Mark does (the little boy, the testing motif, etc.), and it is indeed odd that Bultmann, Fortna and others believe the Fourth Evangelist has added this detail in order to "historicize" the narrative when the two closest examples in terms of genre (Matthew and Luke—if one believes that John used a narrative source like Mark and a discourse source like Q) demonstrate the *opposite* pattern of redacting a written source. No. Mark's and John's distinctive characteristics reflect their proximity to the oral stages of the gospel traditions, not the written, and their similarities/differences with each other reflect an "interfluential" relationship quite possibly occurring during the oral stages of both traditions.[18]

The result of the above findings is that John 6 should indeed be treated as a basic unity, added to the Gospel some time during the late 80's or early 90's, although its oral and written stages of composition must have extended over a generation or more. John's tradition is independent from

---

[18] It cannot be claimed, for instance, that John only drew from the Marcan or pre-Marcan oral tradition. The converse may just as easily have happened, and it is impossible to know which preacher(s) influenced the other(s). Certainly Luke shows signs of following John's lead in departing from Mark and Q (in at least two dozen instances this happens), as does Q (infrequently, but clearly—John 3:35 in Matt.11:27 and Luke10:22, for example). Consider, for instance, that facts that like John and contra Mark, Luke has only one feeding and sea crossing, the confession of Peter follows the feeding of the *5,000* and includes the Johannine *tou theou*, the *right* ear of the servant is severed, the less likely *feet* of Jesus are anointed by the woman—not his head (as in Mark and Matthew), people with the names of Lazarus, Mary and Martha play significant roles in both gospels, and such themes as the Holy Spirit and special concerns for Samaritans and women appear conspicuously close in Luke and John against Mark and Matthew (see Anderson, *Christology,* Appendix VIII, "The Papias Tradition, John's Authorship and Luke/Acts" for further detail). Scholars have routinely explained such similarities on the basis that John drew from Luke or a pre-Lucan tradition. This, however, does not account for the facts that precisely where Luke diverges from Mark, he converges with John, and where Luke and John converge John does not go on and include otherwise distinctive Lucan material by and large. There is no suitable way to explain these facts except to inquire whether Luke may have at times preferred John's tradition to the Marcan. Has Luke 1:2 got anything to do with the Johannine tradition in its oral stages? If so, it would create tumultuous questions regarding one of the "safest" of critical assumptions: that the Fourth Gospel reflects a late—and only late—interpretation of the significance of Jesus' ministry.

the Synoptics in their written forms but probably had contact with the pre-Marcan oral tradition. Luke seems sympathetic to the Johannine rendition of events, nearly always against Mark, and this fact is provocative. John's later material shows affinities with the M tradition in that they both address similar issues: tensions with local Jewish communities and concerns about church governance, for instance, but they deal with them in very different ways. At times John even seems interested in correcting the prevalent view on matters ecclesiological, sacramental and basileiological. These dialogues will be explored later, but for now, the above findings serve as a foundation upon which to construct an effective form-analysis of the Johannine Bread of Life Discourse.

B. Manna as a "Rhetorical Trump" in Ancient Judaism and John

One agrees with Professor Painter[19] that Professor Borgen's monograph on the "Bread from Heaven" motif in ancient Jewish literature (1965) is the most significant work on John 6 so far. Major problems with the work, however, are that not only has it failed to identify the correct homiletical structure of John 6, it has also failed to notice that there are actually *two* "homiletical patterns" when the manna theme is employed in ancient Jewish literature. At least eight times in ancient Jewish literature we have record of manna being used as the Proem text, but this is the minority of the cases, and they nearly all occur together in Exodus Rabbah 25:1-8, where Exodus 16:4 is developed midrashically in eight brief essays. In these midrashim alone (and possibly *Tractate Vayassa* III-IV and a few other midrashim) do we find the manna motif interpreted from the front and developed exegetically. In virtually all the other references to manna in ancient Jewish literature, manna serves as a *secondary* text—a rhetorical trump card—played after declaring one's thesis and identifying desirable and undesirable responses to it.[20]

---

[19] See Painter's response to Borgen's critique (1992) of his work, "Quest, Rejection and Commendation in John 6: A Response to Peder Borgen" (SNTS Johannine writings Seminar, Madrid, 1992).

[20] This is the case in Philo, *Leg. all. III* 162; *Fug.* 137; *Mut.* 259; *Congr.* 158-174; *Mos.* I 196-205; *Mos. II* 258-274; in *Midrash Rabbah*, Genesis XLVIII:10; LI:2; LXVI:3; Exodus V:9; XXIV:3; XXXIII:8; XXXVIII:4; XLI:1; Deuteronomy X:4; and *Exodus Mekilta*, Tractate Beshalla I:201. The rhetorical use of manna is also found pervasively throughout the canonical corpus in such passages as Numbers 11:6-9; 21:5; Deuteronomy 8:3, 16; Joshua 5:12; Psalm 78:23-25; 105:40; 1 Corinthians 10:3; Revelation 2:17; *and* John 6:31 (see Anderson, *Christology*, Ch.3, n. 10).

1. *The rhetorical use of manna pattern in Philo and John*

While Borgen believes he has identified a "homiletical pattern" at work in Philo and John,[21] he sidesteps the fact that none of these passages (except *Exodus Rabbah*, etc.) begins with Exodus 16:4 as the Proem text to be exegeted. In each case other texts are being interpreted, or other points are being made, and the manna motif is brought in to bolster *another* argument or interpretation. This makes it highly doubtful that John 6:32ff. was ever cast in the form of an exegetical exploration in the classical text-centered manner.[22] The form of typical manna rhetoric in ancient Jewish midrashim, Philo, Psalm 78 and in John is as follows:[23]

Table #1, "The Rhetorical Use of Manna Pattern in Ancient Jewish
Literature"

A.) *Main point or text.* A point of argument, exhortation or text to be developed is stated by an author, who calls for a particular action on behalf of his or her audience.

---

[21] While he categorizes various references to the manna motif as "exegetical paraphrase," the homiletical pattern identified by Borgen in Philo (*Mut.*253-63; *Leg. all. III* 162-68) and in John 6, "consists of the following points: (1) The Old Testament quotation. (2) The interpretation. (3) The objection to the interpretation. (4) Point (2), the interpretation, freely repeated and questioned. (5) The answer which can conclude with a reference to point (2), the interpretation. " (*Bread from Heaven*, p. 85).

See, however, T. M. Conley, *Philo's Rhetoric: Studies in Style, Composition and Exegesis* (Berkeley: Center for Hermeneutical Studies, 1987), pp. 56-67, for an unconvinced appraisal, and D. T. Runia's "Secondary Texts in Philo's *Quaestiones,*" in *Both Literal and Allegorical; Studies in Philo of Alexandria's Questions and Answers on Genesis and Exodus*, ed. D. M. Hay (Atlanta: Scholars Press, 1991), pp. 47-80. Runia's three observations are that 1) Philo characteristically invokes *lemmata* (secondary texts) to illuminate a primary *lemma* text, and vice-versa; 2) Philo often moves from one to the other simply on verbal cues versus thematic interests; and 3) Philo's exegetical explorations develop a "main directive idea" rather than a "tight-knit structural coherence" (p. 48). While Borgen is fully aware that Philo never exegetes Ex. 16:4 as a Proem or *lemma* text directly, my contention is that manna in Philo appears to always demonstrate the veracity of *another* point or interpretation.

[22] B. Malina, *The Palestinian Manna Tradition* (Leiden: E. J. Brill, 1968), correctly identifies the rhetorical evolution of the manna motif in ancient Israel, "This development becomes from the prosaic aetiological account of the name 'manna,' an account amplified in Num. 11:6, 7-9, and then used as a springboard for homiletic ends. In this process the manna takes on admirable traits, ending up as heavenly food, the food of angels, rained down by God upon Israel to test and teach the desert generation. " (p. 41) Nonetheless, he errs in viewing John 6:31ff. (with Borgen) as being a "Christian midrash on the manna tradition, a meditation on this tradition in the light of Jesus." (p. 106) Rather, the section is more accurately *a reflection upon the significance of Jesus' works and words*—in the light of the manna tradition—which it supersedes (see Anderson, *Christology*, Ch. 3, n. 10). These are two very different understandings.

[23] A modification of Anderson, *Christology*, *Table 1*, "The Rhetorical Use of Manna Pattern in Ancient Jewish Literature." For a clear identification of this pattern in Philo, see Anderson, *Christology*, *Appendix VII*, "Philo's Use of Manna as a Secondary Text."

B.) *Development of main point using dualistic either/or categories.* This point (meaning of the text) is discussed, usually posing two options: one favorable and the other unfavorable.

C.) *Introduction of manna as a rhetorical trump* (secondary proof-text). The manna motif is introduced and associated with the main point being made by the writer, "proving" its superiority (heavenly origin).

D.) *Continued development and implications.* The discussion continues, and alternative responses to the author's exhortation are associated with earthly bread (or the "flesh"—*sarx*—of quail), in contrast to heavenly "bread," which is clearly superior in terms of origin *and* effect. The secondary text is at times introduced here (D), or in the discussion (at B), as well as at the more common secondary-text location (C).

E.) *Reiteration of main point.* The original appeal (A) or text is reiterated, often with some reference to the life-producing effect of manna and/or the death-producing effect of earthly (inferior) bread.

One finds this rhetorical use of manna as the secondary text used throughout the midrashic passages cited by Borgen, and even in the Philonic texts upon which he constructs his "homiletical pattern" and which he believes are the closest in form to John 6. Another debatable move made by Borgen is to identify John 6:31 as a citation of Exodus 16:4 rather than Psalm 78:24f. The former passage suits his text-exegesis theory of Johannine midrash better (Psalm 78 is not developed midrashically in ancient Jewish literature, while Exodus 16 is.), but the language and rhetorical function of John 6:31 are closer to the latter passage than the former, despite the formal differences between a narrative and exhortative psalm and the literary form of John 6.[24]

---

[24] Certainly, ἄρτον ἐκ τοῦ οὐρανοῦ ἔδωκεν αὐτοῖς φαγεῖν (John 6:31b) is closer to καὶ ἔβρεξεν αὐτοῖς μάννα φαγεῖν, καὶ ἄρτον οὐρανοῦ ἔδωκεν αὐτοῖς (Ps.78:24, LXX B) than it is to ἰδοὺ ἐγὼ ὕω ὑμῖν ἄρτους ἐκ τοῦ οὐρανοῦ (Ex.16:4 LXX B), even with οὗτος ὁ ἄρτος, ὃν ἔδωκεν κύριος ὑμῖν φαγεῖν (Ex.16:15 LXX B) considered alongside it (see E. D. Freed, *Old Testament Quotations in the Gospel of John* [Leiden: E. J. Brill, 1965], pp. 11-16). More significant than the semantic similarities, however, is the rhetorical affinity between John 6:27-58 and Psalm 78. Like Psalm 78:24f., the use of manna in John 6 is elevated ("bread from *heaven*") and used rhetorically to further another argument.

2. *The rhetorical use of manna pattern in Psalm 78.*

Consider, for instance, the formal structure of the rhetorical use of manna pattern in Psalm 78:[25]

> *Table #2,* "The Rhetorical Use of Manna Pattern in Psalm 78"

A.) *Main point of exhortation*: Put your trust in God, oh my people, and do not be like your forefathers (or members of the Northern Kingdom)—a stubborn and rebellious generation. (vv. 1, 7f.)

B.) *Development of point using either/or categories*: God did many miracles inviting their trust (vv. 11-16), but the sons of Ephraim continued to sin, putting God to the test, demanding the food they craved. (vv. 9f., 17-20) Therefore, God's wrath broke out and he sent fire, but they still did not trust. (v. 21f.)

C.) *Introduction of manna as a rhetorical trump*: God even opened the doors of heaven and rained down manna for people to eat, and he gave them the "grain of heaven." Mortals ate the "bread of angels"—as much as they desired. He also rained down flesh (flying birds as thick as sand on the shore), satisfying all their cravings, but despite all this, they went on sinning. Even as the flesh was between their teeth God's anger rose up against them, putting to death even the strongest of them, and yet they still put God to the test. (vv. 23-41)

D.) *Continued development and implications*: God did miraculous signs in Egypt (vv. 42-51) and delivered them from the oppressor (vv. 52-55), but they still put God to the test. (v. 56) Therefore, God was angered. He consumed their young men with fire, put their priests to death by the sword, and rejected the tribe of Ephraim, choosing *Judah* instead.

E.) *Reiteration of main point (A)*: Therefore, God chose David his servant (*and* his monarchy) to be a shepherd to his people and to lead them with skillful hands. Implied exhortation (and threat?): be thankful for God's provision though the Davidic monarchy (pay your taxes, perform your civic duties cheerfully, live righteously, etc.) and do not be ungrateful as were your "grumbling" forefathers in the wilderness, who craved something more. You saw what happened to the Northern Kingdom . . . will *you* be next? (vv. 68-72)

---

[25] This table is adapted from Anderson, *Christology, Table 16,* same title.

This is precisely the same rhetorical use of manna pattern used in John 6, but Borgen's thesis must be amended in one more way. The proponent of the manna motif is portrayed as being neither Jesus nor the narrator, but *the unbelieving crowd*. It is *they* who seek to tempt Jesus into producing more loaves, using Palestinian manna rhetoric to bolster their appeal! In that sense, the function of the Psalm 78:24f. quotation is far less like the expository midrashic form of such passages as Exodus Rabbah 25:1-8, and far more like Satan's use of scripture as a proof-text in the Matthean temptation narrative. (Matt. 4:1-11) Here the Matthean rendition is closer than the Lucan (Luke 4:1-12) to the Palestinian proof-text rhetoric of the Johannine crowd. A.) The request for bread is uttered (Matt. 4:3). B.) Jesus refuses, citing scripture (Deut. 8:3—the Deuteronomic application of the manna motif to the superiority of the Torah) to focus upon the core hunger (need) of humanity, which is spiritual rather than physical (Matt. 4:4). C.) Satan tempts Jesus further, citing scripture (Ps. 91:11f.) and promising that he will be rescued supernaturally (Matt. 4:5f.). D.) Jesus cites scripture back (Deut. 6:16), warning him not to put the Lord God to the test (Matt. 4:7). E.) Satan gets to the overall point and promises Jesus wealth and power if he will bow down and worship him (Matt. 4:8). Jesus refuses and passes the time of testing successfully, fully prepared now to begin his ministry. This stylized dialogue is entirely parallel in function to the crowd's request and dialogue with Jesus in John 6. Here we see clearly the crowd's use of manna as a "rhetorical trump."

3. The crowd's use of manna as a "rhetorical trump" in John 6.

While the Q temptation narrative couches the purification of Jesus' mission as his being tested (and becoming prepared?) before his public ministry begins, John uses the crowd's "tempting" of Jesus ironically. It is actually *they* (as well as the Jews and the disciples) who are tested, and unfortunately they fail the test. The evangelist's employment of Palestinian manna rhetoric here is entirely in order, either as a narratological tool or as a stylized transmission of an actual debate that may have occurred during the ministry of Jesus.[26] The form of the crowd's request is as follows:

Table #3, "The Use of Manna as a 'Rhetorical Trump' by the Crowd in John 6"

A.) *Main point of the crowd's request*: "*How long* have you been here?" (John 6:25; actually inquiring, "And *just how long will it be*

---

[26] In Mark 8:11-13 and Matthew 16:1-4 Jewish leaders request another sign from heaven after the feeding, and this is followed by the disciples' debate over loaves given the dearth of bread in the boat, leading to Jesus' interpretation of the feeding (Mark 8:14-21; Matt. 16:5-12). On the basis multiple attestation, the likelihood of an actual discussion seems plausible. *Table #3* here is adapted from Anderson, *Christology*, *Table 17*, same title.

until we receive *another* feeding?). The ironic character of this odd question is implied by their failure to understand Jesus' mission (v. 14), disclosed by Jesus' knowing response (v. 26), and declared by the evangelist ironically (vv. 32ff.) and explicitly by means of Jesus' assessment of their views (v. 36).

B.) *Development of point using either/or categories*: (In response to Jesus' exhortation to work not for death-producing bread, but the life-producing food which the Son of Man shall give, v. 27) The crowd asks, "What must we do to do (work?) the works of God (and thus receive the life-producing as opposed to death-producing food, v. 28)?" The negotiating implication here is: "We are willing to do *our* part."

C.) *Introduction of manna as a rhetorical trump* (and repetition of main point, A): "Then what sign will *you* show us that we may see and believe you? . . . *Our fathers* ate manna in the desert." (v. 30f.) Clearly the gauntlet is thrown down. They are willing to do their part . . . is Jesus willing to do his? If he is really sent by God (v. 29—like Moses in Deut.18:15-22), can he match the manna-producing wonders of old?

D.) *Continued development and its implications*: The crowd then marshalls scriptural support for their manna-rhetoric, "As it is written, 'He gave them *bread from heaven to eat.*'" (v. 31) By now, the request has become a threat—"If you are indeed sent by God (as the prophet like Moses, who says and does nothing on his own behalf and only what the Father instructs him), let's see some heavenly provision of food." Two implications follow: 1.) "If you are as great as Moses, feed us in the wilderness once more." 2.) "If so, we will believe in you; if you can't, why should we?"

E.) *Reiteration of main point*: "Therefore, they said to him (regarding the bread which comes down from heaven, D), 'Lord, give us this bread all the time.'" (v. 34) The fact that this is portrayed as an ironic misunderstanding is declared by Jesus in v. 36. The crowd is still after their main interest: another feeding (main point A, above).

This pattern is identical to the most typical use of manna in ancient Jewish literature, which is to use manna as a secondary text—a "rhetorical trump," and it illustrates the extended use of irony throughout John 6, further implying its unity. Against Borgen's view that John 6:31 represents the Proem text of the homiletical pattern he describes, one actually finds quite a different pattern. Rather than correcting the sincere exegesis of the crowd in vv. 32ff., the evangelist portrays Jesus as opposing their distortion of the scriptures by using them as a proof-text and failing to comprehend the overall truth to which they point. In their wielding of scriptural knowledge (John 5:39; 6:31), using it for their own ends (John 5:44 and 6:27), they neither are indwelt by the Father's "word" (John 5:38 and 6:45), nor are they willing to "come to" Jesus in order to receive life (John 5:40 and 6:44). Therefore, rather than vv. 31-58 being a unitive Christian midrashic development of Exodus 16:4 in the light of Jesus' ministry, the "Proem text" to be developed "midrashically" is the *works and words of Jesus* (vv. 1-25); and unenlightened manna rhetoric must first be overturned in the testing of the crowd, the Jews, the disciples and Peter. Thus, the manna motif plays a secondary role to the overall theme of *testing*, which is the pervasive and unifying motif of John 6.

C. REVELATION AND RHETORIC IN JOHN: TWO DIALOGICAL MODES OF THE JOHANNINE NARRATIVE

John's narrative has two basic dialogical modes: revelation and rhetoric. The former engages the reader in the divine-human dialogue, calling for a believing response to God's saving initiative in Christ Jesus. The signs narratives, the witness motif, Jesus' "I Am" sayings (and most of the other discourses and narrative) drive home this basic message: God's saving initiative in Jesus invites a believing, human response. Even the purpose of the Fourth Gospel itself is articulated in such terms (John 20:30f.). As S. Schneiders says:

> The central concern of the Fourth Gospel is the saving revelation which takes place in Jesus. This revelation, however, must be understood as a dialogical process of Jesus' self-manifestation as the one being continuously sent by the Father (7:16-18) who is thereby encountered in Jesus (10:30; 14:9-11) and the response of belief on the part of the disciple (17:8).[27]

The Johannine narrative also serves a rhetorical function, and nowhere is this rhetorical mode as extended and effective as in the Johannine misunderstanding dialogue. The purpose of this narrative form is to engage the reader in an imaginary dialogue with Jesus, whereby false and shallow notions of faith are identified and corrected by Jesus, thus exposing error and realigning the belief of the reader in more adequate directions. According to the Russian form-critic, Mikhail Bakhtin, misunderstanding in the novel—or any narrative—*always* serves a rhetorical function:

---

[27] S. M. Schneiders, "Women in the Fourth Gospel and the Role of Women in the Contemporary Church," *Biblical Theological Bulletin* 12 (1982), 39.

The device of 'Not understanding'—deliberate on the part of the author, simpleminded and naive on the part of the protagonist—always takes on great organizing potential when an exposure of vulgar conventionality is involved. Conventions thus exposed—in everyday life, mores, politics, art and so on—are usually portrayed from the point of view of a man who neither participates in nor understands them.[28]

1. *The revelational scenario/discourse as declaration of the divine initiative*
The overall structure of the Johannine narrative moves along in a forward-moving spiral, combining cyclical-repetitive themes with linear-progressive developments. This forward-moving spiral is dialectical on several levels. Most superficially, we see dramatized dialogues between Jesus and his discussants. Then, we read of opposing themes and motifs, placed in juxtaposing tension within the text—obviously a sign of a dialectical (rather than a dogmatic) thinker, seeking to engage his reader in a literary dialogue. Next, we may infer something of the dialectical situation in which the evangelist was writing; but finally and most profoundly, we see in John, articulated more clearly than in any canonical composition, a thorough-going development of the human-divine dialectic wherein humanity is called to an existential, believing response to God's eschatological, saving initiative in Christ Jesus. Most scenarios and teachings depict some aspect of God's saving initiative, accompanied by an illustration of, or an invitation to, believing responsiveness to the divine initiative. This comprises the *revelational* structure of plot progression in John. God or God's agent initiates the potentially-saving dialogue with humanity, and the adequacy of human response produces a result in terms of light and life or darkness and death. This cycle of divine initiative and human response may be portrayed graphically as follows:[29]

---

[28] M. Bakhtin, "Forms of Time and Chronotope in the Novel" in *The Dialogic Imagination*, edited by M. Holquist (Austin, Texas, 1981), p. 164. Johannine use of misunderstanding, of course, is closer to Bakhtin's analysis of the classical Greek biography than the modern novel. See also my paper presented in the New Testament and Rhetoric Section of the National SBL Meetings in Chicago, 1994, "Mikhail Bakhtin and the Corrective Rhetoric of the Johannine Misunderstanding Dialogue."

[29] Not only does the Johannine revelation scenario/discourse describe the sequence of divine initiative—human response (vv. 6, 27, 29, 32f., 35, 37-40, 44-51, 53-58, 63-65), but the narrative also *models such a sequence* where the human-divine dialectic is the main emphasis of the evangelist (vv. 5, 10-13, 19-21, 67). For a schematic outline of how the revelational pattern is juxtaposed with the rhetorical pattern in John 6, see Anderson, *Christology, Table 9*: "Divine Initiative Versus Human Initiative in the Narration of John 6."

Table #4, "Divine Initiative and the Revelational Scenario/Discourse in John"

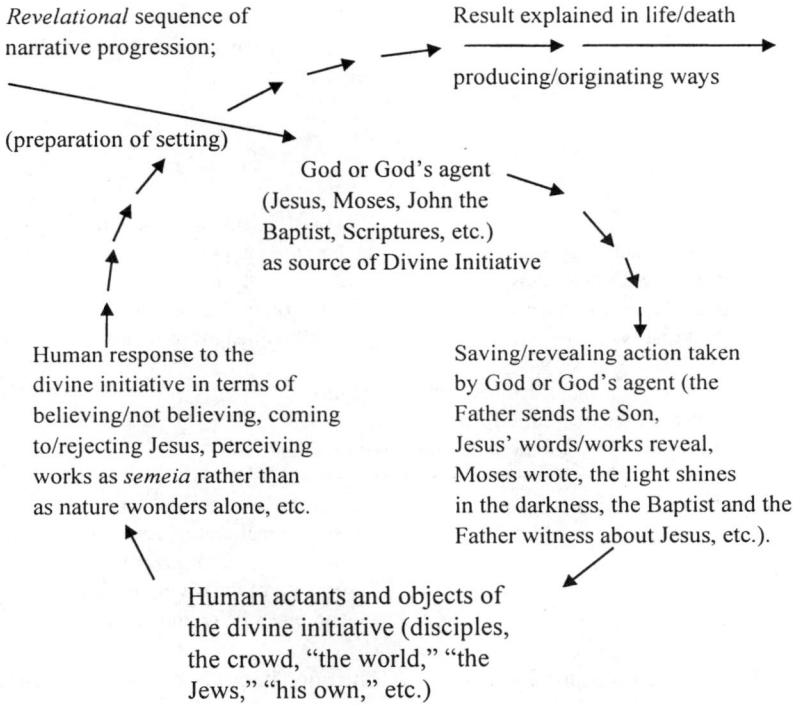

Revelational sequence of narrative progression;

Result explained in life/death

producing/originating ways

(preparation of setting)

God or God's agent (Jesus, Moses, John the Baptist, Scriptures, etc.) as source of Divine Initiative

Human response to the divine initiative in terms of believing/not believing, coming to/rejecting Jesus, perceiving works as *semeia* rather than as nature wonders alone, etc.

Saving/revealing action taken by God or God's agent (the Father sends the Son, Jesus' words/works reveal, Moses wrote, the light shines in the darkness, the Baptist and the Father witness about Jesus, etc.).

Human actants and objects of the divine initiative (disciples, the crowd, "the world," "the Jews," "his own," etc.)

This dialectical structure is identical within the narration of Jesus' signs *and* discourses in John. Both further the kerygmatic interest of the evangelist's understanding of Jesus' mission, and there is no evidence for (or advantage to) assuming that narrative sign and interpretive discourse were *ever* divorced within the Johannine tradition. They both bespeak the human-divine dialectic and call for a believing response to the divine initiative revealed eschatologically in Christ Jesus.

2. The rhetorical function of the Johannine misunderstanding dialogue

On the other hand, where the initiative passes to the discussant and others take the initiative, they often betray a misunderstanding—or a kind of shallow conventionality—and the function of this form will always be corrective and *rhetorical*. Certainly, Professor Painter's outline of the anatomy of the Johannine quest story is helpful here, especially as he outlines the rhetorical function of the objections.[30] As in the structure of the revelational mode of narrative progression, the rhetorical is characterized by its own distinctive pattern:

Table #5, "The Shift to Human Initiative and the Rhetorical Thrust of the Johannine Misunderstanding Dialogue"[31]

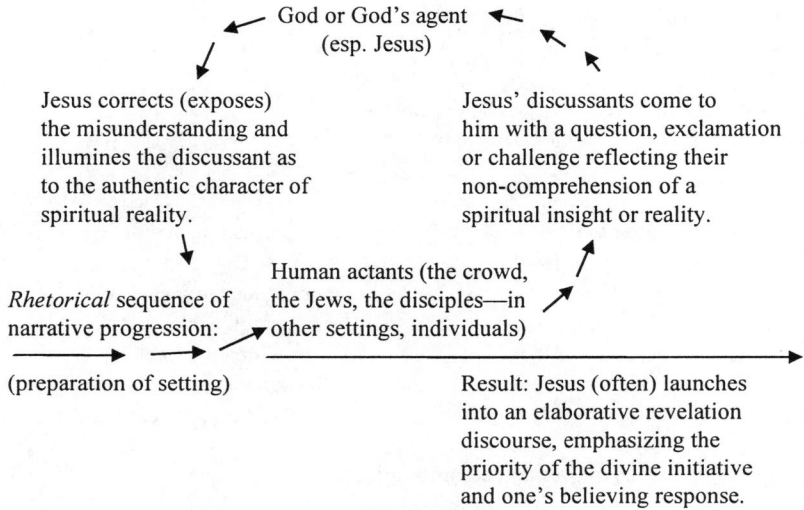

God or God's agent
(esp. Jesus)

| Jesus corrects (exposes) the misunderstanding and illumines the discussant as to the authentic character of spiritual reality. | Jesus' discussants come to him with a question, exclamation or challenge reflecting their non-comprehension of a spiritual insight or reality. |

Human actants (the crowd, the Jews, the disciples—in other settings, individuals)

Rhetorical sequence of narrative progression:

(preparation of setting)

Result: Jesus (often) launches into an elaborative revelation discourse, emphasizing the priority of the divine initiative and one's believing response.

What we have in John 6 is a shifting back and forth between revelational and rhetorical modes of narrative progression marked clearly by the changes of initiative. Interestingly, when the sequence of initiative changes, so does the rhetorical function in most cases.

---

[30] John Painter's insight is especially helpful where he states, "These difficulties or objections are important because it is by means of them that the story teller may wish to change the audience's attitudes." ("Quest, Rejection and Commendation in John 6: A Response to Peder Borgen" 1992 SNTS Johannine Literature Seminar, p. 1). See also Painter's *The Quest for the Messiah: The History, Literature and Theology of the Johannine Community*, 2nd ed. (Nashville: Abingdon, 1993), pp. 33-135, 252-86. Again, to bolster this insight with Bakhtin's judgment, "Stupidity (incomprehension) in the novel is always polemical: it interacts dialogically with an intelligence (a lofty pseudo intelligence) with which it polemicizes and whose mask it tears away." (M. Bakhtin, "Discourse in the Novel" in his *The Dialogical Imagination* [Austin, Texas, 1981], p. 403). While Bakhtin applies this insight to the mimicking function of the misunderstanding protagonist in the modern novel, it works even better where the protagonist's *partners in dialogue* fail to understand—a common rhetorical feature of classical Greek biographical narrative.

[31] Modified from Anderson, *Christology, Table 19*: "Human Initiative and the Rhetorical Misunderstanding Dialogue in John. " See also my 1994 paper mentioned above in note 28.

Table #6, "Transitions Between Revelational and Rhetorical
Modes in John 6"

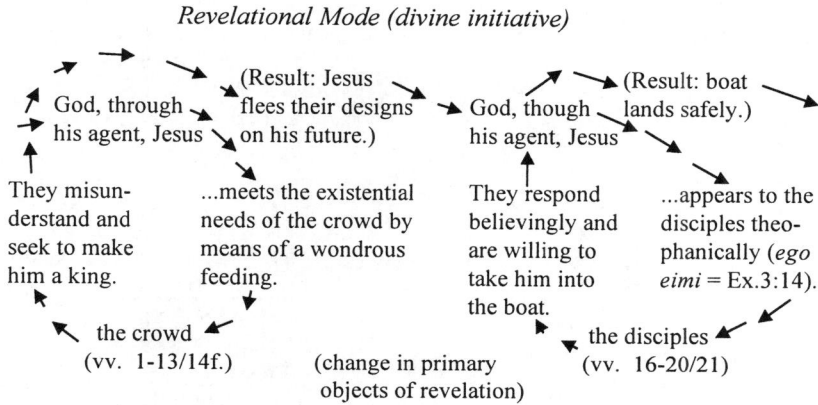

Revelational Mode (divine initiative)

God, through his agent, Jesus

(Result: Jesus flees their designs on his future.)

God, though his agent, Jesus

(Result: boat lands safely.)

They misunderstand and seek to make him a king.

...meets the existential needs of the crowd by means of a wondrous feeding.

They respond believingly and are willing to take him into the boat.

...appears to the disciples theophanically (*ego eimi* = Ex.3:14).

the crowd
(vv. 1-13/14f.)

(change in primary objects of revelation)

the disciples
(vv. 16-20/21)

Reversal of Sequence to Rhetorical Mode (human initiative)

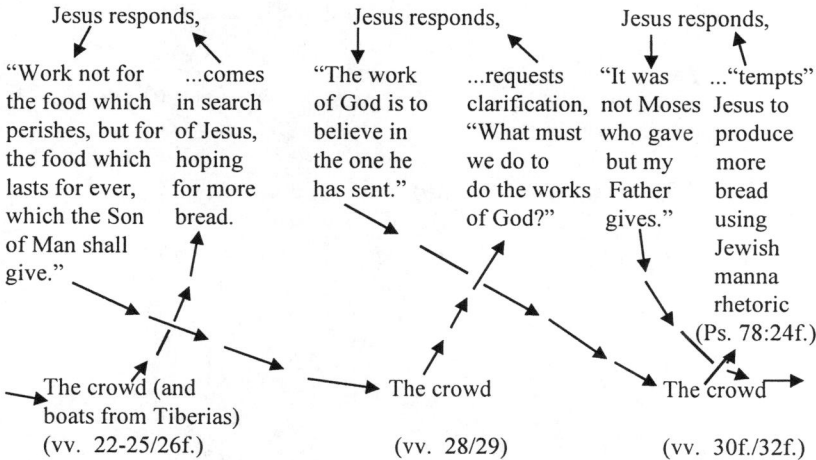

Jesus responds,

"Work not for the food which perishes, but for the food which lasts for ever, which the Son of Man shall give."

...comes in search of Jesus, hoping for more bread.

Jesus responds,

"The work of God is to believe in the one he has sent."

...requests clarification, "What must we do to do the works of God?"

Jesus responds,

"It was not Moses who gave but my Father gives."

..."tempts" Jesus to produce more bread using Jewish manna rhetoric (Ps. 78:24f.)

The crowd (and boats from Tiberias)
(vv. 22-25/26f.)

The crowd
(vv. 28/29)

The crowd
(vv. 30f./32f.)

Jesus responds,
(first discourse)

Jesus responds,
(second discourse)

"I am the Bread of Life. He who believes in me shall never go hungry. ... And I shall raise him up on the last day."

...(still misunderstanding, clarified in v. 36) requests ironically, "Sir (Lord), give us this bread always!"

"No one can come to me unless the Father draws him." (Cites Isa.54:13) "The bread I shall give is my flesh."

"Is this not Mary and Joseph's son whom we know? How can he now say 'I came from heaven'?"

The crowd

(change in discussants)

The Jews grumble,

(vv. 34/35-40)

(vv. 41f./43-51)

Jesus responds,
(third discourse)

Jesus responds,
(revisiting the main theme in v. 27)

"Unless you eat the flesh of the Son of Man and drink his blood you have no life in you. ... He who eats this bread will live eternally."

"How can this man give us his flesh to eat?"

"Does this offend you?... The Spirit is life-producing, the flesh profits nothing. ... The words I have spoken to you are spirit and life. ... No one can come to me unless enabled by the Father."

"This is sure a hard word! Who can go along with it?"

The Jews now fought among themselves, saying,

(setting: the Synagogue in Capernaum; change of discussant)

The disciples also grumbled and said,

(vv. 52/53-58)

(v. 59)

(v. 60/61-65)

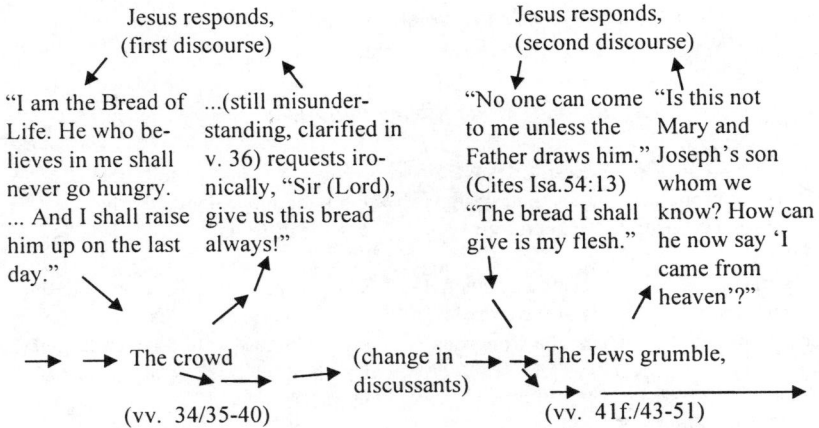

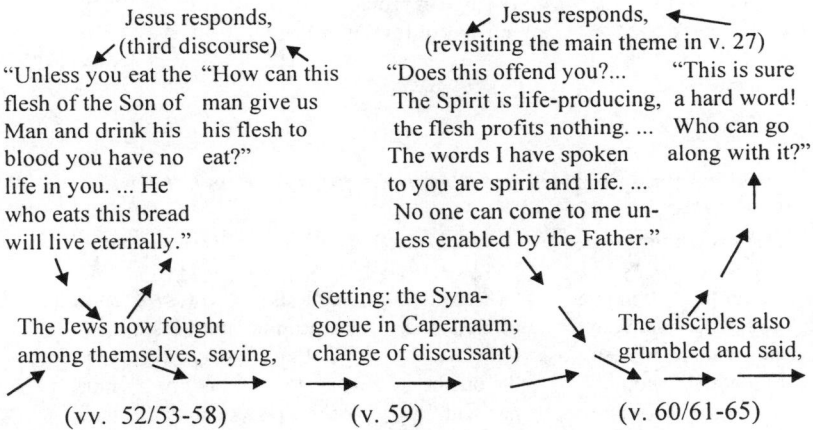

Reversal of Sequence to Revelational Mode (divine initiative)

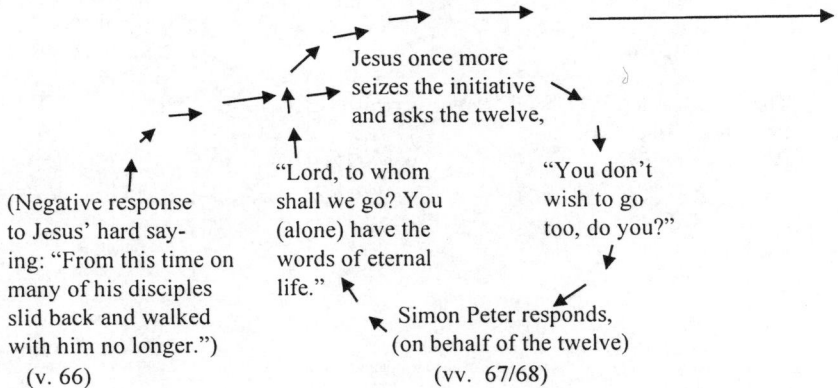

Jesus once more seizes the initiative and asks the twelve,

"You don't wish to go too, do you?"

(Negative response to Jesus' hard saying: "From this time on many of his disciples slid back and walked with him no longer.")
(v. 66)

"Lord, to whom shall we go? You (alone) have the words of eternal life."

Simon Peter responds,
(on behalf of the twelve)
(vv. 67/68)

Reversal of Sequence to Rhetorical Mode (human initiative—implied by Jesus' response)

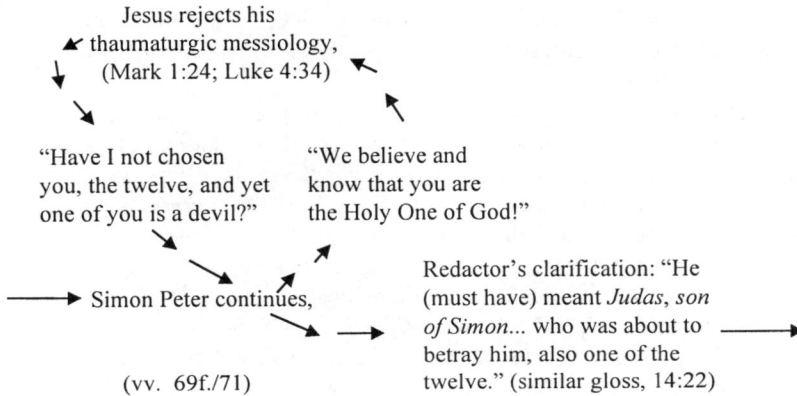

Jesus rejects his
thaumaturgic messiology,
(Mark 1:24; Luke 4:34)

"Have I not chosen
you, the twelve, and yet
one of you is a devil?"

"We believe and
know that you are
the Holy One of God!"

Simon Peter continues,

Redactor's clarification: "He
(must have) meant *Judas, son
of Simon*... who was about to
betray him, also one of the
twelve." (similar gloss, 14:22)

(vv. 69f./71)

Casting the narrative of John 6 in this kind of schema illustrates the theological *and* reader-response interests of the evangelist.[32] They are interwoven into a cyclical-repetitive and a linear-progressive pattern of dialectical narrative, which not only proclaims the divine initiative but models it as well. And, it not only portrays Jesus' correcting his discussants but functions to engage the reader in a saving dialogue with Jesus by assuming him or her into the role of the misunderstanding discussant. It is this latter point that has been under-developed by reader-response analysts.[33] As interesting as many of these studies are, they become most

---

[32] J. D. Crossan, "It Is Written: Structuralist Analysis of John 6" in *Semeia* 26 (1983), 3-21, asks "What would one see if one took John 6 as a unity and officially omitted any historical questioning of the text? What would happen if one attempted by looking at *how* the text means to see *what* the text means?" (p. 3). While Crossan leaves historical/critical discussions out here and simply analyzes the structure of John 6 as it stands, seeking to assess how its earliest audiences may have responded to its content, the above summary of historical/critical findings suggests that this approach *is* warranted. John 6 represents a literary unity which combines signs and discourses in such a way as to "exegete" the meaning of Jesus' works and words for later audiences in the Johannine situation. As the final writing of John 6 probably did not occur until the 80's or 90's, one may also learn something of the history of Johannine Christianity by observing how the "nourishment" which Jesus offers is progressively contrasted to other types of "bread."

[33] On one hand, the works of D. Wead, *The Literary Devices in John's Gospel* (Basel, 1970); R. A. Culpepper, *The Anatomy of the Fourth Gospel* (Philadelphia: Fortress, 1983); P. Duke, *Irony in the Fourth Gospel* (Atlanta: John Knox, 1985); J. Staley, *The Print's First Kiss* (Missoula: Scholars Press, 1987); G. O'Day, *Revelation in the Fourth Gospel* (Philadelphia: Fortress, 1986), and others do the guild a great service in raising Johannine debates above historical/critical impasses and diachronic/synchronic brawls. They help us look at the text afresh, with new eyes, and avail new possibilities for meaningful interpretation.

On the other hand, John was not written as a fictional drama (dramatic though it be) nor as a novel (novelistic though it be). Neither is John an expressionistic or an impressionistic work of art—simply to be appreciated for its form. Its genre is that of a gospel narrative, and it

fully useful when the valuable insights learned about John's dramatic portrayal of the gospel are applied within its historical and socio-religious context. Again, the thesis of this study is to suggest that this historical context will be illuminated by means of considering the false notions of spiritual reality, as represented by Jesus' discussants and his corrective responses to them.

    Another way of putting it is to say that because the literary form of John 6 is a unitive Christian homily, connecting later audiences with the existential significance of the "Bread" which Jesus offers versus less satisfying (death-producing) kinds of "bread," a sequence of acute crises may be inferred from the way the narrative progresses. As the preacher/evangelist tells the story of Jesus' feeding and accompanying events, their various earlier interpretations become the stuff of which later exhortations are made. This is the basic *Sitz im Leben* of the Johannine Bread of Life Discourses. From these exhortations (and at times rhetorical correctives) one may infer specific crises within the evolving historical context of the Johannine audience, and these crises are corroborated by other passages in John, the Johannine Epistles, and the letters of Ignatius.

D. FOUR ACUTE CRISES FACED WITHIN JOHANNINE CHRISTIANITY AS IMPLIED BY JOHN 6

If Bakhtin and Painter are indeed correct, that incomprehension in narrative is always rhetorical (n.30), the failure of Jesus' discussants to understand his deeds and words in John 6 must have been targeted at correcting specific problems in the Johannine audience. Rather than simply telling the story within an abstract setting, the evangelist has specific audiences in mind, whose thinking and actions he desires to correct by means of engaging them in an imaginary dialogue with Jesus. This rhetorical action happens on two levels beyond the *einmalig* level of the events reported. The first represents issues addressed during the oral narration of the events, as

---

purports real events and messages to be responded to by real people in real settings. Therefore, historical/critical issues cannot wholly be left aside for interpretation—even form-analytical interpretation—to reach its fullest potential. Context always affects meaning. While I am not convinced of his views on authorship, M. Stibbe's attempt to combine literary analysis with historical/critical interests seems a profitable way forward (*John as Storyteller* [Cambridge: Cambridge University Press, 1992]; *John* [Sheffield: Sheffield Academic Press, 1993]; and *John's Gospel* [London and New York: Routlege, 1994]; also see Stibbe's collection, *The Gospel of John as Literature: An Anthology of Twentieth-Century Perspectives* [Leiden and New York: E.J. Brill, 1993]). Consider also Margaret Davies, *Rhetoric and Reference in the Fourth Gospel*, JSNTSS 69 (Sheffield: JSOT Press, 1992), for an interdisciplinary approach to literary analysis. Literary studies that will be the most far-reaching and enduring will probably be ones that address adequately the multiplicity of Johannine issues, not just a few.

represented by the way the narrative eventually becomes fixed. This level reflects specific, acute crises (both intramural and extramural) faced by the Johannine community. On this level one may infer the preacher has specific individuals and groups in mind, whose inadequate notions and actions are portrayed as being corrected by the Johannine Jesus as he narrates the story. The second level is often more general, and it involves attempts to preserve earlier traditions and to reach later audiences by means of the written, rather than the spoken, word. In these ways, those whose non-comprehending views are corrected by the Johannine Jesus are *specific individuals and groups*, whose appreciations of the human-divine dialectic require modification. But, these rhetorical devices are also *universalizing*. They appeal to the "light" within every reader, against the ever-encroaching ploys of darkness that so easily beset one's willingness to respond to the divine initiative, tending to replace it with inauthentic trust in human-initiated strategies, which ironically fail so miserably. John 6:25-70 reflects the evangelist's addressing of four such crises and his christocentric responses to them. As the key exhortative text for this section of v. 27, "Work not for death-producing food, but for the eternally life-producing food, which the Son of Man shall give." We will see that each of the misunderstandings betrays a false notion of "food," which is enacted by a particular group representing a perception to be corrected in the Johannine audience by Jesus. Furthermore, with the change of discussant, one may also detect a change in theme, which in turn implies a new epoch and audience targeted by the evangelist. At every turn, the Johannine Jesus corrects these notions and directs the hearer/reader toward a saving/believing acceptance of the "food" to be availed by the Son of Man. While literarily synchronic, the narration of events is rhetorically diachronic.

One more comment about how this dialectical pattern works in John 6. Each of these corrective dialogues has three central parts to it, often with preparative hints before it and a revisiting of the theme after it. The three central parts include: 1.) an *action or teaching of Jesus*, which may be understood on more than one level; 2.) a *misunderstanding statement, question or action* on the part of a new individual or group; and 3.) the *corrective statement or discourse by Jesus*, defining the true way to perceive or respond to the divine initiative and its implications for discipleship. Such an outline produces various sets of double meanings, as part 3 in one dialogue becomes inevitably part 1—the source of misunderstanding for the next.[34] Put in outline form, the four misunderstanding dialogues in John 6 are as follows:

---

[34] This highly interwoven character of the dialectical progression of the Johannine narrative is further evidence of the chapter's unity. Much as Plato has constructed his Socratic dialogues in terms of extended hypothetical syllogisms, for the dual purposes of preserving the teaching of his mentor and refuting his own opponents, the Fourth Evangelist constructs

Table #7, "Discussants, Themes and Audiences in the
Four Misunderstanding Dialogues in John 6"

Discussants	Theme/ Issue	Jesus' Preceding Words or Works	Misunderstanding Action or Statement	Jesus' Response or Discourse
the crowd	physical bread	the feeding of the 5,000	four statements requesting more bread	You did not signs... . "I a am the Bread of life."
the Jews	the bread of the Torah	"I am the Bread coming down from heaven."	"How can he... say 'I have come down from hea- ven'?... give us his flesh to eat?"	"'They shall all be taught by God' ... He who eats of this bread shall live eternally."
the disciples	embra- cing the cross	"Unless you eat my flesh and drink my blood, you have no life."	grumbling, "This is a hard saying! Who can swallow it?"	"The flesh profits nothing... No one can come to me unless the Father draws him."

---

his dialogues/discourses like a snowball, layer upon layer, drawing in specific notions to be corrected by the ongoing voice of the risen Lord as needed within each epoch of the community's history. The audience probably would have heard much of the whole unit, together, many times over many years, and we probably have relatively few interpolations added to the final written version. The one exception in John 6 may be vv. 16-21, which appears to be earlier (certainly more primitive and less developed) than even the Marcan account. It could be that the contents of John 6 were preached mostly without the sea crossing, and that it has been added by the evangelist to make the written rendition more complete. This need not, however, imply John's dependence on the Synoptics. Verse 71, of course, is a clarifying gloss, probably added by the redactor as he inserted John 6 as a unit between chs. 5 and 7.

Discussants	Theme/ Issue	Jesus' Preceding Words or Works	Misunderstanding Action or Statement	Jesus' Response or Discourse
Peter	the be-trayal of Jesus	"You do not wish to leave too, do you?"	"You are the Holy One of God."	"Have I not chosen you, the Twelve, and one of you is a devil?"

The four crises alluded to within the Johannine audience include the following: a.) the physical bread versus the revelational significance of Jesus' ministry reflects an ongoing dialogue between the Johannine view of Jesus' ministry and the prevalent view of mainstream Christianity as represented by all three Synoptic Gospels. This dialogue may have extended from the days of the pre-Marcan tradition through the influence of the written Matthean Gospel (from the 50's or before through the early 90's). b.) The "bread" of the Torah versus the Bread which Jesus gives and is represents the acute dialogue between Johannine Christianity and the local Synagogue over the source of divine authority precipitated by the success of the Christian mission within Judaism. It was most acute within a decade or two of the destruction of the Temple (from the mid 70's to the mid 80's). c.) The challenge to Jesus' disciples to ingest the flesh and blood of Jesus (to participate with him in embracing the cross, v. 51c) would have been felt most acutely during the persecution of Christians in Asia Minor (and elsewhere) by Domitian (from the mid 80's through the mid 90's). During these years, as those who did not participate in public emperor-laud were punished and sometimes executed, Gentile converts to the faith would have been most scandalized by the cost of their new-found religion. In turn, they adopted docetizing (Hellenic) views of Jesus' sufferings in order to excuse their own attempts to retain their Christian identity without having to suffer for it. d.) The juxtaposition of Peter and the Beloved Disciple would have been targeted most acutely toward reversing the institutionalizing tendencies within the mainstream churches (esp. Antiochine influence from the mid 80's through the late 90's). The ambivalent portrayal of Peter in John must have been targeted against the likes of Diotrephes and his kin—those who abused ecclesial power and were threatened by the the Johannine approach to christocracy, the means by which the risen Lord leads the church. A fuller discussion of these evolving challenges follows below.

1. *Misunderstanding Jesus' miracles: John 6:25-40*

Bultmann, Fortna and others are indeed correct to infer a pointed tension between the evangelist's view of Jesus' miracles and their thaumaturgic valuation within the middle/late first-century church. Their assessments of the Fourth Evangelist's partner in dialogue, however, are far too limited and tame. Rather than presume a backwater Jewish/Christian miracle tract for which there is neither convincing empirical evidence nor compelling theoretical advantage, John must be understood as intending to correct the prevalent Christian view of the significance of Jesus' miracles—as reflected in the *entire Synoptic witness*. Unlike the three other crises, the one reflected most explicitly in John 6:25ff. is not limited to a singular event or epoch. Here Jesus is portrayed as overturning the glorious result of *all five* Synoptic feeding accounts, and the Johannine dialogue with those embracing the mainstream view of miracles as "thaumas" may have extended for decades, or even longer.[35]

In the three Synoptic accounts of the feeding of the 5,000 (Mark 6:42; Matt.14:20; Luke 9:17) and in both accounts of the feeding of the 4,000 (Mark 8:8; Matt.15:37) the nearly identical words are used to describe the felicitous result of the feeding: ἔφαγον καὶ ἐχορτάσθησαν ("they ate . . . and were satisfied"). And, in John 6:26 Jesus declares to the misunderstanding crowd: "You seek me *not* because you saw the signs, but because you *ate. . . and were satisfied*" (ἐφάγετε . . . καὶ ἐχορτάσθητε). This is a direct refutation of the prevalent Christian interpretation of the feeding miracle. Put otherwise, the Johannine Jesus is here portrayed as declaring that those who seek Jesus in hopes of more stomach-satisfying bread have missed the whole point of the soul-reaching miracle. Jesus was not a thaumaturge—Marcan, pre-Marcan, or otherwise.[36] He came to reveal,

---

[35] On the earliest end, given the fact that the Johannine and pre-Marcan oral traditions must have enjoyed an "interfluential" relationship, these dialogues could have been as early as the 40's or 50's. On the latest end, the "publication" of Matthew must have caused some renewed speculation about the role of the believer's faith as a facilitator of miracles (as Matthew embellishes this Marcan theme), so this discussion must have continued into the 90's. Within the dialogue/discourse section of John 6 alone, this debate forms something of an inclusio between vv. 25-34 and 66-70.

[36] The Fourth Evangelist need not, and probably did not, have access to written accounts of the Synoptic feeding narratives in order to disagree with their outcomes. Judged by the fact that both Marcan renditions of the feeding portray the *identical* sequence of all sixteen events (Mark 6:30-45; 8:1-10. The crowd gathers, Jesus feels compassion, the disciples inquire about food, Jesus inquires as to the number of loaves they have, and the supply is reported [five loaves and two fish; seven loaves]. Jesus then commands the crowd to sit on the ground, takes the loaves, gives thanks, breaks the loaves and distributes them, doing the same with the fish, and the felicitous result is described [they "ate and were satisfied"]. Jesus finally orders the disciples to gather the left-overs, the number of full baskets is tallied [twelve; seven], the number of the crowd is reported [5,000; 4,000], and Jesus heads off with his disciples in a boat.), it appears that we have one basic set of events that has been reported in slightly different ways. If written when received, it is doubtful that Mark-as-redactor would have

and even to incarnate, the human-divine saving and revealing dialogue, and the physical effect of Jesus' miracles in John is always embellished in order to magnify their revelational value. Semeiology always depletes ontology.

At this point, the difference between the Synoptic and the Johannine views of the relation between miracles and faith is thrown into sharp relief. In the Synoptics, miracles *require* faith. In John, they *lead to it*.[37] According to John, Jesus never intended for all the lame to walk, for all the blind to see, for all the dead to be raised, for all storms to be calmed, or for all the hungry and thirsty to be physically satisfied. In Mark 8:14-21, though, the disciples are chided by Jesus for not believing more fully that Jesus can do such wonders any time he pleases. The purveyors of the Marcan tradition

changed the numbers in a text for symbolic or rhetorical reasons, and indeed, the same basic sequence is also corroborated in John's independent account.

The Mark 8 rendition may reflect the way the feeding narrative was preached throughout the seven churches in Asia Minor (Seven baskets matches the seven elders appointed to watch over Hellenistic churches in Acts 6:1-7; see also the seven churches and their candlesticks in Rev. 2-3. Clearly the number twelve symbolized the twelve apostles, associated originally with Jewish Christianity in Acts 1. Was the number 4,000 associated with another gathering in the desert by another messianic prophet—"the Egyptian" in Acts 21:38?), which by the time Mark began his editing process had already acquired an "explanation passage" (Mark 8:14-21) reconciling it with the difference in numbers in the more widely known feeding of the 5,000 narrative as a dovetail form of integration? On this account, Robert Fowler's extensive treatment of the Marcan feeding narratives (*Loaves and Fishes: the Function of the Feeding Stories in the Gospel of Mark*, SBLDS 54 [Chico: Scholars Press, 1981]) does not convince. While Mark 8:1ff. does have some details in it that are more primitive than those in Mark 6, the "dovetail section" (Mark 8:14-21) already has built into itself a justification for being considered along with the feeding of the 5,000. This unit seems to have been part of the tradition, not the Marcan redaction, and the fact that it justifies itself suggests the priority of the *other* feeding narrative in Mark 6. Luke's redaction of Mark corroborates this judgment.

The significant fact is that in both accounts the value of the feeding is remembered identically as a "wonder of satisfaction," and it is this pre-Marcan (Petrine?) emphasis with which the Fourth Evangelist disagrees. Then again, this emphasis was not solely early, as the Matthean rendition repeats *both* Marcan accounts not long before John was finalized. Thus, the prevalent interpretation of the value of Jesus' miracles as thaumaturgic would have been rife within the oral (and/or written) traditions of the church for at least a half century—and relatively unchallenged (other than locally) until the circulation of John.

[37] For one of the best treatments of this topic, see R. Kysar, "Seeing Is Believing— Johannine Concepts of Faith" in his *John, the Maverick Gospel*, rev. ed. (Atlanta: John Knox Press, 1993), pp. 78-96. See also Anderson, *Christology*, Chapter 7, "The Dialectical Character of John 6;" and P. N. Anderson, "The Cognitive Origins of John's Unitive and Disunitive Christology," *Horizons in Biblical Theology*, June, 1995.

It is interesting to note that both traditions deal with the existential problem of why miracles do *not* happen in their interpretations of Jesus' works. The pre-Marcan tradition (accentuated even more clearly in the Matthean) explains the dearth of miracles as the result of the lack of human faith. "*God did not fail; you* did not believe fully enough. If you would just have *faith the size of a mustard seed...*" the Synoptic explanation must have gone. The Johannine tradition, perhaps even from its early to middle stages (although exact dates are impossible to establish), dealt with the relative dearth of miracles by symbolizing Jesus' miracles as revelatory *semeia*. In that sense, they occupy a christological function within the Johannine kerygma as testimony to Jesus' being sent from the Father (John 6:32f.; 11:27, etc.)—to be responded to accordingly.

have obviously not reflected upon the existential significance of Jesus' miracles in the same way the Fourth Evangelist has. For whatever reason, he has found the mainstream thaumaturgic interpretation of Jesus' miracles to be inadequate. Their import lay in the existentially nourishing conviction that in the storms and deserts of life Jesus calms his disciples and provides daily "bread" for those who trust and abide in him.

On the other hand, Jesus' miracles are heightened in John as nowhere else in the New Testament. Jesus' ministry begins with a "luxury miracle" (John 2:1-11), and Lazarus has been in the tomb four days (ch.11) before being raised up. Furthermore, Jesus declares that his disciples would do *meizona touton* ("greater things than these," whatever that means; 14:12), and promises that whatever is asked in his name (John 14:13f.) will be done. These motifs suggest a tension between the hope that prayers will be answered—with wonders still continuing to happen within the church—and the experienced reality that suffering and death still continue, even for the believer. John's semeiology is a function of the evangelist's approach to theodicy, suggested also by the representation of *pathos* and grieving within the gospel narrative. At the tomb of Lazarus, for instance, Lazarus' sisters, Jesus, and *even the Jews* weep (John 11:33-35); and *both Martha and Mary* exclaim, "Lord, if you had been here, our brother would not have died!" (John 11:21, 32) Whenever and however the crises underlying these emotions may have happened (and they need not have been singular events alone), the evangelist responds to them by existentializing the signs of Jesus.[38] "As wondrous as Jesus' signs must have been, blessed are those who have not seen—and yet believe." (John 20:29) That, for the evangelist, represents the essence of Christian maturity, and he apparently feels called to challenge some of the less reflective approaches to the miraculous ministry of Jesus. Neither are they adequate for faith, in his view, nor does a Christianized form of thaumaturgy represent Jesus' own purpose for performing his signs to begin with. For the Fourth Evangelist, Jesus' signs are functions of his agency christology and basic elements of his kerygma. They confirm that Jesus has been sent from the Father (Deut. 18:15-22), and that through receiving him God's saving initiative is responded to efficaciously, in faith (John 6:35-40).

One more observation here. The narrative means by which the evangelist structures this corrective is to couch it in the crowd's failure to look beyond conventional messianic expectations to the authentic mission

---

[38] At this point, there is little functional difference between the present approach and the excellent essay by R. Fortna in his second monograph ("Signs and Faith" in *The Fourth Gospel and its Predecessor* [Philadelphia: Fortress, 1988], pp. 235-50). Fortna develops the existentializing way in which the evangelist may have re-worked a hypothetical source that was similar to Mark; the present approach does the same, assuming the "partner in dialogue" was the prevalent Christian interpretation of Jesus miracles—a prevailing mind set—as represented in *all five* gospel feeding accounts.

of Jesus. Just as the misunderstanding crowd wanted to sweep Jesus away and make him a prophet-king like Moses (by force!), they have also misunderstood the significance of the feeding. In doing so, the evangelist co-opts the hearer/reader (Jewish prospect, mainstream Christian, or Johannine community member) into the role of the misunderstanding crowd. While there is ample reason to connect the expectations of the crowd in vv. 14f. with vv. 25-34 historically,[39] the evangelist's narrative connection is rhetorical. He portrays the misunderstanding crowd as seeking to coerce Jesus into producing more bread by means of using typical Jewish manna rhetoric. They cite Ps.78:24f. as their "proof-text" and even challenge his messianic identity in hopes of gaining more bread. The scenario is used ironically by the evangelist to show Jesus as "over-trumping" their highest trump card. By contrast to the crowd's manipulative exegesis, Jesus exposits the priority of responding to God's present eschatological activity if one truly hopes for redemption. Traditional stories of God's saving work in the past prefigure God's saving work in the present, but clinging to the former may cause one to miss the latter. The evangelist here works by analogy in reaching his audience. Just as those who wanted Jesus to produce more bread missed his central reason for coming, those who go along with the prevalent Christian mind set that Jesus' miracles were primarily thaumaturgical—to be repeated if the believer can only muster enough faith—will fail to be truly nourished existentially by the "Bread" offered by the Son of Man. His "food" is to do the work of the Father, regardless of temporal outcomes. The original

---

[39] W. Meeks, for instance, has demonstrated clearly that Mosaic Prophet-King messiologies would have been prevalent in Galilee during the first century CE (*The Prophet-King* [Leiden: E. J. Brill, 1967]). Thus, John 6:14f. is not necessarily a Johannine fiction but represents predictable responses to Jesus during his actual ministry—the sort of messiology Jesus disowns most intensely in the pre-Marcan messianic secret motif—and to which the likes of Theudas, "the Samaritan" and "the Egyptian" catered later. Certainly, the Johannine rendition that Jesus fled (φεύγει, in some early mss.) the crowd because they wanted to enthrone him by force is the earliest. It also seems more historically reliable than the more pietistic Marcan one: Jesus departed into the hills to pray (in agreement with Painter, *Quest*, p. 257-66), a theme which Luke also embellishes.

The way all this connects with the request for more bread is that several ancient Jewish documents connect the second Moses (the new Messiah) with once more raining down bread from heaven. According to *Midrash Rabbah* (*Eccles.* 1:9), for instance, "As the first redeemer caused manna to descend, as it is stated, 'Because I shall cause to rain bread from heaven for you (Ex. 16:4),' so will the latter redeemer cause manna to descend." This connects the feeding and requests for another feeding centrally with conventional Palestinian messianic hopes. At stake originally was not just another meal, but popular hopes for the dawning of the New Age—the overthrow of the Romans and the exaltation of the Jewish nation. The realization that such was not the political agenda of Jesus must have caused even some of his original disciples to "turn away and walk with him no longer." (John 6:66) The evangelist builds on those misunderstandings and defections in his addressing later crises facing the Johannine situation.

hearers/readers of this first misunderstanding dialogue probably would have experienced themselves addressed as follows:

— (Says Jesus) "You seek me not because you perceived the signs, but because you ate of the loaves and were satisfied." (v. 26—To experience my miracles as wonders of satisfaction is to miss the whole point of why they were done. Despite what you hear from the rest of the gospel narrators, I never intended simply to fill people's stomachs. I came to lead them to a believing response to God's saving initiative, and the feeding of the 5,000 serves as a symbol of how this new relationship will supply your most basic existential need, which is spiritual.)

— "For the (real) bread of God is the one who comes down from heaven and gives life to the world." (v. 33—Yes, I know that the manna-provision and the recent feeding were wondrous, but these are only anticipators of the ultimate Bread given incarnationally for the life of the world. People who eat physical bread grow hungry again. But those who partake of this nourishment receive life that lasts forever.)

— "For I have come down not to do my own will, but the will of the one who sent me. And this is the will of the one who sent me: that none of those he has entrusted to me shall be lost, but that I shall raise them up on the last day." (v. 38f.—What makes me most like Moses is not the producing of wondrous bread, but the fact that I speak and do solely what the Father has instructed [Deut. 18:15-18]. And this mission is to gather all of those who have been entrusted to me—to care for them and to provide them all they need to survive the ordeals of life. The final goal is to facilitate their [your] faithfulness during difficult times in order that they [you] may be raised up on the last day. This is the will of the Father, and this is what my mission is all about.)

2. *The dialogue with the Synagogue: John 6:29-51*

Notice the overlapping of nuance and meaning between the different kinds of "bread" in John 6. While the debate with the crowd explicitly ends at v. 40, the seeds of the dialogue with the Jews are already planted as early as v. 29. Unlike the first crisis and its corrective implied by the debate of physical bread versus heavenly Bread in John 6, however, the next three crises are more specific in terms of epoch and group. Here we have three sets of dialectical relationships between Johannine Christians and other groups, each of which rises and falls in terms of intensity at sequential—though somewhat overlapping—times in the history of Johannine Christianity.[40] The first of these chronologically, and as presented in the narrative, is the dialogue with leaders of the local Synagogue.

---

[40] In this way, the Johannine Bread of Life Discourse serves the social function of calling to present events in the past in such a way as to create what W. Meeks describes as a

Few books have made more of an impression upon Johannine studies over the last quarter of a century than J. Louis Martyn's *History and Theology in the Fourth Gospel*.[41] In it, Martyn argues successfully that behind the *einmalig* (events reported) level of John's narrative is another level of history—one contemporary with the situation of the evangelist and his audience—suggested by the way the events are narrated. In a nutshell, Martyn reconstructs a scenario which divides the history of Johannine Christianity into three periods. The *Early Period* (from the 60's to the 80's) involved the successful conversion of Jews within a particular Synagogue by means of an evangelist who used a signs gospel to convince Jews that Jesus was the Messiah. Thus, the first Johannine Christians were actually Christian Jews. The *Middle Period* (late 80's-early 90's) saw rising opposition to the Christianizing trend, which led to scriptural debates about the authority of Moses and the Torah (versus Jesus), the devising of the *Birkat ha-Minim* (a curse against "heretics"—specifically "Nazarenes," or Christians), the expulsion of Christians from the Synagogue (they become *aposynagogos*—a technical term for Synagogue excommunication—found in John 9:22; see also 12:42 and 16:2), and the setting up of local councils of Jewish authorities who persecuted (and even executed) some Christian leaders as a disincentive to the movement's growth. Johannine Christians undergo the transition from having been Christian Jews to becoming Jewish Christians. *The Late Period* (inexact—the 90's and later?) saw the transition into an autonomous community. In doing so, broader Christian relations were sought, Gentiles were also evangelized, "Crypto Christians" who stayed in the Synagogue (while maintaining secret identity "for fear of the Jews") were courted by Johannine Christians, and some Johannine Christians were courted back into the Synagogue by the Jews.[42] Dialogues then begin to accelerate with other Christian groups. According to Martyn, the entirety of John should be read against this Jewish/Christian backdrop. The way the story of Jesus is told in John bespeaks the history of the Johannine Community.

"symbolic universe" ("The Man from Heaven in Johannine Sectarianism," *JBL* 91 [1972], 44-72; reprinted in J. Ashton, ed., *The Interpretation of John* [Philadelphia: Fortress, and London: SPCK, 1986], pp. 141-73). Says Meeks, "More precisely, there must have been a continuing dialectic between the group's historical experience and the symbolic world which served both to explain that experience and to motivate and form the reaction of group members to the experience." (Ashton, *Interpretation*, p. 145)

[41] First published in 1968, the book was revised and enlarged in 1979 (Nashville: Abingdon). In his introduction to *The Interpretation of John* (1986), Ashton judges Martyn's book to be "probably the most important monograph on the Gospel since Bultmann's commentary." (p. 5) Given the outpouring of research into the socio-religious situation of the Johannine community over the last two decades or more, especially with reference to local Jewish/Christian relations, Ashton was right.

[42] See Martyn's "Glimpses into the History of the Johannine Community" (reprinted in his *The Gospel of John in Christian History* [New York: Paulist, 1979]) for his clearest outline of the Johannine Community's history (pp. 90-121).

In his massive commentary on the Johannine Epistles and in his book,[43] *The Community of the Beloved Disciple*, Martyn's former colleague, R. E. Brown, refined his scenario. Brown contributed possible explanations for why the Jews became so hostile toward the Christians. He believes that the adding of Samaritan converts with a Mosaic christology influenced Johannine christology toward a pre-existent one, and this caused Johannine Christians to be called "di-theists" by their Jewish counterparts and thus expelled as heretics. Brown also believes that the Johannine defense against the Jewish community eventually led to an internal schism whereby the secessionists moved toward docetism (and eventually gnosticism), and the rest of the Johannine Christians eventually merged with the Great Church. While not all scholars agree with the outlines of Martyn's and Brown's historical sketches, most scholars have become increasingly convinced that underlying John's rendition of the gospel narrative lie penetrating glimpses of Jewish/Christian dialogues in the late first century CE.[44] These sketches are particularly enlightening when interpreting John 6.

According to Martyn,[45] the manna debate in John 6:31ff. is far more than the reflection of an exegetical debate. Disagreeing with Borgen,[46] Martyn claims:

---

[43] See R. E. Brown, *The Epistles of John* (Garden City, N. Y.: Doubleday, 1982); and *The Community of the Beloved Disciple* (New York: Paulist Press, 1979).

[44] Consider, for instance the critical views of S. Katz, "Issues in the Separation of Judaism and Christianity after 70 C.E.: A Reconsideration," *JBL* 103 (1984), 43-76; and R. Kimelman, "Birkat Ha-Minim and the Lack of Evidence for an Anti-Christian Jewish Prayer in Late Antiquity," in *Jewish and Christian Self-Definition*, Vol.2, ed. by E. P. Sanders et al. (London: Fortress, 1981), pp. 226-44. On one hand, Christians and Jews enjoyed a great deal of cooperation and mutual support. On the other hand, few developments began to threaten Judaism from the inside as much as Christian claims to Jesus being the Messiah and Son of God. This is spelled out very clearly in F. Manns' *John and Jamnia: How the Break Occurred Between Jews and Christians c. 80-100 A.D.*, E.t. by M. Duel and M. Riadi (Jerusalem: Franciscan Printing Press, 1988). Consider also the very creative and insightful book by D. Rensberger, *Johannine Faith and Liberating Community* (Philadelphia: Westminster, 1988), which develops the historical and theological implications of the Johannine community's understanding of liberation through Christ in the light of assumed oppression by the local Synagogue. Some of this would of course have applied to other sources of persecution, such as Roman oppression under Domitian. One is also taken by N. Petersen's *The Gospel of John & the Sociology of Light* (Valley Forge: Trinity Press International, 1993), esp. pp. 80-109, regarding John's anti-structuralism, which would not only have been levied against Jewish pressures, but also eventually as a corrective to rising institutionalism in the late first-century Christian (esp. Antiochine) movement.

[45] Martyn, *The Gospel of John in Christian History*, pp. 123-28.

[46] See Martyn's "footnote essay" (ibid., p. 127, n. 188; and also his review of Borgen's book in *JBL* 86 (1967), 44f.) where he argues that Borgen's view that John 6 reflects a countering of Docetists is wrong. Martyn wants to connect John 6 (and the rest of John, for that matter) almost exclusively with the Christian/Synagogue debates in the Johannine dialectical situation but thereby weakens his own case, as ample evidence suggests at least three or four partners in dialogue with the Johannine situation. In doing so, he chides Borgen wrongly for assuming any sort of connection between the Fourth Gospel and the Johannine Epistles—a connection that actually clarifies (and delimits) the Jewish/Christian tensions

John is not saying to the synagogue, "you misread the text. You should read it, 'He gives them bread from heaven to eat.'" Rather, he is emphatically saying:

1. "You are wrong in your identification of the type. It was not Moses but rather God who provided the manna." . . .
2. "The correspondence between type and antitype is fixed by God in his sovereign freedom." . . .
3. "The issue is not to be defined as an argument about an ancient text. It is not a midrashic issue. By arguing about texts you seek to evade the present crisis. God is even now giving you the true bread from heaven, and you cannot hide from him in typological speculation or in any other kind of midrashic activity. You must decide now with regard to this present gift of God." (pp.127f.)

In these observations Martyn is correct, and lucidly so. The evangelist is not simply performing a Jewish midrash on the "correct" meaning of the manna narrative. He shows Jesus declaring that a true exegesis of the scriptures must lead one *beyond* the scriptures to the one to whom they point—the "True Bread" given now, in the eschatological present, for the enlivening of the world. In doing so, Jesus overturns their manna rhetoric and perhaps for the first time in the history of Jewish/Christian manna midrash, he refers to heavenly manna as death-producing: ". . . your forefathers ate *and they died*; the one eating *this* bread bread will live eternally." (vv. 49f., 58) Thus, as Jesus' misunderstanding discussants shift from the crowd to "the Jews," one infers a shifting of the issues being corrected by the Johannine Jesus. No longer is the crisis one of physical bread versus existential nourishment, but it becomes one of members of John's audience wishing to cling to the bread of the Torah versus the Bread coming down from heaven in the eschatological present. Alluded to already in Jesus' refutation of their proof-texting work in verses 32ff., the misunderstanding question of the Jews in vv. 41f. makes this question explicit. Their grumbling (ἐγόγγυζον) is clearly reminiscent of the unbelieving Israelites of Numbers 11-14 as they ask, "Is this not Jesus, son of Joseph, whose father and mother we know? How can he now say 'I came down from heaven?'"

The rhetorical target of this question now becomes specific. It intends to co-opt members of John's audience who, amidst dialectical tensions with the local Synagogue, may be questioning whether Jesus is indeed the Messiah—the Prophet like Moses who says nothing on his own, but only

---

Martyn advocates. The fact is that they confirm a Christian/Synagogue debate *and* a later, docetic schism.

what the Father has instructed—thus, deserving to be treated in all ways like the one who sent him. The rhetoric they get from the Synagogue leaders must have been something like: "We are followers of *Moses*; after all, Moses gave us heavenly manna . . ."; "We obey the *Father* and are *monotheists*. To worship Jesus is to reject the Father and to become ditheists—thus losing your hope for the blessing promised to the children of Abraham"; "We are *scriptural*. After all, 'Man shall not live by bread alone,' but by the Torah—that written deposit of words proceeding from the mouth of God. (Deut. 8:3) If you leave the Synagogue you will not only forfeit your fellowship with the blessed faith, but you will be absented from access to God's instruction. You will move from consolation to desolation. Reject your Christian heresy, or die!"[47] Indeed, by the time 1 John 2:18-25 was written, Johannine Christians had apparently already been purged from the Synagogue, and some of them had been courted back into the Synagogue, perhaps by family and friends. The explanation for their departure by the Elder obviates an antichristic schism involving defectors who left only to return to the Jewish community whence they came. The outline of his appeal is as follows:

Table #8, "The First Antichristic Schism (1 John 2:18-25)—Jewish
Christians Returning to the Synagogue"

— "Little children, it is the last hour, and as you have heard that the Antichrist is coming, even now, many Antichrists have arisen." (v. 18) The Elder explains the threat as the arrival of the eschaton. The predicted Antichrist *has* come, and is even *manifold,* so beware! You too could be misled.

— "They departed from us but were not a part of us—for if they had really been a part of us they would have remained with us; but this just exposes all of them as aliens" (οὐκ εἰσὶν πάντες ἐξ ἡμῶν, v. 19). Obviously, the antichristic schism has occurred by now, and the Elder "explains" this loss to his community as being attributable to the lack of

---

[47] Many of Martyn's observations do seem warranted, for instance: that much of John's community had Jewish origins; that there was an actual purging whereby followers of Christ were singled out and expelled, becoming *aposynagogos*; that upon expulsion, the Johannine community began to take in more Gentile converts; that some members of the Johannine group either rejoined the Synagogue or became underground Christians; and that the evangelist (and the Elder) sought to stave off further defections and continued to argue that Jesus was the Jewish Messiah, greater than Moses, Abraham and the Torah. On the other hand, the dialogue with Judaism was by no means the only source of dialectical tension within Johannine Christianity. Martyn, for instance, is happy to side with Käsemann, *The Testament of Jesus*, E.t. by G. Krodel (London, 1968), in his locating docetizing tendencies within the evangelist's christology, but he does little with Käsemann's main thesis that the evangelist was centrally caught up in a dialectical relationship with the institutional church.

sincerity of those who left. Their abandonment reveals their lack of owning the Johannine community's ideals and commitment to Jesus as the Christ. They *never were* fully (inwardly) a part.

— "But you have an anointing from the Holy One, and you all are in the know" (οἴδατε πάντες, v. 20). They were unenlightened, but you have the Light within you—and among us. We are all taught by God (see v. 27; and John 6:45; Isa. 54:13).

— "I have not written to you because you do not know the truth, but because you do know it, and because no lie can come from the truth. Who is a liar if not the one denying that Jesus is the Christ. *This* is the Antichrist—the one denying the Father and the Son." (vv. 21f.) Here the Elder affirms the universal character of the gospel. It is not simply a matter of one sect over another; it has to do with minding the Truth, which in his view is Christomorphic. Fugitives from the Truth (liars) deny the Father who sent the Son in their rejection of Christ. Those who adhere to the Truth, however, resist the Antichrist and are firmly grounded in their faith.

— "All who deny the Son forfeit the Father also; but the one confessing the Son gets the Father too." (v. 23) At this point the Jewish/Christian tension is absolutely clear. Gentile Docetists would not be worried about losing "the Father," nor would they be reluctant to affirm Jesus as ὁ χριστός. Here we have telling signs of a Jewish-constructed dichotomy: "If you want the Father, you must renounce Jesus as the Christ; if you cling to Christ, *you forfeit the Father!*" To this the Elder responds, "Nonsense! Because Jesus is sent from the Father as his Agent and Son, to receive him is to receive the Father. Conversely, to reject him is to reject/lose the Father who sent him."

— "If what you have heard from the beginning remains in you, you will both abide in the Father and the Son; and this is the promise which he promised us: life eternal." (vv. 24f.) To abide with Christ and his fellowship, in the midst of persecution and social alienation from your families and friends, is to receive an inheritance in the world beyond. You will not only receive the Father's approval, but eternal life through the Son.

All of this matches identically with the misunderstanding dialogue between the Jews and Jesus in John 6.[48] They question *how* he can now

---

[48] It also matches the setting implied by other debates between the Johannine Jesus and the Jews. For instance, U. C. von Wahlde ("Literary Structure and Theological Argument in Three Discourses with the Jews in the Fourth Gospel," *JBL* 103/4 [1984], 575-584; see also his monograph, *The Earliest Version of John's Gospel* [Wilmington: Michael Glazier, 1989] identifies significant similarities of structure between John 6:31-59; 8:13-59; and 10:22-39.

claim to have come down from heaven when they know his earthly origin—
his parents (πῶς νῦν λέγει, v. 42); and *how* he can give us his flesh to eat
(πῶς δύναται . . . δοῦναι, v. 52). Both of these misunderstandings reflect
the scandal of the incarnation and the scandal of the cross. The unbelieving
world asks "*how* is it possible?"; the Christian proclamation is *that* it has
happened—an eschatological event, calling forth a human response to
God's saving initiative. To the Jewish Christian faced with the pressing
decision of whether to rejoin the security and comforts of the Synagogue,
the words of Jesus in John 6 would have offered a great deal of support for
retaining one's Christian loyalties. They probably would have experienced
themselves addressed by Jesus' words as follows:

— "This is the work of God: that you *believe* in the one he has sent." (v.
29—Salvation is not received by keeping the Torah, but by responding to
God's saving initiative in faith.)
— "It was not Moses who gave . . . but my Father who *gives* you the
true Bread from heaven. For the Bread of God is the one who comes down
from heaven and gives life to the world" (vv. 32f.—Your Jewish friends
have the typology wrong. Neither manna nor the Torah were given to make
us Moses' followers, but to point us to the Source of provision *and*
inspiration—God—who has now provided for our needs through the
incarnation.)
— "I am the Bread of Life. The one coming to me by no means
hungers, and the one believing in me will never thirst." (v. 35—In Christ,
God has acted eschatologically, meeting our true needs. As bread and water
meet our physical hunger and thirst needs, so responding to Christ in faith
meets our deeper, spiritual needs.)
— "And this is the will of the one who sent me, that I should lose none
of those he has given me, but that I should raise them all up on the last

---

As to who the audience hearing these stylized debates must have been, von Wahlde correctly
says, "More likely it is intended to confirm those who already believe and to save those who
are in danger of becoming apostate from the Johannine community. These latter are
undoubtedly the Jewish Christians undergoing persecution and expulsion from the
synagogue." (pp. 583f.)   Martyn, *The Gospel of John in Christian History*, also identifies
four contexts in which the discussions of Jesus as the Mosaic Messiah lead to identifying him
as the Son of Man. They include John 3:1-13; 6:14-58; 7:31-8:28; and 9:17-35ff. It is
significant to note that all of the above passages reflect the concerns of the evangelist around
the time the first edition of the Gospel was completed (according to Lindars' theory), and on
this point one takes issue with Manns (*John and Jamnia*) who connects the Synagogue
tensions with the final edition of John. This means that around the time the first edition of
John was completed, and around the time 1 John was written, Johannine Christians faced an
acute crisis (probably in the 80's, with which Manns *would* concur) with the Synagogue.
(This is not to say that the Johannine Gospel and Epistles represent an identical situation—
they probably involve parallel ones, however, if not the same one. Whatever the connection,
the situations were by no means totally disconnected.) A consideration of the supplementary
material added to the final edition suggests that by the time this later material was produced,
another crisis was impending, and probably a docetic one.

day." (v. 39—You are individually and corporately called by God to abide with Christ and his fellowship until the end. It is the Father's will that none of you should be lost, lapsing back into "the world," but that you all should stay and be raised up in the eschaton. I will provide you all you need in order to be faithful till the end.)

— "No one can come to me except the Father . . . draws him . . . ." (v. 44—Even your apparent initiative is already a response to the Father's drawing in your hearts. It is not a matter of permission—this is not a divine regulation: "No one *may* come . . ."—it is a matter of possibility: "No one *can* come . . ." It is impossible to "discover" the truth of the gospel by means of clever exegesis or religious rigor. Saving faith is counter-conventional. It requires paradoxically the abandonment of our confidence in our own abilities to arrive before we can even begin the journey. No one can come by one's own initiative or ingenuity, religious or otherwise. These must be laid at the cross—and repeatedly so—in order to say "Yes" to the saving initiative of God.)

— "It is written in the Prophets, 'And they shall all be taught by God.'" (v. 45.; Isa. 54:13—Don't worry about the threats of the Jews that you will absent yourselves from God's instruction. After all, the very manna passage they cite has a clear reference in Numbers 11 to Moses' climactic yearning: "Would that *all* the Lord's people were prophets, and that the Lord would put his Spirit on them!" v. 29. And this yearning, as foretold by Isaiah, has been fulfilled in the coming of Christ and the sending of the *Parakletos*. What is anticipated in the Jewish scriptures is actualized in the Christian community!)

— "No one has seen the Father, except the one being with God . . . ." (v. 46; 1:18—This is the reason human initiative cannot suffice, and this is the means by which you are taught by God—his *Logos*—who dwelt among us, and whose glory we beheld (1:14). And, speaking of midrash, this one has "exegeted" the Father to us incarnationally (1:18).

— "I am the living Bread which has come down from heaven; If anyone eats of this bread, he will live eternally; and indeed, this Bread is my flesh which I shall give for the life of the world." (v. 51—Two themes are repeated, but the third one is new. To receive Jesus as God's means of saving initiative in the eschatological present is to be assured of eternal life in the eschatological future. This hope, however, is tempered by the cost of discipleship. Just as Jesus' being the Bread of Life will involve him giving his flesh—on the cross—for the life of the world, so the believer must embrace the cross if he or she wishes to receive this Bread. Paradoxically, to receive the promise of life eternal, one must be willing to undergo suffering and death as did the Lord.)

— "Unless you eat the flesh of the Son of Man and drink his blood, you have no life in you. . . Whoever eats my flesh and drinks my blood abides in me and I in him. . . . This is the bread which has come down from heaven; not like that which our fathers ate, and died; the one eating this bread will live eternally." (vv. 53, 56, 58—Now using eucharistic imagery, the appeal for corporate solidarity with Jesus and his community in the face of persecution is brought to the center of the stage. If one hopes to be raised with Christ in the resurrection, one must be willing to go with him to the cross. In so doing one remains with Christ and his community, and Christ also abides with the believer, in strengthening and empowering ways. The heavenly manna so triumphally touted by the leaders of the Synagogue was actually death-producing. Our forefathers ate of it . . . but they died. But this Bread, the flesh of the Son of Man, gives life which is eternal.)

With v. 51c, the theme of suffering is introduced.[49] Until then, the audience has been hearing about the ways God speaks and should be heeded. But now, the cost of believing—potential suffering and even death—is declared bluntly. Verse 51c is not a veiled reference to the eucharist; it is rather, a scandalizing reference to the cross. This would have been absolutely clear to the audiences of the oral and written renderings of this section. Granted, eucharistic language is being used, but the evangelist is *not* saying "Jesus died on the cross in order to bring us the eucharist." Neither is he saying, "God gave manna, and then the Torah, and then the miraculous feeding, and then the Christ Events, and now finally a Christian cultic ritual. Enjoy it or be damned!" No. The eschatology of the evangelist has not changed one bit from its christocentric fulcrum. To follow Jesus will always exact a price—the rejection of the world; and yet, true faithfulness will also involve a reward—abiding with Christ in the eschaton. In furthering the goal of corporate solidarity with Jesus in the face of persecution (by the Jewish leaders first, and later by the Romans), eucharistic imagery is employed as a means of making the point graphically. All of this was first targeted (orally) at the Jewish/Christian members of the Johannine audience during the late 70's and 80's, in the face of pressure to abandon the Christian community and to rejoin the local Synagogue, but it also becomes centrally relevant for averting the next schismatic threat. For those who remain with Jesus and his community, the promise of eternal life is given, as well as the provision of the existential strength to abide in the truth.

---

[49] On this point, Martyn believes that the local Jewish authorities mustered the social and political power to persecute, and even execute, some of the leaders of the Johannine movement as disincentives to their growth (*The Gospel of John in Christian History*, pp. 37-89), and Rensberger's book certainly develops that theme in the light of John's appeal to liberation in Jesus Christ (*Johannine Faith*, pp. 37-134). While some of this may indeed have occurred, it is doubtful that the entire history of individuated Johannine Christianity was spent under an exclusively Jewish cloud. At the least, Johannine Jewish Christians would have been faced with "social martyrdom" as they were forced to make difficult decisions about communal loyalties and commitments of faith. See Anderson, *Christology*, *Table 21*: "Three Acute Intramural Crises Faced by Johannine Christianity."

3. The threat of a second schism involving Gentile converts with docetizing tendencies: John 6:51-66

Notice again the overlapping of meanings with the previous discussants. The third crisis alluded to in John 6 is the temptation of Gentile converts to disassociate themselves with Johannine Christianity, probably in the face of Roman adversity and persecution. As the misunderstanding discussants shift from being the Jews to the disciples, one detects the shift to a situation closer to the immediate audience at the time of the writing of John 6. These disciples are scandalized, not because of the cannibalistic language being used, but because the "Bread" offered them is being served up on a "platter" hewn into the shape of a cross. To ingest Jesus' flesh and blood is to accept the fleshly reality of the incarnation—and its implication—that Jesus' true followers must also be willing to embrace the cross, themselves.

Following the break with the Synagogue, Johannine Christianity began to reach out to Gentiles, and this mission was apparently successful. Then again, there may have been Gentile members of the Johannine movement before that time as well, as the missionary churches of Asia Minor tended to include mixtures of Jewish and Gentile converts. Nonetheless, with the advent of Roman persecution under Domitian, Gentile converts would have been far more scandalized than Jewish ones. From the days of the Maccabeans to the oppositions of Judas the Galilean and the later Zealots, Jews were used to opposing foreign rule and paying a price for their monotheistic commitments. Faced with the challenge to offer emperor-laud or to burn incense in reverence to Caesar, a Jew would commonly have been willing to suffer for refusing such a practice. The average Gentile, however, would have been far more willing to go along with the Roman demand, and far less likely to be willing to undergo suffering for one's faith. This must have been the primary motivating factor underlying their docetizing proclivities. If Jesus did not suffer or corporally die, how could he have expected his followers to suffer corporal persecution—and even martyrdom? Thus, the greatest threat of incipient docetism was not its unorthodox christology—as it related to a system of faith, but its practical implications—as they related to the believer's willingness to undergo suffering and death in the face of Roman persecution. These docetizing Christians also probably sought to legitimize their views by organizing and teaching a docetic rationale for their accommodation to Roman requirements, and leaders such as Cerinthus must have sought to rally support for the emerging party platform. This is precisely what the evangelist is seeking to stave off in John 6:51-66, and what the Elder is seeking to counteract in his antichristic warnings of 1 John 4:1-3 and 2 John 7. Therefore, the history of Johannine Christianity must have been something similar to the following outline:

Table #9, "A Brief Overview of the History of Johannine Christianity"

55-70 CE—Phase 1: *Beginning Chapters*—The gospel comes to Asia Minor. Paul (or another evangelist) "lectures" to "the Jews," and many Jews become followers of "the Way." On the other hand, many are offended and malign "the Way." (Acts 17-19) Apollos, the Fourth Evangelist and others join in the mission, and the evangelist settles down as a local pastoral presence in one of the churches. He brings with him his own independent gospel tradition which has been interfluential with the pre-Marcan (Petrine) tradition.

70-90 CE—Phase 2: *Tensions with the Local Synagogue* (overlapping with Phases 3 and 4)—Following the destruction of the Temple in Jerusalem, a fundamentalistic form of the scripture-based Judaism of the Pharisees begins to replace the Temple-based establishment of the Sadducees. By the mid-70's, this caused local challenges to the "biblicality" of Christian Judaism, and Christians were forced to decide between Christ and their Jewish loyalties. Some persecution, as well as excommunication and even capital penalties, were used by local Jewish leaders to retard the spread of Christianity within Judaism, and the Jewish "mission to the ditheists" partially succeeded in winning some Jesus-followers back into Judaism. 1 John (the first antichristic schism) and the first edition of the Gospel (debates with "the Jews") reflect some of these developments.

81-96 CE—Phase 3: *The Onset of Roman Persecution and the Departure of Gentile Christians* (overlapping with Phases 2 and 4)—Persecution by Domitian (81-96 CE) caused new problems for Johannine Christianity, especially for Gentile Christians. As they were less willing to suffer for their faith, they found it easier to deny their Christian involvements. This caused the Johannine leadership to emphasize the Lordship of Christ (versus Caesar's), the physicality of his suffering and death (versus the teachings of the Docetists) and the final importance of maintaining solidarity with Christ and his fellowship in the face of persecution. During this time, "false teachers" and "false prophets" also arose, advocating a less rigorous form of Christian commitment, bolstered by docetizing christological tendencies and their lax implications for discipleship. These trends are warned about in 1 John and are countered by the incarnational (and anti-docetic) emphases of John's supplementary material. By the writing of 2 John 7, these "Antichrists" have also departed, and those who wished to remain a part of Johannine Christianity while compromising their faith were excommunicated by its leadership.

85-100 CE—*Phase 4: Tensions with the Mainstream Church* (overlapping with Phases 2 and 3)—As evidenced in the M tradition and in the letters of

Ignatius, the centrifugal challenges of Jewish and Roman persecutions led Antiochine Christianity (at least) to erect institutional structures as centripetal means of maintaining connectedness to Christ (and the apostles) and cohesion within the church. The figure of Peter takes on organizing power and vicarious authority, and those who follow in his wake appeal to it as a means of establishing their own positions locally (as did Ignatius, a bit later). Johannine Christianity, however, advocated a pneumatic and familial mode of christocracy (see esp. John 14–16), and this must have threatened Diotrephes and his kin. In 3 John we read that Diotrephes has refused hospitality to Johannine Christians and has excommunicated those who would take them in. This is the final motivator for the Elder's contacting the *ecclesia*, and the witness of the Beloved Disciple was finally compiled and edited in order to declare Jesus' original intention for the governance of his church. John was thus "published" around 100 CE by the compiler (also the Elder) as a christocratic corrective to rising institutionalism in the late first-century church. "His witness is true." (John 21:25) is as much an ecclesial as an historical claim.

While several scholars have done well to illuminate the anti-docetic thrust of the later Johannine material, few have made enough of the connection between docetism as a proto-heretical faith system and the practical implications of docetism during rising persecution by the Romans.[50] In his recent book, R. Cassidy has demonstrated beyond reasonable doubt that scholars who deny any persecution of Christians by Romans in the late first century and early second century are wrong.[51] While "persecution" proper may not be the best way to describe the reality from a Roman perspective (Christians refused to go along with what Roman understandings of civility: honoring the emperor and showing public reverence for the empire), it is fair to say that Romans tried to influence

---

[50] See for instance, P. Borgen (*Bread from Heaven*); B. Lindars, *Behind the Fourth Gospel* (London: SPCK, 1971); U. Schnelle, *Antidoketische Christologie im Johannesevangelium* (Göttingen, 1987), see Linda Maloney's excellent English translation published by Fortress Press, 1992; and R. E. Brown (*Community*, 1979) have correctly noticed John's antidocetic corrective, but the practical (and more acutely, the ecclesiological) implications of docetising beliefs have been underexplored.

[51] While one is not entirely convinced by Cassidy's exegetical moves (*John's Gospel in New Perspective* [Maryknoll: Orbis, 1993]; see my review in *JBL* 114, 2 [1995]) he offers very convincing evidence that based on Pliny's Letter to Trajan (X.96) and Trajan's Rescript (X.97), Christians were being persecuted, sometimes simply for bearing the name "Christian." Says Pliny, "I have asked them in person if they are Christians, and if they admit it, I repeat the question a second and third time, with a warning of the punishment awaiting them. If they persist, I order them to be led away for execution. . . ."

To this, Trajan responds, "These people must not be hunted out; if they are brought before you and the charge against them is proved, they must be punished, but in the case of anyone who denies that he is a Christian, and makes it clear that he is not by offering prayers to our gods, he is to be pardoned as a result of his repentance however suspect his conduct may be." (pp. 89-91)

Christians, sometimes with force, and this was experienced as persecution by Christians. From the excessive tax of two drachmas (identical to the amount of the Jewish annual contribution to the Temple, levied against Jews and some Christians) instituted after the destruction of Jerusalem, to the trial and execution of men, women and children—simply for bearing the name, "Christian" (who did not deny their faith or malign Christ when given the opportunity to escape punishment), Cassidy shows from the Roman records that such a backdrop of persecution must be considered when reading John. Without operating on the assumption of earlier and later material in John, Cassidy nonetheless infers themes that must have been used to bolster the faith and corporate solidarity of Johannine Christians, which Lindars includes as parts of the "supplementary material" added to an earlier edition of the Gospel.[52] In these and other ways, Cassidy adds the backdrop of Roman persecution to Martyn's, Brown's and Rensberger's scenarios illuminating the dialectical backdrop of the Jewish/Christian relations. Both of these crises were real, and an assist from Ignatius may clarify some of the issues at stake for Johannine Christianity.

While Ignatius' seven letters to the churches were probably written a decade or two after John, they nonetheless cast light on the Johannine situation—or at least parallels to it. For instance, the oft-cited "medicine of immortality" reference in Ignatius' letter to the Ephesians (20:2) betrays not a theophagic proclivity in his sacramentology, but rather, a concern for corporate unity in the face of persecution and schismatic tendencies. The full passage (*Eph.*20:1-2) is as follows:[53]

> If Jesus Christ counts me worthy through you prayers, and if it be the (divine) will, I will give you in the second document...[a] further explanation of...Jesus Christ, having to do with faith in him and love of him, with his suffering and resurrection; particularly if the Lord reveals anything to me. All of you, severally and in common, continue to come together in grace, as individuals, in one faith and in Jesus Christ, who according to the flesh was of the family of David, the son of a human and son of God, that you may obey the bishop and the presbytery with

---

[52] For instance, Cassidy interprets the Farewell Discourses and John 21 as needing to be read against the backdrop of Roman persecution (pp. 54-79; see also L. W. Barnard, "St. Clement of Rome and the Persecution of Domitian," in his *Studies in the Apostolic Fathers and Their Background* [New York: Schocken Books, 1966], pp. 5-18), and his interpretation of Jesus' Roman trial and imperial titles applied to Jesus are also well-taken. In doing so, he accentuates the sovereignty and all-sufficiency motifs, as applied to Christ, believing that they functioned to offer a direct counter-balance to Roman claims regarding the deity of the emperor. However, Cassidy does hardly anything with the incarnational—and thus anti-docetic—motifs in John, as they may have helped the believer undergo suffering for one's Lord. This area would be worth exploring.

[53] Cited from W. R. Schoedel, *Ignatius of Antioch* (Philadelphia: Fortress, 1985), p. 95; see also L. W. Barnard, "The Background of St. Ignatius of Antioch," ibid., pp. 19-30.

undistracted mind, breaking one bread, which is the medicine of immortality, the antidote preventing death, but leading to life in Jesus Christ forever.

From this fuller passage it is obvious that the central issue for Ignatius is the corporate unity of the fellowship. In other words, the emphasis in not on the eucharistic *bread* as the *pharmakon athanasias*, but upon the *one* bread (as opposed to factious groups splitting off and having their own fellowship meals) where corporate solidarity is at stake. Clearly this passage harkens back to *Eph.* 7:1-2, which describes factious leaders who "are rabid dogs, biting without warning, whom you must guard against since they are almost incurable. There is *one physician* . . . Jesus Christ our Lord." The central theme here is *oneness*. In the face of the factious tendencies of "rabid dogs," Ignatius emphasizes *one* physician, *one* bishop and presbytery, *one* worship service and the breaking of *one* loaf—the antidote to such schismatic toxins.

A possible explanation for some of these schisms may be alluded to in his letter to the Smyrneans. Here Ignatius connects the fleshly suffering of Christ with his own suffering and participation in the eucharist: (*Smyrn.* 4:2; 6:2-7:1)

> For if those things were done by our Lord (only) in appearance, I too am in bonds (only) in appearance. And why have I given myself up to death, to fire, to sword, to wild beasts? But near the sword, near God; with the beasts, with God; only in the name of Jesus Christ to suffer with him! I endure all things since he, the perfect human being empowers me. . . .
>
> Now observe those who hold erroneous opinions about the grace of Jesus Christ . . . : for love they have no concern, none for the widow, none for the orphan, none for the one distressed, none for one imprisoned or released, none for one hungry or thirsty; they remain aloof from eucharist and prayers because they do not confess that the eucharist is the flesh of our savior Jesus Christ which suffered for our sins, which the Father raised by his goodness.

These passages make it clear that the scandalous result of docetism in Ignatius' view was threefold: first, it made a mockery of Christ's suffering and the martyrdom of contemporary Christians. Ignatius draws the implication into the spotlight: if Jesus did not suffer, then why should we? Precisely the point of the Docetists. Second, this view of cheap grace resulted in the moral failure of its advocates. They failed to hold up their agapeic commitments within the community of faith, and thus the fellowship suffered because of them. Third, they apparently refused to participate fully in the meetings for worship because they did "not confess that the eucharist is the flesh of our savior Jesus Christ which suffered for our sins." It is not clear here whether the emphasis is upon the flesh or the suffering of Christ,[54] but it is clear that their refusal to participate must have divided the community and it disrupted Christian fellowship. The Johannine situation was entirely parallel to these. In the face of Roman harassment and persecution, Gentile Christians (or prospects) found it all too easy to deny the humanity and suffering of Christ, and thereby to try to escape the Roman penalties for being loyal to "the name." They thus made it a practice of denying their Christian involvements and even maligning Christ— perhaps excused in their minds by the notion that a non-suffering Jesus would not expect his followers to suffer and die. When these practices were opposed by the Christian leadership, probably emphasizing the importance of ingesting the flesh and blood of Jesus, the docetizing groups began to break off into quasi-Christian groups, holding their own cultic meetings and developing their own "theological" defense of their assimilating actions: denying the flesh-and-bloodness of Jesus. Representatives then became some of the "false teachers" and "false prophets" mentioned in the Johannine Epistles and the letters of Ignatius. These tendencies may be observed in the second antichristic threat of 1 John 4:1-3 and 2 John 7. Consider the outline of the Elder's antidocetic appeal:

Table #10, "The Second Antichristic Schism (1 John 4:1-3 and 2 John 7)— The Departure of Gentile Christians and their Docetizing Teachings"

— "Beloved, do not believe every spirit, but test the spirits to see if they are of God, because many false prophets have gone out into the world." (1 John 4:1) The warning of a forthcoming threat is issued, and the community member is advised to test the spirits, lest one be deceived by a false prophet. This antichristic threat will be different from the first in terms of christological content and the proselytizing character of its advocates, but beware; do not be deceived.

— "By this you can recognize the spirit of God: Every spirit that confesses Jesus Christ has come in the flesh is of God; and every spirit that does not confess Jesus is not of God." (1 John 4:2-3a) By other appearances, these prophets may seem to be solid Christians, but ask them

---

[54] At this point, Schnelle's argument (*Antidocetic Christology*) is well worth considering. He argues, based on this passage, that because the Docetists here refused to believe that the eucharistic bread was Jesus' flesh, the Fourth Evangelist has called for full participation in the eucharist (John 6:51c-58) as a measured way to confront their docetic beliefs. Still, however, the emphasis must be placed upon the larger corporate and ethical issues rather that ritual ones. The goal of the evangelist was the restoration of Christian unity (and the prevention of further defections), and he used incarnation motifs, an emphasis on the cross, and eucharistic imagery to confront the docetizing tendencies of his audience. Docetism divided precisely because it advocated a gospel of cheap grace in the face of persecution.

about the *flesh and blood of Jesus*, and their teachings will be laid open for scrutiny. These people would not have been of Jewish origin (tending to deny Jesus as the Christ); rather, they would have been of Gentile origin (tending to deny the Christ as incarnated in the man, Jesus), precisely those least inclined to resist assimilation to Roman and/or cultural demands.

— "And this is the spirit of the Antichrist, which you have heard is coming—and even now is already in the world!" (1 John 4:3b) Whereas the first antichristic schism has already departed (1 John 2:18ff.), the second antichristic threat is still on the way. Not only was the first threat different in its beliefs and socio-religious identity, it is also different in terms of timing. The warning is sounded: Beware of the Docetists!

— "For many deceivers who do not confess Jesus Christ as coming in the flesh have gone out into the world. This is the deceiver and the Antichrist." (2 John 7) By this time the docetic threat is not only on the way, but it appears that some of its adherents have also "gone out into the world." The encouragement to remain (v. 9) implies that a second schism has indeed transpired (perhaps the Docetists were expelled from the Johannine community as much as being enticed into newly-formed docetic/Christian groups), and the Johannine Christian is warned to be on the lookout against such false teachers and their divisive tactics.

From these corollaries, one may infer a second schismatic crisis confronting Johannine Christianity, this time involving Gentile Christians with docetizing tendencies.[55] The challenge of Roman persecution and Hellenistic dualism combined here to form the beginnings of docetic christologies, which later evolved into more fully-developed gnosticism. In the "supplementary material" inferred by Lindars, one can readily locate the majority of John's antidocetic material (the Word made flesh, 1:14; blood and water flowing from Jesus' side, 19:34f. ; "unless you eat my flesh and drink my blood . . ." 6:53ff.), and this suggests that Johannine Christianity was faced by the docetizing crisis a few years after the crisis with the

---

[55] Indeed, many scholars lump all three Antichrist passages rather uncritically into the same schismatic soup, but fail to realize the generally flexible character of the term. It was the ultimate slanderous appellative within such a Christocentric setting, and it was used to warn against more than one threat. Given the historical evidence for two external sources of persecution, the opposite differences in christological beliefs between the Antichrist passages, the chronological differences between the times Jewish and Gentile converts would have entered and exited Johannine Christianity (as well as their religious proclivities), and the apparently sequential dealing with two individuated crises (in John, the Johannine Epistles, *and* in the letters of Ignatius), such a view becomes untenable. See also C. C. Richardson for convincing evidence that Ignatius also faced two consecutive threats: a Jewish one and a later docetic one ("The Evidence for Two Separate Heresies," in his *The Christianity of Ignatius of Antioch* [New York, 1967 (1935)], pp. 81-85). While the Johannine situation is not identical to the Ignatian, the parallels are suggestive at least of a similar sequence of ordeals.

Synagogue. This crisis is also alluded to in John 6:51-66, where Jesus' discussants eventually shift to his disciples. They are scandalized by Jesus' words and also begin to *grumble*—like the Jews, a sure sign of their unbelieving inclination (v. 61). Their exclamation and question are, "This is sure a hard word (to stomach)! Who can possibly go along with (swallow) it?" (v. 60) Here the Johannine use of irony works powerfully. On one level, the reader might assume a misunderstanding dialogue on the controversial character of the eucharist might be ensuing. Certainly the language of eating and drinking Jesus' flesh and blood would be offensive to any audience, and real debates on precisely this topic occurred. But on a deeper level, it becomes clear that the subject being discussed is *the cross*: its centrality in Jesus' mission, and the would-be disciple's calling to embrace it in the face of persecution. The disciples in the evangelist's audience would have experienced the dialogue as follows:

— "Indeed, this bread is *my flesh which I shall give for the life of the world.*" (v. 51c—To be my disciple involves the willingness to go with me to the cross. Paradoxically, in losing one's life one finds it. This is the life-producing food offered by the Son of Man.)

— "Whoever eats my flesh and drinks my blood has eternal life, and I will raise him up on the last day." (v. 54—You may think you're about to hear a defense of the eucharist against Jewish charges of "cannibalism," but beware. A far more disturbing message is coming your way. In the light of those docetizing Christians who deny the flesh-and-bloodness of the incarnation, as well as its implications for costly discipleship, you must ingest Jesus' humanity if you wish to share in the benefits of his divinity. If you expect to be raised with him on in the eschaton, you must be willing to suffer and die with him in the present.)

— "Are you scandalized by this? How will you feel when you see the Son of Man ascending to where he was at first?" (vv. 61ff.—Consider your ordeals from the perspective of eternity. Granted, you are offended at bloody talk about the true cost of discipleship, but how will you feel in the eschaton if you take the easy way out for the short term and deny your Lord and his community for the sake of saving your skins? When you see the Son of Man being raised up, triumphant over the powers, and you realize you denied him before humanity and that you will be denied by him before the Father, beware! The final scandal will be *yours and your faithless choices.*)

— "The spirit is that which is life-producing: the flesh profits nothing. The words I have spoken to you are spirit, and they are life; although there are still some of you who do not believe." (vv. 63f.—As we began with at the beginning of this exhortation, work not for the death-producing food, but the life-producing food, which the Son of Man shall give you. My words should offer you consolation: first, because I have promised you an eternal reward for your faithfulness; second, because I will provide you all you need to remain in me; and third, because they are of heavenly origin and are life-producing. That hardship you have wanted to escape, perhaps viewing it as "the bread of affliction," is actually like choosing the flesh of quail over God's eschatological provision. As was the case in the wilderness, those who craved flesh became sick and died. Don't make the same error. Receive the Bread which has now come down from heaven, and be willing to ingest his suffering and death if needed. Doing the work of God will be your true nourishment; the way of the flesh profits nothing!)

— "This is why I have told you that no one can come to me unless the Father has enabled him." (v. 65—Human initiative cannot suffice when it comes to the way of the spirit. Following Jesus is paradoxical, not practical. In responding to the divine initiative, not only must one be willing to set aside one's physical needs, one's religious methods and wisdom, and one's instincts for survival, but one must also lay at the cross one's understandings of how the life of faith ought to work. Even some of you who consider yourselves true followers of mine do not understand or believe. Your only hope is to respond in faith to God's saving initiative. It is not of yourselves, but a gift from God.)

At this, the words and knowings of Jesus are confirmed, and many of his disciples slide back and walk about with him no more (v. 66). The scandalizing words of the Lord are no mere debate over eucharistic rites or answers to Jewish charges of cultic cannibalism. The scandal is that the disciples *have* understood full well the cost of discipleship, but have not comprehended the identity and mission of the Lord. Like the shallow enthusiasm of the crowd which misunderstands the feeding as a political sign (vv. 14f.), even some of Jesus' followers are unwilling to pay the ultimate cost of discipleship. They see the Jesus movement as offering temporal benefits—perhaps even the overthrow of the Romans—but are scandalized when asked to be willing to suffer and die for their Lord. The *einmalig* level of the narrative here pierces the situation of Johannine Christianity. In the light of a second schismatic crisis—a docetizing one led by Gentile Christians—the Johannine Christian is called to remain loyal to the Lord and his community of faith. While eucharistic imagery is used, Johannine Christianity probably does not have a full-blown sacramental ritual as of yet.[56] The "real thing" is *corporate fellowship*, which is

---

[56] At this point, the insight and question articulated by R. Kysar, *The Fourth Evangelist and His Gospel* (Minneapolis: Augsburg, 1975), p. 259, are telling ones: "I believe that the early form of the gospel . . . had no sacramental reference because the johannine community at that time was essentially non-sacramental. Could it be that the absence of the institution of the lord's supper from the fourth gospel is due to the fact that that narrative was not part of the johannine tradition and that the johannine community did not know the institution narratives in any form?"

experienced in the gathered meeting for worship, in fellowship meals, in the caring for the needy within the group and in being willing to confess and suffer for one's Lord. Abiding solidarity with Christ and his community is the central goal of this section's appeal. This is the goal furthered by the use of graphic (and even offensive) eucharistic language, and this is the "hard word" which scandalizes the audience.

4. The portrayal of Peter and Johannine Christianity's dialectical relationship with the mainstream church: John 6:67-70

While indications of this crisis are far more subtle in John 6 than the other ones, they nonetheless are suggestive of other issues beneath the surface and emphasized more clearly elsewhere in the Gospel. Verses 67-70 appear on the surface to deviate from the rhetorical pattern found in the other dialogues of John 6, as well as from the standard revelational pattern. The initiative passes from the discussants to Jesus in v. 67, and Peter appears to make an exemplary confession (vv. 68f.). What is extremely odd is Jesus' negative retort immediately following Peter's confession: "Have I not chosen you, the Twelve? And yet, one of you is a devil!" While this statement is entirely parallel to the Marcan Jesus' response to Peter's reluctance to allow the Son of Man (and his vice-regents) to suffer and die ("Get 'out of my face,' Satan! You are not minding the things of God but the things of humans." Mark 8:33), Jesus' calling Peter "a devil" here is highly problematic. So problematic that it is indeed probable that v. 71 represents the attempt of the compiler to resolve this perplexity.[57] Whatever the case, v. 70 represents Jesus' rejection of Peter's confession, and this implies a misunderstanding somewhere in his statement. This being so, a likely solution is to view the first part of Peter's confession (v. 68) as an adequate response to the question of Jesus; but to see something in his confession—perhaps the second part of it (v. 69) as representing some broader aspect of Petrine understanding which Jesus rejects. One might

---

Historically, this was probably true for some time. The question is how long did it take the Johannine expressions of sacramentality to evolve from human and social (incarnated) realities to ritual and symbolic (eucharistic) ones. Much of John seems to oppose such developments. It is probable that this transition happened, at the latest, after the passing of the Beloved Disciple around the turn of the century. See W. Marxsen, *The Lord's Supper as a Christological Problem*, trans. L. Nieting (Philadelphia: Fortress, 1970); and A. Schweitzer, *The Problem of the Lord's Supper* (1901), English trans. of 1929 ed. A. J. Mattill, Jr. (Macon: Mercer University Press, 1982); and P. N. Anderson, "The 'Medicine of Immortality' in Ignatius and John 6," unpublished paper presented at the Johannine Seminar of the National AAR/SBL Meetings, New Orleans, 1990.

[57] Just as it appears that the compiler has clarified for the reader *which* Judas it was that was speaking in John 14:22 (*not* Judas Iscariot), it appears that he has also solved the perplexity of John 6:70 by explaining parenthetically, "(Jesus did *not* mean Simon Peter, who was a devil, but *Judas, son of Simon* Iscariot, who would betray him later and who must have been alluded to in v. 64b earlier.)" It appears the compiler has "clarified" the meaning of a similar text at John 11:10f.

even infer that the response of Peter comes to a full stop at the end of v. 68, and that the initiative passes from Jesus to Peter in v. 69. With the boldness of his declaration, "We *have believed and known* that . . ." one may detect the evangelist's use of ironic exaggeration—especially, given Jesus' abrupt response to what sounds like a perfectly acceptable and exemplary affirmation. But is it really?

Knowing how to interpret σὺ εἶ ὁ ἅγιος τοῦ θεοῦ (v. 69b) is a difficult matter. Nearly all scholars interpret it as an exemplary declaration of Jesus' holiness and sacred mission, but given v. 70, this explanation is inadequate. Neither is Peter here being cast in the role of the Marcan demoniac (Mark 1:24), even though the confession is identical. What we probably have is a connotation that is fully parallel to Mark 8:32b, where Peter, after making his confession (v. 29), takes Jesus aside and begins to rebuke him for telling the disciples bluntly that the Son of Man must be rejected, suffer and die. At this point Jesus rebukes Peter in Mark, and his reason for doing so in John appears to have been entirely parallel. In Mark, Peter is unwilling for the Son of Man—and especially his followers—to suffer and die. In John, the same concern comes though, and what has been rendered a question by Jesus actually reads better in the declarative: "*I have not elected you*, the Twelve (to escape tribulation, οὐκ ἐγὼ ὑμᾶς τοὺς δώδεκα ἐξελεξάμην), and one of you is a devil (for suggesting so)!" That being the case, one must ask how Peter's confident confession that Jesus is the "Holy One of God" may have been tantamount to his refusal to allow the Son of Man to suffer and die. This query leads in two directions: the first concerns the function of this particular confession in Mark, and the second pertains to its associated meanings beyond Mark.

The demoniac's declaring that Jesus is the "Holy One of God" in Mark sets the stage for Jesus' vanquishing of Satan's reign by his authoritative words and dynamic deeds. Indeed, Jesus promptly exorcizes the man, heals Simon's mother-in-law and begins to proclaim the gospel. Likewise, he designates the Twelve as emissaries, commissioning them to cast out demons and to proclaim the gospel (Mark 3:13-15). As plundering the household of a "strong man" hinges upon first *binding* the strong man (Mark 3:27), so the thaumaturgical work of Jesus and his band prepares the territory for the advance of the Kingdom of God. Jesus' recognition as the "Holy One of God" by the demoniac in Mark 1:24 introduces Mark's Davidic and triumphal basileiology, whereby Jesus sets up his royal kingdom in Zion. This contrasts diametrically to the explanation for why the Judeans failed to recognize Jesus as the Christ in John. They expected (based on their again inadequate exegesis) that the Christ would be a Davidic Messiah from Bethlehem, not a Galilean prophet (John 7:41f.). Does having a Davidic or thaumaturgic messiology, according to John, cause the missing of Jesus' identity and the true character of his kingdom?

As a christological title, ὁ ἅγιος τοῦ θεοῦ occurs elsewhere only in Luke 4:23 in the entire canonical corpus, and here it is simply a repetition of the Marcan passage. On the other hand, τὸν ἅγιον καὶ δίκαιον is found on the lips of Peter in Acts 3:14, ἱεράτευμα ἅγιον and ἔθνος ἅγιον are mentioned in 1 Peter 2:5 and 9, and 1 John 2:20 refers to τοῦ ἁγίου as the source of spiritual unction. The "Holy one of Israel" is mentioned prolifically in Isaiah and some in Zechariah, but it cannot be viewed as identical in meaning, though it is certainly Zionistic and power-oriented.

From these corollaries one may hypothesize that Peter's declaration of Jesus as "the Holy One of God" suggests the following: 1.) Based on Jesus' abrupt response, it was *not* included by the evangelist as an exemplary reference to Jesus' holiness, but served a negative role, probably parallel to Peter's refusal in Mark to allow the Son of Man to suffer and die. 2.) This is closer to the sort of Jewish appellation that Peter would have used and is probably closer to Peter's actual words than the more Hellenized and confessional rendition in Mark.[58] 3.) Ideologically, we have here the portrayal of Jesus' rejecting the typically Davidic Synoptic messiology, just as he had fled the crowd's popularistic designs on his future (vv. 14f.). 4.) Such a portrayal suggests a Johannine inclination to correct the Synoptic view of the Kingdom—how it is established and how it is maintained;[59] and this corrective is illuminated by the juxtaposition of Peter and the Beloved Disciple elsewhere in the Fourth Gospel.

While not described in the context of John 6, the ambivalent relation of Peter to the Beloved Disciple in John is implicated by the ambiguous portrayal of Peter in vv. 68-71. While several scholars have done well to notice this juxtaposed relationship, few have worked out specifically the ecclesial implications as they reflect the Johannine posture toward

---

[58] "The Holy One of God," the "Holy and Righteous One," "Holy Priesthood" and "Holy Nation" are characteristic of the Petrine connection of sanctification with empowerment. Based on the criterion of dissimilarity, ὁ ἅγιος τοῦ θεοῦ would have been far less common than the more predictable Marcan rendition, ὁ χριστός, which is also more Hellenized. If indeed Peter had anything to do with the tradition underlying Mark, as Papias believed, the citation of ὁ ἅγιος τοῦ θεοῦ in Mark 1:24 and John 6:69 may be plausibly traced to the historical Peter (Luke even sides with the Johannine rendition by adding τοῦ θεοῦ to the Marcan ὁ χριστός). It reflects the Petrine understanding of how the Kingdom of God advances, and tellingly, just as the pre-Marcan interpretation of Jesus' miracles in corrected in John 6, apparently so is the pre-Marcan basileiology.

[59] It is wrong to assume that the dearth of Johannine references to the Kingdom of God implies its low priority in the thinking of the evangelist. John uses other terms to describe the Kingdom of God: nouns such as "light," "life" and "truth," and such verbs as "believe," "know" and "love." Furthermore, the two passages describing the Kingdom in John are both corrective in their nuance. John 3:1-8 corrects wooden (institutional?) notions of the Kingdom—it is like the wind of the Spirit; and John 18:36f. challenges institutional claims to authority—Jesus *is* a king, but his Kingdom is one of Truth. These critiques of human instrumentality would have applied to Jewish, Roman *and* evolving Christian forms of institutionalism.

impending mainstream Christian trends.[60] Central to this issue is the fact that the two other dialogues between Peter and Jesus in John *both* portray Peter as misunderstanding the character of servant leadership and agapeic shepherding. In response to Jesus' attempt to model Christian servanthood at the foot-washing scene (John 13:1-17), Peter totally misunderstands the point being exemplified and requests a total immersion. Climactically, Jesus declares, "A servant is not greater than his master, nor is an apostle (ἀπόστολος) greater than the one sending him." (v. 16—Is the Petrine apostolate here being alluded to as competing with Jesus?)

Peter also misunderstands Jesus' intent in the lake-side appearance narrative, where Peter fails three times to understand and respond adequately to Jesus' question (ἀγαπᾷς με?). Granted, many view John 21 as a reinstatement of Peter's authority, but it is not an unambiguous one. Peter is the first to abandon the itinerant ministry of Jesus' band, returning instead to his conventional trade ("I'm going fishing!" v. 3); he does not recognize the Lord on his own but must be guided by the insight of the Beloved Disciple (v. 7); he misunderstands the agapeic instruction of Jesus and is even hurt (ἐλυπήθη) by Jesus' questioning (vv. 15-17); his helplessness in martyrdom is predicted by the Lord (vv. 18f.); and the last glimpse of Peter shows him glaring enviously at the Beloved Disciple saying, "And what about him!" (vv. 20f.), to which the Johannine Jesus responds in ways reminiscent of the Marcan calling narrative, "Follow thou me!" (v. 22, repeated from v. 19).[61] The point of all this is to suggest that the inadequacy of Peter's confession in John 6 probably reflects the

---

60 Such scholars as S. Agourides, "Peter and John in the Fourth Gospel," *Studia Evangelia* 4, ed. F. L. Cross (Berlin: Akademie, 1968), pp. 3-7; A. F. Maynard, "The Role of Peter in the Fourth Gospel," *New Testament Studies* 30 (1984), 531-48; and G. F. Snyder, "John 13:16 and the Anti-Petrinism of the Johannine Tradition," *Biblical Research* 17 (1971), 5-15, have detected clear anti-Petrinism in John. On the other hand, such scholars as Brown, Donfried, and Reumann, et al., *Peter in the New Testament* (Minneapolis: Augsburg, 1973); and K. Quast, *Peter and the Beloved Disciple*, JSNTSS 32 (Sheffield: JSOT Press, 1989) conclude that such a juxtaposition is less telling, as Peter is portrayed with a certain degree of ambiguity in all the gospels. None of these studies, however, has developed the "christocratic" implications of this relationship as they relate to John's ecclesiology and dialectical relationship with rising institutionalism in the late first century church (see my review of Quast's book in *Critical Review of Books in Religion*, 1991). This issue has been explored fruitfully by T. V. Smith, *Petrine Controversies in Early Christianity*, WUNT II 15 (Tübingen: J. C. B. Mohr [Paul Siebeck], 1985), but the particular Johannine scald on the matter deserves further exploration.

61 Indeed, Luke appears to have taken over parts of John 21 for his rendition of the calling narrative in Luke 5. Luke's clear deviation from Mark cannot be explained on the basis of John's dependence on Luke, and the view that John and Luke shared a common source is far more speculative than to hypothesize that where Luke deviates from Mark or Q *and* sides with John may suggest Lucan access to the Johannine tradition. See P. N. Anderson, "Acts 4:20: A First Century Historical Clue to Johannine Authorship?" an unpublished paper presented at the Pacific Northwest Regional AAR/SBL Meetings in Walla Walla, 1992. If Luke did draw from the Johannine tradition, it must have been during the *oral* stages of the Johannine tradition, as issues of sequence and association are better thus explained.

Johannine attitude toward the evolving influence of Peter in the mainstream church around the time the final edition of John was written. A clue to at least one acute crisis in the Johannine situation, which must have exacerbated the need for this corrective, is suggested by 3 John.

In 3 John 9f. Diotrephes "who loves to be their superior" (ὁ φιλοπρωτεύων αὐτῶν), neither receives Johannine Christians nor allows any of his membership to take them in. He "gossips maliciously" about Johannine Christians and even exercises totalitarian authority over his own congregation, being willing to cast out any who should like to extend hospitality to them. Tellingly, the Elder comforts Gaius by telling him that those to whom he has ministered have reported good things about his love to the church (v. 6, ἐκκλησία), and that he has written to the church (v. 9, ἐκκλησία) about Diotrephes. Whomever he may have been, it is obvious from these references that (from the Johannine perspective) Diotrephes must have been a heavy-handed leader aspiring to rule his congregation by means of institutionally-imbued authority, granted from the centralizing church. This obviously betrays an early form of the emerging monepiscopate, rising in Asia Minor during the last two decades of the first century CE, which Ignatius of Antioch seeks to bolster a few years hence. For whatever reason, Diotrephes seems threatened by Johannine traveling ministers and denies them hospitality and access to his group.[62] It is probable that in doing so he has constructed his positional form of leadership on the basis of the tradition, or at least the sentiment, of the Matthean "keys to the Kingdom" passage (Matt.16:17-19), and that he feels justified in wielding his authority on christocratic grounds.[63] This explains

---

[62] Käsemann is indeed correct to infer that Diotrephes is an episcopal leader of sorts, who is threatened by Johannine Christians (*The Testament of Jesus*, 1968). He is wrong, however, in judging the reason for this perceived threat to be the docetizing tendencies of Johannine Christianity. First of all, the Elder and the evangelist have been quite active in opposing such trends, and there is no evidence that even incipient Docetism was ever more than a peripheral phenomenon within this sector of the church. Second, as M. Meye Thompson has pointed out so well in her recent monograph (*The Humanity of Jesus in the Fourth Gospel* [Philadelphia: Fortress, 1988]), the evangelist's christology was absolutely as incarnational as it was elevated. It may have been exalted, but it was never docetizing. Third, far more threatening to Diotrephes' positional authority would have been *the Johannine view of pneumatically mediated and universally accessible leadership of the risen Christ*. The Johannine scandal in Diotrephes' eyes (and rightly so, as far as his aspirations were concerned) was the egalitarian teaching that by means of the *Parakletos*, all believers can be led by Christ (see G. M. Burge's excellent treatment of the Holy Spirit in the Johannine tradition: *The Anointed Community* [Grand Rapids: Eerdmans, 1987]). All of these make it plausible that Diotrephes was probably more threatened by the Johannine pneumatic and egalitarian mode of christocracy which threatened his own position and his (Antiochine?) view of how his own community could be gathered in the face of Roman hardship.

[63] This is not to say that all hierarchical expressions of church leadership misused the image of Peter or the evolving "offices" of the church. This would be no more true than to assume that all forms of charismatic expression had the same faults as Corinthian enthusiasm. It is to say that in at least one case, we have a clear example of institutional authority—and

why the Elder implicates the ἐκκλησία (probably an Antiochine reference) centrally in this crisis, and it must imply his ideological motive for "publishing" the witness of the Beloved Disciple, "whose testimony is *true*" (John 21:25).

At stake in the Elder's motivation to circulate the witness of the Beloved Disciple must have been not simply the preservation of one more gospel narrative, independent though it be, but the desire to declare the original intentionality of Jesus for his church. It is a matter of christocracy—the effective means by which the risen Lord continues to inspire, lead and empower the church—and John poses a familial and egalitarian model over and against the emerging institutional and hierarchical one.[64] When compared with Peter's confession in Matthew 16:16-19, the portrayal of Peter in John 6:67-70 is all the more telling. In Matthew, Jesus imbues Peter (and those who follow in his wake) with christocratic institutional authority; in John, however, Peter is portrayed as acknowledging the living and pneumatic words of Jesus as the only christocratic hope for the Jesus movement. In effect, Peter is here portrayed as *returning* the keys of the Kingdom to Jesus. By means of this deconstructive rendering of Peter's confession, the evangelist clears the ground for his pneumatic and familial ecclesiology developed elsewhere in the Gospel.[65] Notice, for instance, that

---

probably Petrine authority—being wielded in ways that were experienced negatively by some Johannine Christians. This kind of development must have affected the evangelist's appeal to Jesus' original intentionality for his church, and it must have motivated the Elder's desire to circulate such a testimony.

[64] One is indebted to P. Menoud, "Church and Ministry According to the New Testament" in *Jesus Christ and the Faith* (Pittsburgh, 1978), pp. 363-435, for the term, "christocracy" (pp. 407-11). In this essay, Menoud wisely describes the tension between institution and charisma, which existed in the first century church and in every generation before and since. The relevance for the present study is to acknowledge the extent to which rising institutionalism in the late first-century church was experienced as a deviation from nascent Christianity, calling forth a corrective response by the Johannine tradition, which produced a manifesto of radical christocracy—a gospel portrayal of the spiritual means by which the risen Lord will continue to lead the church. This "dialogue" may explain one reason why good biblical traditions continue to come up with variant ecclesiologies. The ecclesiological self-understanding of the historical late first-century church was dialectical, not monological.

[65] In the writings of Ignatius one clearly sees the elevation of Peter and his monepiscopal representative in the local church as the centripetal means of countering centrifugal tendencies in the face of Roman persecution. This is clearly the function of Matthew's supplementing Peter's confession with institutionalizing themes. If one considers an outline of the content of Matthew 16:17-19, one may find remarkably parallel correctives to each of these seven points in John. (See Anderson, *Christology, Table 20*: "Matthew 16:17-19 and its 'Christocratic Correctives' in John.")

See also P. N. Anderson, "'You (Alone) Have the Words of Eternal Life!' Is Peter Portrayed as *Returning* the 'Keys of the Kingdom' to Jesus in John 6:68f.?" (unpublished paper presented at the Johannine Seminar, National AAR/SBL Meeting, Anaheim, 1989); and my essay outlining five aspects of the Johannine Christocratic corrective to institutional developments in the late first-century church in *Quaker Religious Thought* 76 (1991), 27-43). These christocratic correctives include the character of worship, ministry, sacramentality, authority and apostolicity.

while the Beloved Disciple is not entrusted with instrumental keys to the
Kingdom, he is entrusted with *the mother of Jesus* (19:26f.)—an action
suggestive of not only the authority of the Johannine tradition, but also the
relational (familial rather than institutional) character of the church as
having christocratic primacy.

   The point here is that in the face of rising Roman persecution under the
reign of Domitian, the leadership of the mainstream church *and* the Fourth
Evangelist sought to appeal for church unity in the face of schismatic
tendencies, but they did so using diametrically opposite models of
organization. The mainstream church sought to bolster church unity by
raising the value of structured worship and the authority of hierarchical
leadership; the Johannine leadership sought to emphasize the presence of
Christ within the egalitarian fellowship, appealing for corporate solidarity
with Christ and his "family" as an indication of one's love for God and one
another. Each of these had its own strengths and weaknesses, and neither
expression was by any means perfect.[66] By the time 3 John was written and
the final stages of the Gospel were composed, however, the mainstream
"solution" to schismatic defections had itself become a source of division
and alienation for at least one Johannine community. This produced not
merely a complaint about the execution of "right faith and order" within the
church, but a critique of the degree to which rising institutionalism in the
late first-century church represented *the original intentionality of Jesus for
his movement*. This being the case, John 6:67-70 would quite possibly have
been interpreted by the evangelist's audience at the time of the final stages
of writing John 6 (probably in the mid 90's) as follows:

   — (Jesus asking the Twelve) You don't want to leave too, do you?" (v.
67—The testing motif of John 6, begun with the testing of individual
disciples, the crowd, the Jews and Jesus' would-be followers now
culminates with the testing of the Twelve. The crowd misunderstood, the
Jews grumbled and even some of the disciples abandoned Jesus . . . what
will the Twelve do?)

   — (Peter responds) "Lord, to whom shall we go? You have the words of
eternal life." (v. 68—An absolutely shocking statement; especially coming
from Peter—the one everybody has heard received instrumental keys to the
Kingdom! Jesus himself is the source of life-producing words, not his
representatives. Despite what you hear from Diotrephes and his kin,
Christ's life-producing word is available to all believers by means of the
Parakletos, who will sustain you, guide you and convict you of all Truth.
Before Jesus departed he appeared to his own and breathed on
[pneumatized] them, gave them the authority [responsibility] to forgive

---

   [66] See R. E. Brown's excellent treatment of emerging ecclesiologies in the Sub-Apostolic
era (*The Churches the Apostles Left Behind* [New York: Paulist Press, 1984]) and especially
the strengths and weaknesses of each.

sins, and sent [apostolized] them as the Father had sent him [John 21:21-23]. Here Peter, the spokesman of the Twelve, declares the radical possibility of *the apostolicity of every believer*.)

— (Peter continues, a bit overly confident, though) "We have come to believe and know that you are the Holy One of God!" (v. 69—As the demon recognized the true identity of Jesus as the apocalyptic King-like-David, who will sweep out of the skies like Enoch's Son of Man, surely the Romans will be made a footstool for his feet and the heavenly Kingdom of God will once more rule from Zion. Surely this Messiah will be victorious over the Romans, and no harm will come to his vice-regents. Unlike the Jewish messianism of John 6:14f., the mainstream [Synoptic] Christian basileiology will emerge triumphant.)

— (Jesus responds) "I have not elected you, the Twelve [to emerge unscathed from the trials of this age in apocalyptic triumphalism]; and one of you is a devil [for suggesting so]!" (v. 70—Now *this* is an aporia! How can such a devout confession bring such a negative response from Jesus. He must have meant *Judas*, the betrayer, who was alluded to a few verses earlier. Then again, maybe Jesus' reign never involved a foolproof plan to deliver us from all earthly trials. Maybe he expects us to abide with him regardless of the consequences. Now *that* is a test!)

In the light of such hard sayings, especially casting Peter and Synoptic basileiology in critical light, it is easy to see why translators have rendered Jesus' response as a question instead of as a declarative (after all, it does work as a question, although not as well syntactically) and why the compiler has sought to clarify the apparently harsh treatment of Peter by adding v. 71. As the compiler inserted John 6 between chapters 5 and 7, he probably doctored this aporia of portrayal. He obviously has harmonized John 18:1 to accommodate the insertion of chs.15–17 between chs.14 and 18. Furthermore, just as he has clarified which is *not* the wicked Judas (John 14:22), and just as he has sought to elevate the presentation of Peter in the material added in the epilogue (ch. 21), so he has also "clarified" for the reader that Jesus was not addressing *Simon* Peter son of John, but Judas Iscariot son of *Simon*, the one alluded to in v. 65, who would later betray the Lord. The first audiences, however would not have been privileged to this softening gloss, and they would have understood full well the ecclesiological implications of the evangelist's pointed crafting of the story. Here the ideological corrective returns to the critique of Synoptic thaumaturgy highlighted in v. 26 (crisis #1), and this is further evidence of the long-term duration of that critique. To follow Jesus is to embrace the offence of the incarnation. Even Christian (not just Jewish) thaumaturgy and triumphalism must be laid at the foot of the cross—precisely the reason the evangelist's message was, and often continues to be, misunderstood.

E. Synthesis

While John 6 has evoked the most prolific combination of literary, historical and theological debates of any single unit in the Fourth Gospel, this complexity also produces an equal degree of interpretive richness when considered comprehensively. Because John 6 represents a basically unitive written composition, preserving an independent oral tradition which elaborated homiletically on the meaning of Jesus' words and works for later generations, some of the issues faced by Johannine Christians are mirrored in the misunderstandings of Jesus' discussants and his corrective responses to them. In this sense, John 6 is literarily synchronic, but rhetorically diachronic. At every turn, the audience is called to work for life-producing rather than death-producing "food," and this appeal must have meant different things at various times in the community's history. In that sense, while the formal *Sitz im Leben* of John 6 was constant, the situational contexts in which its content was delivered homiletically continued to evolve.

Ironically, classic Jewish manna-rhetoric is overturned by the Johannine Jesus, as he corrects superficial understandings of the physical benefits of Jesus miracles, represented by the prevalent, thaumaturgical valuing of Jesus' wonders. The evangelist points instead to their revelational significance as *semeia*. And, in the face of Jewish appeals for Johannine Christians of Semitic origin to return to the local Synagogue, Jesus not only overturns their exegesis, but he exposes their absolute failure to understand the eschatological workings of God—in the past *and* in the present—thus running the risk of missing their reward in the afterlife. The Gentile Christian is also addressed existentially in John 6. Faced with a second round of persecution, this time from the Romans, members of Johannine Christianity are called to reject absolutely the docetizing tendencies of those who believe a non-suffering Lord would excuse their accommodating to the requirement of emperor-laud—at the penalties of harassment, suffering and even death. Eucharistic imagery is used to bolster the appeal for corporate solidarity with Christ and his community in the face of such hardships, and the cost of discipleship involves the ingesting of, and identification with, Jesus' Bread: the incarnated flesh of the Son of Man, given for the life of the world.

In the face of coping with persecution, Johannine Christians also become maligned by ecclesial groups who attempt to overcome schismatic tendencies by increasing structural authority and value. In the midst of these intramural dialogues, the pneumatically mediated and egalitarian model of christocracy is raised as representing Jesus' original intentionality for his church, and the Johannine Christian is called to resist "safer" innovations, clinging instead to the life-producing words of Jesus. Structurally and theologically, the narrative of John 6 calls for an abandonment of human-originated ploys and methods in exchange for responding to the saving initiative of God, as revealed through Jesus the Christ. Ironically, however, all of this leads to a final and ongoing paradox for the interpreter: to understand and believe the text fully is to fully release one's dearly-held conclusions—even exegetical ones—to the priority of responding to the divine initiative which, like the daily-given manna, comes through and beyond the revelatory text. Κύριε, πάντοτε δὸς ἡμῖν τὸν ἄρτον τοῦτον.

JESUS AND THE QUEST FOR ETERNAL LIFE[1]

John Painter

That John 6 was intended as a relatively self-contained unit is clearly signalled by the evangelist, who has commenced chapters 5, 6, and 7 with μετὰ ταῦτα,[2] a formula that marks a new beginning. Yet there has long been controversy regarding the unity and integrity of the chapter and its present place in the Gospel. Although it is argued that the chapter was based on tradition and developed through successive editions of interpretation, it is also asserted that the resulting composition constitutes a unified though developing interpretation of the tradition.

Concerning the tradition used by John it is argued that, though independent of the Synoptics, John has made use of Synoptic-like tradition and that John 6 provides evidence of a developing and yet unified interpretation of that tradition. The tradition was the basis of successive editions of the chapter. The hypothesis of a developing interpretation of the tradition provides a basis for understanding the shift of John 6 from a position before John 5 to its present position following that chapter.

Recognition and characterization of the tradition is an important beginning in the attempt to understand John 6. A second step is to note the signals indicating changes of time, place and audience which coincide with changes of literary *genre*. Changes are signalled from the crowd at Capernaum (6:22-40) to the Jews in the synagogue at Capernaum (6:41-59) to the mass of disciples and "the twelve" at some unspecified location (6:60-71). There are two references to each audience in the narrative of these sections (6:22, 24, 41, 52, 60, 66, 67, 71) and a Son of Man saying in each of Jesus' responses, to the crowd (6:27), the Jews (6:53), and the disciples (6:62). Changes of *genre* from quest (6:1-35) to rejection (6:41-59 and 6:60-66) to commendation (6:67-71) stories confirm these divisions. There is also a transition from the emphasis on the emissary christology in the quest story to the soteriology of the rejection stories. These changes, brought about by the evangelist's developing interpretation, led to the relocation of the chapter, which once followed John 4. Relocation was relatively easy (though some *aporiai* can be recognized) because chapters 5 and 6 are more or less self-contained and John 7 marks a new beginning.

---

[1] The basis of this study was given as a short main paper at the Cambridge *SNTS* Meeting in 1988 and appeared under the title "Tradition and Interpretation in John 6," *NTS* 35 (1989), 421-50. More developed forms appeared in *The Quest for the Messiah* (Edinburgh: T & T Clark, 1991 and 1993) under the title "The Messiah as the Bread of Life."

[2] See 3:22; 5:1, 14; 6:1; 7:1; 13:7; 19:38; 21:1, in all eight times. The slightly more specific μετὰ τοῦτο is used four times in 2:12; 11:7, 11; 19:28.

The transition from quest to rejection stories is evidenced by a change of dialogical pattern which can be detected by the quotation formulae:

1. In the feeding story (6:1-15) there is dialogue between Jesus and his disciples. Three sayings of Jesus to the disciples are introduced (6:5, 10, 12) and two sayings of the disciples to Jesus (6:7, 8). Jesus initiated the dialogue to test Philip, who fails the test. But Andrew, who is again introduced as the brother of Simon Peter (6:8 and see 1:40) to remind the reader of the initial quest of Andrew, shows a glimmer of comprehension. Those (οἱ ἄνθρωποι) who saw the sign also make a confession about Jesus. But this is apparently done in his absence and manifests their misunderstanding. As in 1:47-49 Jesus displays supernatural knowledge, this time to escape from the misguided attempt to make him king, 6:15. Interestingly, in 1:50 Nathanael mistakenly confesses Jesus as king, a confession that Jesus corrects with a saying about the exalted Son of Man.
2. In the narrative of the sea-crossing (6:16-21) only one saying of Jesus is introduced though the story is told from the perspective of the disciples. The specific reference to their fear (6:19) and their failure to speak to Jesus further manifests their lack of comprehension.
3. In the dialogues between Jesus and the crowd (6:22-35) there are four sayings of the crowd to Jesus (6:25, 28, 30, 34) and four responses by Jesus to the crowd (6:26, 29, 32, 35). This makes clear the initiative of the crowd and the responsive nature of Jesus' sayings.
4. The ultimatum of Jesus in 6:36-40 is formally addressed to the crowd, though there is no indication of their response to these pronouncements on their unbelief. The request of the crowd (6:34) and the self-revelation of Jesus (6:35) have not prepared the reader for this devastating verdict. The crowd is given no opportunity to reply to the stern pronouncement of their fate by Jesus in words that have the appearance of a collection of sayings on the subject of unbelief.
5. Neither the Jews (6:41-59) nor the mass of disciples (6:60-66) speak to Jesus though Jesus does react in two stages (6:43, 53 and 6:61, 65) to what he knows they are saying about him (6:43, 53 and 6:61, 65). It may be that here also we are meant to think in terms of Jesus' supernatural knowledge.
6. In the dialogue between Jesus and the twelve two sayings of Jesus are introduced (6:67, 70) and one by Peter speaking for the twelve (6:68).

Neither the Jews (6:41-59) nor the mass of disciples (6:60-66) speak to Jesus though he does know what was being said about him and reacts with pronouncements in the form of ultimatums which bring out the lack of genuine dialogue. There are dialogues between Jesus and the disciples (the twelve) and the crowd, portrayed as potential disciples. Indeed the dialogical pattern is strongest in 6:22-35 dealing with Jesus and the crowd. This section stresses the initiative of the crowd and the responsiveness of Jesus to their approach. The Jews and the mass of disciples move towards the inevitable rejection of Jesus. Yet surely the crowd ought not to be portrayed more positively than the mass of disciples! This suggests that the story of the crowd is earlier than the story of the mass of disciples, the latter reflecting the period subsequent to 70 CE, probably from the time of crisis for Jewish believers within the synagogue. The evidence in John 6 suggests that a series of editions expanded the Gospel in various ways. In the end the evangelist has made use of these expansions to produce a narrative development so that the resulting chapter is a literary unity. What enables the critic to penetrate beneath this surface unity is the evangelist's failure to introduce the changing groups in his normal fashion and the resulting aporiai.

A. TRADITION

1. John 6 and the Synoptics

Evidence that John was dependent on the Synoptics is often found in the overall agreement of order between John and Mark within which close verbal parallels occur.[3] When allowance is made for the duplicate feedings in Mark the evidence of John 6 provides as strong a case for this point of view as anything in the Gospel.

	John	Mark
Multiplication for 5000	6:1-15	6:30-44
Walking on the Sea	6:16-24	6:45-54
Request for a sign	6:25-34	8:11-13
Remarks on bread	6:35-59	8:14-21
Faith of Peter	6:60-69	8:27-30
Passion theme: betrayal	6:70-71	8:31-33[4]

As in Mark, the feeding is followed by the sea crossing, with Jesus walking on the water. Further agreements with the Markan order include the demand for a sign, elements of the discourse on bread, the confession of Peter and the passion theme. Hence a tradition with something like the Markan order underlies John 6. But there is evidence that suggests that a theory of Synoptic dependence involves serious problems.

i. Much of the evidence of the relation of John 6 to the Synoptics concerns tradition that, at first glance, could be attributed to dependence on

---

[3] See C. K. Barrett, *The Gospel According to St John,* 2nd ed. (Philadelphia: Westminster, 1978), p. 43, for "a list, which is certainly not complete, of corresponding passages which occur *in the same order* in both Mark and John." Barrett notes in particular that the sequence of the feeding and the walking on the lake "is not readily explicable except on the hypothesis of literary relationships." One may ask, however, whether the dependence is direct or indirect, because Mark could have taken over the sequence from his tradition. To this view Barrett can respond, "Anyone who after an interval of nineteen centuries feels himself in a position to distinguish nicely between 'Mark' and 'something much like Mark' is at liberty to do so." *John,* p. 45.

[4] See R. E. Brown, *The Gospel According to John* (Garden City, N.Y.: Doubleday, 1966), 1:238.

Mark. The evidence, however, turns out to be more complex because John is sometimes closer to Matt. or Luke than to Mark and some differences from all of them are not easily explained in terms of redactional tendencies.

a. Tradition common to Matt., Mark, and Luke:
John 6:9 (Matt. 14:17; Mark 6:38; Luke 9:13). But John, exactly as Matt., has πέντε ἄρτους and where the Synoptics use ἰχθύες John uses ὀψάρια. The latter could be due to Johannine editing (see John 21:13). Although John 21 is an appendix, it probably contains tradition from the Johannine school.
John 6:13 (Matt. 14:20; Mark 6:43; Luke 9:17) though δώδεκα κοφίνους is exactly as Matt..
John 6:30 σημεῖον (and Matt. 16:1; Mark 8:11; Luke 11:16).

b. Tradition common to Matt. and Mark:
John 6:5, though John has θεασάμενος ὅτι πολὺς ὄχλος while Matt. 14:14 and Mark 6:34 have εἶδεν πολὺν ὄχλον.
John's use of πόθεν relates to the second feeding of Matt. 15:33; Mark 8:4.
John uses ἀγοράσωμεν while Matt. 14:15; Mark 6:36 use ἀγοράσωσιν.
John 6:10 uses χόρτος; Matt. 14:18 (χόρτου) Mark 6:39 (χόρτῳ).
John uses ἀνέπεσαν as in Mark 6:40, but see the second feeding Matt. 15:35 and Mark 8:6.
John uses ἄνδρες πεντακισχίλιοι as in Matt. 14:21; Mark 6:44.
John 6:11 and Matt. 15:36; Mark 8:6 (the second feeding) use εὐχαριστήσας but εὐλόγησεν is used by Matt. 14:19; Mark 6:41; Luke 9:16 in the first feeding.
John 6:15 and Matt. 14:23; Mark 6:46 use εἰς τὸ ὄρος but John "adds" αὐτὸς μόνος and Matt. has κατ' ἰδίαν and both Matt. and Mark "add" προσεύξασθαι.
John 6.17 has ἐμβάντες εἰς πλοῖον ἤρξοντο πέραν τῆς θαλάσσης εἰς Καφαρναούμ. Compare Matt. 14:22; Mark 6:45 which use ἐμβῆναι εἰς τὸ πλοῖον καὶ (αὐτὸν, Matt. only) εἰς τὸ πέραν (πρὸς Βηθσαϊδάν, Mark only). Both Matt. and Mark go on (with minor variations) to indicate that the disciples did this while Jesus dismissed the crowd. This differs from John, where it is Jesus who withdrew from the crowd. The destinations of John and Mark also differ. Minor variations in wording are more serious obstacles to a theory of Synoptic dependence in the light of these observations.
John 6:19, θεωροῦσιν τὸν Ἰησοῦν περιπατοῦντα ἐπὶ τῆς θαλάσσης and see Matt. 14:26; Mark 6:49.
John 6:20, ἐγώ εἰμι, μὴ φοβεῖσθε and see Matt. 14:27; Mark 6:50 both of which add θαρσεῖτε. Mark, like John, uses the introductory formula λέγει αὐτοῖς.

John 6:21, εἰς τὸν πλοῖον as Matt. 14:32; Mark 6:51.
John 6:24, ἀνέβησαν (or ἐνέβησαν), see Matt. 14:22 and Mark 6:45.

c. In the few cases where John is related to Mark alone the evidence remains complex.
John 6:1, ἀπῆλθεν and Mark 6:32 ἀπῆλθον and see John 6:27.
John 6:2, πολύς and Mark 6:33 πολλοί.
John 6:5, and Mark 6:36 φάγωσιν.
John 6:7, διακοσίων δηναρίων ἄρτοι and Mark 6:37 δηναρίων διακοσίων ἄρτους.
John 6:10 and Mark 6:40 ἀνέπεσαν and see Mark 8:6 and Matt. 15:35.
John 6:20 and Mark 6:50 λέγει αὐτοῖς.

d. Dependence on Mark will not explain those cases where:

1. Only John and Matt. agree:
John 6:10, οἱ ἄνδρες τὸν ἀριθμὸν ὡς πεντακισχίλιοι and Matt. 14:21 ἄνδρες ὡσεὶ πεντακισχίλιοι.
John 6:13 and Matt. 14:20 δώδεκα κοφίνους.
John 6:19 and Matt. 14:24 σταδίους.
John 6:19, ἐφοβήθησαν and Matt. τοῦ φοβοῦ, and later of Peter, ἐφοβήθη, Matt. 14:30.
John 6:68 and Matt. 16:16 Σίμων Πέτρος. See also the references to John 6:9, 13 in a. above.

2. John has tradition common to Matt. and Luke:
John 6:2, ἠκολούθει δὲ αὐτῷ ὄχλος πολὺς and compare Matt. 14:13; Luke 9:11 which introduce the theme of the crowds following Jesus οἱ [δὲ] ὄχλοι ἠκολούθησαν αὐτῷ whereas Mark mentions πολλοί and does not refer to following, though this might be implied. It could be argued that John's ὄχλος πολύς is a combination of Mark's πολλοί and Matt.'s and Luke's ὄχλοι. Alternatively it might derive from a variant tradition. See also John 6:69 ὁ ἅγιος τοῦ θεοῦ and Matt. 16:16 ὁ Χριστὸς ὁ υἱὸς τοῦ θεοῦ and Luke 9:20 τὸν Χριστὸν τοῦ θεοῦ and Mark 8:29 has simply ὁ Χριστός.

3. John agrees with Luke alone:
John 6:1. Neither John nor Luke mentions a boat at this point. While Luke does not recount the return sea-crossing John does and has to introduce the boat at that point suggesting that the two stories were once separate but had become joined in the tradition used by John yet without introducing the first sea-crossing as do Mark and Matt.

John 6:5, ἐπάρας οὖν τοὺς ὀφθαλμοὺς is a Lukanism, see Luke 6:20; 16:23; 18:13. This however might be a case of Johannine editing rather than Lukan dependence, see John 4:35; 17:1.
John 6:42, οὐχ οὗτός ἐστιν Ἰησοῦς ὁ υἱὸς Ἰωσήφ; and Luke 4:22 οὐχὶ υἱός ἐστιν Ἰωσήφ οὗτος;

While some of these points of contact might be a result of coincidental editing, the obvious implication is that, if John is to be understood on the basis of dependence on the Synoptics, it must be dependent on the three of them and, given the creative kind of composition John is, this does not seem likely.[5]

That the theory requires dependence on Matt., Mark and Luke is surely less credible than if John could be understood on the basis of Mark alone. For example, I would judge that Matt. dates from about the same time as John. John itself bears the marks of a long process of composition. Given the completion of John around the same time as Matt., a theory of substantial dependence on Matt. is hardly credible.[6] Further, the differences between John and the Synoptics need to be noted. Though many of these could be due to Johannine editing, it is likely that John has made use of a variant source of the feeding and other traditions now recorded in John 6. Other evidence can be given to support this view.

ii. There were several variant traditions of the feeding story and the subsequent sea-crossing. Two of these were known to Mark and agreements between Matt. and Luke against Mark suggest that they knew yet another version of the feeding story. John's account of the feeding story resembles aspects of both of Mark's accounts as well as the variant in Matt. and Luke. At no point do John's agreements occur where we have demonstrable Markan, Matthaean or Lukan redaction. It is more likely that John made use of a Synoptic-like variant of the traditions than a patchwork from all that is now found in Matt., Mark and Luke.

iii. While some of the variations from the Synoptics in John's feeding story are a consequence of the evangelist's editing,[7] there are others which are derived from the tradition. Both Matt. and Luke, like John, refer to the

---

[5] See now Moody Smith, *John Among the Gospels: The Relationship in Twentieth–Century Research* (Minneapolis: Fortress, 1992), p. 180.

[6] This judgement need not be based on the two document hypothesis though that is the assumption of this chapter. The early stages of John (perhaps even earlier than Mark) already made use of the feeding story as the evidence of the expansion and modification of it shows.

[7] Touches of the evangelist's hand are to be noted in the telling of the story itself: the time reference (μετὰ ταῦτα); the note indicating that the Passover is the feast of the Jews; the dialogues with Philip and Andrew; the direct commands by Jesus and his distribution of the food. The account of the sea-crossing also has some differences from the Synoptics for which the evangelist might be responsible; the account is more compressed and instead of the stilling of the storm there is a miraculous arrival at the destination.

crowd *following* Jesus to the desert place. Only John explains why.[8] They followed him seeing the signs he did on the sick, 6:2. John also tells of the crowd's response to the feeding miracle, 6:14-15. They confessed him to be the prophet and attempted to make him king, a political motif not likely to have been added by John. It was to escape from this that Jesus withdrew, not to pray (as in Matt. 14:23; Mark 6:46). In Matt. and Mark, following the feeding and at Jesus' command, the disciples embarked in the boat leaving Jesus. But no-one asked him how he would follow them. Only then did he dismiss the crowd and go further up the mountain to pray, an apologetic motif emphasizing Jesus' piety. In John Jesus fled from the crowd, leaving the disciples at the same time. When evening came the abandoned disciples attempted to make their way back across the lake. This is a more natural sequence of events and without apologetic motif or evidence of Johannine themes. Here John appears to have preserved primitive elements of the tradition.

iv. The Synoptics cannot account for a number of the traditions used in John, notably the healings of John 4:46-54; 5:1-9; 9:1-11. In addition John 2:1-11 and the underlying tradition of 11:1-44 should perhaps be added. It is enough to show that a number of important Synoptic-like stories cannot have been derived from the Synoptics and are unlikely to be Johannine creations but have probably been drawn from another source[9] from which have come also the basic traditions now in John 6. According to Moody Smith, "The distinctive character of the Johannine narrative material within the Gospel strongly suggests a principal source (or sources) and one independent of the Synoptics."[10] There is, however, need to distinguish the distinctive character of the Gospel, which is, at least in part, a result of the evangelist's interpretation of tradition, from the Synoptic-like character of that tradition.

2. The Traditional Stories in John 6:1-21

Synoptic parallels make quite clear that John 6 has been developed on the basis of a sequence of traditional material. The appropriate approach for the detection and identification of the underlying tradition begins by noting agreements with the Synoptics. But it is unlikely that the tradition was confined to this material. Departures from the Synoptics should be examined with a view to ascertaining whether these have arisen in the

---

[8] That Jesus should flee to a desert place at the execution of John the Baptist (see Mark 6:14-29 and parallel) is reasonable enough. This does not explain why the crowd followed him.

[9] C.H. Dodd, *Historical Tradition and the Fourth Gospel* (Cambridge: Cambridge University Press, 1963), argued, in case after case, that the traditions he had isolated were not derived from Matt., Mark and Luke though they were Synoptic-like.

[10] D. M. Smith, "Johannine Christianity," *NTS* 21/2 (1975), 229.

tradition or are due to the evangelist's handling of his material. Without the control of the Synoptic comparison, this task, though necessary if we are to appreciate the evangelist's achievement, is hazardous.

   i. The miraculous feeding (6:1-15). Unlike Matt. and Mark neither John nor Luke mentions the departure of Jesus in a boat, though John, in agreement with Matt. and Mark, introduces the boat for the return journey. This probably indicates that the feeding and the sea-crossing were once independent stories that had come to form a sequence in the traditions used by Mark and John.[11] It is unlikely that Mark and John independently created the sequence. In John the general directions imply a desert place,[12] which is explicit in Matt. and Mark. Given that John has reproduced, from the tradition, the account of the political response of the crowd, it may be that he has de-emphasized the desert place because Jesus' decision to lead the crowd there might imply complicity with their political intentions. Matt. and Luke indicate that the crowd followed Jesus, implied in Mark and explicit in John who alone indicates the reason, ὅτι ἐθεώρουν τὰ σημεῖα ἃ ἐποίει ἐπὶ τῶν ἀσθενούντων.[13] The reason was probably given in John's source and might have been suppressed in the Synoptics. In Matt. and Mark Jesus' flight to the desert place followed the execution of John the Baptist. This does not explain why the crowds should have followed him. John's source answers this question.

   Whatever the crowd expected, in the wilderness Jesus performed a sign of deliverance.[14] Paul Barnett[15] has argued that in Josephus there is evidence of a class of "sign prophets" and that the pattern of the prophet, sign (Exodus motif), wilderness location, crowd as audience, is significant,

---

   [11] That neither Luke nor John mention the departure in a boat and Luke does not follow the sequence of the miraculous feeding with the miraculous sea crossing support this view. The tradition used by John stands between Mark and Luke. John makes no attempt to explain from whence the boat comes.

   [12] This is complicated by verses 22-24, which are not part of the tradition used by John and probably contain an interpolation. See R. Schnackenburg, *The Gospel according to St John*, 2:33.

   [13] This use of τὰ σημεῖα ἃ ἐποίει ἐπὶ τῶν ἀσθενούντων has the specialized sense of "miracles of healing" which appears to be derived from the source. R. T. Fortna, "Source and Redaction in the Fourth Gospel's portrayal of Jesus' Signs," *JBL* 89 (1970), 160, has argued that the source did not speak of "seeing" signs. Such reference, he thinks, was introduced by the evangelist. It is uncertain whether the correct reading in 6:2 is ἑώρων or ἐθεώρουν. It is argued that the latter is an assimilation to 2:23. If that is the case ἐθεώρουν is used in 2:23; ἑώρων is used in 6:2; and ἰδόντες in 6:14. According to Ed Freed, this variation of vocabulary is characteristic of the evangelist and not the tradition, see "Fortna's Signs-source in John," *JBL* 94 (1975), 563-79. But if Fortna is correct the source may have indicated that the crowd followed Jesus "because of the signs he performed on the sick." These distinctions are less convincing if a loose collection of tradition is in view rather than a complex signs source or Gospel.

   [14] See Josephus, *AJ* xx.168,188, and especially *BJ* ii. 259; vi.285.

   [15] "The Jewish Sign Prophets," *NTS* 27/5 (1981), 679-97.

suggesting some relation between Jesus and the sign prophets.[16] While each intended the sign to show that he was "the prophet," because the promised deliverance was not achieved we find a class of failed sign prophets. Of special importance, for an understanding of Jesus' miracle in the wilderness is Theudas,[17] who, according to Josephus, promised to part the Jordan, allowing his followers safe passage, thus re-enacting the Exodus:

> During the period when Fadus was procurator of Judaea, a certain impostor (γόης) named Theudas persuaded the majority of the crowd (τὸν πλεῖστον ὄχλον) to take up their possessions and to follow him to the Jordan River. He stated that he was a prophet and that at his command the river would be parted and would provide them an easy passage. With this talk he deceived many. Fadus, however, did not permit them to reap the fruit of their folly, but sent against them a squadron of cavalry. (Josephus, *AJ* xx.97-99)

Because Jesus was the first of those known to us (only John the Baptist was earlier, and he did no sign, John 10:41), Barnett suggests that Jesus himself, and the proclamation of his signs, might have "set this pattern." But it is hardly likely that later Jewish movements would have patterned themselves on Jesus or that Josephus was influenced by the Jesus movement in his portrayal of them.

R. A. Horsley has responded critically to Barnett's article.[18] He rightly asserts that the accounts of both Josephus and John must be treated critically in the awareness that they are not straightforward accounts of what happened. His analysis of Josephus leads to the conclusion that the first century prophets were of two kinds: the individual oracle prophets and those who led popular prophetic movements. The latter, he thinks, arose from among the common people and were concerned with the deliverance of the the common people from the socio-economic oppression of the day. He stresses that the association with deliverance is essential to this movement though signs are not. Here Horsley's own summary account (8-9) hardly bears out his insistence that deliverance was essential while signs

---

[16] *AJ* xix.162; xx.167-172,188; *BJ* ii.258-263; vi.285-286. In *BJ* vi.286 Josephus mentions a multitude of such prophets. That they were perceived to be prophets by the masses is clear from his reluctant naming them as such though he himself uses the term γόης of them.

[17] See D. Aune, *Prophecy in Early Christianity and the Ancient Mediterranean World* (Grand Rapids: Eerdmans, 1983), pp. 127-28, who argues that Theudas saw himself as "the prophet like Moses."

[18] "Popular Prophetic Movements at the Time of Jesus: Their Principal Features and Social Origins," *JSNT* 26 (1986), 3–27 especially 4-10, 15.

were not. True, the prophets were perceived as deliverers. But how were they recognized in the first place? The accounts in Josephus suggest that Exodus type signs played some part in this,[19] but Horsley fails to note that the promised parting of the Jordan river and the promise that the walls of Jerusalem would fall down constitute signs even if they are not so called by Josephus. That he does not use the terminology there suggests that Josephus has no particular reason for introducing the view but that it represents the popular perception of the movement.[20] If Horsley is only concerned to show that the descriptive title "sign prophets" is not the most apt for this movement he has gone too far in his attempt to break the link with signs because, even though these prophets were concerned with deliverance, they were recognized through the promise or performance of Exodus-type signs.[21]

According to John, the crowd which followed Jesus into the desert place responded to him in a way consistent with the perception of him in these terms (6:2, 14-15). Because it is a position rejected both by the evangelist and the tradition used by him it is likely that it represents a pre-crucifixion response. Indeed it is unlikely that such an overtly political motif would have been added. This suggests a known Jewish tradition which led to the recognition of Jesus as a sign prophet, that is, the prophet legitimated by sign(s). Recognition that there was a group of such prophets only reveals those who failed to be legitimated. That is, they failed to deliver. This would account for the disparaging view of the movements that we find in Josephus.

Rabbinic statements affirm that just as the first redeemer (Moses) brought down the manna, so also will the latter redeemer. While these references are somewhat later than John, 2 Baruch 29:8, which is more or less contemporary with John, tells that the manna will come again at the dawning of the new age.[22] The narrative of the feeding miracle in John, but not those in the Synoptics, reflects this expectation which appears to be related to the expectation concerning the sign prophet.[23] That would not be

---

[19] *AJ* xx.97, 169-71; *BJ* ii.261-2. See also *AJ* xviii.85-86; and *BJ* ii.259; *AJ* xx.167-8. The final reference describes a number of "deceivers and imposters" (obviously the evaluation of Josephus rather than their followers) who led their followers out into the wilderness anticipating that God would give them "signs of liberation." This generalized account makes explicit what is implicit in the other accounts.

[20] Contrary to Horsley, "Popular Prophetic Movements," p. 25, n. 22.

[21] See Schürer, *The History of the Jewish People in the Age of Jesus Christ*, ed. G. Vermes et al. (Edinburgh: T. & T. Clark, 1973–87), 2:603-06.

[22] See C. K. Barrett, *St. John*, pp. 288f. and R. Schnackenburg, *The Gospel according to St. John* (New York: Seabury, 1968–82), 2:449, n. 110 for references.

[23] Such figures are referred to as "millennial prophets" by J. D. Crossan, *The Historical Jesus: The Life of a Mediterranean Jewish Peasant* (San Francisco: Harper, 1991), p. 158.

surprising if that expectation were based on Deut. 18:15, 18.[24] It would make sense of the response of the crowd in the Johannine account. According to the story, the crowd followed Jesus out into the desert because of the signs he was performing. In the desert Jesus replicated the giving of the manna by Moses. It is not surprising that the people[25] should perceive Jesus to be the prophet (6:14) and that they should attempt to make him king.[26] Moses was the prophet-king.[27] That Jesus was the prophet-king is the view of those who witnessed the sign, 6:14-15.[28] Thus we are warned against insisting that the categories of eschatological prophet and messianic king were always viewed separately. Clearly they are closely related by those depicted in John 6:14-15 and this should not be seen as a Johannine or early Christian construction but as a popular perception of Jesus in response to his signs and the feeding sign in particular.

Horsley wishes to distinguish the popular prophetic movements from overtly political movements (Sicarii and Zealots) and popular messianic movements. The distinction between those who sought deliverance by armed uprising and those who waited to participate in the deliverance wrought by God is probably clearer in theory than actuality. The War Scroll of Qumran suggests that with the dawning of God's deliverance the children of light would be engaged in the battle as an essential part of the forces of God.[29] The key was to know when was God's time to act. Certainly the

---

[24] Such figures are referred to as "millennial prophets" by J. D. Crossan, *The Historical Jesus: The Life of a Mediterranean Jewish Peasant* (San Francisco: Harper, 1991), p. 158 because it shows that, for the Qumran Community, the Teacher was not just one prophet amongst many and indeed may have been identified with the coming Prophet.

[25] Here John does not speak of the crowd but of the ἄνθρωποι. John's use of οἱ ἄνθρωποι (the people) is probably intended to indicate that not all of the crowd saw the sign (see 6:26) and specifies those who did, 6:14. While the Synoptics have no equivalent to John 6:14-15 both Matt. and Mark refer to the ἄνδρες who were fed, and in this they are followed by John 6:10. Matt. adds χωρὶς γυναικῶν καὶ παιδίων.

[26] See J. L. Martyn, *History and Theology in the Fourth Gospel* (New York: Harper & Row, 1968), pp. 98-101.

[27] See Wayne Meeks, *The Prophet-King* (Leiden: E. J. Brill, 1967).

[28] The vast majority of mss read σημεῖον, but p[75] B a boh read σημεῖα, which is probably an assimilation to John 6:2. Thus the singular should be read. It refers specifically to the feeding and does not include the healings. If, as argued, the confession of Jesus as the prophet-king is inadequate (according to John) the illuminating study of that name by Wayne Meeks does not penetrate the depths of the Johannine mystery. See now John Ashton, *Understanding the Fourth Gospel* (Oxford: Clarendon, 1991), p. 100, n. 76.

[29] Yigael Yadin *The Scroll of the War of the Sons of Light against the Sons of Darkness* (Oxford: Oxford University Press, 1962), p. 15, says that the purpose of the scroll "was to supply an urgent and immediate need, a guide for the problems of the long predicted war, which according to the sect would take place in the near future." The association of zealot tendencies with heavenly and earthly messianic figures at Qumran is argued by R. Eisenman and M.Wise, *The Dead Sea Scrolls Uncovered* (Rockport, MA: Element, 1992), especially on the basis of materials until recently unpublished.

Romans would have found difficulty in distinguishing the two types of prophet deliverers, as is indicated by the case of the self-styled prophet in the time of Fadus.[30] Horsley (5) rightly stresses that we do not have access to the intentions of the various prophets. Nor do we have access to their actions but only to the perception of their actions as reported.[31] That Jesus was perceived by the masses as the prophet is inherently probable. It is also probable that, in popular perception, the prophet was not sharply distinguished from the Messiah.[32]

Horsley's distinctions might correspond more precisely with the intentions of the leaders of various movements. The problem, acknowledge by Horsley, is that we do not have direct access to the evidence of those intentions but only to the perception of the movements by others. While differences do emerge it is clear that various leaders had to struggle against a generalizing interpretation of their roles and movements. Both Horsley and Crossan acknowledge that the Romans tended to interpret the various movements in socio-political terms and to suppress them even where, on the evidence of Josephus, that suppression does not appear to be justified.[33] In reading Josephus critically or "against himself" the evidence confirms that in popular perception traditions were assimilated. John 6:14-15 confirms this while emphasizing that both Jesus and John reject this popular perception.

Reference to "the feast of the Jews," has all the hallmarks of the evangelist's hand,[34] but the Passover theme itself probably belonged to the traditional story giving force to Jesus' sign of feeding the crowd in the wilderness. The evangelist has not simply taken over the reference to the Passover. Birger Olsson referred to the Sinai screen of 1:19–2:11.[35] In John 6 the evangelist has interpreted the traditional material through a Passover/Exodus screen. The Synoptics tell of Jesus' early Galilean

---

[30] See the quotation of *AJ* xx.87-99 above. Gerd Theissen, *The Shadow of the Galilean* (Philadelphia: Fortress, 1987), reconstructs the story of Jesus to show that although Jesus did not lead a revolutionary movement against the Romans they *perceived* him as a political threat and executed him.

[31] In the case of Jesus we also have access to the perception of his words and the significance of this should not be minimized. As G. Vermes has frequently noted, the significance of Jesus' teaching sets him apart from other popular prophetic movements in his day.

[32] See Schürer, *History*, 2:598-606.

[33] See Crossan, *The Historical Jesus*, pp. 159ff.

[34] See 2:13, 23; 6:4; 11:55; 12:1. On each of the three occasions the Passover is described as a feast of the Jews.

[35] *Structure and Meaning in the Fourth Gospel* (Lund: C. W. K. Gleerup, 1974), pp. 102-09. There he says, "I use 'screen' and not 'pattern' or 'structure' or 'motif' because of its dynamic character and its usefulness in the semantic structure of a text and postsemantic processes behind a text." (p. 102, n. 29). "The Sinai screen explains the composition and many of the details...[and] confirms the total interpretation." . . . "The narrator saw in his material an equivalent of the events that once took place at Sinai, . . . " (p. 109).

popularity but they mention no attempt to take him by force (ἁρπάζειν) and to make him king. This attempt explains Jesus' withdrawal into the mountainous region alone. Matt. 14:23 and Mark 6:46 explain this withdrawal as being προσεύξασθαι, which might be the implied purpose of the original withdrawal, according to Matt. and Mark. In John Jesus' calculated withdrawal itself shows his rejection of the attempt to make him king.[36] While we would not expect an actual crowd, intent on making Jesus king, to take his refusal so easily, it is important to remember that, from the point of view of the story, Jesus' rejection was both clear and final. There is nothing to be gained by telling that the crowd persisted in its intent. Indeed, it was the evangelist's purpose to proceed to the next scene.

It is unclear what christological perception was communicated in the traditional story as distinct from the christology of the crowd which it reported. It is possible that the story was intended to proclaim Jesus as the eschatological deliverer. Fragments of this position are to be found in 6:27, 39, 40, 44, 54. The emphasis is on the food (βρῶσις) which the Son of Man[37] will give (δώσει) and the resurrection on the last day. It seems that the tradition proclaimed Jesus as a man approved of God by signs and wonders,[38] exalted to God's right hand as the judge elect of all the world. Both christologies (that of the crowd[39] and that of the traditional story[40]) proposed corporate solutions to the envisaged problem. The crowd looked for a political resolution to the Roman occupation, while the traditional story looked for an apocalyptic solution to the ills of the world. Because, as we shall see, the traditional story has become absorbed into the evangelist's quest story development (6:1-40) the apocalyptic eschatology remains only as a relic alongside the christology of the quest story. This suggests that the evangelist did not reject that eschatology but made an emissary christology the focus of the quest story. This christology made Jesus the source of life for the believer in the present.

ii. The miraculous sea-crossing (6:16-21). The evangelist agrees with Mark (and Matt.) in telling the story of the miraculous sea-crossing following the feeding story because it was already attached to his story of

---

[36] In 6:15 the use of πάλιν indicates a further movement into the deserted mountainous region.

[37] The first Son of Man saying (6:27) is in the quest story (1-35); the second (6:53) in the controversy with the Jews (6:41-59); and the third (6:62) in the controversy with the disciples (6:60-66). Traditional third person Son of Man sayings and third person Father/Son sayings are reworked with characteristically Johannine "I" sayings in the first person, or "my Father" sayings. This reworking is a Johannine characteristic. See also the discussion of 5:19-30 in chapter 5 of my *The Quest for the Messiah*, "The Paradigm of Rejection."

[38] See Acts 2:22-36; 3:19-21.

[39] Synoptic parallels show that reference to the crowd is traditional.

[40] Clearly the crowd in the story and the story as a whole give expression to rival christologies. Thus political messiahship was already rejected in the tradition used by John.

the feeding, though the evidence suggests that the stories were originally independent. His account of the miraculous sea crossing is much briefer than those of Matt. and Mark which, apart from Matt.'s addition of Peter's walking on the water, are quite similar. They differ from John in that, according to their accounts, Jesus enters the boat and the storm ceased whereas, in John, Jesus' appearance and self-identification miraculously coincides with the boat reaching its destination.[41]

In all three accounts Jesus identifies himself with the words ἐγώ εἰμι· μὴ φοβεῖσθε.[42] It is sometimes argued that this is used by the evangelist as a theophany formula.[43] Against this view: 1.) The evangelist has simply taken this over from the tradition and has made nothing of it. 2.) Mark portrays the amazement of the disciples, and notes their lack of understanding (Mark 6:51-52), and Matt. (14:33) has the disciples proclaim "Truly you are Son of God," though this response is to the miracle rather than Jesus' words. But John has no confession from the disciples, which would be expected if this were a revelation formula. In John it is only noted that the disciples wished to take Jesus into the boat, having identified who it was. Whether this happened remains unstated. Instead we are told that immediately the boat reached its destination. 3.) While the frequent use of ἐγώ εἰμι in John suggests something significant, appeals to various examples where God himself as speaker reveals himself using *ani hu* (Exod. 12:12; Isa. 45, especially verses 5-8, 18-22) do not provide a basis for interpreting the Johannine use because in all of these instances it is clear that God is the speaker, "I am the Lord, and there is no other." Here in John 6:20 the "I am" is simply an identification, "It is I/me."[44]

All of this suggests that the evangelist is not narrating a theophany through his telling of the sea crossing. He tells the story because it was already attached to the feeding story. But he has used the story to good effect. This story dramatically separates Jesus from the crowd which had followed him into the desert. Separation could have been achieved simply by Jesus' withdrawal into the wilderness of the mountain. But that would have been an ambiguous action in relation to the political affirmation for which the desert was the legitimate milieu. The story of the sea-crossing was used because it lay ready at hand to make the point of Jesus' rejection of the political role while, at the same time, separating Jesus from the crowd. That separation was then used to emphasize the renewed seeking of Jesus by the crowd "on the next day."

---

[41] See Psalm 107:29-30. In the Psalm the stilling of the storm and the arrival at the desired destination occur together and perhaps this is also presupposed in John.

[42] In both Matt. and Mark this saying is prefixed by θαρσεῖτε.

[43] See B. Gärtner, *John 6 and the Jewish Passover* (Lund: C. W. K. Gleerup, 1959), pp. 17-18, 28 and P. Borgen, *Bread from Heaven* (Leiden: E. J. Brill, 1965), p. 180.

[44] Thus C. K. Barrett, *St John*, p. 281.

B. INTERPRETING THE TRADITION

It is notable that in the narrative description: in 6:22-35 there are two references to the crowd (6:22, 24); in 6:41-59 there are two references to the Jews (6:41, 52); in 6:60-66 there are two references to the disciples (6:60, 66); and in 6:67-71 there are two references to the twelve (6:67, 71).[45] This balance does not seem to be accidental. Rather the evangelist appears to have developed further discourses on the basis of the quest story of 6:1-35 of the first edition. Verses 36-40 are based on the concluding pronouncement of the quest story. In this section (36-40) we also find remnants of the eschatological messiahship[46] which the tradition used by the evangelist had offered as an alternative to the rejected political messiahship of 6:15. But the primary function of this section is to form a transition to the rejection of Jesus by the Jews and the mass of disciples in 6:41-66. Of course this also means that the quest of the crowd has ended in failure and it is said that they have seen and not believed, 6:1-40. The function of verses 67-71 is less clear. It could be that they make a hybrid of the rejection story by introducing an element of commendation, the twelve, through Peter, being commended for exemplary faith.

1. The Quest Story of 6:1-40: First Edition

i. Quest stories in John. The case for recognizing a quest story in John 6 is facilitated by the recognition of the genre and its use in earlier parts of the Gospel.[47]

The anatomy of the quest story can be set out as follows:
1. A quester approaches with an implied or explicit request for help.
2. The quest dominates the story, holding the episodes together.
3. The quester is important and not a mere foil for Jesus as the opponent frequently is in objection/rejection stories.
4. The quest story is longer than other pronouncement stories because there are difficulties that must be overcome. These difficulties or objections are important because it is by means of them that the storyteller may wish to change the audience's attitudes. This is certainly true of the quest story of John 6, see especially 6:27, 32.
5. The quest story, unlike the traditional story of John 6, focuses attention on the quest of the individual and emphasizes the need for individual

---

[45] Jesus also refers to the twelve in 6:70.

[46] See the reference to the Son of Man (in 6:27) and the use of the future δώσει. This future tense is later taken up in an "I" saying by Jesus in 6.51 ἐγώ δώσω and see 4:14. The future tenses in chapter 6 appear to point forward to a future event while in 4:14 Jesus was referring to a present possibility, see 4:10. There are traces of a continuing future eschatological dimension in John 6; see 6:27, 39, 40, 44, 54.

[47] See chapter 4, "Quest Stories in John 1-4," in my *The Quest for the Messiah*.

response, 6:35. Though Jesus was speaking to the crowd he called for individual response, "the one who comes to me . . . the one who believes in me . . . ." This accentuates the way the corporate quest has been reinterpreted in individual terms. The stress on the individual might well be intended by Tannehill when he says, "The story concerns a person in quest of something important to human well-being."[48]

6. In John what is important to human well-being at a physical level becomes the symbol of well-being at a spiritual level, see 4:10; 6:27. The quest is transformed by redirection from ordinary water and bread to life-giving water and bread, indeed, bread from heaven. It is fundamental to John's symbolic discourse that the material world, with its sources of life, cannot satisfy the human quest for life though it can and does point beyond itself to the transcendent source of all life.

7. The pronouncement by Jesus holds the key to the resolution of the quest, see 6:35.

8. The result of the quest is indicated, see 6:36.[49]

Here a pattern emerges that is recognizable elsewhere, including John 6.[50] The transformation of the opening series of quest stories by the insertion of 1:51 is also relevant to John 6 where the focus has been moved from a miracle worker christology to an exalted Son of Man christology. See 6:62.

ii. The quest story of 6:1-40. Reading 6:1-15 from the perspective of the quest story we note the initiative of the crowd which followed Jesus (ἠκολούθει δὲ αὐτῷ) seeing the σημεῖα he performed. The crowd was rewarded and they were fed by Jesus. This suggests a successful quest. But the story is not yet finished. The crowd's quest to make Jesus king was frustrated by his premature withdrawal. Here an action provides the objection to the quest which now appears to have failed. But the story still continues and is taken further by 6:16-21 which dramatizes Jesus' separation of himself from the crowd. Had the wilderness withdrawal been used for this purpose the crowd, renewing its seeking of Jesus, would have come again to him in the desert place, the location associated with the sign prophet, which role Jesus had rejected. Instead of this it was necessary for the crowd to come seeking him in Capernaum.

---

[48] See R. Tannehill, "Pronouncement Stories," *Semeia* 20 (1981), 9.

[49] In his review of the first edition of *Quest* K. Grayston wrote "*Quest* corresponds to the frequent Johannine use of *zetein*" (*Epworth Review* [May 1993], 111). This totally ignores the literary analysis of the quest story and partially ignores the thematic complex of "following," "seeking" and "finding" which signals quest in John.

[50] See especially the motifs of "following," "seeking," and "finding" in 1:37, 38, 40, 41, 43, 45; 6:2, 24-26 and the connection of events by the use of τῇ ἐπαύριον, 1:29, 35, 43; 6:22.

The use of τῇ ἐπαύριον in 6:22[51] ties the following events, dialogues, and discourses, to the sea-crossing, which is integrally related to the feeding story, 6:1-21. Thus, "on the next day" the story of the crowd that commenced in 6:2 is taken up again with all the appearances of a successfully completed quest. The crowd which had followed (ἠκολούθει) Jesus to the place of the feeding miracle (6:2) now comes again seeking Jesus (ζητοῦντες τὸν Ἰησοῦν), 6:24;[52] and indeed finds him (εὑρόντες αὐτόν) 6:25. Yet again what follows shows that the quest failed. Jesus' response (6:26) is provided with characteristic Johannine quotation formula,[53] and introduced by a solemn double amen-saying.[54] In this saying Jesus acknowledged the crowd's quest, ζητεῖτέ με. But it is no longer the quest of 6:1-15, οὐχ ὅτι εἴδετε σημεῖα. Note especially 6:2,14. While the crowd had followed Jesus because they saw the signs he was performing in healing the sick, only some of the crowd (οἱ ἄνθρωποι) saw the sign of the feeding. All were fed, but only some saw the sign and they sought to make Jesus king, 6:14-15.

Jesus' departure from the desert place left no doubt that he had rejected the perception of him as a sign prophet (prophet-king). Yet the crowd still sought him because they had eaten of the loaves and were satisfied.[55] This saying of Jesus (6:26) is not a reproach. Rather it draws attention to the christological vacuum left by the rejection of the political role. The crowd no longer sought him as one who had given a sign of liberation. They sought him because he satisfies the hungry ("you ate of the loaves and were satisfied"). It is this theme of satisfying the hungry that the discourse develops. But to do this a distinction must be made (in verse 27) between the loaves that have been eaten, that is, the food (βρῶσις) which perishes, and the food (βρῶσις)[56] which gives eternal life. Through the dialogues of

---

[51] See 1:29, 35, 43; 6:22; 12:12. The expression is used elsewhere in the NT only in Matt. 27:62; Mark 11:12; and Acts 10:9, 23, 24; 14:20; 20:7; 21:8; 22:30; 23:32; 25:6, 23. Its use appears to be characteristic of John and Acts but it is notably absent from Luke!

[52] It is not likely that the evangelist intended his readers to understand that there were two crowds, one which had seen the feeding miracle and the other which had not, though this is advocated by M. E. Boismard and adopted by R. E. Brown, *John*, 1:259.

[53] "Jesus answered them and said." The same formula is used with an *amen*-saying in 3:3; 6:26 and introducing other sayings of Jesus in 1:48, 50; 3:10, 13; 6:29, 43; 7:16, 21; 8:14. Other quotation formulae are used in another ten *amen*-sayings while the remaining thirteen *amen*-sayings are without quotation formulae as they do not commence a Jesus- saying.

[54] See 1:51; 3:3, 5, 10, 11; 5:19, 24, 25; 6:26, 32, 47, 53; 8:34, 51, 58; 10:1, 7; 12:24; 13:16, 20, 21, 38; 14:12; 16:20, 23; 21:18. Nothing can be deduced concerning the authenticity of the sayings from the use of this formula. In John 6 two *amen*-sayings occur in the quest story and two in the story of conflict with the Jews.

[55] For the use of ἐχορτάσθητε see Mark 8:8.

[56] The term is used in 6:27 in the quest story and 6:55 in the story of Jewish rejection. In the latter it is used to introduce the idea of the true food and drink, the flesh and blood of Jesus, symbols of the giving of his life in death.

6:25-36 we are led, with increasing expectation, to the request of the crowd, κύριε, πάντοτε δὸς ἡμῖν τὸν ἄρτον τοῦτον (6:34)[57] and finally to the pronouncement of 6:35.

Yet surprisingly, in the end we are told that the crowd's quest ended in failure, 6:36. The surprise is heightened by the expectation of success given by the request of 6:34 which resonates with the sound of the request of the Samaritan woman (4:15) which foreshadowed a successful quest, not only for the woman, but also for the people of her town. Both the Samaritan woman and the crowd in John 6 misunderstood the nature of the water/bread that Jesus offered. Misunderstanding is a common means by which clarification is made on the way to understanding and belief. Because this was the case with the Samaritan woman the reader has every reason to expect that the crowd that has resolutely followed Jesus across the lake and back to Capernaum will also succeed in its quest now redefined by Jesus. Thus the pronouncement of their unbelief (6:36) comes as a shocking announcement. Further, 6:36-40 is made up of a collection of isolated sayings which form a transition to the rejection story of 6:41ff. and was probably added when the quest was transformed into rejection. The collection of sayings is quite different from the set of short dialogues between Jesus and the crowd up to this point.

In the quest story 6:27 should be seen as a new objection to the renewed quest of the crowd. Their quest is now for the perishable food. They are told that it does not satisfy, that it does not give eternal life. For this they need the food which the Son of Man will give to them. In 6:27 we have the first in a string of what were unrelated traditional sayings linked by the association of works (ἔργα) and sign (σημεῖον).[58] In this first saying the crowd is exhorted to "work . . ." (ἐργάζεσθε). The term βρῶσις is used rather than ἄρτος. The food which perishes is distinguished from the food which abides to eternal life. The Son of Man is named as the giver. It is said that he will give (δώσει) the food which abides. What is essential to well-being at a physical level has become symbolic of the source of spiritual well-being.

The theme of working (6:27) is thematically related to 5:17[59] and linguistically linked to working the works of God (6:28), which is probably

---

[57] See 4:15 κύριε, δός μοι τοῦτο τὸ ὕδωρ,... The reader is obviously expected to recognize the echo of this request in 6:34.

[58] That 6.27-30 is based on tradition is shown by Synoptic parallels and the linking of unrelated sayings by common words.

[59] "Work" involves the expending of effort to produce an effect. In 5:17 the question concerns the expending of such effort on the Sabbath. The specific work on the Sabbath to which reference was made in 5:17 was indeed a σημεῖον. But what was prohibited on the Sabbath was the expending of effort to produce an effect whether or not a miracle was involved.

to be understood in the sense of signs. But this is redefined by Jesus in terms of believing in the one sent by God, 6:29. To believe Jesus (6:30) is to believe in the one whom he (God) sent (6:29) which, in the dialogue, it is assumed, refers to Jesus, which the crowd understood. Because of this the crowd demanded a sign. The demand, as Synoptic parallels show, is from the tradition. It may be that John has added the purpose "that we may see and believe you," and the interpretation of the demand in terms of τί ἐργάζῃ, 6:30. Thus, in the demand by the crowd, signs and works are here equated. For the evangelist Jesus' works included the signs he worked because the whole mission of Jesus is summed up as his work, 4:34. But the crowd demanded to see a sign that would authenticate that Jesus was the one sent by God.

The demand for a sign is strange in the context of this chapter in which the performance of a notable sign has been recognized, 6:14. Even stranger is the nature of the demanded sign, 6:31. The crowd appealed to "our fathers," a term used of the generation that came out of Egypt.[60] They appealed to the fathers because they ate manna in the desert. This becomes a crucial issue in the subsequent conflict with the Jews, 6:49, 58. There Jesus recalls the assertion of 6:31a (not the text of 6:31b), but adds "your (the) fathers" who ate the manna are dead, proving conclusively that the manna was not the life-giving bread from heaven, a distinction dependent on 6:27 and 6:32-33. Nor did Jesus' feeding miracle provide the true bread from heaven, and this is the point of 6:27. Only in 6:35 is the true bread from heaven identified.

What did the crowd seek in asking for a legitimating sign (6:30)? It was not to the repetition of the sign that the appeal to Scripture[61] refers but to the original event. By analogy this reference could be understood as the call for a new feeding miracle such as Jesus had recently performed. This would imply that the crowd was blind to that sign but 6:14-15 hardly confirms this.

For the text of 6:31b appeal is generally made to Neh. 9:15; Ps. 78(77):24; and Exodus 16. Here it is appropriate to discuss the important and influential thesis of Peder Borgen.[62] Borgen thinks that both John and

---

[60] See further in 6:49, 58 and 1 Cor. 10:1. In 6:49 Jesus refers to "your fathers" distinguishing himself from those for whom they are "our fathers." In 6:58 Jesus refers to "the fathers" which is more neutral. In the rabbinic literature *aboth* (fathers) is used of the ancestors of the nation. The term is used by the Samaritan woman of the ancestors of the Samaritans in 4:20 and specifically of the patriarch Jacob in 4:12.

[61] The quotation formula καθώς ἐστιν γεγραμμένον occurs here and at 12:14. It appears to be the Johannine variation of the very common καθώς γέγραπται. John 6:45 has the variation ἐστιν γεγραμμένον ἐν τοῖς προφήταις. See also 7:38. On the quotation formulae see E. D. Freed, *Old Testament Quotations in the Gospel of John* (Leiden: E. J. Brill, 1965).

[62] *Bread from Heaven.*

Philo[63] made use of midrashic techniques that provide a pattern for dealing with the manna tradition. The pattern involves the use of a text from the torah (Exod. 16:15) in 6:31b followed by a text from the prophets (Isa. 54:13) in 6:45a. The primary text is interpreted by breaking it up and substituting new words for words that appear in the text thus bringing new insights to the text. Persuasive as some aspects of this thesis are there are certain problems that need to be addressed.

1. The first Scripture quotation (6:31b) is closer to Ps. 78(77):24 than Exod. 16:15 even if this is combined with 16:4. Precise identification of the Scripture quoted has not been possible.[64] Georg Richter suggests that the quotation is not from the OT but from a Jewish manna tradition.[65] The quotation formula must cast some doubt on this suggestion but the difficulty of identifying the text with a specific citation from the torah must cast doubt on Borgen's hypothesis.

2. Borgen's hypothesis disregards the narrative context of the discourse. Indeed he suggests that the feeding miracle is merely the excuse for the discourse. If this were the case the complex narrative elements of the chapter would be inexplicable. Rather they are to be seen as decisive indications of transformation in the discourse.

3. Borgen sets the discourse as a whole in the context of the Johannine struggle with a form of docetism similar to that which is illustrated in the writings of Ignatius. How this correlates with the use of techniques of Palestinian midrashim is difficult to assess. It also fails to do justice to much of the material which seems to have been shaped in the dialogue and conflict with the synagogue. That does not exclude the possibility that late elements in the discourse reflect the conflict with docetism within the Johannine community. Borgen's hypothesis fails to take account of the layers in the discourse though these should not be attributed to different authors.

4. The text upon which the discourse as a whole is based is 6:35 not 6:31b though 6:31 as a whole is used (with 6:27) in leading up to the pronouncement of 6:35. Thus Borgen's thesis need not be rejected but it should be modified so that the midrash of John 6 is seen to have its basis in the authoritative (for the evangelist) words of Jesus which come to light in the structure of the quest story.

The crowd's appeal to the manna tradition (6:31b) provided Jesus with the position against which he could pit his own. Here (6:32-33) the words of Jesus make certain modifications to what was asserted by the crowd.

---

[63] See *Leg. all.* iii.162-168; *Mut.* 253-263.

[64] See also 7:38. Freed thinks that the evangelist modified the quotations to suit his own purpose.

[65] *Studien zum Johannesevangelium* (Regensburg: Pustet, 1977), pp. 211-29.

1. It is said that the giver is "my Father" not Moses,[66] though previously (6:27) it has been asserted that the Son of Man will give the abiding food (βρῶσιν).

2. The gift is to the crowd (ὑμῖν) not to those who came out of Egypt (αὐτοῖς).

3. Jesus asserts gives (δίδωσιν) not gave (ἔδωκεν) or will give (δώσει), 6:27.

4. He refers to the true bread from heaven.

5. The true bread from heaven is designated the bread of God.

6. It is identified with he (or that which)[67] who comes down from heaven giving life to the world, 6:33.

7. That which/the one who comes down from heaven gives (διδούς) life to the world, 6:33.[68] It is because it/he gives life to the world that it/he is called "the bread of God."

The crowd obviously assumed that ὁ καταβαίνων referred to the bread. But why should they think of Jesus as the giver if he has said that it is his Father who gives this bread? (6:32). This can only mean that the crowd, provisionally at least, has accepted Jesus as the emissary of God (6:29), that is, the Son of Man whom, he has said, "will give" the food that abides to eternal life (6:27). This food is the true bread from heaven so that what Jesus says the Son of Man "will give" is identical with what he says "my Father gives" (6:32). Apparently there are two givers but only one giving and one gift.[69] That this point was perceived is implied in that after Jesus has spoken of the Father the crowd requests, "Lord, always give us this bread." This implies that the crowd now perceives Jesus as the Son of Man, the emissary of God who will give the bread of God.[70] What persuaded them of this? Jesus performed no further sign such as was demanded in

---

[66] This assumes that the "he" who "gave" (ἔδωκεν) was understood to be Moses. Naturally this is not clear.

[67] Because ἄρτος is masculine it is unclear whether ὁ καταβαίνων should be translated as "he who" or "that which."

[68] In 6:33 "descending" (καταβαίνων) and giving (διδούς) are present participles, see also 6:50. The aorist participle (καταβάς) is used in 6:41, 51, 58 and 3:13. The aorist participles indicates the specific, historic nature of the descent while the present participles signify the characteristic action of the redeemer. With both the aorist and present participles Jesus speaks in the third person either of "he" or "it" (the bread). The perfect tense καταβέβηκα is used by Jesus in "I" sayings in 6:38, 42. The other side of the descent is the ascent of the Son of Man, 6:62, see also the use of ὕψωσεν in 3:14 which is the equivalent of ἀναβέβηκεν in 3:13. The Son of Man who descended from heaven is the only one to have ascended ("to heaven" is implied).

[69] Compare the discussion of 5:17 in *The Quest for the Messiah,* chapter 5, II.2. "The Text."

[70] The request marks real progress towards the recognition of Jesus' relation to God even if residual misunderstandings remain.

6:30. Jesus in John allows that belief on the basis of his signs/works is a valid starting point, 5:36; 10:25, 38; 14:11, but here it is Jesus' words that overcome the demand for a sign and lead to the request of 6:34, κύριε, πάντοτε δὸς ἡμῖν τὸν ἄρτον τοῦτον. At this point the quest appears to be on the threshold of success.

The ambiguity of ὁ καταβαίνων in 6:33 is then clarified by the climactic concluding pronouncement of Jesus in 6:35: ἐγώ εἰμι ὁ ἄρτος τῆς ζωῆς· ὁ ἐρχόμενος πρὸς ἐμὲ οὐ μὴ πεινάσῃ, . . . The self-identification of Jesus with the life-giving bread is both a new objection to the quest of the crowd, which has progressed to recognize Jesus as the emissary of God, and a clarification of their misunderstanding of the nature of the bread. At this point John's symbolic use of bread brings out the soteriological implications of his christology over against the Jewish symbolic use with reference to the Torah. At this point a real choice has to be made.[71]

Given that the stress is on the crowd's quest, and that they have appealed to the manna, the bread from heaven, Jesus is saying that he, not the manna is the bread from heaven,[72] just as he has said that his father, not Moses, gives the true bread from heaven, 6:32. In 6:35 bread from heaven, which could mean bread rained down from the sky like the manna (6:33), is interpreted as the life-giving bread. Hence, the fact that those who ate the manna are dead is evidence that the manna was not the true life-giving bread, as will be argued in 6:49, 58. Thus "from heaven" no longer simply indicates the origin of the bread. Rather it is an indication of the quality of the life given by this bread. It is the life of the age to come that is offered by Jesus in the present.[73] He has offered it in such a way that it is clear that individual response to Jesus is necessary if the life of the age to come is to be enjoyed. Thus the quest story focuses attention on the person of Jesus as the fulfilment of the quest.

The implied contrast with Jesus is the Law of Moses, represented by the symbol of the manna, the bread from heaven.[74] Naturally this contrast, inherent in the quest story, belongs to the dialogue between the Johannine

---

[71] To complete the quest story all that now remains to be done is for the narrator to announce the success or failure of the quest. The surprising failure of the quest is announced in the words of Jesus in 6:36.

[72] See R. Bultmann, *The Gospel of John* (Philadelphia: Westminster, 1971), p. 225, n. 3. Bultmann argues that 6:35 (as well as 6:41, 48, 51) is an example of *recognition formulae*. "This formula is also found in sacred language, sometimes in such a way that by the ἐγώ εἰμι something which men are looking at or already know is given a new interpretation" . . . "It is used as a revelation formula proper (i.e. where the speaker, being present, reveals himself by the ἐγώ εἰμι as the one whom people were waiting for or looking for)."

[73] In rabbinic statements the manna has become the symbol of the new age, Ecclesiastes R. 1.128. See Barrett, *St. John*, p. 288.

[74] See Proverbs 9:5; Genesis R. 70.5; Str.B. II. 483f.

Christians and those Jews who, though not yet believers, were open to the appeal of Jesus.[75] At this stage it is belief in Jesus as the emissary[76] from heaven (from God) that is held out as the fulfilment of the quest. A definite individual response is called for if the life Jesus offered is to be enjoyed. The story concludes with Jesus' proclamation of the failure of the crowd's quest (6:36), forming a transition to the rejection stories.

It is likely that the conclusion to the quest story in the first edition was more open than this. But as the story now stands the note of rejection is sounded for the first time in 6:36 which now marks the failure of the quest. Yet at no point in the dialogues between 6:22-36 does the crowd reject Jesus or his words though (as is expected in a quest story) Jesus does offer objections to their understanding and in this way the crowd is led to request of Jesus, "Κύριε, always give us this bread," a request that resonates with the successful request of 4:15. An expectation of success for this quest is thus established. Jesus then identifies himself with the bread of life (6:35) which clarifies the nature of the bread that he offers. Without any further response from the crowd Jesus pronounces that they have not believed. The reader has not been prepared for this negative evaluation of the crowd's quest.

The movement of the story suggests, as we have seen, that the negative conclusion was not original. This observation is made probable by the transitional nature of verses 36-40 which appear to be a collection of traditional sayings. The saying introduced by "But I told you..." has no precise earlier reference,[77] though 6:26 could be in view. If so, then a new negative interpretation is given to that saying and this supports the suggestion that a new negative conclusion was given to the story in the second edition. The point of the saying (6:36) is now to introduce the theme of unbelief. Jesus proclaims the failure of the crowd's quest thus providing a transition to the rejection stories. When the audience is next identified (6:41) it is no longer described as "the crowd," but as "the Jews" and the theme of the possibility of coming to Jesus being dependent on the Father (6:37) is now stated in negative terms. No one is able to come unless he is drawn by the Father, 6:44. The theme of raising up on the last day those

---

[75] It would become a basic tool in the struggle with the synagogue reflected in later parts of the discourse.

[76] The emphasis on the emissary is made through the use of ἀπέστειλεν, 6:29, 57; πέμψαντος, 6:38; ὁ πατὴρ ὁ πέμψας με, 6:44; and indirectly ὁ ὢν παρὰ τοῦ θεοῦ, 6:46 and reference to the Son of Man as τοῦτον γὰρ ὁ πατὴρ ἐσφράγισεν ὁ Θεός, 6:27.

[77] It is characteristic of Jesus in John that he quotes his own earlier sayings, sometimes exactly, sometimes with less than clear reference. Thus 3:7 refers to 3:3; 3:28 to 1:20; 4:53 to 4:50; 5:11 to 5:8; 6:36 possibly to 6:26; 6:41 to a combination of 6:33 and 35; 6:65 to 6:37 etc.

who come is also repeated, 6:39, 44. Thus 6:36-40 belongs with 6:41ff. and the transformation of the quest story into a rejection story.

The importance of the quest story *genre* in John is difficult to overestimate.[78] The use of the first of the great symbolic "I am" sayings as the climactic pronouncement of the quest story of John 6 alerts us to the theological significance of this particular quest story. The use of the symbolism of bread within this quest story suggests that, although the context implies a contrast is being made between Jesus' understanding of bread and the Jewish understanding of the *manna* as a symbol for the Law, a more universal application is in order. That the crowd was fed by Jesus and comes again seeking bread confirms this. Bread was for them the means of sustaining life. It was for this reason that bread, the manna, became a symbol for the Law. The logic of the symbolism is dependent on the perception that "the life is more than food."[79] The great religions of the world have all recognized that physical existence does not exhaust the meaning and purpose of human life. The contrast is not between bare existence and the desired quality of life which today is often invoked in discussions of *euthanasia*.[80] In such discussions bread is not a symbol but the desired reality. In other words, physical life is the reality and bread is the means of supporting this. But for the life of which Jesus speaks he is himself the bread, that is, the source, the means of supporting that life. The viability of this use of language arises from the fact that material possessions do not satisfy the human quest/thirst/hunger for life. Death, which terminates physical life is one reason for this. More significant, however, is the human quest for some meaning in the context of a world that so often seems meaningless and purposeless. In the midst of competing ideologies, one of which was the Jewish understanding of the Law, John proclaimed Jesus as the bread of life, the source of true life.

2. The Rejection Stories of 6.36-71: Subsequent Editions.
i. Transition (6.36-40). The whole of this section appears to be a transitional addition. Indeed, it was this addition that gave the negative conclusion to the quest story. While the dialogues of 6:26-35 arise from the feeding story of 6:1-15, find focus in 6:31, and reach their climax in the pronouncement of 6:35, the sayings of Jesus in 6:36-40 are an elaboration of the "believing"/"coming" idea of 6:35. They also introduce the theme of being cast out (cf. 9:34). Unlike the Jewish authorities of 9:22, 34, Jesus will not

---

[78] See the conclusion to chapter 4, "Quest Stories in John 1-4" in *The Quest for the Messiah* for a statement concerning the relevance of John's use of quest stories to an understanding of the social context and theological message of the Gospel.

[79] See Matt. 6:25ff.

[80] Here, when the desired quality of life is irrevocably lost it is sometimes argued that the self-determined termination of life is justifiable.

cast out those who come to him. This theme signals coming conflict. The subsequent discourse is, as a whole, developed on the basis of the saying of Jesus in 6:35.[81] Neither of the Scripture texts quoted in 6:31 and 6:45 deals with the question of "coming" to Jesus. This is a central theme of the Jesus saying in 6:35 and it is the recurrent theme of 6:36-71.[82]

Picking up the negative conclusion of 6:36, "You have seen and you have not believed,"[83] 6:36-40 provides a transition to 6:41-59 by giving an explanation, in predestinarian terms, for the relative failure of the mission to the synagogue while, at the same time, proclaiming the benefits for believers.[84] Jesus said that everything[85] the Father gives him comes to him and he does not cast them out because he has come down from heaven[86] to do the will of the Father, the one who sent him. Those who come to him, who see him and believe, he will raise up on the last day.[87] The assertions concerning his Father and his descent from heaven provide the basis for the murmuring[88] rejection by the Jews in 6:41-59.

ii. Rejection by the Jews (6:41-59). This phase is signalled by the indication of the changed audience. The audience is specifically "the Jews" and the location for the discourse the synagogue, 6:59. Two things are clear:

---

[81] John 5:17 is another text with the discourse of 5:19-30 based on it. On this see chapter 5, "The Paradigm of Rejection" in *The Quest for the Messiah*.

[82] See 6:37, 44, 45, 65. If we add to this the parallel theme of 6:35, "believing," the dependence of 6:36-71 on 6:35 becomes even more obvious. See 6:40, 47, 64, 69. Then there is the reiteration of the basic affirmation of 6:35 in 6:48, and with slight variation in 6:51. The themes of eating and drinking in 6:50-58 also arise from the affirmation of 6:35 which indicates the satisfaction of hunger and quenching of thirst.

[83] Although me is well attested by the majority of mss including p[66] and probably p[75] as well as B D K L, it should probably be omitted along with ℵ A it [a b e q] syr[c s]. The introduction of "me" is more easily accounted for than its omission. The point is that they have seen the sign of the giving of the bread from heaven and yet have failed to believe in the one who is himself the bread of heaven.

[84] The combination of first and third person self-references in Jesus' description of his relation to the Father so characteristic of 5:17-30 is also characteristic of 6:37-40, 43-51. In the majority of cases in John 6 Jesus speaks of himself in the first person but the use of "the Father" in 6:37 (not "my Father") implies "the Son" which we find in 6:40 and there Jesus refers to "the Son" as "him." In 6:44 Jesus refers to "the Father who sent me" mixing implied third person with first person. The third person combination of "the Father" with "the one who is from God" is found in 6:46. The third person "This is the bread coming down out of heaven" (6:50) is combined with first person "I am the living bread which came down out of heaven" (6:51). In this case the third person self-references are more appropriate because of the use of the bread symbolism.

[85] "Everything" (πᾶν) 6:37, 39, becomes "everyone" (πᾶς) 6:40, and see 6:45.

[86] See 6:38 and 6:33.

[87] See 6:39, 40, 44, 54.

[88] The reference to murmuring is an echo of the murmuring of the fathers in the wilderness, Exod. 16:2, 8f. Such murmuring was regarded as unbelief, Ps. 105:24-25 LXX. In John the murmuring of the Jews is mentioned in 6:41, 43 and the murmuring of the disciples in 6:61. We have here evidence of the Passover/Exodus screen through which this tradition has been interpreted.

1. The evangelist does not normally alternate between "the crowd" and "the Jews" when referring to the same group.[89] The Jews of 6:41, 52 can hardly be identified with the many disciples of 6:60, 66 or "the twelve" of 6:67, 71. If these terms distinguish different groups it seems clear that the crowd is to be distinguished from the Jews also.

2. The evangelist can hardly have intended to suggest that the dialogues and discourses between Jesus and the crowd as well as between Jesus and the Jews, had taken place in the synagogue at Capernaum.[90] That is the venue for Jesus' debate with the Jews (Jewish experts on the Law).

It is argued here that the change of terminology from the crowd to the Jews indicates a change of audience and a change of time, and that the note concerning the synagogue in 6:59 indicates a change of location. 6:41-59 reflects the struggle between the Johannine Christians and the synagogue. For this context "the Jews" is the appropriate term of reference. They do not represent the Galilean crowd which had followed and subsequently come seeking Jesus. They are the Jews of the synagogue.

There is no suggestion that the "murmuring" of 6:41 and "fighting" of 6:52 caused a division amongst the Jews such as is to be noted in 10:19 and in relation to the Pharisees in 9:16, to which 10:19 probably refers. Rather these references to murmuring (6:41, 43, 61) recall the murmuring of the Israelites against God and Moses (Exod. 15:24; 16:2, 7, 8, 9, 12; Num. 14:2, 27, 29, 36; 16:11, 41; 17:5, 10) which is interpreted as unbelief (Ps. 105:24-25 LXX). Consequently the Jews now repeat the unbelief of the *fathers* in the wilderness. Even though they ate the manna they died. Given that the Exodus context is explicit in the dialogues (6:31, 49, 58) it is extraordinary that John Ashton suggests that "their murmuring (γογγυσμός, v. 41) is prompted more by bewilderment than real antagonism."[91] On the contrary, the murmuring is to be understood as unbelief and the rejection of God and his messenger, not now Moses but Jesus.

The alternation between Pharisees (9:13-17, 40) and the Jews (9:18-23; 10:19-20) and the indication that both groups were divided with regard to

---

[89] Discussions of the evangelist's use of "the Jews" tend to isolate 6:41 and 6:52 as a special case. The assumption is that the evangelist has used the term of the Galilean crowd, hence it cannot here mean the Judaeans as it does in 7:1. See U. C. von Wahlde, "The Johannine 'Jews': A Critical Survey," *NTS* 28/1 (1982), 33-60. While he has suggested that "the Jews," on the one hand, and the "Pharisees," "chief priests," and "rulers" on the other, belong to two different strata or sources (see U. C. von Wahlde, "The Terms for Religious Authorities in the Fourth Gospel: A Key to Literary-Strata?" *JBL* 98/2 [1979], 231-53) this has not been argued concerning the use of "the crowd" in 6:22, 24, which is presumably the audience as far as 6:35(40), and "the Jews" of 6:41, 52, are presumably the audience until 6:59. The evangelist indicates by this change that there are in fact two different audiences, times and places.

[90] C. K. Barrett (*John*, p. 300) notes that "the discourse with its interruptions suggests a less formal occasion than a synagogue sermon."

[91] *Understanding*, p. 200.

their attitude to Jesus, the majority in each case being against him, suggests that we have there reference to the same group by different names. The same cannot be said concerning the references to the crowd and those to the Jews in John 6.[92] The crowd, though it has misunderstood Jesus, requests that Jesus should always give them the bread of which he has been speaking, 6:34. The clarification of misunderstanding is a standard way in which characters within the story (Nicodemus, the Samaritan woman) are led to a more adequate understanding of Jesus. This expectation is raised as Jesus progressively corrects and clarifies the expectations of the crowd leading up to the final clarification of 6:35.[93] On the other hand the Jews do nothing but raise *objections* to what Jesus has said. They represent the hardening attitude of the synagogue to the Johannine Christians and this part of the discourse gives us the response of the Johannine Christians at this stage of the conflict with the synagogue. It is based on the text given by Jesus in 6:35.

The *objection* of the Jews in 6:41-42 is to the christology of the quest story. They objected to Jesus' claim to be the emissary of God, the bread which comes down (6:33, 50) or came down (6:41, 51a) or has come down (6:38, 42) from heaven.[94] Jesus responded by asserting that only those drawn and taught by the Father could come to him (6:44-45), taking up the theme of 6:35, 37-38 and providing a rationale for the rejection that the Johannine community was experiencing. Their rejection sealed their election by God while those who rejected them revealed only that they were not drawn and taught by the Father. The unique role of the emissary is emphasized in 6:46[95] and the necessity of believing in him is stressed in 6:47. All of this only repeats, in more provocative and confrontational terms, what has already been asserted. But it leads on to a more scandalous assertion, that the bread which must be eaten is Jesus' flesh which he says "I will give (δώσω)[96] for the life of the world," 6:51b. This assertion only antagonizes the Jews who then ask amongst themselves "how can this man give us his flesh to eat?"(6:52). Jesus then asserted the necessity of eating

---

[92] John 7:12, 40-44 attest the σχίσμα in the crowd but there is no identification with the Jews who were feared by the crowd, 7:13.

[93] Of course the reader is also led in a progressive process of understanding and this is the real purpose of the telling of the story.

[94] ὁ καταβαίνων, 6:33, 50; ὁ καταβὰς, 6:41, 51a; καταβέβηκα, 6:38, 42.

[95] Compare ὁ ὢν παρὰ τοῦ θεοῦ, 6:46 with ὁ ὢν εἰς τὸν κόλπον τοῦ πατρός, 1:18.

[96] See 6:27. Hans Weder, "Die Menschwerdung Gottes: Überlegungen zur Auslegungsproblematik des Johannesevangeliums am Beispiel von Joh 6," *ZTK* 82 (1985), 325-60, especially 352-55 rightly stresses the centrality of the incarnational theology. Thus, without importing the specific reference to John 1:14 into John 6, if John uses the language of an emissary christology it is also clear that the emissary comes from God and has become flesh.

the flesh of the Son of Man and drinking his blood (6:53), which is even more scandalous and provocative. While this language is influenced by the Eucharistic practice of the early church,[97] and the controversy reflects Jewish accusations concerning cannibalism,[98] that is hardly the point of the statement. Just as eating and drinking are symbols of coming and believing in Jesus' person in 6:35, so now in 6:51 what is intended is belief in the life-giving function of the giving of Jesus' life for the world.[99]

Far from answering the objection of 6:41-42, this assertion only heightens the problem, 6:52. What is more, Jesus does not attempt to minimize the scandal but goes on to assert that "unless you eat the flesh of the Son of Man and drink his blood you do not have life in yourselves," 6:53. As in the earlier statement, eating and drinking are symbols for coming and believing, not now simply in the person of Jesus, as the use of flesh and blood indicates, but belief in the efficacy of his death. Characteristically for John, Jesus' language moves from the third person idiom of 6:53 (Son of Man) to the first person language of 6:54-57. At the heart of this development is a passion prediction concerning the Son of Man which is based on tradition. Thus in the rejection story attention has moved from the call to belief in the person of Jesus as the emissary of God (in the quest story) to belief in the saving efficacy of his death. No doubt is left that the Jews rejected this call.

iii. Rejection by the disciples (6:60-66). Next we have the change from the synagogue, where the Jews formed the audience, to an unspecified situation where disciples constitute the audience. John 6:59 indicates the synagogue location up to that point (ταῦτα εἶπεν) and implies a new context for what follows. Indeed 6:60 is the first indication of a large number of disciples. It does not fit easily with earlier references to the disciples in 6:3, 8, 12 where, almost certainly, the twelve are in view as reference to the twelve baskets probably confirms, 6:13.[100] Now it is a large number (πολλοί) of disciples who find Jesus' word hard (σκληρός ἐστιν ὁ λόγος), and are scandalized (σκανδαλίζει) by it, so that it causes them to murmur (γογγύζουσιν), and ultimately to defect, 6:60-61, 66.

---

[97] This view finds support in the Madrid SNTS seminar paper by Maarten J. J. Menken, "John 6.51c-58: Eucharist or Christology" (1992).

[98] See Origen, *Celsus*, VI.27, *GCS* 3.97.

[99] From this perspective it is unnecessary to propose a redactional addition in 6:51c-58.

[100] Each basket represents one of the disciples collecting the fragments left-over. Reference to "the twelve" is specific in 6:67-71. The "twelve" also seem to be assumed in the story of the sea-crossing (6:16-21) because a large crowd of disciples would not have fitted into a small boat. The earliest edition of the story included only Jesus, the small group of disciples and the crowd. It is the addition of the Jews and the mass of disciples that has produced untidy transitions in the narrative. But these additions were made necessary by the course of history and the evangelist's interpretation of the tradition in relation to this.

There is no indication that the murmuring indicates a division. The many, who are here mentioned, all defect. Because John now deals specifically with the defection of disciples it is improbable that 6:41-59 should be interpreted in terms of dissension within the Johannine community. But the murmuring of the disciples arose on the same grounds as that of the Jews of 6:52-59. While this confirms that two different groups were in view the problem remained the same. That problem concerned the developing Johannine christology, explicitly in relation to the death and exaltation of Jesus. Apparently these were Jewish believers within the synagogue who were unable to follow the evangelist in the development of a more exalted christology. They may have been secret believers within the synagogue who, when a crisis arose in confrontation with the synagogue, fell away from faith. At least, that was their position as perceived by John.

Evidently what scandalized the disciples was Jesus' discourse (6:53-58) about eating his (or the Son of Man's) flesh and drinking his blood.[101] In response to the murmuring Jesus asked (6:62) "What if you see the Son of Man ascending (ἀναβαίνοντα) where he was formerly?"[102] That ascent, or being lifted up (ὕψωσεν, see 3:13-14), refers to Jesus' death on the cross by means of which he is exalted in saving efficacy, 12:32. The interpretation of the saving efficacy of Jesus' death probably emerged in the struggle with the synagogue and many believers found the view unacceptable. That the words about eating Jesus' (or the Son of Man's) flesh and drinking his blood were not meant in a materialistic sense is clear from the quest story itself (6:35) and further clarified by 6.63. Set in the narrative context of Jesus' ministry, the words should have been free from that misunderstanding. Even so it was the words of 6:53-58 that scandalized the many disciples and this scandal was not removed by the provoking words of 6:62-63. It was this provocation[103] which led to the apostasy of the "many disciples," 6:66. This passage might well reveal the conflict with the synagogue when many of those who believed either defected or became secret believers. It reflects a time of division amongst the Johannine Christians, a schism that left the evangelist and his supporters in the minority. It is unlikely that this defection reflects the schism of 1 John

---

[101] ἀκούσαντες refers to a specific conversation as does the σκληρός λόγος, 6:60. The question of how this was overheard need not be raised because 6:60-66 is a literary development on the basis of the previous story.

[102] While we may ask whether this (ἀναβαίνοντά) is perceived as a possible aid or a greater problem, no direct answer is given. The question produces no positive response from the disciples but rather accentuates or brings out the difficulty and leads to the defection of the mass of disciples.

[103] This is the force of the ἐκ τούτου which probably means both "from this time" and "for this reason."

2:19[104] because the grounds of apostasy are the same as those for the rejection of Jesus by the Jews.

In terms of the rejection story, the pronouncement remains that of the the quest story, that is, 6:35. It is elaborated in various ways in both stories of rejection, by the Jews and the mass of disciples. No new definitive pronouncement emerges in either of these stories. This alerts us to the fact that we do not have here self-contained rejection stories but adaptations on the basis of a quest story. It is the pronouncement of 6:35 and elaborations of it to which both the Jews and the mass of disciples object. The elaborations in what follows do not lessen, but in fact heighten their grounds for rejecting Jesus. The actual rejection of Jesus by the Jews is implied and the rejection by the mass of disciples is clearly stated, 6:66. While rejection stories are polemically spoken against the Jews and apostates, they are addressed to the Johannine community as an assurance to those rejected by men that they are chosen by God.[105]

iv. The twelve: commendation or condemnation? (6:67-71). That leaves only "the twelve," represented by Peter. Tradition provided the basis for the confession of Peter as the spokesman for the faith of the disciples,[106] in John, for "the twelve." This suggests that we have a contrast between the rejection story of 6:60-66 and the commendation story of 6:67-71.[107] The behaviour of the many is not to be followed; the confession of Peter is to be emulated. If this reading is persuasive we should perhaps attribute this part of chapter 6 to the latest edition of the Gospel along with chapter 21. There we find evidence of an attempt to reconcile the beloved disciple and his tradition with Peter (and "the twelve"?).[108]

It is notable, however, that Jesus in no way commends Peter for his confession, as he does in Matt. 16:17. The form of the confession in John, "you are the holy one of God," differs from the Synoptics, "you are the Christ," Mark 8:29; "you are the Christ the son of the living God," Matt. 16.16; "the Christ of God," Luke 9.20 and in John Jesus does not refer to his death, as he does in the Synoptics.[109] In Matt. and Mark the confession of Peter is followed by Jesus' passion prediction, Peter's objection and Jesus' rebuke, "Get behind me Satan, you are a scandal to me, because you do not think the thoughts of God but of men," Matt. 16:23; Mark 8:33. In John there is no rebuke to Peter. Instead Jesus refers to Judas Iscariot, the betrayer, as a devil, 6:70-71. That looks like a transfer of the rebuke from

---

[104] *Pace* R. Schnackenburg, *John*, 2:3ff.

[105] This is especially clear in the rejection story of John 9 where the once blind man, cast out from the synagogue, was received by Jesus, 9:34-38.

[106] See Mark 8:29 and parallels.

[107] In both John 6 and 9 rejection stories are combined with commendation stories.

[108] There is first the reinstatement of Peter, 21:15-19, followed by the statement of the relative roles of Peter and the BD, 21:20-23.

[109] See Mark 8:31 and parallels.

Peter to Judas. It could be, however, a way of casting doubt on the credibility of "the twelve" as a group, including Peter as spokesman. The episode concludes by noting that Judas was εἷς ἐκ τῶν δώδεκα, 6:71. In the light of this conclusion the words of Peter's confession need to be re-examined.

The title "holy one of God" is known to us nowhere else in John and in the Synoptics only on the lips of the demon-possessed, Mark 1:24; Luke 4:34. The use of this title in Peter's confession has been something of a puzzle. Because it is a *hapax legomenon* in John it is not likely that it represents an important Johannine title. Nor does it seem to have a discernible nuance arising from the context of Peter's confession. Given the Synoptic accounts of Peter's confession it is unlikely that it was derived from the tradition. It may be that the use of the title confessed by the demon possessed is no coincidence but places Peter in the role of the Satan. Alternatively, the point of the use of the title, "holy one of God," might be to draw attention to the revelation involved in the confession. Just as the demons confessed by supernatural knowledge, so now Peter's confession is a result of divine revelation, see Matt. 16:17. Given that "the twelve" are contrasted with "the many" it seems right to understand 6:67-71 as a commendation story aimed to reconcile the community of the BD with the tradition of Peter, but there are some puzzling and conflicting signals that disturb this reading of the story.

C. CONCLUSION

The traditional feeding story dramatized Jesus' rejection of the political role of the sign prophet proclaiming him instead as the eschatological judge. The evangelist himself transformed the tradition, turning it into a quest story. The quest story depicts the crowd seeking Jesus. Just as the Samaritan woman sought water at Jacob's well, so now the crowd seeks bread. Just as Jesus distinguished the water of the well from the water which he gives, so in chapter 6 he distinguished the bread which perishes from the bread which abides. The request of the woman (4:15) is remarkably like the request of the crowd (6:34). The similarities suggest that the two chapters originally belonged together. In one there is the offer of the life-giving water and in the other there is the offer of the life-giving bread. Here we have the two fundamental and universal symbols of the sources of life which have universal appeal. The symbols also have a particular resonance for Judaism. The well is the Law,[110] though the well actually represents the water which it contains and this is apparent also in John 4. Bread, the manna, also

---

[110] See *CD* VI.4. Jesus also is the spring/well from which issues the life-giving water, 7:37-39. He is the giver of the life-giving water, 4:10, 13-14.

became a symbol for the Law.[111] In using these symbols the Jesus of John set himself in opposition to Moses and the Law as the giver/mediator of life. Here the evangelist has used a Passover/Exodus screen to interpret the tradition and this screen provided a resource for use in the conflict with the synagogue.

The quest of the crowd itself provides evidence of the failure of the Law to bring life. The quest story, developed on the basis of the traditional story, leads through the request of the crowd to the climactic pronouncement of Jesus in 6:35. This saying is not only the climax of the quest story, it is the text upon which the dialogues and discourses which follow are developed. These follow because of the reaction of the synagogue to the success of the Johannine Christians. That reaction created conflict and what follows in 6:36-71 is in response to conflict. The placing of chapter 6 immediately after chapter 4 belongs to the first edition and constitutes an appeal to sympathizers and secret believers within the synagogue.

In the light of 6:36-71 it is easy to see that John 6 has become predominantly concerned with rejection. The quest story has now been modified so that the theme of rejection by the crowd, the Jews and the mass of disciples becomes dominant. The use of the term *rejection* here draws attention to the way objections raised lead to the rejection of Jesus and ultimately to his execution. This theme demands that the chapter be placed in the conflict section of the Gospel after chapter 5. This new position has caused problems for the itinerary of Jesus' ministry, leaving rough seams between chapters 4 and 5, 5 and 6, 6 and 7. Evidently the evangelist considered the thematic structure of the Gospel to be more important than a straightforward description of Jesus' itinerary. It is, however, perplexing to find evidence of sophisticated literary developments alongside poorly integrated material. Three basic responses have been made to this problem:

1. Literary sophistication is attributed to the source (thus Haenchen) alongside the ineptness of the evangelist;
2. Disruptions are explained by some accident to the completed Gospel (Bultmann);
3. Disruptions are explained as a result of the death of the evangelist prior to the completion and publication of the Gospel (see 21:20-25).

In this study the third response is accepted along with the recognition that the order of the text, as it is, suggests the priority of thematic structure over geographic itinerary. Thus John 6 has become predominantly focused on rejection and the appropriate place for this chapter is in chapters 5-12. Chapter 5 is the appropriate introduction to the rejection section because it

---

[111] See *Str.B.* II, 483f. noting Proverbs 9:5; Genesis R. 70.5.

introduces the two specific objections to Jesus: as a Law (Sabbath) breaker and a blasphemer, a man claiming divine status for himself. It also sets the pattern of the response of Jewish rejection, 5:16, 18.

In the rejection section of John 6 there is a development in christological perception. Whereas the crowd that followed Jesus into the desert perceived him to be a sign prophet, a messianic political deliverer, the traditional story proclaimed Jesus as the future eschatological judge/deliverer. But in the quest story of the first edition there is an emphasis on Jesus, not Moses as the emissary of God, as the life-giver and that Jesus not the Law is the life-giving bread, This interpretation developed in the period of dialogue and apologetic approach to the synagogue. There are two stages in this development. In the first Jesus is understood to be the Messiah/Son of Man, the giver of the eschatological bread from heaven, 6:27, 34. But there is a significant development of the Jewish expectation because Jesus is himself the life-giving bread, 6:35. In the conflict that develops the stress falls on the necessity of Jesus' death in order that, as the bread of life, he should bring life to the world, 6:51. To some extent this development merely made explicit what was implicit in the symbolism of the bread of life, 6:35. Just as bread sustains physical life, so Jesus gives eternal life. But whereas 6:33 seemed to imply that the bread gave life to the world by coming down from heaven, now it becomes clear that the bread must be eaten. At this point, by introducing the symbols of hunger and thirst the evangelist has transformed the notion of bread into food and drink that sustain life. Eating and drinking are symbols of coming to Jesus and believing in him, 6:35. While coming is symbolic of believing, the point of this set of symbols (as it is developed in 6:51-58) is that belief in Jesus takes account of his death for the life of the world.

Robert Fortna is right in seeing the development from christology to soteriology.[112] In this chapter we have traced a development from the belief in the eschatological deliverer and judge of the traditional story and belief in the heavenly emissary of the quest story to the theme of the saviour whose death brings life to those who believe in him, the glorified, exalted Son of Man, glorified and exalted by way of the cross. This theme emerged in the conflict with the synagogue. Reference to the death of Jesus could not but draw attention to the Jewish involvement in the execution of Jesus. But while this polemic is spoken against the Jews and apostates from within the community, it is spoken to the community to assure them that though they have been rejected by men they are the chosen of God. The development represents another stage in the evangelist's quest for the Messiah, now a Messiah who brings life through giving up his own life. Indeed we can say that in the quest for the Messiah John has developed his own distinctive

---

[112] See R. T. Fortna, "From Christology to Soteriology," *Interpretation* 27 (1973), 31-47. Fortna rightly recognizes that christological belief has soteriological consequences.

christology and with this has produced his characteristic understanding of salvation.

In John 6 the quest for the Messiah turns out to be an expression of the universal quest for life. For John this quest finds its fulfilment in Jesus as the emissary from God who not only reveals God but in his life, death/resurrection/exaltation/glorification is the action of God bringing life to the world. This emphasis not only produced conflict with the Jews, it was to bring conflict within the Johannine community, first as in 6:60-66, then in a conflict over the role and significance of Jesus' earthly life which was to be manifest in a schism specifically mentioned in 1 John 2:19.

JOHN 6: TRADITION,
INTERPRETATION AND COMPOSITION

Peder Borgen

In 1975 I had the privilege of reading a paper at the twenty-sixth Biblical Conference of Louvain, Belgium, under the chairmanship of Professor M. de Jonge. Ten years later I served as the local host of the 40th General Meeting of *Studiorum Novi Testamenti Societas* at the University of Trondheim, Norway, and the President in charge was Professor de Jonge. On many other occasions I have had the privilege of learning greatly from his scholarship and of being enriched by his friendship. It was therefore with pleasure and gratitude that this essay was first published as a contribution to his Festschrift in 1993. In the essay I shall add some insights on a question which has engaged me for many years, the intriguing ch. 6 in the Gospel of John.

There are many puzzling problems in chapter 6. First, the collective designations of people vary. In 6:1-40 one reads about the disciples (vv. 1-21), the crowd, ὁ ὄχλος, the men, οἱ ἄνθρωποι, and then, in 6:41-58 the term "the Jews," οἱ Ἰουδαῖοι, is used. Finally, when the general reaction to Jesus' discourse is told in 6:60-71, only the reaction of many among the disciples, οἱ μαθηταί, etc. are mentioned. Second, the term "sign," σημεῖον (σημεῖα) seems to have different meanings in vv. 2 and 14, and in v. 26, and v. 30. Although the crowd, according to v. 14 has seen a sign, they still ask for one in v. 30, and Jesus says in v. 26 that the crowd does not seek him because they saw a sign, although according to vv. 14-15 they saw the sign and therefore thought he was a prophet and wanted to make him king. Third, there is the long-debated question of relating the eucharistic formulations in vv. 51ff. to the preceding section of Jesus' discourse.[1]

In *Bread from Heaven*[2] I concentrated on the analysis of John 6:31-58, understood as an exposition of the scriptural quotation in v. 31b, "bread from heaven he gave them to eat." There is a need for looking more closely at chapter 6 as a whole and its thematic ties to the end of chapter 5, however. More recent scholarly analysis both by others and myself should also be brought into the investigation.

A. JESUS IS NOT JUST THE PROPHET-LIKE-MOSES, JOHN 6:1-21

The persons mentioned in this section are: Jesus, the disciples (with name-specifications in vv. 5-8), a lad (v. 9), and a large crowd (vv. 2 and 5: ὁ

---

[1] See commentaries and the survey given by L. Schenke, "Die literarische Vorgeschichte von Joh 6,26-58," *BZ* 29 (1985), 68-75.

[2] NovTSup 10 (Leiden: E. J. Brill, 1965).

ὄχλος) and the people (vv. 10 and 14 οἱ ἄνθρωποι, numbering 5000, v. 10).
In v. 4 there is a reference to "the Jews." The two stories narrate the actions
and reactions among Jesus, the disciples and the crowd. Oral dialogue takes
place between Jesus and Philip/Andreas in vv. 5-10a, and words said by Jesus
as a greeting to the disciples are recorded in v. 20. There is no dialogue
between Jesus and the large crowd/the people, but a report on what the people
said (among themselves) is given in v. 14: ". . . they said, 'This is indeed the
prophet who is to come into the world.'"

This section begins with a general statement about "the signs which Jesus
did on those who were diseased" (v. 2) and then one particular sign follows,
the feeding of the 5000 (vv. 3-13). In vv. 14-21 the effects of the event are
described—on the one hand the effect on the people and subsequently on
Jesus (vv. 14-15), and on the other hand on the disciples and Jesus (vv. 16-
21).

The story of the feeding of the 5000 in John 6:1-13 renders one version of
a tradition which is narrated in all the four gospels, Matt. 14:13-21; Mark
6:32-44, and Luke 9:10-17. The brief subsequent section, John 6:14-15, has
no parallel in the synoptic gospels. These verses show the effect which the
event had on the crowd, and how Jesus reacted to the crowd's understanding
and action. The crowd understood the feeding miracle to have a meaning
beyond itself. They thought the event showed Jesus to be prophet and king
(like Moses[3]), "When the people saw the sign which he had done, they said,
'This is indeed the prophet who is to come into the world!' (v. 14);
'Perceiving then that they were about to come and take him by force to make
him king, Jesus withdrew again to the hills by himself'" (v. 15).

In John 6:16-21 the crowd is not in the picture, but "his disciples" who are
seen as a distinct group. They got into a boat and crossed the sea. While a
strong wind was blowing and the sea was becoming rough, Jesus came to
them "walking on the sea and drawing near to the boat" (v. 19).

The two stories primarily tell about how Jesus acted in feeding the crowd
and how they reacted—they wanted to make him king. This led to a
responding action on Jesus' part—he withdrew to the hills. The reaction of
the disciples was also in the form of an action—they went away across the
sea.

While maintaining that the evangelist interpreted the feeding miracle
meaningfully, J. Painter thinks that the same evangelist reported the story of
the sea-crossing because it was already attached to the feeding story in the
received tradition. But, according to Painter, the evangelist has used the story

---

[3] See esp. W. A. Meeks, *The Prophet-King*, NovTSup 11 (Leiden: E. J. Brill, 1967).

to good effect as it dramatically separates Jesus from the crowd which had followed him into the desert.[4]

When Painter interprets the sea-crossing (6:16-21) as an extension of the story of the miraculous feeding (6:1-15), he does not take seriously the fact that the disciples and Jesus are the persons mentioned in the sea-crossing, and not the crowd. The story of the crossing of the sea, therefore, has quite a central function. It makes clear that although Jesus withdrew from the crowd, the opposite happened to the disciples: he acted by miraculously coming to them.[5] Here, as elsewhere, John has made the traditional story express an idea which was central to him. The crowd misjudged the meaning of the feeding miracle, while the disciples had an authentic and epiphanic encounter with Jesus.

The works done by Jesus are called signs. What is the definition of the term "sign," $\sigma\eta\mu\epsilon\hat{\iota}ov$, in this context? John describes the miracles of Jesus both by the term "works," $\xi\rho\gamma\alpha$, as in 5:36, and by the term "signs," $\sigma\eta\mu\epsilon\hat{\iota}\alpha$, as in 6:2. The term "sign" suggests that the miracle has a function beyond itself in the form of carrying a certain meaning or creating a certain effect. The meanings or effects may vary somewhat, and the precise and detailed description of the term must therefore be made within the context in which it is used. In 6:14-15 the designation "sign" implies that the feeding miracle was understood to have a function beyond itself and to activate the people's expectations of a coming prophet/king. By withdrawing from the people at that point Jesus made clear that they had misunderstood the significance of his actions.

B. THE SON OF MAN—THE FATHER'S ACCREDITED ENVOY, JOHN 6:22-27

Verses 6:22-24 seem at first to be very confused, and the apparent obscurity has caused several variant readings to appear in the manuscripts.[6] The structure of the verses takes on meaning, however, when one realizes that John here repeats phrases from and makes references to the preceding stories and adds interpreting words.[7] In this way it is seen that in v. 22 he refers to the

---

[4] J. Painter, *The Quest for the Messiah* (Edinburgh: T. & T. Clark, 1991), pp. 226-27. The same view was already expressed in J. Painter, "Tradition and Interpretation in John 6," *NTS* 35 (1989), 430-31.

[5] See Borgen, *Bread from Heaven*, p. 180, n. 1: "According to v. 15, the feeding miracle brought the people to the non-spiritual and external wish to make Jesus king. For the disciples, on the other hand, it resulted in a theophanic encounter with the Son of God, vv. 16-21. C. K. Barrett, *The Gospel according to St. John*, 2nd ed. (London: SPCK, 1978), pp. 279-80, finds this interpretation to be plausible.

[6] See Barrett, *John*, p. 285.

[7] Cf. R. Schnackenburg, *Das Johannesevangelium, 2. Kommentar zu Kap. 5–12* (Freiburg: Herder, 1971), pp. 44-47. Schnackenburg attempts to reconstruct a picture of the details in the

story of the crossing of the sea by the disciples (vv. 16-21). In vv. 23-24a he refers to the story about the feeding, while in vv. 24b-25a the crowd is brought to the destination of the disciples' crossing, Capernaum. Some of the repeated words are common to both stories, of course. In the following the words from the two stories are underscored.

From the crossing of the sea:

v. 22   ὁ ὄχλος ὁ ἑστηκὼς πέραν τῆς θαλάσσης εἶδον
         ὅτι πλοιάριον ἄλλο οὐκ ἦν ἐκεῖ εἰ μὴ ἕν, καὶ
         ὅτι οὐ συνεισῆλθεν τοῖς μαθηταῖς αὐτοῦ ὁ Ιησοῦς εἰς
         τὸ πλοῖον
         ἀλλὰ μόνοι οἱ μαθηταὶ αὐτοῦ ἀπῆλθον.

From the feeding of the 5000:

v. 23   ἄλλα ἦλθεν πλοιάρια ἐκ Τιβεριάδος ἐγγὺς τοῦ τόπου
         ὅπου ἔφαγον ἄρτον [εὐχαριστήσαντος τοῦ κυρίου].[8]

v. 24   ὅτε οὖν εἶδεν ὁ ὄχλος ὅτι Ιησοῦς οὐκ ἔστιν ἐκεῖ οὐδὲ
         οἱ μαθηταὶ αὐτοῦ.

To Capernaum:

         ἐνέβησαν αὐτοὶ εἰς τὰ πλοιάρια καὶ ἦλθον εἰς
         Καφαρναοὺμ ζητοῦντες Ιησοῦν.

v. 25   καὶ εὑρόντες αὐτὸν πέραν τῆς θαλάσσης εἶπον αὐτῷ

The elaborations emphasize that Jesus was not found with his disciples when they crossed the sea. Neither was he present at the place where the feeding miracle took place. After searching in vain in these two places, the crowd looked for Jesus in Capernaum where they found him. They asked where he had been:

v. 25: And having found him . . . they said to him:
       'Rabbi, when did you come here?'
v. 26: Jesus answered them,
       'Truly, truly, I say to you,
       You seek (ζητεῖτε) me, not because you saw signs,
       but because you ate your fill from the loaves.
v. 27: Do not labour for the food which perishes,
       but for the food which endures to eternal life,

---

movements of the crowd(s) as to timing and geography. His analysis demonstrates, however, that the text as it stand is not consistent.

[8] See Schnackenburg, ibid., about the words in brackets which are lacking in some mss. and may be an added gloss.

which the Son of Man will give to you;
for this is the one whom God the Father has sealed.'

Jesus criticizes the crowd for having searched for him for the wrong reason
(v. 26) and then challenges them not to labour for perishable food, but for
food which endures to eternal life, which the Son of Man will give, for on him
God the Father put his seal.

It is important to notice that the main point in v. 27 is not the search by the
crowd nor the choice as such with which Jesus confronts them but the seal
which God the Father put on the Son of man. In order to understand this
saying the term σφραγίζω, "to seal," must be examined. The use of the word
here is debated by the exegetes.[9] B. F. Westcott has suggested that the sealing
refers to Jesus' consecration unto death by the Father.[10] A similar argument is
entertained by J. Marsh, who sees the aorist as a "prophetic perfect," which
refers to the future glory of the cross and resurrection.[11] For B. Lindars the
sealing tells that Jesus is chosen or marked out.[12] M.-J. Lagrange and G. H. C.
Macgregor think that it is the authority of Jesus' miracle-working power that
is referred to, including the miracle of the incarnation itself.[13] R. E. Brown
emphasizes the idea that God sets his seal on the Son, not so much by way of
approval, but more by way of consecration.[14] C. K. Barrett understands 'the
sealing' to mean that it is "God the Father who attests to the authority and
truth of Jesus."[15]

Moloney follows Barrett and defines the meaning in this way: "What is
being said here is: 'You must work for the bread which endures for eternity;
that bread will be given to you in the revelation of the Son of man. It is to the
Son of man, and to him alone, that God has given such authority; what he
reveals is the authentic revelation of God.'"[16] This understanding by Barrett
and Moloney is appropriate to the use of the term σφραγίζω here. An even
more precise meaning can be given, however. In Liddell and Scott's Greek-
English lexicon the meaning of the word in John 6:27 and 2 Cor. 1:22 is
defined as "accredit as an envoy."[17] This interpretation is confirmed by the

---

[9] For the following, see F. J. Moloney, *The Johannine Son of Man* (Rome: Libreria Ateneo
Salesiano, 1978), pp. 113-14.

[10] B. F. Westcott, *The Gospel according to John* (London: Murray, 1892), p. 100.

[11] J. Marsh, *Saint John* (Harmondsworth: Penguin, 1968), p. 295.

[12] B. Lindars, *The Gospel of John* (London: Oliphants, 1972), p. 255.

[13] M.-J. Lagrange, *Évangile selon saint Jean*, 3rd ed. (Paris: Lecoffre, 1927), p. 173; G. H. C.
MacGregor, *The Gospel of John* (London: Hodder & Stoughton, 1928), pp. 138-39.

[14] R. E. Brown, *The Gospel according to John I–XII*, AB 29 (Garden City, NY: Doubleday,
1966), p. 261.

[15] Barrett, *John*, p. 287.

[16] Moloney, *The Johannine Son of Man*, p. 114.

[17] H. G. Liddell and R. Scott, *Greek-English Lexicon* (1940; rpt. Oxford: Clarendon, 1958), p.
1742.

equivalent Hebrew and Aramaic word חם, to seal, which, as seen from M. Jastrow's Dictionary, is the technical term for sealing and signing as a witness.[18] An understanding along this line has been suggested by R. Schnackenburg: "Just as the One Sent by God (3.34) brings the testimony about the Father (cf. 3.35) from the heavenly world, so also the Father gives testimony about the Son (5.32, 37; 8.18)."[19]

The verb in John 6:27 has aorist form and refers to the sealing as a past event. This event is probably the commissioning of the Son of Man as the Father's emissary, as the Son of Man who descended from heaven (John 3:13).[20] This commissioning is indicated several places in John, as in John 12:49: "For I have not spoken of myself, but the Father who sent me, has himself given me commandment what to say and what to speak."[21]

C. THE MANNA-BREAD FROM HEAVEN, THE SIGN OF THE SON OF MAN,
JOHN 6:28-59

This section, John 6:28-59, consists of a dialogue between "they," that is, the crowd (vv. 28, 30, 34) and Jesus (vv. 29, 32, 35) which results in reactions and objections among the Jews (vv. 41, 52) followed by comments and answers given by Jesus (vv. 43, 53).

In John 6:59 it is written that Jesus said this in a Synagogue, as he taught at Capernaum. C. K. Barrett comments: "At v. 24 we learned that the scene was Capernaum, but the discourse with its interruptions suggests a less formal occasion than a Synagogue sermon."[22] Against Barrett, it must be said that questions and answers, direct exegesis and problem-solving exegesis were part of the discourses in the Synagogue. All of these elements are found in rabbinic midrashim, as for example in *Mekilta on Exodus*, as well as in Philo's commentaries. A glimpse into such practice is given by Philo in his description of the Therapeutai. When they assemble the leader "examines

---

[18] M. Jastrow, *A Dictionary of the Targumim, the Talmud Babli and Yerushalmi, and the Midrashic Literature* (Israel, no date), pp. 513-14.

[19] Schnackenburg, *Das Johannesevangelium*, p. 50.

[20] See P. Borgen, "The Son of Man Saying in John 3:13-14," in Borgen, *'Logos Was the True Light' and Other Essays on the Gospel of John* (Trondheim: Tapir, 1983), pp. 138-42. As for the concept of agency in John, see Borgen, *'Logos Was the True Light,'* pp. 121-32. See further J.-A. Bühner, *Der Gesandte und sein Weg im 4. Evangelium* (Tübingen: Mohr-Siebeck, 1977).

As Jewish background material for God's, the Father's, sealing of the Son of Man, one might refer to the figures of Logos, Metatron and Yahoel, upon whom the name of God was, as understood from exegesis of Exod. 23:20: ". . . for My name is on him"; Philo, *Migr.* 173-75; *b. Sanh.* 38b; *3 Enoch* 12:5; *Ap. Ab.* 10. See P. Borgen, "Heavenly Ascent in Philo: An Examination of Selected Passages," in J. H. Charlesworth and C. A. Evans, eds., *The Pseudepigrapha and Early Biblical Interpretation* (Sheffield: JSOT Press, 1993), pp. 246-68.

[21] See P. Borgen, "The Use of Tradition in John 12:44-50," *NTS* 26 (1979), 18-35.

[22] Barrett, *John*, p. 300.

(ζητεῖ) some points in the sacred writings, or also solves (ἐπιλύεται) that which is propounded by another" (*Contempl.* 75). The term ζητέω and the composite verb ἐπιζητέω are used elsewhere in Philo's writings when an exegetical question is raised, such as in *Opif.* 77, "One might examine (ἐπιζητήσειε) the reason because of which . . . ," cf. *Spec.* 1:214; *Leg. all.* 1:33; 1:48; 1:91; 2:103, and *Quaest. in Gen.* 1:62 (Greek fragment). Answers and solutions are given, and in *Leg. all.* 3:60 the verb λύω is used, corresponding to the use of the composite verb ἐπιλύω used in *Contempl.* 75. In *Contempl.* 79 the leader is said to have discoursed, διαλέγομαι, and since questions and answers were part of the discourse, the verb means "discuss." In Philo's commentary *Questions and Answers on Genesis and Exodus*, a question or a specific view is introduced by simple formulas, for example by phrases such as "some say" (*Quaest. in Gen.* 1:8; 2:64, and 3:13, cf. *Opif.* 77); or just "why" (*Quaest. in Gen.* 1:1; 2:13, 64, etc.) or "what" (*Quaest. in Gen.* 2:15, 59).

Thus in Philo's expositions, such as those seen in the *Allegorical Commentary* and elsewhere, direct exposition of a scriptural quotation is often interrupted by a question or an objection, and in *Quaest. in Gen.* a question is raised at the very outset, and direct exegesis and objections may then be given, as for example in *Quaest. in Gen.* 2:28.

The question:
"What is the meaning of the words
'He brought the spirit over the earth and the water ceased'?"
Interpretation:
"Some would say that by 'spirit' is meant the wind through which the flood ceased."
Objection and alternative interpretation:
"But I myself do not know of water being diminished by wind . . .
Accordingly, (Scripture) now seems to speak of the spirit of the Deity . . ."

Against this background the following conclusion can be drawn: in John 6:30ff. John draws from the gospel tradition the claims that Jesus was asked to give a sign and that he gave his answer.[23] When John elaborates upon this tradition in 6:30-58, he develops the exegesis of an Old Testament quotation into learned midrashic expositions. Thus, the reference to a Synagogue as the setting (John 6:59) is appropriate.

The analysis from John 6:28 should be continued against the background of these observations. John 6:28 is a further discussion of the word ἐργάζεσθε in v. 27. The crowd asks Jesus: "What must we do, then, to 'work' the works of God (ἐργαζώμεθα τὰ ἔργα τοῦ θεοῦ)?" Although the term in v. 28 means

23 See John 2:18; Matt. 16:1ff./Mark 8:11ff.; cf. Matt. 21:23ff./Mark 11:27ff./Luke 20:1ff.

"perform a work" and not as in v. 27 "to work for food" it has vv. 22-27 as background—the crowd acted wrongly and misunderstood the multiplication of the loaves to mean that the eschatological manna miracle was of earthly nature. Jesus corrects them and tells them to work for the food which endures to eternal life. In vv. 28ff. the crowd then logically asks what they shall do to receive the proper food.

In John 6:28 the crowd asks Jesus to define his understanding of the notion "the works of God," that is, the works willed by God. In v. 29 Jesus defines the term, but in the singular, "this is the work (τὸ ἔργον) of God, that you believe in him whom he sent." On this basis they ask Jesus to provide the legitimation so as to demonstrate that he is to be identified as "him whom he (God) sent."[24] The question about the works/work which the crowd was to perform, has in this way been related to what Jesus could do to demonstrate his own identity as the Father's commissioned envoy (v. 30). "So they said to him, 'then what sign do you do (ποιεῖς), that we may see, and believe you? What work do you perform (ἐργάζῃ)?'" The dialogue form is appropriate to such a change of meaning given to ἐργάζομαι and ἔργα/ἔργον in vv. 28ff.

In v. 31 they refer to the manna miracle: "Our fathers ate the manna in the wilderness; as it is written, 'He gave them bread from heaven to eat.'" This reference is strange, since according to vv. 14-15, as a reaction to the multiplication of the loaves, they understood Jesus to be a prophet, that is, the prophet like Moses (Deut. 18:15, 18). If so, they already regarded the feeding miracle to be an eschatological event corresponding to the manna miracle in the desert (Exod. 16). Against this background the repeated reference to the manna miracle in John 6:30-31 is puzzling, since they seemingly once more ask for the same sign that they already had experienced.

Exegetes have suggested various solutions to this problem. R. E. Brown states that it is difficult to reconcile the request for bread (vv. 30-31) with the indication that this is the same crowd that saw the multiplication of the loaves the day before. In his comments on v. 14 he writes: "Most likely this is a reference to the expectation of the prophet-like-Moses . . . for in v. 31 these people draw a connection between the food supplied by Jesus and the manna given by Moses."[25] As a response to Brown's interpretation, one must say that in v. 14 the crowd already seems to have understood the feeding miracle as an event corresponding to the manna miracle, since they thought that Jesus was the prophet-like-Moses. If so, Brown does not explain why the crowd in vv. 30ff. again ask Jesus to perform the manna miracle as a sign.

R. Schnackenburg thinks that vv. 2 (signs = healing miracles) and 15 (they wanted to make him king) express the misinterpretation of the signs by the crowd, while v. 14 formulates the understanding as intended by the Evangelist

[24] On agency in John, see references in n. 20.
[25] Brown, *John*, p. 234.

–Jesus was to be confessed as the prophet-like-Moses who actually exceeded Moses. When according to v. 31 the crowd asked for a sign similar to the manna given in the desert, it is to be seen as a literary device used by the Evangelist: "Wenn man diese Überleitung als literarisches Vorgehen des Evangelisten betrachtet, fällt die mehrfach erwähnte Schwierigkeit weg (oder wird begreiflich), dass die Teilnehmer an der Speisung ein Verlangen äussern, da sie nach dem von Jesus gewirkten Zeichen und ihrem eigenen Bekenntnis (V 14) als erfüllt ansehen sollten."[26] M. J. J. Menken rightly objects to Schnackenburg's interpretation, that it is the same crowd who pronounces both the confession of 6:14 and the question of 6:30-31, and John does not indicate in his text a shift from one level of meaning to another.[27]

According to E. Haenchen the contradiction between the request for a sign in John 6:30-31 and the sign mentioned in v. 14 should not be taken seriously: ". . . der Evangelist will hier keine psychologisch durchsichtige Darstellung der Reaktionen bei den Hörern bringen. Die Zeichenforderung der Juden zeigt freilig einmal, wie unfähig die Menschen sind, die erlebten Zeichen als solche zu erfassen. Zum andern schafft der Evangelist sich damit den Übergang zum eigentlichen Thema, dem er zustrebt: das Himmelbrot."[28]

The contradiction disappears, however, if one understands vv. 30-31 along the lines suggested by Menken.[29] Then these verses are to be seen precisely as a restatement of the crowd's view that the feeding miracle corresponded to the manna miracle and thus legitimated Jesus as the prophet-like-Moses (vv. 14-15). In their view, since Jesus already had legitimated himself as a prophet by the feeding miracle, they now needed another sign which would demonstrate that he was the one sent by the Father, that is, the Son of Man who was sealed by the Father, God (vv. 27-29). The correct meaning of vv. 14-15 and vv. 30-31 is then: since the feeding miracle was the eschatological manna miracle, Jesus had legitimated himself as the prophet-like-Moses. Now in vv. 27-29 he seemed to imply that he was the Son of Man, the Father's (heavenly) commissioned envoy. Therefore there was the need for (another) sign which would demonstrate that this was the case.[30]

---

[26] Schnackenburg, *Das Johannesevangelium*, p. 53; see also pp. 31-32. Painter, *Quest*, pp. 230-31 seems mainly to see John 6:31 as a verse which introduces the theme of manna as a crucial issue in the subsequent conflict with the Jews, 6:49-58.

[27] M. J. J. Menken, "Some Remarks on the Course of the Dialogue: John 6:25-34," *Bijdragen, tijdschrift voor filosofie en theologie* 48 (1987), 141.

[28] E. Haenchen, *Das Johannesevangelium: Ein Kommentar* (Tübingen: Mohr-Siebeck, 1980), p. 321.

[29] Menken, "Some Remarks," pp. 145-46.

[30] This distinction between two levels of Christology is formulated by M. De Jonge, *Jesus: Stranger from Heaven and Son of God* (Missoula, Montana: Scholars, 1977): ". . . it is evident that this identification of Jesus with the Mosaic Prophet, though perhaps pointing in the right direction, does not really explain the secret of Jesus' coming. Jesus' reaction towards the ideas of the crowd in the following discourse is entirely negative. In that chapter not the similarities but the dissimilarities receive all emphasis . . . it is clear, however, that the unique relationship

John 6:30ff. can be paraphrased in this way: The crowd said, "What sign
do you do so that we may see, and believe that you are God's heavenly-sent
envoy, the Son of Man, who is sealed by the Father? The manna sign which
we experienced in the feeding miracle was a sign which, in our mind, showed
that you were the prophet-like-Moses, but it did not legitimate you as God's
heavenly-sent envoy, the Son of Man." Jesus answered, "You have
misunderstood the manna miracle. It was not given by Moses, nor now by the
prophet-like-Moses, but it was the gift from heaven, given by the Father, and
I am (myself) the manna/bread."

Thus in vv. 32ff. Jesus, by means of his exegesis of v. 31b "bread from
heaven he gave them to eat," demonstrated that the Scriptures bore witness to
him (5:39) and that Moses wrote about him (5:46). The giving of the manna,
rightly understood, was a sign about Jesus (not just as a prophet-king, but) as
the one who came down from heaven.

From 6:30-40 there is an exegetical dialogue between Jesus and "they,"
that is the crowd, and from vv. 41-58 there are exegetical objections voiced
among the Jews, followed by statements given by Jesus.

John 6:31-58 has many midrashic features. As shown in my book *Bread
from Heaven* there are such features in vv. 32-33. Jesus develops philological
exegesis and states in v. 32 that his Father and not Moses is the subject of the
verb "to give" (ἔδωκεν, Hebrew נתן) in the Old Testament text. Moreover, the
verb is not to be read as past tense, δέδωκεν (ἔδωκεν), but in the present
tense, δίδωσιν. By means of midrashic exegesis, Jesus corrects the crowd
when they refer to the manna/bread from heaven (v. 31) as a sign of the
prophet-like-Moses.

Jesus' understanding of the Old Testament quotation follows in v. 33,
introduced by γάρ:[31] "For *the bread* of God is that which (or he who) comes
down *from heaven*, and gives life to the world." (The words from the Old
Testament quotation are italicized). According to Jewish traditions the Torah,
given at Sinai, gave life to Israel or the world (*Tanh. Shem.* 25; *Mek. Exod.*
15:26; *Exod. Rab.* 29:9). Thus, "the bread of God" in John 6:33 has the role
of the Torah. This understanding presupposes the identification of the
manna/bread from heaven with the Torah, as exemplified in Philo, *Mut.* 253-
63 and *Mek. Exod.* 13:17. Moreover, in the expository application in John
6:32 the third person plural pronoun "them" (αὐτοῖς) has been interpreted as
"you" (ὑμῖν). In John 6:34 "they" (the crowd) ask for this Torah-bread from
Jesus: "Lord, give us this bread always."[32] The exposition in vv. 32-33 made

_____

between Jesus and God is underlined by means of the expression 'my Father' (vv. 32, 37, 40, 44,
and especially v. 46) and the notion of 'descent from heaven' (v. 33, 41, 42, 50, 51)."

[31] Cf. Philo, *Deter.* 47-48, with exegesis of Gen. 4:8: "it must be read in this way: 'Cain rose
up and slew himself,' not someone else. For (γάρ) . . ."

[32] Painter, *Quest*, p. 233, asks why the crowd according to John 6:34 should think of Jesus as
the giver if he has said that it is his Father who gives this bread? Painter's answer is that the

clear that God the Father gives the bread, but does not make explicit what
kind of bread it is. The formulations seem to indicate that the bread means the
wisdom of the life-giving Torah, and the crowd asks Jesus to give them this
bread always, presumably as a teacher who gives the people the wisdom of
the God-given Torah. Thus they had not recognized Jesus' identity, that he
himself was the one who came down from heaven.[33] Then Jesus makes
explicit his exegetical application of the Old Testament quotation (v. 31b) to
himself in v: 35: "I am *the bread* of life; he who comes to me shall not
hunger, and he who believes in me shall never thirst."

J. Painter regards John 6:35 as the pronouncement to which the dialogues
of 6:25-36 lead. According to him, this verse is the text upon which the
discourse as a whole is based. Thus the Old Testament quotation in 6:31b
does not serve as the text, but v. 31 as a whole is used to leading up to the
pronouncement of 6:35.[34] It must be said that Painter does not define the
relationship between vv. 31 and 35 in an adequate way. The Old Testament
quotation in v. 31b and the pronouncement in v. 35a are tied together in the
way formulated in 5:39: "it is they (the Scriptures) that bear witness to me."
Thus, on the basis of this hermeneutical key the pronouncement in John
6:35a, "I am *the bread* of life," renders the precise meaning of the central
term in the Old Testament quotation in v. 31b "*bread* from heaven he gave
them to eat." The scriptural text in v. 31b bears witness to Jesus.

Moreover, although v. 35 gives the precise meaning of the Old Testament
quotation, it does not function as the text since it does not form the basis for a
subsequent expository structure. The Old Testament quotation in v. 31b
serves as such a text, however. In a systematic way the words from the Old
Testament quotation are repeated and paraphrased. Only words from the first
part of the quotation, "he gave them bread from heaven," are repeated and
paraphrased and discussed in vv. 32-48. The last word, "to eat" is then added,
so that the whole quotation is interpreted in vv. 49-58. Moreover, themes
from the Old Testament quotation are developed in a systematic way.

1. vv. 32-49. In vv. 32-34 it is made clear that it is the Father who "gives
the bread." Then in vv. 35-49 the theme is Jesus as the "bread."

2. vv. 49-58: In vv. 49-51a the focus is on the effect of the "eating of the
bread"—it gives eternal life. This theme is continued in vv. 51b-58, but here

---

crowd, provisionally at least, has accepted Jesus as the emissary of God (6:29), that is, the Son of
Man. It is not necessary to go quite as far as Painter does, however. Against the background of
6:31-33 the crowd might understand Jesus to be a teacher who through his teaching brings the
Torah-manna which gives life. They would then understand Jesus to be a teacher who follows the
principle formulated in 5:39: "You search the Scriptures, because you think that in them you have
eternal life."

[33] Against Painter, *Quest*, p. 233, who thinks that "the crowd, provisionally at least, has
accepted Jesus as the emissary of God (6:29)."

[34] Painter, *Quest*, pp. 229 and 232.

with the emphasis on the idea that the bread is the flesh of Jesus as the "Son of Man" (referring back to the Son of Man in v. 27) which he "shall give for the life of the world."

The conclusion is that the Old Testament quotation in v. 31b serves as a text, while Jesus' word in v. 35 gives the precise expository meaning of the word "bread" in the quotation.

Painter's hypothesis of a distinction between quest stories as John's first edition and rejection stories as his second edition breaks down in 6:36-40. According to him the quest is made by the crowd, and the "Jews" (vv. 41 and 52) are the ones who reject. Verse 36 tells that the crowd rejected, however: they "do not believe." To Painter this causes embarrassment: "surprisingly, in the end we are told that the crowd's quest ended in failure, 6:36. But 6:36-40 is made up of a collection of isolated sayings forming a transition to the rejection story of 6:41ff."[35] According to Painter "*the* Jews" are the group associated with rejection. He does not give a plausible reason why John, who, according to Painter, is himself responsible for both editions, here pointedly states that "*they*," that is, *the crowd* (cf. v. 24) rejected Jesus. Painter indicates that the crowd's unbelief in v. 36 shows that the quest story ended in failure. If so, there is no real distinction between the quest story and the rejection story.

In John 6:35b-40 the identification of the manna/bread with Jesus (v. 35a) is related to the main point in the dialogue of vv. 29-30, believing in him whom the Father, God, has sent. Verse 35b refers to "coming" and "believing." In v. 36 Jesus accuses the crowd, saying that they "do not believe." Then vv. 37-40 combine the idea of "coming" and "believing" with the idea of Jesus as "the one sent by the Father." The section is an elaboration of the words "from heaven" in the Old Testament quotation in v. 31b, a phrase which is repeated in v. 38, and is an integral part of the dialogue about "the Son of man" and "the one whom God sent."

In the study "God's agent in the Fourth Gospel,"[36] I have shown that in vv. 38-40 halakhic principles of a commissioned envoy are applied to Jesus, the one whom the Father sent. One such principle was that it was a legal presumption that an agent, that is, one who is sent, would carry out his mission in obedience to his sender. In accordance with this principle, Jesus was an obedient agent who did as the Father had commanded. He said, "I have 'come down *from heaven*' (see v. 31b 'from heaven') not to do my own will, but the will of him who sent me." The will of the sender is then defined in vv. 39-40.

---

[35] Ibid., p. 229. See also pp. 236-37.
[36] See reference in n. 20.

Another halakhic principle of agency is also used, that in the context of a lawsuit the sender transferred his own rights and the property concerned to the agent. The will of the sender, the Father, in John 6:39 is based on this transfer: "This is the will of him who sent me, that all he has given me . . . ." The transfer is even more pointedly stated in John 17:6: "thine they were, and thou gavest them to me . . . ." The same idea is also formulated in 6:37: "All that the Father gives me . . . ."

The Jews' objection to Jesus' exegesis in 6:41-42 is formulated with a term from the story about the manna, Exod. 16:2, 7, 8: they "murmured" (ἐγόγγυζον), John 6:41, cf. v. 43. The objection has the form of an exegetical problem formulation followed by a solution, parallels to which are found in the midrash and in Philo. The exposition consists of the following points:

1. The Old Testament quotation: John 6:31, "Bread from heaven he gave them to eat."

2. The interpretation of the quotation: 6:41, "he (Jesus) said, 'I am the bread which came down from heaven'" (words taken from vv. 35 and 38).

3. The basis for the questioning of Jesus' exegesis: 6:42, "They said, 'Is not this Jesus, the son of Joseph, whose father and mother we know?'"

4. The questioning of the interpretation: 6:42, "how does he now say 'I have come down from heaven?'"

5. The answer to the objection and the solution of the problem: 6:43ff., "Jesus answered and said to them, 'Do not "murmur" among your-selves. . . .'"

In Jesus' answer the word "he who believes . . ." in v. 47 refers back to vv. 35 and 29-30, and the words, "I am the bread of life" in v. 48 repeats v. 35a, which in turn is the interpretation of the word "bread" in the scriptural quotation in v. 31b.

In *Bread from Heaven*, I have referred to the corresponding points of exegetical exchange which are found in *Mek. Exod.* 12:1 and 12:2 and in Philo, *Mut.* 141a, 142b-44.[37]

It is noticeable that the objection in John 6:41ff. is not raised by the crowd, but by "the Jews," ὁι Ἰουδαῖοι. Painter draws extensive conclusions from this introduction of the term "the Jews" in John 6:41: "It is argued here that the change of terminology from the crowd to the Jews indicates a change of audience and a change of time, and that the note concerning the Synagogue in 6:59 indicates a change of location. John 6:41-59 reflects the struggle between the Johannine Christians and the Synagogue. For this text 'the Jews' is the appropriate term of reference. They do not represent the Galilean crowd which had followed and subsequently come seeking Jesus."[38] Against Painter it must be said that the reason for this change of terminology cannot be that

---

[37] Borgen, *Bread from Heaven*, pp. 80-83.
[38] Painter , *The Quest for the Messiah*, p. 237.

"the Jews" rejected Jesus, while the crowd did not. On the basis of the text, it might even be said that "the Jews" who "murmured" expressed scepticism about Jesus' exegesis,[39] while "they," that is the crowd, rejected Jesus outright, as stated in v. 37,[40] and nothing in v. 41 indicates a different time and location from the setting of the preceding verses.

Several scholars think that "the Jews" in John 6:41 refers to "the crowd" (6:22, 24) and thus does not carry the usual meaning of the Jewish authorities.[41] There is one observation which indicates that the term "Jews" also here refers to the Jewish authorities, but in the role as midrash scholars. In John 6 the "crowd" wants to make Jesus a king, they seek him and address him as rabbi, and make requests to him. They do not perform scholarly midrashic exegesis, however, as rabbi Jesus and "the Jews" do. Thus "the Jews" in John 6:41 and 52 are the midrashic experts, as distinct from the common people, "the crowd." As Jesus and "the Jews" in John 5:10-18 had a halakhic and midrashic exchange on the commandments about the Sabbath in the Law of Moses, so rabbi Jesus and "the Jews" in 6:41ff. and 51ff. had a scholarly midrashic exchange. The difference is that the Jewish authorities in 5:10-18 persecuted Jesus and sought to kill him, while the Jewish scholars in 6:41 and 52 expressed objection to Jesus' application of the scriptural quotation about the bread from heaven (v. 31b). Thus the attitude of "the Jews" in John 6:41 and 52 is similar to the attitude associated with the term in 1:19; 2:18, 22, where the designation expresses scepticism and unbelief, but not hostility. In 6:41, 52 "the Jews" represent those who, as stated in 5:39, execute (professional) midrashic exegesis of the Scriptures, but refuse to accept that the Scriptures bear witness to Jesus.

Jesus' answer leads in 6:49ff. into further elaboration of the application to himself of the scripture quotation in v. 31b to himself. Now the word "to eat" (φαγεῖν) from v. 31 is introduced and is placed in the centre of the exposition to the end, v. 58.[42] As Jesus did in v. 32, he also here criticizes the misunderstanding expressed by the crowd in vv. 14-15, 26 and 31.

In John 6:51b the "bread" of the scripture quotation in v. 31b is interpreted as Jesus' "flesh." This application of the scriptures to Jesus is again met with

---

[39] J. Ashton, *Understanding the Fourth Gospel* (Oxford: Clarendon, 1991), p. 200: ". . . called οἱ Ἰουδαῖοι (6:4, 41, 52), but their 'murmuring' (γόγγυσμός, v. 41) is prompted more by bewilderment than by real antagonism."

[40] Painter, *The Quest for the Messiah*, p. 238, ignores Jesus' word to the crowd that they do not believe, v. 36, and writes: "The crowd, though it has misunderstood Jesus, requests that Jesus should always give them the bread of which he has been speaking, 6:34. On the other hand the Jews do nothing but raise *objections* to what Jesus has said. They represent a hardening attitude of the Synagogue . . . ." Against Painter it must be said that objections do not represent a hardening attitude when compared with the attitude of unbelief of the crowd.

[41] See the survey in U. C. von Wahlde, "The Johannine 'Jews': A Critical Survey," *NTS 28* (1982), 33-60.

[42] Concerning the use of τρωγεῖν in vv. 54-58, see Borgen, *Bread from Heaven*, pp. 92-93.

exegetical objection in dispute among "the Jews" (v. 52). Also the objection
here has the form of an exegetical problem formulation followed by a
solution, parallels to which are found in the midrash and in Philo. The same
five points as found in vv. 41-48 are also found here, except point 3, which in
an explicit way stated the basis for the questioning of Jesus' exegesis in vv.
41-48.

1. The Old Testament quotation: John 6:31, "Bread from heaven he gave
(ἔδωκεν) them to eat (φαγεῖν)."

2. The interpretation of the quotation: 6:51, .". . . the *bread* (ὁ ἄρτος) which
I *shall give* (δώσω) for the life of the world is my 'flesh' (ἡ σάρξ)."

3. The basis for the questioning of Jesus' exegesis (the basis is implied in
point 4).

4. The questioning of the interpretation: 6:52, "The Jews then disputed
among themselves, saying, 'How can this man *give* (δοῦναι) us his "flesh"
(τὴν σάρκα) *to eat* (φαγεῖν)?'"

5. The answer to the objection and the solution to the problem: 6:53ff, "So
Jesus said to them, 'Truly, truly I say to you . . . .'"

In 6:53-58 there is an expository elaboration on the theme of eating in v.
31, tied together with the theme of the Son of Man in vv. 53 and 27, and the
theme of the one whom the Father sent in vv. 57 and 29. It should be added
that the formula used when raising the question in John 6:52, πῶς δύναται,
corresponds to the technical midrashic term כיצד.[43]

Although the exposition in John 6:31-58 consists of dialogue and scholarly
exchanges, there are several unifying threads which demonstrate that the
passage is composed as a whole—throughout the words "Bread from heaven
he gave them" (v. 31b) are built into the formulations, and from 6:49 and
onwards the word "to eat" from v. 31 is added. Moreover, the statement "our
fathers ate manna in the wilderness" (v. 31) is repeated with some changes in
v. 49 and in v. 58. These threads which run through 6:31-58 demonstrate that
the passage as a whole is composed to serve as a scriptural debate in response
to the question raised in v. 30: "Then what sign do you do, that we may see,
and believe you? What work do you perform?"

D. THE REACTION AMONG THE DISCIPLES, JOHN 6:60-71

It is surprising that the subsequent section of John 6:60-71 reports the reaction
among the disciples. They have not been mentioned in 6:25-59, although their
presence must then be presupposed. The section refers at several points back
to the earlier parts of the chapter. The disciples are mentioned several times in

[43] Ibid., pp. 89-90; W. Bacher, *Die exegetische Terminologie der jüdischen Traditionsliter-
atur* (1899; Leipzig: rpt. Darmstadt, 1965), p. 77.

6:3-21 and also in 6:22-24. The disciples "murmured" (γογγύζουσιν), 6:61, just as "the Jews" did (6:41). This "murmur" has its background in Exod. 16:2 and shows that the scriptural story about the manna still serves as frame of reference. The word in 6:62 ("If then you see the Son of Man ascending to where he was before?") presuppose the words about the Son of Man in 6:27, 53 and the words about (his) descent from heaven (6:38, 41, 51).[44] The term "flesh" occurs in 6:63 and back in 6:51-56.[45] Some of the disciples "do not believe" (6:64) just as with the crowd (6:36). John 6:65 cites a previous saying of Jesus, actually a composite of words from 6:37 and 6:44. In contrast to the unbelief of the crowd (6:36) and of some of the disciples (6:64) Peter, representing "the Twelve," says that they have believed (6:69). Thus Peter gives a positive response to Jesus' word in 6:29: "This is the work of God, that you believe in him whom he has sent."

These observations demonstrate that the section 6:60-71 is an integral part of the chapter. How is its function to be defined in a more precise way? At the outset it is to be noticed that the subsequent result of the feeding miracle for the disciples is the walking on the sea in 6:16-21—Jesus miraculously came to the disciples (6:16-21) after he had withdrawn from the crowd who mistakenly wanted to make him king (6:14-15). The works of Jesus, that is, the healing miracles, the feeding miracle and the walking on the sea, bore witness to him and the disciples experienced an epiphanic encounter with him.

Jesus' words about perishable and life-giving food and about the Father bearing witness about the Son of Man were addressed to the crowd (6:27). His words about believing in him whom God sent, and his application to himself of the scriptural word about the manna-bread from heaven, resulted in unbelief by the crowd and in exegetical objections stated by the Jewish scholars (6:28-58). Thus it remains to learn how the disciples reacted to the witness to the Son of Man, given by the Father (6:27-28), who sealed and sent him (6:27-28), and by the Scriptures (6:31-58).

Then from 6:60-71 we learn that the reaction among the disciples was divided—many said that Jesus' discourse was a hard saying, and they subsequently left him. Peter, representing the Twelve, accepted Jesus' words. Thus they accepted that God bore witness about him and so also did the Scriptures: "You have the words of eternal life; and we have believed, and have come to know, that you are the Holy One of God" (6:68-69). As for

---

[44] It is difficult to define the exact meaning of John 6:62 because it has the protasis, but lacks the apodosis. See commentaries, and Borgen, *Bread from Heaven*, p. 187, Moloney, *The Johannine Son of Man*, pp. 120-23; and L. Schenke, "Das johanneische Schisma und die 'Zwölf' (Johannes 6:60-71)," *NTS* 38 (1992), 113ff.

[45] Concerning the meaning of John 6:63 in relation to 6:51-56, see commentaries, and Borgen, *Bread from Heaven*, pp. 181-83; Schenke, "Das johanneische Schisma," pp. 109, 114-17.

Jesus' "words (ῥήματα) of eternal life" it is to be noticed that according to 5:47 the writings of Moses and the words of Jesus coincide: "but if you do not believe his (Moses') writings, how shall you believe my words (ῥήματα)?" Moreover, John 10:36 makes evident that "the Holy One of God" means consecrated by God and sent by Him into the world: ." . . him, whom the Father consecrated (made holy) and sent into the world."[46] Thus, the christological designation used by Peter has the same meaning as that expressed by the designations used in 6:27, "on him the Father has set his seal," and in 6:29, "him whom he has sent."[47]

E. THE TRANSITION FROM JOHN 5 TO JOHN 6

The transition from John 5 to John 6 represents one of the most striking aporias of the Fourth Gospel. In ch. 5 Jesus was in Jerusalem, and in ch. 6 he is in Galilee and goes to the other side of the Sea of Galilee (6:1ff.). Then he comes to Capernaum (6:24, 59). Moreover, there is in John 7:23 a reference back to the healing story in 5:1-18, and both 5:16-18 and 7:1ff. report that "the Jews" persecuted Jesus and wished to kill him. Scholars such as Bultmann and Schnackenburg thus reverse the order of chs. 5 and 6, and Lindars and Ashton regard ch. 6 as an addition made by the evangelist himself.[48]

The present study is an analysis of ch. 6. Thus it would go beyond the limits of this paper to deal with its relationship to ch. 5, especially since such an undertaking would necessitate a thorough examination of this latter chapter. Some observations might be listed, however, as a point of departure for further research on the subject.

It might prove fruitful to investigate whether points in John 5:31-47, the final part of the discourse of Jesus in 5:19-47, serve as the thematic background of ch. 6. If so, such a thematic connection would indicate that ch. 6 is in its right and original place in the Gospel. These points from ch. 5 may also give an important insight into the composition of ch. 6.

Such an approach was indicated in an embryonic form in my book *Bread from Heaven*. I suggested that John 6:31-58 might be an elaboration upon and an illustration of points discussed in 5:37-47. The conclusion was: "The close connection between John 5:37-47 and 6:31-58 speaks against any

---

[46] Cf. Brown, *John I-XII*, p. 298; Schnackenburg, *Das Johannesevangelium*, pp. 110-11; Barrett, *John*, p. 307.

[47] There is no need in this essay to discuss whether John 6 implies an antidocetic polemic. See commentaries, and Borgen, *Bread from Heaven*, 183-92; Schenke, "Das johanneische Schisma," pp. 105-21.

[48] R. Bultmann, *Das Evangelium des Johannes* (Göttingen: Vandenhoeck & Ruprecht, 1941), pp. 154-77; Schnackenburg, *Das Johannesevangelium*, pp. 6-114; Lindars, *John*, pp. 50, 206-09, and 234; Ashton, *Understanding the Fourth Gospel*, pp. 200-01.

rearrangement of the sequence of chs. 5 and 6 in spite of the obvious geographical discrepancies (ch. 5 in Jerusalem; ch. 6 at the sea of Galilee, etc.)."[49]

The most obvious point deals with the interpretation of Scriptures (5:39-40) for which 6:31-58 is an illustration. References back to 5:39 have already been made in the present study. The connection is then as follows: in John 5:39-40 a hermeneutical principle is formulated—(v. 39) "You search the Scriptures, because you think that in them you have eternal life; and it is they that bear witness to me (v. 40); yet you refuse to come to me that you may have life." The same principle is also found in 5:46-47: "If you believed Moses, you would believe me, for he wrote of me. But if you do not believe his writings, how will you believe my words?" Then in ch. 6 a quotation from the Scriptures is given in v. 31, "as it is written, 'He gave them bread from heaven to eat,'" and midrashic interpretations and diverse responses are seen in vv. 32-59, and various attitudes are also pictured in vv. 60-71. Thus John 6:31-58 serves as an illustration of the searching of the Scriptures mentioned in John 5:39-40. The phrase ἐρευνᾶτε (τὰς γραφάς) in John 5:39 is even a Greek equivalent for the technical term for performing midrashic exegesis.

This link between chs. 5 and 6 provides a basis for investigating whether other connections might be found. John 5:36 might give us a lead. According to this verse Jesus' works bear witness to him: ". . . the works which the Father has granted me to accomplish, these very works which I am doing, bear me witness that the Father has sent me." The line here may be drawn to 6:1-13. If so, light might be thrown on the puzzling verse 6:2—why should the evangelist here report that the crowd followed Jesus because they saw the signs which he performed on those who were diseased? Actually only one healing is reported by him to have taken place in Galilee (4:46-54). Seemingly, E. Haenchen is right when he states that the context does not explain why it is said that a large crowd followed Jesus. The verb ἠκολούθει even has imperfect form to show that the crowd's following of Jesus was a lasting phenomenon![50] The preceding context, that is, John 5:36, may provide a clue. This verse says that Jesus' works, τὰ ἔργα, bear witness to him, and 6:1-13 may be meant to illustrate this witnessing function of the works, first by giving a summary statement about Jesus' healing activity in v. 2[51] and then

---

[49] Borgen, *Bread from Heaven*, p. 152, with the quotation taken from n. 2.

[50] Haenchen, *Das Johannesevangelium*, p. 300: "Das eine grosse Menge Jesus folgt (Imperfekt der Dauer!), wird hier aus dem Kontekst freilich nicht verständlich." Cf. Schnackenburg, *Das Johannesevangelium*, p. 17: "Woher die grosse Volksmenge stammt, die hier unvermittelt auftaucht, wird nicht gesagt. Von einem 'Nachfolgen' so vieler Menschen ist sonst nirgends im Joh-Ev die Rede . . . ."

[51] Summarizing statements about Jesus' healing activity are found in Matt. 4:23-25; 9:35; Acts 2:22; 10:38. See also John 20:30.

reporting in vv. 3ff. more specifically on how Jesus' feeding miracle bore witness to him.

Also John 5:37, "And the Father who sent me has himself borne witness to me," might prove to be of interest. Does the evangelist here think of a particular occasion or a particular kind of witness? Scholars have made several different suggestions. It has already been mentioned above that Schnackenburg has joined the idea about the testimony of the Father, in John 5:37 with John 6:27b where it is said that it is the Father, God, who sealed the Son of Man and bore witness to him as His envoy.[52]

If further analysis offers support for these suggestions, then there are three witnesses. First, Jesus' works (v. 36), secondly, the Father who sent him (v. 37), and thirdly, the Scriptures (vv. 39-40 and 46-47). It is interesting to note that three corresponding sections seem to be found in ch. 6 since the main focus in vv. 1-21 is on Jesus' works as signs,[53] in vv. 22-27 on the Father and in vv. 28-71 on the Scriptures.

F. SUMMARY

1. Jesus is not just the Prophet-like-Moses, John 6:1-21

The two traditional stories about the feeding of the multitude and the crossing of the sea in John 6:1-21 primarily report how Jesus acted in feeding the crowd and how they reacted: they thought the feeding was a new manna miracle and that Jesus was the prophet-like-Moses, and they wanted to make him king. This reaction, in turn, led to a further action on Jesus' part—he withdrew to the hills. The reaction of the disciples as a distinct group was also in the form of an action—they went away across the sea and Jesus miraculously came to them.

2. The Son of Man—the Father's Accredited Envoy, John 6:22-27

In 6:22-24 John repeats phrases from and makes references to the preceding stories and inserts additional interpretation. In this way it is seen that in v. 22 he refers to the story of the crossing of the sea by the disciples (vv. 16-21). In vv. 23-24a the story about the feeding is referred to, while in v. 24b-25a he brings the crowd to the destination of the disciples' crossing, Capernaum. In this way it is shown that the crowd was searching for Jesus.

The concluding point in v. 27 is not the search of the crowd nor the choice as such with which they are confronted by Jesus, but the seal which God the Father put on the Son of Man. The word σφραγίζω and its Hebrew and

---

[52] Schnackenburg, *Das Johannesevangelium*, p. 50.

[53] See Borgen, *Bread from Heaven*, p. 180: ". . . the feeding miracle offers an example of the works mentioned in 5:36."

Aramaic equivalents, are technical terms for sealing and signing as a witness. Thus, the Son of Man (and not the prophet-like-Moses) gives the bread which which endures for eternal life.

3. The Manna-bread from Heaven, the Sign of the Son of Man, John 6:28-59

The structure of John 6:28-59 is as follows: Against the background of the general statements about "the Son of Man" and "the one who is sent" by God (6:27, 29) the question is raised whether Jesus is "the Son of Man" and "the one who is sent" by God (6:30). Exchanges on the scriptural story about the giving of the manna follow in 6:31-58, with particular focus on the interpretation of the quotation "bread from heaven he gave them to eat" (6:31b). In this way it is made clear that Jesus himself is the manna-miracle, as the bread/the Son of Man who came down from heaven (6:31-58).

The common people, "the crowd" addresses Jesus as "rabbi" (6.25) and asks questions (6:25, 28, 30, 34), while Jesus and "the Jews" practise scholarly midrashic exegesis. Jesus accuses "the crowd" of unbelief (6:36), and he criticizes "the Jews" because they object to his application of the scriptural quotation to himself (6:43ff. and 54ff.).

4. The Reaction among the Disciples, John 6:60-71

From 6:60-71 we learn that the reaction among the disciples was also divided—many disciples left him. Peter, representing the Twelve, accepted Jesus' words. Thus they acknowledged that both God and the Scriptures bore witness about him, "You have the words of eternal life; and we have believed, and have come to know, that you are the Holy One of God" (6:68-69). John 10:36 makes evident that "the Holy One of God" means consecrated by God and sent by him into the world. Thus, the christological designation used by Peter has the same meaning as that expressed by the designations used in 6:27 and in 6:29.

THE STRUCTURE OF JOHN 6

Johannes Beutler, S.J.

The sixth chapter of John appears as a kind of summary of the Gospel of John and its riddles. On the one hand, we have here a condensation of the theological statements of the evangelist about the unique importance of Jesus Christ for the faithful and for the world. On the other hand, we find in this chapter also a condensation of the problems of the interpretation of the Fourth Gospel. Unclear still is the integration of this chapter in its context. How does Jesus get to Galilee unexpectedly at the beginning of the chapter, and why does he leave Galilee again at the end of the chapter? Would chapter 7 not fit better with chapter 5 as the preceding context, and could the original position of chapter 6 not have been immediately after chapter 4?[1] Or was it perhaps added to the gospel secondarily by the evangelist?[2] The literary unity of the chapter itself is also disputed. Particularly the transition within the discourse in the Bread of Life—from the bread which Jesus *is* to the bread which he *gives* as eucharistic food—is attributed to two different redactional layers of the gospel by some interpreters.[3] In the perspective of this hypothesis the announcement of the bread which the Son of Man will give in 6:27[4] and the threefold reference to the coming resurrection of the dead in 6:39, 40, 44 may also be attributed to this "sacramental" layer.[5] But there are also other proposals of literary criticism in John 6.[6]

---

[1] So among more recent commentators R. Bultmann, *Das Evangelium des Johannes*, KEK, 2 (Göttingen: Vandenhoeck & Ruprecht, 1941), pp. 154f.; R. Schnackenburg, *Das Johannesevangelium II*, HTKNT, 4/2 (Freiburg-Basel-Wien: Herder and Herder, 1971), pp. 5-14. A position after 10:21 is envisaged by M. Shorter, "The Position of Chapter VI in the Fourth Gospel," *ExpTim* 84 (1972-73), 181-83.

[2] So with good reasons B. Lindars, *The Gospel of John*, NCB (London: Oliphants, 1972), pp. 50, 234; R. Kieffer, *Johannesevangeliet*, 2 vols., Kommentar till Nya Testamentet, 4 (Uppsala: EFS, 1987-88), here 1:159f.

[3] Cf. besides Bultmann, *Das Evangelium des Johannes*, pp. 161f.; G. Bornkamm, "Die eucharistische Rede im Johannes-Evangelium," *ZNW* 47 (1956), 161-69; E. Lohse, "Wort und Sakrament im Johannesevangelium," *NTS* 7 (1960-61), 110-25, esp. 117-20; G. Richter, *Studien zum Johannesevangelium*, ed. by J. Hainz, BU 13 (Regensburg: F. Pustet, 1977), 174-78 and passim; E. Haenchen, *Das Johannesevangelium*, ed. by U. Busse (Tübingen: J. C. B. Mohr, 1980), 329-32; J. M. Perry, "The Evolution of the Johannine Eucharist," *NTS* 39 (1993), 22-35.

[4] Cf. Bultmann, *Das Evangelium des Johannes*, p. 166; Richter, *Studien*, p. 91 etc.; Haenchen, *Das Johannesevangelium*, p. 320.

[5] So already Bultmann, *Das Evangelium des Johannes*, p. 162.

[6] Cf. particularly L. Schenke's effort to show the existence of a collection of dialogues prior to the evangelist, which already comprehended parts of John 6: L. Schenke, "Die formale und gedankliche Struktur von Joh 6, 26-58," *BZ* 24 (1980), 31-41; id., "Das Szenarium von Joh 6, 1-25," *TTZ* 92 (1983), 191-203; id., "Die literarische Vorgeschichte von Joh 6, 26-58," *BZ* 29 (1985), 68-89; id., "Der Dialog Jesu mit den Juden im Johannesevangelium: Ein Rekonstrukionsversuch," *NTS* 34 (1988), 573-603; id., "Das

There are also ongoing disputes about the extent and identity of possible sources of the narrative and of the discourse material in John 6 and about a possible dependence of the evangelist or one of his sources or redactions upon the Synoptic Gospels.[7]

Recently there has been an increasing interest in the general structure of the chapter. Different perspectives are possible here and have in fact been chosen. On the one hand, the theories of literary criticism have influenced the proposals regarding the structure of the chapter, as we can see from different recent commentaries and monographs. The best known example is the alleged transition from a christological to a eucharistic section within the discourse on the Bread of Life in John 6:51c.[8] On the other hand, form criticism has contributed to the elaboration of the structure of the discourse on the Bread of Life. One well-known example is Peder Borgen's[9] proposal that a Jewish homiletic pattern lies behind this discourse, according to which we would have in John 6:32-58 two parts inspired successively by the two elements of the initial quotation of 6:31: "He gave them bread from heaven" and "to eat."

While such proposals of a structural analysis of the chapter finally remain indebted to a diachronic approach, an increasing number of proposals in English and French speaking research regarding the overall structure of John 6 are based on purely formal observations without an historical point of view. Here too different methods are possible and have in fact been applied. In French speaking research we note the influence of

---

Johanneische Schisma und die Zwölf (Johannes 6,60-71)," *NTS* 38 (1992), 105-21. A successive quest and rejection story is presumed by J. Painter, "Tradition and Interpretation in John 6," *NTS* 35 (1989), 421-50; cf. id., *The Quest for the Messiah* (Edinburgh: T. & T. Clark, 1991), pp. 215-44.

[7] Cf. most recently P. W. Barnett, "The feeding of the multitude in Mark 6/John 6," in D. Wenham and C. Blomberg, ed., *The Miracles of Jesus*, Gospel Perspectives, 6 (Sheffield: JSOT Press, 1986), pp. 273-93; J. M. Sevrin, "L'écriture du IVe évangile comme phénomène de réception: L'exemple de Jean 6," in id., *The New Testament in Early Christianity: La réception des écrits néotestamentaires dans le christianisme primitif*, BETL, 86 (Louvain: Louvain University Press, 1989), pp. 69-83; and C. Riniker, "Jean 6,1-21 et les évangiles synoptiques," in J. D. Kaestli, J.-M. Poffet, and J. Zumstein, ed., *La communauté johannique et son histoire: La trajectoire de l'évangile de Jean aux deux premiers siècles*, La monde de la Bible (Genève: Labor et Fides, 1990), pp. 213-47; E. Ruckstuhl, "Die Speisung des Volkes durch Jesus und die Seeüberfahrt der Jünger nach Joh 6,1-25," in F. van Segbroek et al., ed., *The Four Gospels*, Festschrift F. Neirynck, BETL, 100 (Louvain: Louvain University Press, 1992), pp. 2001-19; F. Vouga, "Le quatrième évangile comme interprète de la tradition synoptique: Jean 6," in A. Dennaux, ed., *John and the Synoptics*, BETL, 101 (Louvain: Louvain University Press, 1992), pp. 261-79; I. Dunderberg, *Johannes und die Synoptiker: Studien zu Joh 1-9* (Helsinki: Suomalainen Tiedeakatemia, 1994), pp. 125-74.

[8] So, besides the authors mentioned in note 3, R. E. Brown, *The Gospel According to John*, 2 vols., AB, 29 (Garden City, N.Y.: Doubleday, 1966), 1:268-94, and M. Gourgues, "Section christologique et section eucharistique en Jean VI - une proposition," *RB* 88 (1989), 515-31.

[9] P. Borgen, *Bread From Heaven: An Exegetical Study of the Concept of Manna in the Gospel of John and the Writings of Philo*, NovTSup, 10 (Leiden: E. J. Brill, 1965).

French semantics and semiotics. Interest is centered around the meaning of signs and their mutual relationship in sense lines and oppositions.[10] Scenic comments are often overlooked. In anglo-saxon research, mainly from the North American continent, such scenic remarks generally find stronger emphasis. Two contributions to John 6 from vol. 26 of *Semeia* (1983) may demonstrate this perspective. Here Gary A. Phillips (see note 15, below) structures the chapter according to actants or groups of acting or speaking subjects in seven sections, with two subsections for the discourse in the Bread of Life: Jesus' discourse with the "multitude" (vv. 22-40) and his discourse with the "Jews" (vv. 41-58). The story of the miraculous feeding is also divided by Phillips into two subsections: Jesus with the disciples (vv. 1-13) and Jesus with the multitude (vv. 14f), so counting Jesus' walking on the sea and the two final sections—vv. 60-65, "many disciples," and vv. 66-71, Peter and the Twelve—we have the seven sections which we mentioned initially. Although the division of the feeding story and the discourse on the Bread of Life in two sections remains doubtful to me, Phillip's proposal contains so many positive elements that I should like to base my own structural analysis largely on it. What I see positively in his proposal is the structuring of Jesus' discourse on the Bread of Life according to interactions between Jesus and his audience. Structuring the discourse in this way is not accepted generally and is accepted only in part by J. Schneider[11] and somewhat more by R. Kieffer. Positive also is Phillip's distinction of scenes according to indications about time, place, participating persons, and the attitude of these persons toward each other, which Phillips adopts from his American tradition of interpretation. Additions and corrections to Phillip's contribution can be found in the article by John D. Crossan in the same volume. He renounces both the division of the feeding story and of the discourse on the Bread of Life into two sections, since he recognizes in the first case the continuity of locale and participating persons, and in the latter the identity of the "multitude" of vv. 22-40 with the "Jews" in v. 41. Important in Crossan's article[12] is the insight that there is an inclusion between the feeding story with Jesus and

---

[10] Cf. besides Gourgues, "Section," and Kieffer, *Johannesevangeliet* (Swedish commentary by a French author); Ph. Roulet and U. Ruegg, "Étude de Jean 6. La narration et l'histoire de la rédaction," in Kaestli, Poffet, and Zumstein, ed., *La communauté johannique* (see note 7), pp. 231-47; J. Calloud and F. Genuyt, *L'Évangile de Jean*, vol. 1 (L'Arbresle: Centre Thomas More; Lyon: Centre pour l'Analyse du Discours Religieux, 1989); X. Léon-Dufour, *Lecture de l'Évangile selon Jean*, vol. 2 (Paris: du Seuil, 1990).

[11] J. Schneider, "Zur Frage der Komposition von Joh 6, 27 - 58 (59)," W. Schmauch, ed., *In memoriam E. Lohmeyer* (Stuttgart: Evangelisches Verlagswerk, 1951), pp. 132-42. Cf. also J. A. Grassi, "Eating Jesus' Flesh and Drinking His Blood: The Centrality and Meaning of John 6:51-58," *BTB* 17 (1987), 24-30, here pp. 25f.; T. L. Brodie, *The Gospel According to John* (New York and Oxford: Oxford University Press, 1993).

[12] J. D. Crossan, "It Is Written: A Structuralist Analysis of John 6," in: D. Patte, ed., *Narrative and Discourse in Structural Exegesis: John 6 and 1 Thessalonians*, Semeia, 26 (Chico: Scholars Press, 1983), pp. 3-21, here p. 4.

the disciples as actants in 6:1-15 and the conclusion of the chapter in 6:66-71, where we again find Jesus with the smaller group of his disciples (here the "Twelve") alone. Here we find an orientation of structural research which we should like to pursue.

A. PURPOSE AND METHOD

On the basis of these contributions from international research we should like to elaborate an overall structure of John 6 that abstracts from the prehistory of the chapter. Fundamental for our analysis is the division of the chapter into scenes separated from each other by indications of time and locale, and participating persons and their relations to each other. In this respect the discourse on the Bread of Life will present itself as a literary unit which—with its framing—reaches from v. 22 to v. 59. We shall try to structure it according to the interactions and the dialogue between Jesus and the multitude or the "Jews" respectively, and this will lead us to six subsequent sections. Our working hypothesis, from which we start, supposes that both the chapter as a whole and the discourse on the Bread of Life in its midst form a chiastic pattern, with the discourse at the center of the chapter and the first self-proclamation of Jesus as the "Bread of Life" in v. 35 as the turning point of the discourse.

Our proposal distinguishes itself from previous efforts to find a concentric structure in John 6[13] mainly by the fact that it takes its starting point from the scenic structure of the chapter and not primarily from semantic observations. Such observations shall be added to our analysis only secondarily. We also leave aside a detailed linguistic and syntactic analysis of the chapter since our interest is focused on a first orientation to the text. We shall emphasize particularly references to time and locale in our text, but also participating persons and groups of persons. Within the discourse also references to the supposed time and locale in the speech itself will turn out to be useful indicators for determining the structure of the text. In addition, the change of grammatical subject will be important. So, the indicators of the narrative framework find their correspondence within the direct speech and turn out to be relevant for the structure of the text. We may add some formal observations concerning individual subsections, like inclusions, chiasms, or parallelisms.

---

[13] Cf. M. Girard, "L'unité de composition de Jean 6, au regard de l'analyse structurelle," *EeT* (O) 13 (1982), 79-110; Calloud-Genuyt, *Évangile*, p. 138; Crossan, "It Is Written," p. 15 (with at least a threefold division of the text); M. Roberge, "La composition de Jean 6.25b-34," *LTP* 50 (1994), 171-86.

The axial arrangement which emerges from our research does not mean that the real message of the chapter has to be found at the turning point, that is to say in the very center of the discourse. The only thing we can say is that here the central subject of the discourse that is relevant for the understanding of the whole discourse is expressed particularly clearly. In respect to text pragmatics, the chapter leads without doubt toward the concluding section: the decision of faith in "God's Holy One" who reveals himself in his word and offers himself in bread and wine. The situation of decision comes out more and more clearly from the middle of the chapter, so particularly the second half of the chapter will show a movement toward the end.

B. THE SCENIC GENERAL STRUCTURE

The narrator's references to time, locale, and participating persons already allow a preliminary division of the chapter into scenes. The general indications about time, which situate the reported events either according to absolute chronology (in the evening, in the morning) or to a relative one (after this, on behalf of this), seem to be particularly relevant. Such indications appear in vv. 1, 16, 22, 60, and 66. In v. 1, the narrator refers to chapter 5 with a vague "after this." The reference to "Passover, the great Jewish festival" in v. 4 situates the content of the narrative in theological perspective and does not form the beginning of a new narrative unit. The temporal clause in v. 12 forms a transition inside the feeding story, but does not lead to a new section as such, since the locale, the participating persons, and the quality of interaction remain unchanged. The same holds true of the sequence of events in the three following verses.

Important again is the chronological reference in v. 16. It locates the following events according to absolute chronology: it is "at nightfall." That "darkness had fallen" in v. 17 does not add anything particular to this setting. There are no more temporal references until v. 22. Here, the next morning has been reached. In the entire dialogue between Jesus and the multitude of the "Jews" up to v. 58 there are no further temporal references on the level of the narrative framework. We only have reactions from Jesus' listeners that lead to a continuation of Jesus' discourse.

We come next to temporal references with the two formulas of introduction in vv. 60 and 66. With the concluding remark in v. 59, the discourse on the Bread of Life has come to an end. The following participle, connected with οὖν refers to the discourse and reports the reaction of many of the listeners. In a similar way in v. 66 we hear about a new reaction from the disciples of Jesus to the words of Jesus caused by the previous critical reaction. The initial ἐκ τούτου has at least some temporal connotation and separates the section that extends to v. 71 from the preceding one. With the μετὰ ταῦτα we have—as with the one at 6:1—the beginning of a new section in the macro context. References to the locale complement our observations about the temporal structure of the chapter and confirm our previous results. The territory beyond the Sea of Galilee or of Tiberias, which is named in 6:1, forms the framework for the feeding story through v. 15. The mention of the "mountain" that Jesus went up in vv. 3 and 15 forms an inclusion within this story. This mountain has to be located within the territory mentioned previously.

The following story of the walking on the sea is held together by references to the sea (here called θάλασσα). The local name, "Capernaum" in v. 17, seems to be anticipated and prepares for the mention of the place in the next section. Further local references inside the section describe vertical and horizontal movements of the disciples and of Jesus; they go down to the sea (v. 16), enter the boat (v. 17), and row about 25 or 30 stadia (v. 19). Jesus first does not come and then comes to them walking on the sea (vv. 17 and 19), and immediately they reach the opposite shore (v. 21). All this takes place in a sequence of events that is held together by the sea.

More difficult to determine are the local references in the next verses. Since authors generally do not place the beginning of the discourse on the Bread of Life before v. 26, they consider vv. 22-25 to be a transitional section.[14] The concluding remark in v. 59 about the locale of the event in the synagogue of Capernaum appears to some interpreters to be unmotivated and insufficiently prepared. But it probably concludes not only the controversial dialogue of Jesus with the "Jews" in vv. 41-58, but the whole dialogue composition from v. 22. The mention of Capernaum in v. 24 (with the preparation in v. 17) at the end of the verses which prepare for the first word from the multitude in v. 25, seems to bear some importance. The additional boats, which appear in v. 23 a bit like a "deus ex machina," allow the multitude to get from the other shore to Capernaum and to seek and to find Jesus there. That they meet Jesus in the synagogue is neither affirmed nor denied, but follows from v. 59.

In the verses 60-71 the remark in v. 66 seems to be of some significance: from this moment on many of Jesus' disciples turned away from Jesus (literally "drew back") and did not follow him any longer. On the one hand, it spells out the consequence of the complaint of many disciples among the listeners in v. 60. On the other, it forms a transition to the decision of the

---

[14] See for instance Schnackenburg, *Johannesevangelium*, 2:43; Brown, *John*, 1:257 (vv. 22-24). What has been rightly observed is that the multitude's question in v. 25 alludes to Jesus' surprising appearance on the other shore. So the multitude did not understand Jesus' walking on the sea as a sign, as it had not understood the multiplication of the loaves as a sign. The positive role of this sign as such is played down by M. Roberge, "Jean 6, 26 et le rassasiement eschatologique," *LTP* 45 (1989), 339-49.

Twelve claimed by Jesus. So the remark of v. 66 separates the subsections vv. 60-65 and 66-71 from each other and connects them at the same time.

The picture we have achieved so far becomes clearer when we look at the participating persons or groups of persons in the different scenes. Vv. 1-15 are held together by the naming of the multitude, the disciples of Jesus, some disciples named individually (Philip and Andrew, brother of Simon Peter), and the boy with the five barley loaves and the two fish. In vv. 16-21 we see Jesus alone. In vv. 22-59 the disciples do not appear (although their presence has to be supposed because of vv. 60-71), but we find Jesus in dialogue with the multitude (vv. 22-40) or with the "Jews" (vv. 41-58). Vv. 60-65 speak of an interchange between Jesus and certain disciples who had belonged to the audience of the discourse of the Bread of Life. In vv. 66-71 the number of the disciples who had been bewildered is isolated from the group of the Twelve, and they are addressed separately with Peter as speaker and Judas Iscariot as a negative contrasting figure.

Precisely these persons or groups of persons allow us to correlate the five scenes we have obtained so far (vv. 1-15, 16-21, 22-59, 60-65, 66-71) in a concentric pattern. Only in the first and the last scene do we encounter disciples named individually. Jesus' relation to them can be characterized in a way similar to that proposed by G. A. Phillips:[15] as Jesus puts Philip on trial with his initial question in v. 5 (see v. 6!), so in v. 67 he forces his disciples to decide for or against him. Peter's confession of faith in vv. 68f. does not find a correspondence in such a confession from the disciples, but rather in the word of the multitude calling Jesus the Prophet who was to come into the world (v. 14). Of course, this word remains ambiguous, as the following verse shows, and for the moment Jesus remains alone. The disciples sail away without him.

Linguistically the number twelve connects the first and the last scene (we encounter the word only here in John with the exception of 11:9 and 20:24); so the twelve baskets prepare for the faith of the group of Twelve. Theologically there is a progression from faith based on signs which have been seen (vv. 2 and 14) to faith based on the word of Jesus (v. 68). The title "God's Holy One" in the final sections goes beyond the one of the "Prophet" who was to come into the world in the first section.

There is less contact between the second scene (vv. 16-21) and the fourth one (vv. 60-65). The most important element is the "disciples." In both scenes none of them is named individually. The situation is comparable. Again there is a test of faith. In both cases the disciples, or some of them, are moving away from Jesus. The comforting coming of Jesus walking on the sea corresponds to the challenging word of Jesus calling for decision in the second section (vv. 60-65). Both sections have in

---

[15] G. A. Phillips, "'This Is a Hard Saying: Who Can Be Listener to it?' Creating a Reader in John 6," in D. Patte, ed., *Narrative and Discourse in Structural Exegesis: John 6 & 1 Thessalonians*, Semeia, 26 (Chico: Scholars Press, 1983), pp. 23-56, here pp. 30, 42.

common the "seeing," related to Jesus—in the first instance seeing Jesus as the one who came down from them mountain and approached his disciples (v. 19), in the second seeing him as the one who is parting and ascending (to his Father, v. 62).

So we have in the center the discourse on the Bread of Life with its framing in vv. 22-59. It refers to the double narrative of vv. 1-15, 16-21, and it prepares the two sections about the decision of faith in vv. 60-65, 66-71.

C. THE STRUCTURE OF THE DISCOURSE ON THE BREAD OF LIFE

That the discourse on the Bread of Life encompasses vv. 22-59 is not generally agreed upon. Because of the self-identification of Jesus as the "Bread of Life," many interpreters make the discourse start in v. 35.[16] Others see the beginning in v. 31 or 32, where the subject of the Bread from Heaven occurs for the first time.[17] Still other interpreters recognize with good reasons the connection between v. 27 and the concluding section of the discourse (vv. 52-58) and make the discourse start in v. 27.[18] In our opinion, the scenic composition of the discourse has to be respected as well when we ask for its overall structure. Six times we encounter a speech or a word of Jesus by which he answers a question, a word, or a reaction of his listeners. The first interchange is introduced from v. 22 onward.[19] The multitude is described on its way to Capernaum seeking Jesus. This quest culminates in the first question of the multitude in v. 25, which is answered by Jesus' first response in vv. 26f.

The conclusion of the discourse is clearly marked by v. 59. According to Carl J. Bjerkelund we have here a "clause of precision," such as we find elsewhere in the Gospel of John and in comparable texts of its literary milieu. With this sentence, not only a section of the discourse but the discourse as a whole is located and situated in the history of salvation. Since, according to Bjerkelund, in the preceding discourse of Jesus there is no sufficient basis for a real new start (likewise the transition from the

[16] So among others Brown, *John*, 1:268; Girard, "L'unité."

[17] So Borgen, *Bread from Heaven*; cf. Schenke, "Struktur."

[18] So Bultmann, *Das Evangelium des Johannes*, p. 161; Schneider, "Frage"; C. J. Bjerkelund, *Tauta Egeneto: Die Präzisierungssätze im Johannesevangelium*, WUNT, 40 (Tübingen: J. C. B. Mohr, 1987), p. 90; starting already with v. 26 Schnackenburg, *Johannesevangelium*, 2:43; Lindars, *John*, p. 249; Haenchen, *Johannesevangelium*, p. 316; Roulet and Ruegg, "Étude," p. 235.

[19] The macro context of the discourse starts with v. 22 for Kieffer, *Johannesevangeliet*; C. K. Barrett, *Das Evangelium nach Johannes*, KEK Sonderbund (Göttingen: Vandenhoeck & Ruprecht, 1990; Eng. 2nd ed., Philadelphia: Westminster, 1978), p. 294; cf. Schnackenburg, *Johannesevangelium*, 2:41, and others.

"multitude" [vv. 22-40] to the "Jews" [vv. 41-58] does not seem to be such a basis),[20] we simply have to assume that the whole discourse on the "Bread of Life" has to be located in the synagogue in Capernaum. We only have to recognize (against Bjerkelund), that it does not start as late as v. 27, but is introduced already in v. 22.

If we structure the discourse of Jesus in this way by interchange of speech, we immediately notice strong contacts between the first and the final section with its subsequent "clause of precision," that is between vv. 22-27 on the one hand and vv. 52-59 on the other. The inclusion we find here particularly between v. 27 and the final section has been noticed also by Bjerkelund and other scholars before him.[21] This observation leads us to the question whether the four remaining sections may not betray a similar symmetrical relationship. This seems to be the case in fact, so that there is a correspondence between vv. 28f. and 41-51 as well as between vv. 30-33 and 34-40. Let us start the verification of our hypothesis with the safest starting point, that is to say with the correspondence between vv. 22-27 and the one hand and 52-59 on the other.

The first coincidence which strikes us is the scenic framework, which locates the events at Capernaum (vv. 24 and 59 respectively). This local name does not occur again in the whole of the discourse. The arrival at Capernaum had been prepared for already in v. 17. For the rest this local name occurs only in these two sections.

The temporal reference in v. 22 marks, as we saw, a new greater section. It has not direct equivalent at the end of the discourse except the οὖν in v. 60 which introduces the reaction of many of the listeners.

In the first exchange of dialogue, v. 25 with the question of the crowd and v. 26 with the beginning of Jesus' answer, look back to the two scenes in vv. 1-15 and 16-21. Of course, they also prepare for the following sections. The purpose of these verses is to expose the deeper meaning of the feeding of the multitude, but also of the unexpected appearance of Jesus on the other side of the sea as "signs." What this means concretely is shown by v. 27. It contains a number of elements which occur again in the final section in v. 51 (a thematic announcement of the final section) or 52 to 58 respectively. Such common elements are, among others,

- the mention of the "Son of Man" (in the discourse only vv. 27 and 52)
- the "giving" of a gift by Jesus (in the discourse only v. 27 and 51f.)
- the "food" (βρῶσις) (vv. 27 and 55, only other instance 4:32)
- "remaining" (in the discourse only v. 27 and v. 56).

---

[20] Different from this view: Phillips, "This Is a Hard Saying," pp. 38, 42; Painter, "Tradition," pp. 443f.

[21] See above, note 4.

The linguistic contacts we have shown are too strong to be explained by chance. So, we should consider v. 27 as an announcement of verses 51 or 52 to 58, as do most authors who consider vv. 51c-58 to be a secondary addition. They normally suppose secondary redaction in v. 27 also.

Does this mean that vv. 22-27 have a "eucharistic" meaning? This does not look very probable; they merely allow for such an interpretation. Perhaps there is an indirect hint at the coming eucharistic section in the expression "the bread over which the Lord gave thanks" in v. 23. It appears rather unmotivated in this context, because no reason is given why just this element has been chosen from the preceding feeding story. Apparently the way in which Jesus gave the bread to the crowd, that is to say that he "gave thanks" and so "gave" it to them was important for the narrator in his flashback in v. 23. So, a hidden hint at the eucharistic meaning of the "Bread of Life" in the final section of the discourse is at least possible.

The contacts between the second and the fifth exchange of dialogue (vv. 28f. and 41-51) are less obvious and undoubtedly weaker than those between the first and the last. The connection between the first and the second exchange of dialogue is given by the theme of "working" (ἐργάζεσθαι). The listeners have heard that they should work for something, but they have not understood for what. They want to do "the works of God." Jesus makes clear to them that they do not have to do a number of pious works but only have to allow God to do his one work. The genitive, "the work of God," refers here to God as acting subject rather than as someone who claims the work (cf. 4:34; 17:4).[22] The only work which God will do consists in faith in the one whom he has sent.

If we understand our little section this way, it prepares in fact for vv. 41-51. Here again there is talk about the one who has "sent" Jesus (v. 44, here expressed by the verb πέμπω instead of ἀποστέλλω; the verb occurs also in vv. 38f.) or "from whom" Jesus is (v. 46), but he is interpreted here as the Bread which came from heaven. Again there is talk of the necessity of faith (v. 47, cf. previously vv. 30, 35f., 40). Particularly striking is the common idea that coming to Jesus or faith respectively appears as God's work (see above to v. 29 and cf. vv. 44f.). This idea is found only in these two subsections. If the "Jews" mentioned in v. 41 think they can know about the origin of Jesus by referring to Joseph as his father and to his mother, just by this opinion they block their access to knowledge about his true origin and mission. It seems that precisely this apparent knowledge makes "Jews" (vv. 41, 52) out of the "people" who are still open in the decision for Jesus (vv. 22, 24).

In the third and fourth exchange of dialogue (vv. 30-33, 34-40) the contacts also remain more conceptual than verbal, at least in the sense that we hardly meet expressions which are limited to these two sections. The

---

[22] Cf. Brown, *John*, 1:262 (as a possibility); Kieffer, *Johannesevangeliet*, 1:168.

connection of the third exchange of dialogue with the second one is made by the resumption of the theme of "working." The crowds have not grasped the invitation of Jesus to permit the work of God to be realized in them, so they ask again for a sign worked by Jesus so that he might be legitimized in their eyes. Again, they refer to a scriptural quotation that has not yet been located with certainty (vv. 30f.). The basis of their argument is that seeing a sign can lead to faith in a prophet. Apparently they are little bothered by the fact that they just now have been witnesses of such a sign. Jesus does not answer their demand directly, but rather refers to the sign just worked, vis. the bread given by God himself, not Moses, and this not once upon a time but now. It is qualified as "true," "real" bread, "which gives life to the world." Important here is the transition from an event in the past, which helped only a limited number of human beings for a certain time, to an event in the present with universal salvific importance.

The crowds, according to their intervention in v. 34, have only grasped that Jesus offers a heavenly bread, a gift of God, for the present. So their only request is that Jesus might give them this bread forever. With this they remain on the level of the request of the Samaritan woman to conceives Jesus' water of life as a fountain to fill her jar (cf. 4:15). But Jesus promises a food that does not allow hunger or thirst any longer. New here in v. 35 is Jesus' self-identification with the "Bread of Life." As in vv. 30-35 there is here a connection between seeing and believing. It has only been modified: the task is no longer to come to faith by seeing a sign—the Bread of Life given by God—but to recognize the Bread from Heaven in the person of Jesus and to believe in him (vv. 36 and 40). Precisely in this consists the decisive correspondence, but also the fundamental difference between vv. 30-33 and 34-40.

Of course, many in the crowd proved unable to encounter Jesus in this way. This fact is not simply due to their personal failure, but to their lack of the gift of faith in Jesus. Otherwise, by seeing Jesus they would have come to faith and would have found in him eternal life—leading to the future resurrection of the dead on the last day.

If we bring the two sections vv. 30-33 and 34-40 to this short common denominator, we see clearly their correspondence. The subject is on the one side seeing the Bread from Heaven and believing, on the other the origin of the Bread from heaven and its identity. At the turning point there is the first self-identification of Jesus as "the Bread of Life" (v. 35). It fills with content what is meant by the "Bread from Heaven," and at the same time prepares for the second half of the discourse on the Bread of Life, in which Jesus first appears as the "true Bread from Heaven," before the thought finally returns to the bread, which Jesus at the same time is and gives (vv. 53-58).[23]

D. SUMMARY

The discourse on the Bread of Life with its narrative framework has turned out as a coherent and well-structured literary unit. The two miracle stories at the beginning (vv. 1-15, 16-21) along with the double narrative about the consequences of the discourse (vv. 60-65, 66-71) form a double frame into which the discourse itself (vv. 22-59) seems to be integrated. The discourse itself seems to be built chiastically around the first self-predication of Jesus, "I am the Bread of Life," in v. 35 as beginning of the fourth of six exchanges of dialogue between Jesus and the crowd or the "Jews" respectively. Here we notice strong correspondences between the first and the last exchange of dialogue and remarkable correspondences between the second and the fifth as well as between the third and the fourth respectively. The framing of the discourse by vv. 22-27 and 52-59 turned out probable particularly because of the function of v. 27 as preannouncement of vv. 52-59. This correspondence was the starting point for our research into the parallel arrangement of the following subsections. Here we showed at least indications of a further parallelism between the scenes. Undoubtedly, work will have to continue on this subject.

If these conclusions should prove correct, this would be a strong argument for the internal coherence of the existing discourse on the Bread of Life including its so-called "eucharistic" section. "Eating" and "Drinking" of flesh and blood of the Son of Man would no longer be a eucharistic alternative to faith in Jesus as the Bread of Life, but the concrete form in which faith in Jesus is practiced in the celebration of the community. Particularly vv. 60-71 show that the controversy confronted not only the "Jewish" listeners but also and above all the group of his disciples with the necessity of making a decision about Jesus.

The framing of the whole chapter by sections particularly interested in the disciples (vv. 1-15, 16-21 on the one side, and vv. 60-65, 66-71 on the other) highlights the pragmatic interest of the author in leading the disciples to a decision of faith. This faith, in turn, has to grow from a belief based on

---

[23] A turning point of the discourse is also seen in v. 35 by M. J. J. Menken, *Numerical Literary Techniques in John*, NovTSup, 55 (Leiden: E. J. Brill, 1985), pp. 138-88. From this moment onwards Jesus' dialogue partners do not talk with him any longer, but only with each other. Less convincing appears to us Menken's proposal to start a new section with v. 51c and his recourse to numerical statistics. For the scriptural quotations in John 6 see now his recent fine contribution, *Old Testament Quotations in the Fourth Gospel: Studies in Textual Form*, Contributions to Biblical Exegesis and Theology, 15 (Kampen, NL: Pharos, 1996).

the seeing of signs to a faith that is finally based on the word of Jesus: "Lord, to whom shall we go? Your words are words of eternal life" (v. 68).

THE FUNCTION OF PROLEPSIS
IN THE INTERPRETATION OF JOHN 6

Francis J. Moloney, SDB

Two problems interlock in all scholarly discussion of John 6:1-71: the content of Jesus' discourse as a whole, and the interpretation of 6:51c-58. Is the discourse eucharistic? If not, what is the role of vv. 51c-58, where the eucharistic themes of eating and drinking are found? Was this section added to an originally sapiential discourse?[1]

A. READING JOHN 6:1-71

John 6 is a story which forms part of a larger story. The scene is set in vv. 1-4, as place, time, characters, and setting are established. From vv. 5-15 the reader encounters the report of the multiplication of the loaves and fishes and its aftermath. Jesus, the disciples, and the crowd go in different directions as the disciples cross the sea, only to be met by Jesus in the midst of a storm, and brought safely to land in vv. 16-21. Thus far the narrative flows along logical lines.[2] In vv. 22-24, the elements provided in vv. 1-4 (place, time, characters, and setting) are again established. The original location and grouping of vv. 1-4 have been upset by the voyage of the disciples and their encounter with Jesus in vv. 16-21. All three characters (Jesus, the crowds, and the disciples) have gone their separate ways by v. 17, although Jesus has rejoined the disciples by v. 21. In order to involve the people, the disciples, and Jesus in a discussion and a discourse over the bread from heaven, which has the miracle of the gift of the bread (vv. 5-15)

---

[1] For a survey of the discussion see F. J. Moloney, *The Johannine Son of Man,* 2nd ed.; BibScRel 14 (Rome: Libreria Ateneo Salesiano, 1978), pp. 89-95. For scholarship since then, see M. Roberge, "Le discours sue le pain de vie, Jean 6,22-59. Problèmes d'interprétation," *LTP* 38 (1982), 265-99, and M. J. J. Menken, "John 6,51c-58: Eucharist or Christology," *Bib* 74 (1993), 1-6.

[2] There are, of course, quite a few historical and exegetical difficulties. The miracle of the multiplication, followed by an encounter on the sea follows the Synoptic order of these events, and there are some close contacts, especially between the Johannine and the Markan accounts of the feeding miracle (see Mark 6:31-44; 8:1-10). For an analysis which details these parallels, and supports some form of dependence upon the Synoptic tradition, see C. K. Barrett, *The Gospel According to St John: An Introduction with Commentary and Notes on the Greek Text* (London: SPCK, 1978), pp. 271-78. See also U. Schnelle, *Antidocetic Christology in the Gospel of John: An Investigation of the Place of the Fourth Gospel in the Johannine School* (Minneapolis: Fortress Press, 1992), pp. 105-07, 111-12. Schnelle suggests that the John 6:1-15 rests on a pre-Markan narrative, but had its own Johannine development while 6:16-21 is independent. For a detailed and comprehensive rejection of any theory of dependence, see C. H. Dodd, *Historical Tradition in the Fourth Gospel* (Cambridge: Cambridge University Press, 1963), pp. 253-87; R. E. Brown, *The Gospel according to John,* AB 29-29a (Garden City, NY: Doubleday, 1966-1970), 1:236-44.

as its point of reference, the groups must be reunited. Thus vv. 22-24 must be read as a second introductory passage.

The division of the discourse on the bread from heaven follows criteria provided by the movement of the discussion between Jesus and the crowd and "the Jews." On six occasions, first the crowd and then "the Jews" pose questions to Jesus (vv. 25, 28, 30, 34, 41-42, 52).[3] These questions steer Jesus' discourse in a slightly different direction, until it is closed by the narrator's remark: "This he said in the synagogue, as he taught at Capernaum" (v. 59). Indeed, John 6:25-59 is not properly a discourse; it is more a series of brief discourses, united around the theme of the bread from heaven, which unfolds under the stimulation of questions posed to Jesus.[4]

A final scene is dedicated to the response of the disciples to the word of Jesus, and from within the wider group of the disciples, to the further response of the Twelve (vv. 60-71). In this finale to the chapter κρίσις comes into play. The reader has, on earlier occasions, read of the division which the presence of Jesus would create (see especially 3:11-21, 31-36; 5:27-29). In 6:60-71 it takes place among the disciples as they respond to the word of Jesus.[5]

In terms of its overall shape, and on the basis of indications within the text, the narrative of John 6 unfolds in the following six-stage fashion:

1. *6:1-4:* An introduction to the narrative (where? when? who? why?).

2. *6:5-15:* The account of the miracle of the loaves and fishes which leads to the crowd's decision that Jesus is the one who is to come, Jesus' awareness that they wish to make him king, and his flight from that place.

3. *6:16-21:* Jesus, who has ascended the mountain in v. 15 is no longer present. The disciples leave the crowd and set off across the sea. In the midst of a storm, Jesus comes to them, reveals himself to them as ἐγώ εἰμι, and they come safely to shore.

---

[3] J. Painter, *The Quest for the Messiah,* 2nd ed. (Edinburgh: T. &. T. Clark, 1993), pp. 278-79, argues that (among other things) this shift from the crowd to "the Jews" indicates two stages in the composition of the discourse. The earlier stage is marked by a misunderstanding quest, while the latter by hostility and rejection.

[4] C. J. Bjerkelund, *Tauta Egeneto: Die Präzisierungssätze im Johannesevangelium,* WUNT 40 (Tübingen: J. C. B. Mohr [Paul Siebeck], 1987), pp. 89-93, and X. Léon-Dufour, *Lecture de l'Evangile selon Jean,* 2 vols., Parole de Dieu (Paris: Editions du Seuil, 1990), 2:128, point to the mention of Capernaum in v. 24 and v. 59 as indicating the external limits of the discourse.

[5] For a survey of scholarly opinion on the structure of John 6, see M. J. J. Menken, *Numerical Literary Techniques in John: The Fourth Evangelist's Use of Numbers of Words and Syllables,* NovTSup 55 (Leiden: E. J. Brill, 1985), pp. 186-88.

4. *6:22-24:* A second introduction (where? when? who? why?).

5. *6:25-59:* The discourse on the bread from heaven. It takes the form of a discussion between Jesus and the crowds and "the Jews," where the latter raise a series of misunderstanding questions or statements which enable the thematic development of the discourse. More attention will be given to the internal shape of the discourse below, but the themes dealt with are determined by the following interventions from either the crowd or "the Jews":
   - v. 25: "Rabbi, when did you come here?"
   - v. 30: "Then what sign do you do?"
   - v. 34: "Sir, give us this bread always."
   - v. 42: "Is this not Jesus, the son of Joseph, whose father and mother we know? How does he now say, 'I have come down from heaven?'"
   - v. 52: "How can this man give us his flesh to eat?"

6. *6:60-71:* A κρίσις is created by the word of Jesus, and there are two responses:
   (a) vv. 60-65: "Many of the disciples" find the word of Jesus too hard, and leave him.
   (b) vv. 66-71: Peter, in the name of the Twelve, confesses that Jesus alone has the words of eternal life. But even among those who commit themselves to the word of Jesus, there is the possibility of failure, as Jesus warns of Judas' future betrayal.

This reading of John 6 argues for its unity. The epoch-making study of P. Borgen convinces me that the so-called discourse is a homiletic midrash upon a text provided by Jesus' interlocutors in v. 31: "He gave them bread from heaven to eat."[6] The first part of the discourse (vv. 32-48) is a

---

[6] There is no Old Testament passage which explicitly states: "He gave them bread from heaven to eat," and various suggestions have been made. Borgen claims that Exod. 16:4, 15 are combined to form the text, while Exod. 16:2 is used in the midrashic paraphrase (P. Borgen, *Bread from Heaven: An Exegetical Study of the Conception of Manna in the Gospel of John and the Writings of Philo*, NovTSup 10 (Leiden: E. J. Brill, 1965), pp. 40-42. See also E. D. Freed, *Old Testament Quotations in the Gospel of John*, NovTSup 11 (Leiden: E. J. Brill, 1965), pp. 11-16; J.-N. Aletti, "Le discours sur le pain de vie. La Fonction des citations de L'Ancien Testament," *RSR* 62 (1974), 190-191; G. Reim, *Studien zum alttestamentlichen Hintergrund des Johannesevangeliums*, SNTSMS 22 (Cambridge: Cambridge University Press, 1974), pp. 12-15. Not all would agree. Notably, C. K. Barrett, "The Flesh of the Son of Man," in *Essays on John* (London: SPCK, 1982), pp. 39-40, and Painter, *Quest*, pp. 271-73, have argued for Ps. 78:24. For details of this debate at an earlier stage, see Moloney, *Son of Man*, p. 96 n. 63. Rightly, F. Manns comments: "Il s'agit vraisemblablement de text d'Ex 16.4 et 16,15, passage qui sera médité dans le Ps 78,24 et en Ne 9,15" (*L'Evangile de Jean à la lumière du Judaïsme*, Studium Biblicum Franciscanum Analecta 33 [Jerusalem: Franciscan Printing Press, 1991], p. 153).

midrashic paraphrase of the words of Scripture: "He gave them bread from heaven," while the latter part (vv. 49-58, some of which [vv. 51c-58 is often regarded as a later introduction of eucharistic material)[7] is a midrashic paraphrase of the words of Scripture: "to eat." Over the latter part of the discourse, a paraphrase of the earlier words ("he gave them bread from heaven") continues, but the paraphrase of the action of eating predominates.[8]

B. READING THE PROLEPSES IN JOHN 6

1. The Prolepsis of 6:12-13[9]

The account of the miraculous provision of food for the multitude largely follows the traditional shape of a miracle: the problem is stated, the miracle is worked and there is a reaction of wonder from those present.[10] But the author insinuates another perspective into the telling of this traditional story. A major element in this is the treatment of the κλάσματα, the gathering of the broken pieces, so that they might not perish in vv. 12-13. The account of gathering the fragments uses words which were used in the early Church to speak of the Eucharistic assemblies. Τὰ κλάσματα was used to speak of the eucharistic species (Didache 9:3, 4).[11] Similarly, συνάγειν (vv. 12, 13) was used to indicate the gathering of the faithful at the Eucharistic celebration (Didache 9:4; 1 Clement 34:7, and Ignatius, Letter to Polycarp 4:2).[12] Given the eucharistic hints behind vv. 1-15 as a whole, some connection with the celebration of the Eucharist is present, but we must not lose contact with the

---

[7] On this discussion, see Moloney, Son of Man, pp. 98-107.

[8] See Borgen, Bread from Heaven, pp. 28-57. For a summary, see Moloney, Son of Man, pp. 95-98.

[9] A prolepsis is a form of "anachrony" (Genette) which occurs when the regular sequence of events (story time) is disrupted by reference to events which look to the future for their resolution. Another form of anachrony (also called "narrative time") is a looking back to events which happened before the time of the story. This is called "analepsis." On the temporal features of narrative, see G. Genette, Narrative Discourse: An Essay in Method (Ithaca: Cornell University Press, 1980), pp. 33-84. See also S. Rimmon-Kenan, Narrative Fiction: Contemporary Poetics, New Accents (London: Methuen, 1983), pp. 46-51; M. G. Brett, "The Future of Reader Criticisms?" The Open Text: New Directions for Biblical Studies? ed. F. Watson (London: SCM Press, 1993), pp. 13-31. Brett's remarks on "Chronological Reading: A Distinctive Method" (pp. 17-20) apply to this reading of John 6. See also below, note 22.

[10] On this, see R. Bultmann, The History of the Synoptic Tradition (Oxford: Blackwell, 1968), pp. 218-31. See also idem, The Gospel of John: A Commentary (Oxford: Blackwell, 1972), pp. 210-11.

[11] On the close relationship between the Johannine details and the eucharistic prayer in the Didache, see C. F. D. Moule, "A Note on Didache IX 4," JTS 6 (1955), 240-43; Brown, John, 1:247-48.

[12] For the references, see Barrett, St John, pp. 276-77.

flow of the world of the narrative in our search for a world behind it. While it is sometimes claimed that the text means "the gathering by God of his elect,"[13] this may be reading too much into it. The reader reads nothing more than the gathering of the κλάσματα by the disciples.[14]

Jesus has fed a multitude in a way that recalls a Christian celebration of the Eucharist, but this feeding has taken place at Passover time, when the gift of the manna was recalled. The disciples are commanded to gather the fragments of this original meal, ἵνα μή τι ἀπόληται. The author uses language which recalls the practice of the Exodus people, gathering the manna each day, and eating it until they have had their fill (see Exod. 16:8, 16, 18, 21).[15] Unlike the Markan account, Jesus shows no interest in gathering the fragments of τὰ ὀψάρια, only of τὰ κλάσματα (see Mark 6:43).[16] However, in the desert, Moses commands that the manna was not to be stored. Any manna that was collected and put away perished (Exod 16:20-21). But the bread provided by Jesus will not perish.[17] Jesus' gift to people who come to him in search of bread (see v. 5) must not be lost, and the disciples are to see to its preservation: "Gather up the fragments left over, that nothing may be lost" (v. 12).

Often in Johannine sacramental material, the author is concerned to show the reader, now distant from the events in the story, that she or he is still part of the story.[18] This is the point of Jesus' final command to his disciples who do as they are told. The language used by the narrator makes it clear to the reader that the κλάσματα are still available, and that these fragments come directly from this feeding miracle as "the Passover, the feast of the Jews, was at hand" (v. 4). The disciples gather (συνήγαγον), they fill (ἐγέμισαν) twelve baskets with the κλάσματα from the five barley loaves (see v. 9) which had been left by those who had eaten (v. 13). The author has linked the present reader of the text with the people in the

---

[13] Barrett, *St John*, p. 277; J. M. Perry, "The Evolution of the Johannine Eucharist," *NTS* 39 (1993), 25. Against this, see Léon-Dufour, *Lecture*, 2:113 n. 42; Dodd, *Tradition*, p. 268.

[14] This is certainly the case for the implied reader. Centuries of reading within a Christian community may lead a real reader to see eucharistic overtones. See below, note 22. Much is made of the Jewish notion of God's blessing in the gift of the surplus. See D. Daube, *The New Testament and Rabbinic Judaism* (London: Athlone, 1956), pp. 36-51; Dodd, *Tradition*, p. 424 n. 4. While there may be traces of this, there is no mention of "surplus," but τὰ κλάσματα.

[15] The verb συνάγειν is used by Moses as he directs the Israelites to gather manna in LXX Exod. 16:16.

[16] See Brown, *John*, 1:234.

[17] See Léon-Dufour, *Lecture*, 2:112-13. Only on the Sabbath eve were the Israelites allowed to collect for two days, as no manna was provided on the Sabbath (see Exod. 16:22-30).

[18] Implied, intended, and real readers are being involved in the story. See below, note 22. On this, see F. J. Moloney, "When is John Talking about Sacraments?" *AusBR* 30 (1982), 10-33.

story who had eaten. Looking back to the fundamental text of Exod. 16, the reader is informed that, unlike the manna in the desert given by God to the ancestors of Israel, the κλάσματα given by Jesus on the occasion of the Passover feast have not perished. The traditional number 12 indicates a collection complete in itself,[19] and this collection of κλάσματα is gathered by the disciples, obedient to the command of Jesus. As the Jewish feast of the Passover approaches, Jesus provides a miraculous feeding for a multitude. The reader senses, from the beginning of the narrative (vv. 5-6) that this feeding is linked to a food which only Jesus can give. The disciples are unable to transcend the purely physical impossibility of feeding such a crowd (vv. 5, 7). Paralleling, and yet surpassing the gift of the manna in the desert (see Exod. 16; Lev. 11), Jesus feeds the multitude, and begins a feeding that endures, as the fragments are gathered into 12 baskets. Is it mere chance that the only other uses of the number "12" in the Johannine narrative are associated with "the Twelve," mentioned at the close of the account of the events beside the lake (see 6:67, 70-71) and in localising Thomas as "one of the Twelve" (20:24)? A Christian reader may sense that the enduring availability of τὰ κλάσματα is in some way associated with believing (6:67-69) and failing (6:69-70; 20:24) disciples.

2. The Prolepsis of 6:27

On arrival at the discussions between Jesus, the crowd and "the Jews" at Capernaum, the reader has encountered two introductions (vv. 1-4, 22-24) which answered the questions, who? where? when? and why? and two miracle stories (vv. 5-15, 16-21) which were shaped in an identical fashion: a setting, a problem, the miraculous actions and words of Jesus and a response. The discourse, interspersed with questions, has its own shape, determined by its unique literary form within the overall story of the deeds and words of Jesus on the occasion of the celebration of the Jewish feast of the Passover.

A closer reading of the several interventions and the words of Jesus which follow them discloses the following narrative shape:[20]

vv. 25-29: "Rabbi, when did you come here?" (v. 25). This trivial question leads Jesus to instruct on the need to search for the food which endures to eternal life, belief in the one whom God has sent. This sets

---

[19] See Léon-Dufour, *Lecture*, 2:111-12.

[20] This is not to accept the suggestions of B. Gärtner, *John 6 and the Jewish Passover,* ConNT 17 (Lund: Gleerup, 1959); E. J. Kilmartin, "Liturgical Influence on John 6," *CBQ* 22 (1960), 183-91, and D. Daube, *The New Testament and Rabbinic Literature,* pp. 36-51, 158-69, that the questions and answers echo the Jewish Passover *Haggadah.* They form part of the Johannine misunderstanding technique. On this, see Brown, *John,* 1:266-67.

the theme for the rest of the discourse: the search for the true bread from heaven which gives eternal life.

vv. 30-33: "Then what sign do you do?" (v. 30). Jesus is asked for miracle working credentials which surpass Moses' gift of manna in the wilderness (vv. 30-31). Jesus points to the gift of another bread from heaven, the true bread from heaven, perfecting the former gift of God in the Manna dispensed by Moses.

vv. 34-40: "Lord, give us this bread always" (v. 34). Responding to a demand for a bread that will fulfil the crowd's limited understanding of its needs, Jesus presents himself as the true bread from heaven, the only one able to make God known and give eternal life.

vv. 41-51: "Is not this Jesus, the son of Joseph, whose father and mother we know? How does he now say, 'I have come down from heaven'" (v. 42). The question of origins is explored. Jesus is able to give the bread from heaven which will raise up the believer to eternal life because he comes from heaven. His flesh is the bread which gives life to the world.

vv. 52-59: "How can this man give us his flesh to eat?" (v. 52). A final question leads to Jesus' teaching on the need to eat the flesh and to drink the blood of the Son of Man, the bread sent by the Father which perfects the bread given to the ancestors in the desert.

The strategic location of statements, questions or objections from Jesus' interlocutors is fundamental to the narrative shape of the discourse-discussion of the bread from heaven.[21] The reader follows the words of Jesus as he responds to the queries and objection of his interlocutors. This reading produces an ever-deepening appreciation of Jesus' presentation of himself as the true bread from heaven.[22]

---

[21] Menken, *Numerical,* pp. 159-60, is opposed to this. He claims "the interruptions in 6,41-42.52 do not have a function in the progression of the discourse." I attempt to show that they do in Chapter 2 of my *Signs and Shadows: Reading John* 5-12 (Minneapolis: Fortress Press, 1996).

[22] I am using "reader" in a number of ways. Some clarification is called for. My primary concern in this paper is to trace the implied reader (generally simply "reader"). This heuristic device is a sequential or chronological reader who does not know what will happen later in the narrative flow. However, the Johannine implied reader is already credited with a basic knowledge of the Christian story. Elements of the story are presupposed as known as they are never explained: e.g. baptism (1:33; 3:3-5), messianic hopes fulfilled in Jesus (1:35-51) resurrection (2:22), the death of Jesus (3:13), a Christian mission (4:31-38), Eucharist (6:11-13). Of course, much more is supposed (e.g. knowledge of Greek, Jewish thought and practices, some idea of the geography of Palestine etc.). Narratives are successful, however, when a certain mutuality is created between the implied reader in the text and the original intended reader(s) of the text, in this case the Johannine Christians. I will call them the

Jesus' critical understanding of the motivation for the crowd's presence with him at Capernaum enables him to shift the discussion to another form of nourishment (vv. 26-27). They seek more food from Jesus, but they are to work (ἐργάζεσθε) not for the bread (v. 26: ἄρτος) which fills their bellies, nor a food which perishes (τὴν βρῶσιν τὴν ἀπολλυμένην), but upon the food which endures (v. 27a: τὴν βρῶσιν τὴν μένουσαν). The reader recalls an earlier use of this expression, as Jesus has used it to speak of the driving force which motivates his life's task: "I have food (βρῶσιν) to eat of which you do not know . . . My food (ἐμὸν βρῶμα) is to do the will of him who sent me and to accomplish his work" (4:32, 34). There is a form of nourishment which transcends all earthly bread, and this food must be the goal of the people's searching; it is upon this that they must work. The reader also recalls a more recent event: the gathering of the fragments ἵνα μή τι ἀπόληται (v. 12). Is there a link between the possibilities of an ongoing availability of the κλάσματα provided by Jesus and gathered by the disciples into twelve baskets (vv. 12-13), and the need to work, not for a food which perishes, but upon another food which will endure to eternal life (v. 27)? At this stage of the narrative no answer is provided to this question which occurs to the reader, but a beguiling question is raised.[23]

If Jesus' food was the perfection of God's will (4:32-34), what is to be the food of the people? In a prolepsis, Jesus points forward to a food "which the Son of Man will give to you" (v. 27b).[24] The enigmatic title "the Son of Man" is introduced at a crucial stage in the encounter between Jesus and would-be believers.[25] The reader is aware that Jesus is the Son of Man (1:51; 3:13-14; 5:27), and is also aware that the Son of Man is the only revealer who can claim to have come from God (3:13), to make God known (1:51) by means of a "lifting up" (3:14). The acceptance or refusal of this revelation will bring about judgment (5:27). But a great deal of this revelation lies in the future. Both 1:51 and 3:14 looked to the future for their fulfilment. Whatever the reader's suspicions about the two meanings of the verb ὑψωθῆναι might be, for the characters there is to be some future moment in the story when the revelation of God will take place in the lifting

---

"intended reader." Narratives maintain their attraction if they continue to appeal to a subsequent "real reader," distant in time, place, culture and the social conditioning of the intended reader. For more detail on my ideas of "the reader," see F. J. Moloney, *Belief in the Word: Reading John 1-4* (Minneapolis: Fortress Press, 1993), pp. 9-21; idem, "Who is 'the Reader' in/of the Fourth Gospel?" *AusBR* 40 (1992), 20-33. As S. Chatman has remarked, "When I enter the fictional contract I add another self: I become an implied reader." *(Story and Discourse: Narrative Structure in Fiction and Film* [Ithaca: Cornell University Press, 1978], p. 150). On this, see Moloney, *Belief,* pp. 20-21.

[23] See Brown, *John,* 1:261.

[24] There are many witnesses (Sinaiticus, Bezae, Old Latin, Curetonian Syriac) which have the present tense, but p[75] tips the scale in favour of the future. See Brown, *John,* 1:261; C. K. Barrett, *St John,* p. 287; Manns, *L'Evangile,* p. 143.

[25] For a detailed study of 6:27, see Moloney, *Son of Man,* pp. 107-15.

up of the Son of Man. The reader certainly suspects that this moment will be upon the cross, but still wonders how a "lifting up" can also be a revelation of God.[26] Much more needs to be read before an answer to that problem will emerge. But the food which the Son of Man will give will endure for eternal life. The promise of a nourishment which would provide life responded to the expectations of Israel. The Law provided life for those who lived by it (see Sir. 17:11; 45:5; *Mekilta* 15:26; *Exod. Rabbah* 29:9; *Deut. Rabbah* 7:3),[27] and they "laboured" (ἐργάζεσθαι) to have this life from the Law. Jesus' words point to an alternative nourishment as the source of eternal life, the gift of the Son of Man.[28]

Yet, whatever difficulty the characters in the story, and even the reader, may have in fully understanding this promise, Jesus Christ, the Word of God who became flesh and dwelt among us to make God known (1: 14-18), speaks with an unquestionable authority as he affirms that God the Father has set his seal upon the Son of Man: τοῦτον γὰρ ὁ πατὴρ ἐσφράγισεν ὁ θεός (v. 27c).[29] The emphatic use of οὗτος singles out the Son of Man. There is a uniqueness about the nourishment which will be given by the Son of Man because it is "God the Father who attests the authority and truth of Jesus."[30] As an author puts his own seal on a missive to show its authenticity and to give it authority,[31] so has God the Father done with the Son of Man, his unique mediator between heaven and earth. He is the one who has come down from heaven (see 1:51; 3:13), bearing the credentials of God the Father (6:27c). Whatever difficulties this prolepsis might create for the reader, the promise has been uttered by the most authoritative character in the story.[32]

---

[26] See above, note 22. The reader knows that Jesus died on a cross, but does not know that this was a ὑψῶσις. The Johannine version of the story is entirely new, and yet to be fully discovered by the reader.

[27] See Borgen, *Bread from Heaven*, pp. 148-49; Léon-Dufour, *Lecture*, 2:132.

[28] I have attempted to indicate a subtle shift in meaning in the use of ἐργάζασθαι in v. 27. The accepted meaning of "work for" is used for a food produced by human labour, but the gift of the nourishment provided by the Son of Man requires another meaning. I have rendered it "work upon." On this, see BAGD, 307, s.v. ἐργάζομαι, para 2e. This also provides a good parallel with the Rabbinic tradition of "working upon" Torah.

[29] The aorist refers back to the ἐγένετο of 1:14, the moment in history when ὁ λόγος πρὸς τὸν θεόν (1:1) became flesh. See Moloney, *Son of Man*, pp. 114-15. Other scholars prefer Jesus' baptism, or the descent of the Spirit. For surveys, see Brown, *John*, 1:261-62; Barrett, *St. John*, p. 287; Léon-Dufour, *Lecture*, 2:133 n. 94.

[30] Barrett, *St. John*, p. 287.

[31] LSJ, p. 1742. See also BAGD, p. 804.

[32] It could be claimed that God, the Father of Jesus is the most authoritative character in the Fourth Gospel. However, God never enters the narrative in person. God is uniquely and authoritatively represented in the human story by the person and the voice of Jesus. John 6:27c re-affirms this, but it is not new (see esp 1:1-18; 3:11-21, 31-36).

3. The Prolepsis of 6:35

Perfecting God's gift of bread through Moses, Jesus promises a bread which
will give life to the world (vv. 32-33). The crowd is delighted to hear of
such a bread, and makes a request which parallels the Samaritan woman's
request for the living water which would free her from the necessity of
coming to the well for ordinary water. As the woman had said, κύριε, δός
μοι τοῦτο τὸ ὕδωρ (see 4:15), the Jewish crowd at Capernaum now asks,
κύριε, πάντοτε δὸς ὑμῖν τὸν ἄρτον τοῦτον (6:34). The crowd is anxious to
have this bread, but misunderstands its nature. They ask Jesus to give them
this bread πάντοτε. They suggest that the bread of heaven be given again
and again.[33] It is to this request for bread that Jesus, for the first time, passes
to the first person, correcting the misunderstanding, and carrying his self-
revelation further. He identifies himself as that bread: ἐγώ εἰμι ὁ ἄρτος τῆς
ζωῆς (v. 35).[34] The discussion now takes on an eminently christological
character, as Jesus claims to be the bread who will provide nourishment and
satisfy the thirst of all who would come to him. As with all the ἐγώ εἰμι
sayings with a predicate, Jesus is not so much describing who he is, as what
he does. He nourishes with a bread which produces life.[35]

The idea of a heavenly bread is widespread in Old Testament and Jewish
thought, and it comes from the biblical story of the gift of the manna.[36] The
manna came to be interpreted, especially in the Wisdom traditions, in terms
of word and instruction (see especially Sir. 24:19, 21; Prov. 9:5). The
nourishing bread for Israel is Torah.[37] Jesus claims that he is now the

---

[33] In a stimulating deconstructive reading of John 4, 7 and 19, S. D. Moore, "Are there
Impurities in the Living Water that the Johannine Jesus Dispenses? Deconstruction,
Feminism, and the Samaritan Woman," *BibInt* 1 (1993), 207-27, claims that in 4:7-15 the
desire of Jesus, itself a response to the desire of God (see 4:34 etc.), is just as great as the
desire of the woman. Indeed, "desire" is a key to the reading of the Fourth Gospel: "God's
desire is a black hole that slowly draws the Johannine cosmos into it" (p. 226). In 6:34 the
desire of Jesus to offer himself as the bread of life (see 6:35: πώποτε), and the desire of the
crowd to have the bread again and again (πάντοτε), are at odds. See M.-J. Lagrange,
Évangile selon Saint Jean (Ebib; Paris: Gabalda, 1936), p.176; R. Schnackenburg, *The Gospel
according to St John*, HTCNT 4/1-3 (London: Burns & Oates; New York: Crossroad, 1968-
82), 2:43.

[34] On the christological use of ἐγώ εἰμι with a predicate see, among many, the excellent
surveys of Bultmann, *John*, pp. 225-26 n. 3, and Barrett, *St John*, pp. 291-93.

[35] See Schnackenburg, *St John*, 2:79-89, esp. pp. 88-89.

[36] It is found in both Judaism and in other ancient religions. See, for references, W. Bauer,
Das Johannesevangelium erklärt, 3rd ed.; HKNT 6 (Tübingen: J. C. B. Mohr [Paul Siebeck]
1933), p. 97 (Judaism), p. 100 (other religions); Schnackenburg, *St John*, 2:42-44. For the
close relationship which exists between Wisdom, Jewish traditions and the johannine use of
bread, see Borgen, *Bread from Heaven*, pp. 147-58.

[37] See, for a discussion, C. H. Dodd, *The Interpretation of the Fourth Gospel* (Cambridge:
University Press, 1953), pp. 336-37. On the rabbinic nature of vv. 34-40, see Borgen, *Bread
from Heaven*, pp. 69-80.

nourishing bread from heaven; he perfects the former gift of the Torah. Gone are all the limitations of a chosen people, as Jesus promises the satisfaction of the needs of anyone who would come to him (ὁ ἐρχόμενος πρὸς ἐμὲ); they will not hunger. Anyone who would believe in him (ὁ πιστεύων εἰς ἐμὲ) will not thirst. The two expressions "to come to . . . to believe in," set in close parallel, mean one and the same thing.[38] The reader senses that those who come to Jesus find rest from the never-ending search for Wisdom: "Those who eat me (Wisdom) will hunger for more, and those who drink me will thirst for more" (Sir. 24:21. See also Isa. 49:10). No longer will Moses, the manna, Wisdom or Torah, provide for the deepest needs of humankind, but Jesus will satisfy all hunger and thirst.

There is a close link with Wisdom traditions here, but there is also a promise that Jesus will provide both food and drink.[39] Both of the verbs are in the future: "shall not hunger" (οὐ μὴ πεινάσῃ) and "shall never thirst" (οὐ μὴ διψήσει πώποτε). The reader again encounters a prolepsis, an emphatic promise that belief in Jesus will eventually provide a totally satisfying food and drink.[40] When might this happen? What might this food and drink be? The link with the Wisdom traditions indicates to the reader that the revelation of God in Jesus surpasses and perfects the Law. But the memory of the unresolved prolepses involved in the gathering of the κλάσματα so that they might not perish (vv. 12-13), and the promise that the Son of Man would give a bread which, unlike the bread of Israel's ancestors, would endure to eternal life (v. 27), remains with the reader. He or she reads on in an attempt to discover if the narrative will resolve the promise of the future gift of food and drink which will never perish, forever satisfy all hunger and thirst (v. 35). What might this food and drink be, and when will Jesus provide it for all who come to him and believe in him?[41]

4. The Prolepsis of 6.51c

There is a close parallel between the words of Jesus in v. 50: "This is the bread which comes down from heaven . . . ," and v. 51: "I am the living

---

[38] See Brown, *John*, 1:269.

[39] As D. A. Carson, *The Gospel according to John* (Grand Rapids: Eerdmans, 1991), p. 289, points out, if Sir. 24:21 provided background for the author, "what he writes is in marked contrast." But the theme of both eating and drinking, present in Sir. 24:21, suits the author's purpose well. See B. Lindars, *The Gospel of John*, NCB (London: Oliphants, 1972), pp. 259-60. Painter, *Quest*, pp. 273-75, claims that v. 35 is the turning point of the narrative. He argues (p. 215) that a second edition of an original quest story (vv. 1-35) is to be found in the rejection stories which follow (vv. 36-71).

[40] The twofold use of οὐ μὴ and the use of πώποτε (subtly correcting the crowd's πάντοτε [v. 34]) provides the emphasis.

[41] Brett, "The Future of Reader Criticisms?" pp. 18-20, points to some confusion between the 'implicit' reader and the 'historical' reader in some contemporary reader-oriented studies. But both, in different ways, search for an answer to the questions: what might this bread be, when and how will the gift take place? See above, note 22.

bread which came down from heaven . . . ." Reflecting upon the Exodus
story in a paraphrase of the words "He gave them bread from heaven to eat"
(Exod. 16:4, 15) provided by the question raised by the crowd in vv. 30-31,
the theme of eating has emerged. However, the reader sees nothing more in
the emergence of this theme than a reminiscence of what happened in the
wilderness. Moses pointed to the manna and proclaimed: "This is the bread
which the Lord has given you for food" (Exod. 16:15). But the ancestors of
Israel ate of the bread, and yet they died (John 6:49). This is obvious, as
they are no longer present, and the death of Moses is recorded in the Law
itself (see Deut. 34:5-8). But now there is another bread from heaven, οὗτος
ἐστιν ὁ ἄρτος ὁ ἐκ τοῦ οὐρανοῦ καταβαίνων . . . ἐγώ εἰμι ὁ ἄρτος ὁ
ζῶν ὁ ἐκ τοῦ οὐρανοῦ καταβάς. The reader already knows of a bread
coming down (καταβαίνων) from heaven to give life (v. 33), and has heard
Jesus claim to be this bread of life (v. 35a). The change from the present
participle (v. 50: καταβαίνων) to the aorist participle (v. 51: καταβάς)
allows the reader to create the scene: Jesus points to himself as he
emphatically claims "I am the bread which *came* down from heaven,"
present among you, nourishing and revealing God to you. As Moses pointed
to the manna and said: "This is the bread" (Exod. 16:15), now Jesus points
to himself saying: "This is the bread" (John 6:50). He then repeats his claim
in the first person (ἐγώ εἰμι . . .), but by means of an inceptive aorist points
back to the basis for such a claim (v. 51). Jesus' coming into the human
story, when ὁ λόγος σὰρξ ἐγένετο (1:14), initiated the presence of the
true bread from heaven which can lay unique claim to provide a
nourishment which makes God known. Eating of this bread from heaven
eliminates the reality of spiritual death.

There is nothing eucharistic about this claim. Going beyond anything
that the Law could offer, Jesus is the revelation of God, making God known
to all who come to him so that they may have eternal life (vv. 46-47). In
doing this he perfects the former gift of the manna, the Law (v. 48), and
proof of this can be seen in the fact that those who ate of the former manna
are now dead (v. 49). The nourishment which Jesus provides will give
people everlasting life, because Jesus has come from God to make him
known (v. 50-51ab). This is not new for the reader, who has already
accepted the earlier words of Jesus to "the Jews": "He who hears my word
. . . has passed from death to life" (5:24).

There has been a gradual intensification of the concentration upon the
person of Jesus: "This is the bread . . ." (v. 50a), "I am the bread . . ." (v.
51a). This focus upon Jesus now culminates in a surprising fashion as Jesus
informs "the Jews" of a future gift: "The bread which I shall give is my

flesh for the life of the world" (v. 51c).[42] There are many elements in v. 51c
which lead scholars to find contacts with Johannine eucharistic traditions (ὁ
ἄρτος, σάρξ, ἐγὼ δώσω, ὑπέρ),[43] but the reader recalls 1:14 where σάρξ
was used to speak of the presence of the Word among us in the historical
human being, Jesus Christ (see 1:17).[44] After all that has been said to this
point, the reader understands that Jesus, the true bread which has come
down from heaven, will make God known by a gift of himself for the life of
the world.[45] It is a startling turn for the discourse to take, but Jesus' words
say no more nor less than that he will give himself totally for the life of the
world. What will this be? How will it happen?

As in all the proleptic statements of some future encounter between the
darkness and the light (1:5), the hour of Jesus (2:5) and his being lifted up
(3:14), much of what has been said remains a mystery to the reader, but
there are already some solid hints that Jesus is heading for death at the
hands of "the Jews." They rejected him at the Temple in 2:13-23, and the
encounter between Jesus and "the Jews" on the occasion of the Sabbath
concluded in a decision that Jesus must be killed (5:18). Connections are
being made by the emerging reader. However, the manner in which Jesus'
experience of death will provide nourishment for the life of the world still
remains incomprehensible. Nevertheless, the reader accepts the promise of
Jesus, the most authoritative character in the story. But "the Jews" do not. A
claim to give his flesh for the life of the world can only bring dispute, shock
and horror to the Jewish listeners who take his words on their face value.[46]

The future tense of the verb in Jesus' promise, ὁ ἄρτος δὲ ὃν ἐγὼ
δώσω, must be taken seriously.[47] It is not the first time in the narrative
where Jesus has promised a future gift. The words of Jesus, pointing to the
future gift of his flesh for the life of the world (v. 51c) remind the reader of

---

[42] Following p[66], p[75], Vaticanus, Bezae, Old Latin, Vulgate, Sinaitic Syriac, Curetonian
Syriac and Sahidic. There are many attempts to smooth out this difficult expression. For a
discussion, see Barrett, St John, p. 298.

[43] See, for example, J. H. Bernard, A Critical and Exegetical Commentary on the Gospel
according St John, 2 vols.; ICC (Edinburgh: T. & T. Clark, 1928), 1:clxx-clxxi; J. Jeremias,
The Eucharistic Words of Jesus (London: SCM Press, 1966), pp. 106-08; Brown, John,
1:284-85; Schnackenburg, St John, 2:54-56.

[44] In Mark 14:22 (and parallels) the bread is identified with σῶμα, and there has been
much discussion over the the alternatives of σάρξ and σῶμα, as translations of the Hebrew
בָּשָׂר. See, for a summary, Barrett, St John, pp. 297-98; Brown, John, 1:285. The author's use
of σάρξ to speak of the flesh of Jesus is determined by its use in 1:14.

[45] See Moloney, Son of Man, p. 115. For a detailed analysis, coming to this conclusion see
Léon-Dufour, Lecture, 2:159-62. See also Menken, "John 6,51c-58," pp. 9-13.

[46] The disputing (ἐμάχοντο οὖν . . . οἱ Ἰουδαῖοι) continues the theme of the
"grumbling" from Exod. 16. It appears in Exod. 17:2, with the same meaning as the verb
γογγύζειν in Exod. 16:7-8 and John 6:41, 43. See also Num. 11:4. See Schnackenburg, St
John, 2:60; Léon-Dufour, Lecture, 2:162 n. 148.

[47] See also Menken, "John 6,51c-58," pp. 13-15. Menken sees the importance of the future
tense and rightly links it to the cross.

two earlier prolepses in the narrative. In 6:12-13 the disciples were commanded to gather the κλάσματα so that they might not be lost. But why are the twelve baskets to be preserved? Eclipsing Moses' command that bread not be stored (see Exod. 16:19-20), Jesus' command has been obeyed, and the reader wonders what the collection of the κλάσματα might mean. In 6:27 Jesus urged the crowds not to labour for a nourishment which would perish, but for a food which would endure, to be provided by the Son of Man. Is there a link between the gathering of the κλάσματα so that they might not perish (6:12: ἵνα μή τι ἀπόληται), and the future gift of the food of the Son of Man, surpassing all food which perishes (v. 27: τὴν Βρῶσιν τὴν ἀπολλυμένην)? If so, what might this food be, and when might the gift take place? A further prolepsis occurs in v. 35. Jesus' claim to be the bread of life led to the promise that anyone who comes to him will not hunger, and anyone who believes in him will not thirst. There is to be a definitive food and drink which will forever satisfy the needs of all who believe in Jesus. When will this food and drink be provided? What will it be? For the moment the reader can only read on, hoping to find some solution to these problems. Jesus has been arguing throughout his discussion with the crowd and "the Jews" that the gift of the nourishment provided by the Law has been surpassed by the gift of the true bread from heaven, the revelation of God in and through Jesus. The reader reasonably awaits some explanation of how this will take place.

For the moment the reader can only read on, hoping to find some solution to these problems. Jesus has been arguing throughout his discussion with the crowd and "the Jews" that the gift of the nourishment provided by the Law has been surpassed by the gift of the true bread from heaven, the revelation of God in and through Jesus. Now more has been promised: through the total gift of himself, Jesus will provide nourishment for the world (6:51c). The reader reasonably awaits some explanation of how this will take place.

5. A Solution Emerges in 6:53-54

"The Jews'" hostile rejection of his outrageous suggestion not only takes the discussion further, but raises the question facing the reader: "How (πῶς) can this man give us his flesh to eat?" (v. 52). Their complaint about Jesus' origins has provided Jesus the opportunity to address the crucial question of his origins with God, the basis for his ability to make God known (vv. 41-51). His closing words in that section of the discussion now lead to a further question which will lead to the clarification of how the revelation of God will take place in and through the gift of the Son of Man (see v. 27), how all who come to him and believe in him will no longer hunger or thirst (see v.

35), how his flesh will give life to the world (v. 51c).[48] The narrative is working at at least two levels. The question raised in v. 52 is a rejection of Jesus' outrageous suggestion for "the Jews" as characters in the story. But for the reader it is a question which needs to be answered in the further unravelling of Jesus' perfection of the Mosaic bread from heaven given through Jesus' gift of himself as the true bread from heaven. Unlike the bread in the wilderness (see Exod. 16:20), the bread given by Jesus has been gathered so that it might not perish (vv. 12-13). The reader now knows that it will give life to the world (v. 51c). But how does this happen?

"The Jews" remain at a purely physical level and ask how the flesh of a human being could be the bread which is to be eaten for the life of the world (v. 52). The idea is abhorrent, but only because "the Jews" are not prepared to go beyond anything which they cannot control or understand. Like Nicodemus, who understood rebirth in a crassly physical fashion (3:4), "the Jews" limit Jesus' words to a physical eating of the body of the person standing before them. There is a profound misunderstanding here.[49] Again, as in v. 26 and v. 32 Jesus opens his response to his opponents' question with a double "amen."[50] He unflinchingly insists upon a gift of flesh and blood for life. He first says it negatively: whoever does not eat of the flesh and drink of the blood of the Son of Man has no life (v. 53); and then positively, identifying himself as "Son of Man": "whoever eats my flesh and drinks my blood has eternal life now and will be raised up on the last day" (v. 54). The paraphrase of the verb "to eat" in the midrashic exposition of the Exodus passage provided in v. 31: "He gave them bread from heaven to eat," reaches its highpoint. There can be no doubt that behind these words of Jesus lies a Christian community which celebrated the Eucharist. The use of the very physical verb τρώγειν in vv. 54 and 56-57, a word which indicates the action of a physical crunching with the teeth,[51] renders

---

[48] There is no break at v. 48 (against, for example, Carson, *John*, p. 294), nor does a new section begin with v. 51c. On this, see Barrett, *St John*, p. 296. Most commentators and critics, impressed by the eucharistic possibilities of v. 51c, read 51c-58 as a unit.

[49] Moore, "Are there Impurities?" pp. 222-23, argues that Jesus himself does not understand that the supposed distinction between the physical and the spiritual is not true. In a faulty use of 1:51 (and of C. K. Barrett!), Moore claims that Jesus "dissolves the partition between the two realities possible" (p. 222). "What Jesus says is contradicted by what he is" (p. 223). But behind "bread of life," which Jesus claims to be (v. 35), is not some "spiritual reality" but the Law, as it has been understood in the Wisdom traditions. The discourse is at all times on the level of the physical. The intended readers are told that they have not lost the authentic teaching of God, the Manna of the Law, in their separation from the synagogue (see 9:22; 12:42; 16:2). The person and teaching of Jesus have perfected that former gift (see 1:16-17). On 1:51, see Moloney, *Son of Man*, pp. 23-41. On 1:16-17, see idem, *Belief*, pp. 45-51.

[50] Although not present at the opening of each of Jesus' responses (see v. 35, which has its own solemn opening: ἐγώ εἰμι ὁ ἄρτος τῆς ζωῆς, and v. 44, where Jesus reprimands "the Jews" on account of their murmuring) the presence of the double "amen" on three out of five occasions (vv. 26, 32, 53) is an indication of the staged unfolding of the argument.

[51] BAGD, p. 829; LSJ, p. 1832. But Barrett, *St John*, p. 299, remarks: "It is very improbable that John saw any special meaning in the word and distinguished it from other

concrete the notion of the eating of the flesh of Jesus. The implied reader senses eucharistic references in Jesus' words, but this is not the main thrust of the argument.[52] Flesh and blood also emphasise that it is the flesh and blood life of the Son of Man which is life-giving food.[53] Any Christian reflection upon the eating of a bread which is the flesh of Jesus (see v. 51) would be influenced by eucharistic thought and language, but the argument of vv. 25-51 continues into vv. 52-59. The celebration of the feast of the Passover and the contrast between the gift of Moses and the gift of Jesus, the unique revelation of God, so central to the discussion so far, remain at the centre of the discussion between Jesus and "the Jews."

The reader also senses the culmination of a series of prolepses which began with the miracle of the loaves and fishes. There the disciples gathered τὰ κλάσματα so that they would not perish (vv. 12-13). Then, in v. 27 the crowd was told not to work for a food which perishes, but for the food which will endure to eternal life, the food provided by the Son of Man, upon whom God the Father had set his seal. At the height of his use of Wisdom motifs to explain his presence as the life giving bread, Jesus has promised that those who come to him and believe in him will never hunger nor will they thirst (v. 35). Later, in v. 51c, a further promise was made: Jesus will provide a bread for the life of the world, and that bread is his flesh. Through the total gift of himself, Jesus will provide a food for the world. While "the Jews" ask how Jesus can give his flesh to eat, the reader asks how the total self-gift of Jesus will provide a food which will not perish, but will provide a nourishment for the world. As the ancestors of Israel were nourished by the gift of the Torah, Jesus will nourish the whole world with the gift of himself. But how?

The answer is provided by the description of Jesus' self-gift as the gift of his flesh and his blood. Israel was nourished by the eating of the manna, perennially recalled in the nourishment provided for them by their total receptivity to and absorption of the Law.[54] Now "the Jews" are told of the absolute need for eating of the flesh and drinking of the blood of the Son of Man (vv. 53-54). Flesh is to be broken and blood is to be spilt. The reader has been aware for some time that violence is in the air. After earlier skirmishes which did not augur well for future relationships (see esp 2:13-23), the decision by "the Jews" to kill Jesus has already been made (see

---

words for eating." See also Menken, "John 6,51c-58," pp. 16-18. For the position adopted, see Brown, *John*, 1:283, and especially C. Spicq, "τρώγειν: Est-il synonyme de φαγεῖν et d' ἐσθίειν dans le Nouveau Testament?" *NTS* 26 (1979-80), 414-19.

[52] The reader has not been instructed on Eucharist, but knowledge of it is presupposed in 6:11-13. See above, note 22.

[53] Barrett, *St John*, p. 299; Brown, *John*, 1:282.

[54] For a collection of Jewish material on this "absorption" of the Law, see H. Odeberg, *The Fourth Gospel Interpreted in its Relation to Contemporary Religious Currents in Palestine and the Hellenistic-Oriental World* (Uppsala: Almqvist, 1929), pp. 238-47.

5:16-18). Jesus now associates the separation of flesh and blood in a violent death as the moment of his total giving of himself. This will be the time and the place where Jesus will offer his broken body and his spilt blood, his whole self, as the bread which will give life to the world (see v. 51c).

The reader has also been told of a future "lifting up" of the Son of Man in 3:14. The use of the double-meaning verb ὑψωθῆναι informed the reader that there would be a moment in the future when the Son of Man would be lifted up from the ground, just as Moses had lifted up the serpent in the wilderness, but that this "lifting up" would also be an exaltation.[55] The reader knows that there is a conflict between light and darkness that does not overcome the light (1:5) and that Jesus will be rejected by "his own" (1:11). The reader has heard of some future "hour of Jesus" which has not yet come (2:4), has had the first hints of a conflict between Jesus and "the Jews" (2:18-20) and a promise that the Son of Man must be "lifted up" as Moses lifted up the serpent in the wilderness (3:14). These hints have blossomed into a decision that Jesus must be killed (5:16-18). Now, the Son of Man has been inserted into this ever-increasing bank of knowledge for the second time. There can be no mistaking the message: Jesus, the Son of Man, will give of his whole self for the life of the world (6:51c) by means of a violent encounter between himself and his enemies (1:5, 11; 2:18-20; 3:14; 5:16-18) in which his body will be broken and his blood spilt (6:53-54). This is the enduring gift which the Son of Man will give, the food that will not perish (v. 27) but will satisfy forever all hunger and thirst (v. 35).

The reader is now more fully informed that there will be something unique about the death of Jesus. The early Christians had to grapple with the reality of the death of Jesus. It was "stumbling block to Jews and folly to Gentiles" (1 Cor. 1:23), but a historical reality which could not be ignored. Thus, all four Gospels had to tell a story of the cross which made sense of such a tragic and bloody event.[56] The reader is aware of the story of the cross but is meeting, for the first time, an evolving understanding of this event as a life-giving lifting up of Jesus which makes God known in a way previously performed by the Law. The Son of Man will offer this nourishment not only to Israel, but to the whole world. There is a growing bank of knowledge which leads the reader further into the narrative in anticipation of a story of broken flesh and spilt blood, but more is at stake. The reader is by now aware that the story of the crucifixion of Jesus in the Johannine Gospel will do more than report the events. It will tell of a crucifixion which is also an exaltation, and the revelation of God in a life-giving gift to the whole world which perfects everything that had been done

---

[55] On 3:14, see Moloney, *Son of Man*, pp. 59-65; idem, *Belief*, pp. 117-18.

[56] Much has been written on this. See, for example, F. J. Matera, *Passion Narratives and Gospel Theologies: Interpreting the Synoptics through their Passion Stories*, Theological Inquiries (New York: Paulist Press, 1986).

for Israel through the Law.[57] As once Israel ate of the manna in the desert, and was nourished by its adhesion to the Law given at Sinai, now the world is summoned to accept the further revelation of God which will take place in the broken body and the spilt blood of the Son of Man. In this way they will have life, now and hereafter (vv. 53-54).[58]

The crucial affirmation of vv. 53-54 both explains how the flesh of Jesus will give life to the world (see v. 51c) and leads the reader further into a story which will reveal how the flesh and the blood of the Son of Man will make God known. These events are yet to be narrated. Such claims are further reinforced through vv. 55-57. Earlier parts of the discourse are recalled as Jesus insists that his flesh ἀληθῶς ἐστιν βρῶσις, and his blood ἀληθῶς ἐστιν πόσις. [59] In a play on words, Jesus recalls for the reader his promise of the βρῶσις which the Son of Man would give (v. 27), and his claim that over against all other bread from heaven, and especially the gift of the Law from heaven, the Father gives τὸν ἄρτον ἐκ τοῦ οὐρανοῦ τὸν ἀληθινόν (v. 32). He is that true bread from heaven (v. 35). As Barrett paraphrases, "My flesh and blood are what food and drink should be, they fulfill the ideal, archetypal function of food and drink, that is in giving eternal life to those who receive them."[60] It is on the basis of the whole discourse that Jesus can lay claim to his flesh and his blood as authentically (ἀληθῶς) food and drink.[61]

But what of the eucharistic background to this final part of the discourse, highlighted by the words ἄρτος, βρῶσις, σάρξ, αἷμα, πόσις τρώγειν and πίνειν? While the author is not primarily concerned with the presence of Jesus in the celebration of the Eucharist, the paraphrasing of the word "to eat" from v. 31 summons up eucharistic language.[62] The reader also recalls Jesus' command to his disciples to gather τὰ κλάσματα after the multiplication of the bread. The broken pieces are gathered into twelve baskets so that they might not perish (vv. 12-13). For the reader, the shadow of the κλάσματα falls across a discourse which deals with a nourishment which will endure (v. 27). This nourishment is Jesus, the life-giving bread from heaven which will satisfy all hunger and thirst for those who believe in him (v. 35); it is Jesus' flesh, given for the life of the world (v. 51c). Although the main message of the author has looked to Jesus' self-gift on

---

[57] For a detailed study of v. 53, arguing for its primary reference being the crucifixion, see Moloney, *Son of Man,* pp. 115-20.

[58] See Léon-Dufour, *Lecture,* 2:169; Menken, "John 6,51c-58," pp. 16-18.

[59] Following the first hand of Sinaiticus, Bezae, Koridethi, Athos, Old Latin, Vulgate, Sinaitic Syriac, Curetonian Syriac and the Peshitta, I am reading ἀληθῶς, rather than ἀληθής. See Barrett, *St. John,* p. 299.

[60] Barrett, *St John,* p. 299.

[61] For Léon-Dufour, *Lecture,* 2:166-67, v. 55 is the pivot of vv. 53-57 and the link between vv. 53-58 and vv. 25-51.

[62] See Menken, "John 6,51c-58," pp. 6-9.

the cross (vv. 51c, 53-54), the reader senses eucharistic possibilities. In vv. 53-57 the author has no hesitation in using eucharistic language as it serves his purposes well, and brings to partial resolution the prolepsis which began with the gathering of the κλάσματα in vv. 12-13.[63]

There is no break in the argument at v. 51c, as eucharistic terms enter and multiply through vv. 53-57, after the question of v. 52.[64] Throughout the discourse Jesus is presented as the true bread from heaven, replacing the former bread from heaven, the manna of the Law. The reader is being asked to be receptive to the revelation of God which will take place in broken flesh and spilt blood (vv. 53-54), a never failing (v. 35) nourishment which the Son of Man will give (v. 27). But the Christian reader asks: where do I encounter this revelation of God in the flesh and blood of the Son of Man? By means of the underlying eucharistic language the author insinuates an answer: it is in the Eucharist where one can encounter the flesh and blood of Jesus the Christ, and the κλάσματα consigned by Jesus to his disciples (vv. 12-13) have lurked behind the story reminding the reader of such celebrations. The author is working at two levels here. The main thrust of the discourse is to point to Jesus as the revelation of God, the true bread from heaven, perfecting God's former gift, the bread of the manna. The use of the κλάσματα in vv. 12-13, the promise of a future gift of a food which the Son of Man would give in v. 27, the reference to satisfying food and drink in v. 35, and the further promise of the gift of the flesh of Jesus for the life of the world in v. 51c, however, keep the eucharistic question alive. Eucharist is recalled through the use of eucharistic terminology as the verb "to eat" is paraphrased in vv. 49-58. This recollection plays a secondary, yet important role. It renders concrete, in the Christian understanding of the implied reader, and in the eucharistic practice of the intended reader, the Johannine community, what the author has spelt out through the discourse.

C. CONCLUSION

Johannine Christianity was not the product of an intellectual assent to a preached message. The Johannine Eucharist was a place where one could come to eternal life. Encountering the flesh and blood of Jesus (vv. 53-54), the believer was called to make a decision for or against the revelation of God in that encounter (vv. 56-58), gaining or losing life because of it (vv. 53-54).[65] The author is not interested in sacramental ritual, or theories of the

---

63 These unexplained further eucharistic hints indicate that the reader's knowledge of Eucharist is presupposed. See above, note 22.

64 Against, for example, Brown, *John,* 1:284: "In this section the eucharistic theme which was only secondary in vss. 35-50 comes to the fore and becomes the exclusive theme."

65 As E. C. Hoskyns, *The Fourth Gospel,* ed. F. N. Davey (London: Faber & Faber, 1947), p. 297, puts it: "First, redemptive significance is assigned to the death of the Son of God, who is to offer His Flesh as a sacrifice for the life of the world; secondly sacrificial significance is

real presence of Jesus, but in the call to recognise the revelation of God in the κλάσματα, the broken pieces which remained after Jesus' initial feeding with bread (vv. 12-13). These κλάσματα will not perish (v. 12) as they are part of the food which will not perish, but which will endure to eternal life (v. 27). Jesus provides food and drink that never fails (v. 35) through the revelation of God in the flesh and blood of the Son of Man (vv. 53-54). Much of this message is still a puzzle to the reader. The link between the death of Jesus on the cross and the revelation of God in and through that death is yet to be discovered (see, for example, 13:31-32). So too is the link between the lifting up of Jesus on the cross, and nourishment which flows from the pierced one upon the family of Jesus (see 19:25-37). It is the revelation of God in and through Jesus' being lifted up on the cross which gives life, and the κλάσματα of the eucharistic celebration is the memory, the זִכָּרוֹן of the cross for the Johannine community.

The critical reader can glance forward to these passages (13:31-32; 19:25-37) for reassurance that a certain "reading" of the text is going in the right direction, but the implied reader must wait until the end of the story for an explanation of these mysteries.[66] A full understanding of the κλάσματα (vv. 12-13), the future gift of the Son of Man (v. 27), totally satisfying food and drink (v. 35), Jesus' flesh as food for the life of the world, and the eating of the flesh of the Son of Man and drinking his blood (vv. 53-54), still lies ahead. But the reader trusts in Jesus' assuring words that only here can be found a life-giving mutual indwelling between the believer and Jesus, the sent one of the living God (vv. 56-57). The reader does not question these promises made by the most authoritative character in the story, Jesus Christ, the only begotten Son of the Father, the incarnation of the pre-existent Word (see 1:1-18). Such assurances make the need to discover the full truth of these matters more urgent. "Narrative texts implicitly keep promising the reader the great prize of understanding later."[67]

---

assigned to the Eucharist, which is at once the concrete commemoration of the sacrifice once offered and the guarantee of its efficacy." On this, see F. J. Moloney, "John 6 and the Celebration of the Eucharist," *DRev* 93 (1975), 243-51.

[66] I have introduced another reader! The critical reader is a real reader who approaches the text in a scholarly, critical fashion, looking back and forth through and behind the text for links which may explain the passage under scrutiny. On "the critical reader," see R. M. Fowler, "Who is 'the Reader' in Reader Response Criticism?" *Semeia* 31 (1985), 5-10.

[67] S. Rimmon-Kenan, *Narrative Fiction: Contemporary Poetics*, New Accents (London: Methuen, 1983), p. 125.

JOHN 6:15-21: JESUS WALKING ON WATER
AS NARRATIVE EMBODIMENT
OF JOHANNINE CHRISTOLOGY

Gail R. O'Day

It is very easy for the narrative of Jesus walking on water in John 6:15-21 to disappear into the broad sweep of John 6:1-71. The feeding miracle (6:1-14), Jesus' dialogue with the crowd (6:26-34), and the bread of life discourse (6:35-59) are mutually reinforcing of interrelated narrative and theological themes—Jesus as the one who feeds (6:11, 27, 35, 51, 53-58); the food/bread that endures to and gives eternal life (6:12, 27, 39-40, 47-51, 58); Jesus as both gift of God and giver of that gift (6:6, 11, 29, 32-33, 35, 45, 57). With the exception of the words ἐγώ εἰμι in v. 20, 6:15-21 contains no verbal echoes of its surrounding context, no explicit cross referencing of themes. The seeming detachment of this passage from the larger context leads most commentators to read 6:15-21 as supplementary to the main themes of John 6 at best, irrelevant to those themes at worst.

A. JOHN 6:15-21 AND EARLY CHRISTIAN TRADITION

The governing view of John 6:15-21 among Johannine interpreters is that its inclusion in John 6 is a result of its linkage with the feeding miracle in early traditions about Jesus. C. K. Barrett, for example, notes that this miracle has "very little to do with the Johannine context," and serves only as a "traditional bridge," included because "it was firmly fixed in the tradition along with the miracle of the five thousand."[1] Even Raymond Brown, who is more positive in his assessment of the contribution this story makes to John 6, sees the inclusion of 6:15-21 as due solely to the requirements of tradition: "Since it would have been simpler for the fourth evangelist, if he were simply a creative artist, to have placed the discourse on bread immediately after the multiplication, his inclusion of the walking on the sea indicates that he was controlled by an earlier tradition in which the multiplication and the walking on the sea were already joined."[2]

But is this explanation for the inclusion of the story at this juncture in the gospel satisfactory, given what the rest of the fourth gospel narrative reveals about the evangelist's handling of tradition? The fourth evangelist unquestionably used traditional material as a building block in the composition of the gospel narrative, but it is difficult to make a compelling

---

[1] C.K. Barrett, *The Gospel according to St. John*, 2nd. ed. (Philadelphia: Westminster Press, 1978), p. 279.
[2] Raymond E. Brown, *The Gospel According to John (I-XII)*, AB 29 (New York: Doubleday, 1966), p. 252.

case that he was constrained in his composition by any conventional ordering or joining of events in the tradition (or traditions) to which he had access. The Fourth Gospel contains many narratives that point to the fourth evangelist's respect for, yet almost complete interpretive freedom with, received tradition: for example, his reframing of the call of the first disciples (1:35-51); the ways in which he recasts healing traditions to incorporate large sections of dialogue (cf. John 5:1-18 and Mark 2:9-10; John 9:1-41 and Mark 8:22-26; 10:46-52; Matt. 12:22-37);[3] his elaborate reworking of Jesus' trial before Pilate (18:28–19:16a).

The fourth evangelist's freedom in narrating the cleansing of the temple provides a useful analogue for assessing his handling of traditional material in John 6:15-21. The evangelist is not controlled by the connection in early Christian tradition of this dramatic incident from Jesus' ministry with Jesus' passion entry into Jerusalem (cf. Matt. 21:12-13; Mark 11:15-19; Luke 19:45-48). Rather, the fourth evangelist moves the temple scene to the beginning of the gospel narrative (John 2:13-22) because of the symbolic value it has for him. This story, in combination with the Cana wine miracle (2:1-11), thus becomes the inaugural event of Jesus' ministry. Together the two stories point the reader toward the Gospel's governing theme: Jesus is the locus of God's presence on earth.

Indeed, one of the distinguishing characteristics of the literary and theological style of the Fourth Gospel is the way in which the fourth evangelist is simultaneously conserving and creating in his handling of traditions about Jesus. The evangelist shapes his work as storyteller-interpreter in accordance with his understanding of the teaching work of the Paraclete. The Paraclete will remind the community of what Jesus said (14:26), and the Paraclete will also guide the community into fresh encounters with the words of Jesus in the future (16:12-15). Traditions about Jesus are simultaneously remembered and interpreted in this Gospel,[4] and there is every reason to assume that both traits are operating in the evangelist's handling of the sea walking tradition. That Jesus walking on water is included at all (note its absence in Luke) and in this particular location in John 6 derives from narrative and theological strategy and not simply the requirements of the tradition.[5]

---

[3] See similarly, L. T. Witkamp, "Some Specific Johannine Factors in John 6:1-21," *JSNT* 40 (1990), 51.

[4] See Gail R. O'Day, *John*, NIB, vol. 9 (Nashville: Abingdon Press, 1995), pp. 773-78.

[5] One of the few Johannine commentators who sees literary and theological intentionality in the evangelist's use of the sea walking tradition is Rudolf Schnackenburg, *The Gospel according to St. John*, vol. 2 (New York: Seabury, 1982), pp. 25, 28-29. This passage has also been largely ignored in monographs and articles. Two recent exceptions are John Paul Heil, *Jesus Walking on the Sea* (Rome: Biblical Institute Press, 1981); and L. T. Witkamp, "Some Specific Johannine Factors in John 6:1-21," *JSNT* 40 (1990), 43-59.

B. THE NARRATIVE FOCUS OF JOHN 6:15-21

1. "He withdrew again to the mountain by himself" (6:15)

One clue to the evangelist's strategy can be found in the way he makes the transition from the feeding miracle to the story of Jesus walking on the sea. John is alone among the gospels in narrating the crowd's response to the feeding miracle (6:14; cf. Matt. 14:20-21; Mark 6:42-43; 8:8-9; Luke 9:17). The crowd's exclamation that Jesus is "the prophet who is to come into the world" establishes several important continuities between this miracle and the larger gospel context. The miracle is explicitly called a "sign" (v. 14a; σημεῖον), nomenclature that links this miracle with two earlier Galilean miracles (2:1-11; 4:46-54). More importantly, that the crowd's declaration of Jesus as prophet is based on this sign recalls the earlier reaction of the Jerusalem crowd to Jesus (2:23), a reaction that Jesus did not trust (2:24-25). Verse 14 thus introduces a note of ambiguity into the scene—"prophet who is to come into the world" is an appropriate, if incomplete, recognition of Jesus' identity (cf. 1:45; 4:19, 25; 9:17), but it is evoked solely by a sign.

Verse 15 very quickly resolves this ambiguity. As at 2:24-25, Jesus knows in advance what the people are thinking. The people's intent forcibly to make Jesus king underscores the distance between Jesus and the crowd, a distance that is given physical expression when Jesus withdraws to the mountain by himself. It is a central theme of this gospel that no one can force Jesus to do anything—his mother cannot force him to attend to the wine shortage at the Cana wedding (2:4); his brothers cannot force him to go to Jerusalem for the feast (7:6-10); neither the crowds here nor the authorities later can take Jesus by force (7:43; 8:20; 18:6). Jesus acts solely in response to the work God has given him to do, and Jesus' kingship will be initiated by his free gift of his life on the cross (10:18; 18–19; esp. 18:4, 33-37; 19:1-5, 11, 14-16, 19-22), not by the forcible actions of this crowd or even his disciples (18:10-11, 36).[6]

The conclusion of the feeding miracle in John thus stands in marked contrast to the conclusion of this story in the other Gospels. In Matthew and Mark, the feeding miracle concludes with Jesus' simple dismissal of the crowds (Matt. 14:23a; Mark 6:46a), rather than with his escape from them. Jesus then ascends to the mountain by himself (Matt. 14:23b; Mark 6:46b), but only in John is this ascent explicitly linked with Jesus' rejection of the crowd's response to him.

Jesus' escape to the mountain also informs the way the sea walking narrative begins. In Matthew and Mark, Jesus makes his disciples get into the boat as a prelude to his dismissal of the crowds (Matt. 14:22; Mark 6:45); the disciples' embarkment thus serves as a narrative link between the

---

[6] See Wayne A. Meeks, *The Prophet-King: Moses Traditions and the Johannine Christology* (Leiden: E. J. Brill, 1967), pp. 63-81; O'Day, *John*, NIB, 9:816-23, 829-30.

two stories. In John, however, Jesus ascends the mountain before the
disciples depart, and indeed, the disciples, not Jesus, take the initiative for
their embarking across the Sea of Galilee in Jesus' absence (6:16-17).
Although it is commonly held that the notation in v. 17b that Jesus "had not
yet come to them" anticipates Jesus' coming to the disciples across the sea,
in the context of 6:15, the notation's purpose may be to remind the reader
that Jesus is still on the mountain. Jesus' escape to the mountain in 6:15 sets
the final tone for his relationship to the crowd who witnessed the feeding
miracle and shapes the disciples' actions in the subsequent narrative.

The traditional link between the feeding miracle and Jesus walking on
the sea thus is altered in John. In Matthew and Mark, the two miracles are
narrated as two parts of a continuous story, but in John that seamless
continuity is interrupted by Jesus' abrupt ascent of the mountain. (The break
in continuity can also be seen in the awkwardness of the crowd's discovery
of Jesus' departure in 6:22-24). The disciples' departure in the boat belongs
wholly to the second story. Moreover, unlike in Matthew and Mark, where
Jesus' mountaintop ascent is portrayed as a time of prayer (Matt. 14:23b;
Mark 6:46b),[7] Jesus' solitary presence on the mountaintop in John clearly
signals Jesus' rejection of the crowd's interpretation of the miracle and its
misplaced political intentions toward him. By positioning Jesus'
unambiguous rejection of these intentions as the transition between the two
miracles,[8] the fourth evangelist shifts the narrative focus away from the
feeding miracle per se and towards questions of Jesus' identity. This focus
on Jesus' identity provides the critical link between the two miracles with
which John 6 opens.

2. "I AM; do not be afraid" (6:20)

As is universally recognized, the Johannine version of the story of Jesus
walking on the sea is briefer and more tautly recounted than those found in
Matthew and Mark. All three versions share core details and vocabulary: the
disciples are on the sea in the evening (Matt. 14:24; Mark 6:47; John 6:17);
Jesus walks (περιπατέω) upon the sea (θάλασσα; Matt. 14:25; Mark 6:48;
John 6:19); Jesus speaks the words, ἐγώ εἰμι μὴ φοβεῖσθε (Matt. 14:27;
Mark 6:50; John 6:20). Yet despite these common traits, there are

---

[7] Both Schnackenburg, *John*, 2:20, and Heil, *Jesus Walking on the Sea*, p. 76, read this verse
through the lens of the Matthean and Markan versions and interpret Jesus' solitary presence as a
time of communion with God, but the context seems to put the verse's weight on Jesus' ascent as
rejection, not as a time of prayer.

[8] This understanding of 6:15-21 contrasts with that of John Painter, *The Quest for the
Messiah: The History, Literature and Theology of the Johannine Community*, 2nd edition
(Nashville: Abingdon Press, 1993), pp. 266-68, who maintains that Jesus' withdrawal into the
wilderness is ambiguous, so "the story of the sea-crossing was used because it lay ready at hand
to make the point of Jesus' rejection of the political role while, at the same time, separating Jesus
from the crowd."

significant differences among all three stories, but especially in the Johannine version.[9]

The beginnings of the story in Matthew and Mark emphasize similar features. The distress of disciples in the boat in the rough sea is underscored ("the wind was against [ἐναντίος] them"; "beaten by waves [βασανιζόμενον]"; "struggling in their rowing [βασανιζομένους ἐν τῷ ἐλαύνειν]"; Matt. 14:24; Mark 6:48). These introductory details follow the conventions of a miracle story by depicting the situation of need, in this case, distress at sea, that Jesus' miracle will correct. The description of the disciples' distress in Matthew and Mark has important echoes of traditions of distress at sea found in the OT. Ps. 107:26-27 evokes the plight of sailors who are buffeted by high seas; their rescue comes from God who answers their cries for help and calms the seas (Ps. 107:28-32). In Jonah 1:13, the sailors' struggle to row in the tempestuous sea is narrated, and again, rescue is effected through God's intervention (Jonah 1:14-16).

That Jesus comes across the sea to the disciples in response to their distress highlights Jesus' act as one of rescue at sea (Matt. 14:25; Mark 6:48) and links it with these earlier stories of God's rescue of sailors at sea. This link is confirmed by the cessation of the wind at the end of the pericopae in Matthew and Mark (Matt. 14:32; Mark 6:51; cf. Ps. 107:29; Jon. 1:15).

In John, by contrast, the frame of a rescue story is missing. The disciples' distress in the boat is not highlighted at all. The power of the wind and the attendant roughness of the sea are described in 6:18, but the effect of these factors on the disciples is not noted. The focus is on the power of the wind and sea, not the disciples' need of rescue. Jesus' movement towards the disciples thus is not portrayed as motivated by their distress. Indeed, the reader is given no hint of Jesus' presence until the narrator records that the disciples "saw Jesus walking on the sea and coming near the boat" (6:19). In Matthew and Mark, the narrator seems to stand at the shoreline with Jesus, but in John the story is narrated from the disciples' perspective. This shift in perspective moves the opening emphasis of the story away from what Jesus *does* (Jesus' rescue of the distressed disciples) and places it on what the disciples *see* (Jesus walking on the water). The Johannine story of Jesus walking on water is a story of theophany, not rescue. It is a story of the revelation of the divine in Jesus.

As with the distress/rescue motifs in Matthew and Mark, there is also important OT precedent for the theophanic dimension of images of walking on water.[10] A core OT symbol of the character and identity of God is God's

---

[9] For a thorough discussion of the similarities and differences of the three versions, see John P. Heil, *Jesus Walking on the Sea.*

[10] For a full discussion of the various OT texts that provide background for this dimension of the story, see Heil, *Jesus Walking on the Sea,* pp. 37-58.

power over the chaos of the sea. Job 9:8 describes God's identity and power as creator by asserting that God "trampled the waves of the sea." This verse recalls God's conquest of the powers of the sea as evidence of God's conquest of the forces of chaos at creation. This dimension is especially clear in the MT of Job 9:8, which speaks of God trampling on the back of the sea dragon. In Ps. 77:19 and Isa. 51:9-10, this creation imagery is joined with another theophanic motif—God's deliverance of God's people through the water of the Reed Sea at the Exodus. God's dominance over the sea leads to the redemption of God's people (cf. also Isa. 43:16). These elements are also in the background of Matthew and Mark, but they take second position to the distress at sea traditions. In John, theophany traditions dominate. When Jesus walks across the rough sea in John 6:19, Jesus acts as only God acts, sharing fully in God's dominion over the waters of chaos.

The primary theophanic focus of John 6:15-21 is confirmed by comparing the disciples' response to Jesus' appearance in Matthew and Mark with their response in John. Two key elements characterize the disciples' response in Matt. 14:26 and Mark 6:49-50a: the disciples think that the figure walking across the water toward them is a ghost (φάντασμα) and they are terrified (ἐταράχθησαν) by that sight. The focus of this response is on the disciples' terror and their mistaken perception of who it is that walks upon the water. Jesus' words in Matt. 14:27 and Mark 6:50b explicitly address that focus. Jesus' opening words, θαρσεῖτε, respond directly to the disciples' terror; his second response, ἐγώ εἰμι, "It is I," explicitly states his identity for them. The disciples can take heart, because Jesus is coming to their rescue.

The balance of elements in this sequence is substantively, albeit at first glance subtly, different in John. There is no mistaken identity in the Johannine account. John 6:19 states quite clearly that the disciples recognize Jesus as the one who is walking on the sea (θεωροῦσιν τὸν Ἰησοῦν περιπατοῦντα ἐπὶ τῆς θαλάσσης; cf. the use of the pronoun αὐτός and not the proper noun Ἰησοῦς in Matt. 14:25-26 and Mark 6:49-50a). The terror of mistaken identity is eliminated completely. The disciples' response to the sight of Jesus walking on the sea, then, is not terror at the sight of a ghost, but fear that is the fear and awe of God. (English translations [e.g., NRSV] blur the important difference and distinction in verb use to describe the disciples' response in John—not ἐταράχθησαν as in Matthew and Mark, but ἐφοβήθησαν.) As Bultmann has eloquently stated, the disciples "are awe-struck by the miracle of the manifestation of the divine."[11]

It is this fear, and this fear only, that Jesus addresses in his words to the disciples (6:20). The disciples are not encouraged to take heart. Rather, the

---

[11] Rudolf Bultmann, *The Gospel of John* (Philadelphia: Westminster Press, 1971), p. 215.

words that appropriately accompany a theophany are spoken by Jesus, ἐγώ εἰμι μὴ φοβεῖσθε. In Jesus' words in 6:20, it is clearest how the fourth evangelist has taken traditional material and shaped it to reflect his own theological interests. The phrase, ἐγώ εἰμι, which was found in the tradition and which is appropriate as an identification formula in its Matthean and Markan contexts, is transformed and given its special Johannine meaning in John 6:20. The expression ἐγώ εἰμι is a revelatory formula here, not a formula of simple identification. The disciples in John do not need to be told that it is Jesus who walks on the water; they already know that. Rather, they need revealed to them the meaning of what they see: how is it possible that Jesus walks across the water. This revelation is at the heart of Jesus' words in 6:20.

Both elements in Jesus' response derive from the OT repertoire of theophanic language and imagery. Jesus' words ἐγώ εἰμι in 6:20 should not be translated as a simple identification formula, "It is I," but should be translated as an absolute ἐγώ εἰμι, "I am."[12] As Jesus walks across the water, he identifies himself with the divine name, "I AM," and thereby provides the meaning of his miraculous act. This usage of the "I AM" seems to be modelled after the use of the divine name in the LXX of Second Isaiah (Isa. 43:25; 51:12; 52:6). The fourth evangelist portrays Jesus as speaking of himself with the same language that provides Yahweh's self-identification in Second Isaiah.

The words, "do not be afraid," are also a standard element of theophanies (e.g., Gen. 15:1; Luke 1:30). Of even more importance for the use of these words in John 6:20, these words, like the "I AM," also constitute the distinctive speech of Yahweh in Second Isaiah (e.g., Isa. 43:1; 44:2, 8). They are the words of the salvation oracle (cf. Lam. 3:55-57), words of comfort and redemption spoken by Yahweh to Yahweh's people. In speaking these words, Jesus speaks God's own words of hope and promise. In both Jesus' deed—walking across the sea—and words, "I AM, do not be afraid," Jesus identifies himself as wholly one with God.

Jesus' self-revelation is followed by the immediate landfall of the disciples' boat (6:21). In this landfall, the Johannine story incorporates the distress/rescue motif that shapes the walking on water stories in Matthew and Mark. Most commentators speak of this landfall as a second miracle, and not only is it second, but also secondary. The primary focus of John 6:15-21 rests on the theophany of Jesus walking on water; the safe conclusion of the disciples' sea-crossing is narrated as almost an afterthought. In John, the disciples' safe passage is only a corollary of the central miracle—that in Jesus the fullness of God is revealed.

---

[12] O'Day, *John*, pp. 596, 602. Raymond Brown correctly suggests that in 6:20 the evangelist may be "playing on the ordinary and sacral use of ἐγώ εἰμι." *The Gospel according to John, I-XII*, p. 534; see also p. 254.

C. JOHN 6:15-21 AS NARRATED CHRISTOLOGY

The above exegetical analysis has attempted to show the ways in which the fourth evangelist has shaped the traditional story of Jesus walking on water to focus the reader's attention on this miracle as theophany. The story has been streamlined to highlight what the evangelist takes to be its theological core—the revelation of God in Jesus. With this reading of the text in view, it is now possible to ask about the narrative and theological function of such a theophany at this juncture in the Fourth Gospel.

1. The relationship of John 6:15-21 to John 5:19-47

In his classic study of John 6, Peder Borgen reflected briefly on the possible relationship between the bread of life discourse and the discourse in John 5:31-47. Borgen suggested that the homily in John 6:31-58 could be read as an illustration of the searching of the scriptures mentioned in John 5:39-40, and concluded that "John 6,31-58 is therefore an elaboration upon and an illustration of the points discussed in 5,37-47."[13] In a more recent article, Borgen has expanded on his earlier observation. He examines more broadly the relationship between John 5 and John 6, and suggests that John 5:31-47 may serve as the thematic background for all of John 6.[14] In addition to the link between John 6:31-58 and John 5:39-40, Borgen also notes the possible connection between John 5:36 and John 6:1-13. The feeding miracle may be intended to illustrate that Jesus' works bear witness to him. Jesus' words about the witness of the Father in 5:37 may also provide the background for 6:27b.

As Borgen himself notes, his comments are important for what they say about theories of displacement to explain the relationship between chapters 5 and 6 in John and about the evangelist's compositional strategy.[15] Borgen has unnecessarily limited the range of comparison between the discourse of John 5 and John 6, however. Borgen has focused only on the second half of the discourse in John 5, and as such has examined how the witnesses to Jesus referred to in 5:31-47 (his works, the Father, the scriptures) are illustrated in the feeding miracle and bread of life discourse in John 6. If one expands the area of inquiry to include the first half of the discourse in John 5, 5:19-30, other connections between John 5 and 6 become visible.

John 5:19-30 expand on Jesus' words in 5:17 ("My Father is still working, and I also am working") to offer a fully developed discourse on

---

[13] Peder Borgen, *Bread from Heaven: An Exegetical Study of the Concept of Manna in the Gospel of John and the Writings of Philo*, NovTSup 10 (Leiden: E. J. Brill, 1965), p. 152. See also p. 180.

[14] Borgen, "John 6: Tradition, Interpretation, and Composition," in *From Jesus to John: Essays on Jesus and Christology in Honor of Marinus de Jonge*, ed. Martinus C. de Boer, JSNTSS 84 (Sheffield: JSOT Press, 1993), pp. 287-89.

[15] *Bread from Heaven*, p. 152, n.2; "John 6," p. 188.

the co-working of Father and Son. From its opening affirmation that "whatever the Father does, the Son does likewise" (5:19), this discourse then names two activities traditionally associated with God alone in which the Father and Son now share: giving life (5:21, 26) and judgment (5:22, 27). Jesus' relationship with God is described here in terms of the works they share: to see Jesus' works is to see the works of God (cf. 5:23-24).

This discourse becomes a suggestive backdrop against which to place the theophany of John 6:15-21, because John 5:19-30 provides the theological lens through which to interpret this miracle. When Jesus walks across the sea, he enacts another of God's works—God's ability to control the waters of chaos—and so illustrates the truth of John 5:19ff. Jesus shares fully in God's work (cf. 4:34); the works of God are fully revealed in Jesus. The identity of God and Jesus in their works is confirmed by the words that Jesus speaks as he walks across the sea, "I AM" (6:20). The miracle story of 6:15-21 works in tandem with John 5:19-30 to embody for the reader one of the evangelist's pivotal theological beliefs, Jesus' sharing in the character and identity of God.

2. The relationship of John 6:15-21 to the rest of John 6

Many interpreters identify the function of John 6:15-21 in its larger John 6 context primarily as one of contrast with the feeding miracle. Painter, as noted above, sees the function of the passage to separate Jesus from the crowd of 6:1-14 and so underscore the contrast between Jesus and the crowd. Borgen sees the function of the passage in the contrast it establishes between the experience of the crowd and that of the disciples: "The crowd misjudged the meaning of the feeding miracle, while the disciples had an authentic and epiphanic encounter with Jesus."[16] Brown, too, notes that the miracle serves as a "corrective of the inadequate reaction of the crowd to the multiplication."[17]

Yet such contrastive readings seem to ignore the full sweep of John 6. In John 6:60-71, there is a divided response to Jesus among the very disciples who witnessed Jesus' self-revelation, with many (πολλοί) of his disciples leaving him. It is hard to make the case that the disciples provide a positive model in contrast to the crowd's negative one on the basis of that textual data. Moreover, John 6:15-21 is noteworthy for its reserve in depicting the disciples' response to Jesus' self-revelation. Matthew devotes an extended section to the response of Peter as an individual disciple and of the group (Matt. 14:28-33), whereas Mark quite explicitly points to the disciples' continuing hard-heartedness (Mark 6:52). John 6:21a narrates simply that

---

[16] Borgen, "John 6," p. 270. See also Marinus de Jonge, *Jesus: Stranger from Heaven and Son of God: Jesus Christ and the Christians in the Johannine Perspective*, SBLSBS 11 (Missoula, MT: Scholars Press, 1977), p. 129.

[17] Brown, *The Gospel according to John (I-XII)*, p. 255.

the disciples wanted to take Jesus into the boat. While it may be tempting to read into this comment an affirmation of the disciples' joyous reception of Jesus,[18] it is nonetheless worth noting that the disciples' desire involves an act of taking (λαμβάνω) not totally dissimilar from the crowd's grasping desire at 6:14.

Readings that focus on John 6:15-21 primarily as a story of contrast also tend to miss the narrative and theological value of the theophany in its own right. In the context of John 6, this miracle functions as the evangelist's commentary on the "sign" of 6:1-14. For a sign to be of theological value in the fourth gospel, those who witness the sign must see in and through the particular event (turning water into wine, 2:1-11; the healing of the royal official's son, 4:46-54; the feeding of the five thousand) to that to which the sign points (cf. 6:26). John 6:15-21 positions Jesus as the interpreter of the sign. When he withdraws to the mountain, Jesus signals that the correct interpretation of the sign is not that he is the prophet-king like Moses. When Jesus walks across the sea and identifies himself with the "I AM," he gives the sign its full and true meaning. The theophany of 6:18-20 reveals that to which the sign of 6:1-14 points: Jesus' identity as the incarnation of God.

Together, then, the feeding miracle and the story of Jesus walking on water provide the context for the remainder of John 6. Jesus' conversation with the crowd in 6:25-34, for example, must be read with both events in view. The theophany of Jesus walking on water gives an added dimension to Jesus' words about the Son of Man on whom "God the Father has set his seal" (6:27), as well as Jesus' description of the work of God in 6:29. The "I AM" of 6:20 provides the theological grounding for Jesus' subsequent "I am" statements in 6:35, 41, 48, 51.[19] By providing the reader with a vivid enactment of the relationship of Jesus and God, the narrative of 6:15-21 anticipates the theological move from Jesus as the giver of bread, as he is in the miracle of 6:1-14, to Jesus as the bread of God that comes down from heaven (6:31-58). It is as the one who walks upon the sea, who shares fully in God's work, that Jesus is the bread from heaven.

3. The relationship of John 6:15-21 to the larger Fourth Gospel narrative

The theophany narrative of John 6:15-21 puts into story form the theological claim that has been echoing since the opening lines of the Fourth Gospel. The Prologue informs the Gospel reader that Jesus is the incarnate Word of God, and the rest of the Gospel demonstrates and serves this central claim: "In the beginning was the Word, and the Word was with God, and the Word was God" (1:1) . . . "the Word became flesh and dwelt among us" (1:14) . . . "No one has ever seen God. It is God the only Son, who is close to the Father's heart, who has made God known" (1:18). Far

[18] So Witkamp, "Some Specific Johannine Factors in John 6:1-21," p. 54.
[19] Schnackenburg, *The Gospel according to St. John*, 2:27.

from being peripheral to the Johannine context and themes, John 6:15-21 provides a bold and vivid demonstration of the unity of God and Jesus, the Father and the Son.

The most succinct and direct articulation of this claim is found in John 10:30: "The Father and I are one." This verse states in summary form what Jesus said at length in the discourse of 5:19-30. "One" (ἕν) is neuter, not masculine; Jesus is not saying that he and the Father are one person, nor, to use the language of later Christian doctrine, of one essence or nature. Rather, he is saying that he and the Father are united in the work that they do. This verse states directly what Jesus' works throughout the Gospel have already shown: Jesus shares in God's work and power.[20]

The narrative and theological function of John 6:15-21 becomes even clearer when read in the light of John 10:30. The power that enables Jesus to feed the multitudes is not the power of either a prophet or a king. Rather, it is the power of the one who walks across the sea. That is, it is the power of God. The story of Jesus walking on water thus functions in the Fourth Gospel as a narrative embodiment of the Gospel's christology. Just as John 10:30 provides a verbal summary of the Gospel's central claim about God and Jesus, John 6:15-21 offers a narrative summary of the same claim. The theophany narrative is emblematic of the theological reality in which the entire Gospel is grounded.

---

[20] See O'Day, *John*, pp. 676-79.

THE DISMANTLING OF DECISIONAL FAITH:
A READING OF JOHN 6:25-71

Robert Kysar

The discourse segment of John 6 has been the subject of frequent investigations.[1] Often it has been read in terms of its relationship with Hebraic and Jewish themes[2] and often in search of its sacramental meaning.[3] The symbolism of the language attributed to Jesus in these verses has intrigued scholars for centuries, and its pivotal role in the whole narrative of chapters 1 through 12 is clear to some interpreters.[4]

This reading of 6:25-71 does not intend to minimize the importance of other investigations but only to supplement them. My interest here is in the exploration of the general function of the language of the passage on and in the reader. The method used in this essay asks how the discourse/dialogue of verses 25-71 functions in its narrative context; how the language performs in a particular reading experience. Hence, I am concerned with what the text does to a particular reader. The conviction underlying this method is that the whole of the passage may impact readers in some unusual ways.[5]

---

[1] For a recent bibliography on John 6 see George R. Beasley-Murray, *John*, Word Bible Commentary, vol. 36 (Waco, TX: Word Books, 1987), pp. 81-82.

[2] For example, Peder Borgen, *Bread from Heaven: An Exegetical Study of the Concept of Manna in the Gospel of John and the Writings of Philo*, Supplements to Novum Testamentum, vol. X (Leiden: E. J. Brill, 1965).

[3] For instance, C. K. Barrett, "'The Flesh of the Son of Man' John 6:53," *Essays on John* (Philadelphia: Westminster Press, 1982), pp. 37-49. A more recent discussion is found in Craig R. Koester, *Symbolism in the Fourth Gospel: Meaning, Mystery, Community* (Minneapolis: Fortress Press, 1995), especially pp. 257-262. For the literature and interpretations of the issue of the Eucharistic references of 6:25-71 see Kysar, *The Fourth Evangelist and His Gospel: An Examination of Contemporary Scholarship* (Minneapolis: Augsburg Publishing House, 1975), pp. 252-55, 257-59.

[4] For example, Thomas L. Brodie understands it to be the climax of Part 2 (2:23-6:71) of "Book One" (chapters 1-12). *The Gospel According to John: A Literary and Theological Commentary* (New York/Oxford: Oxford University Press, 1993), p. xii. William Loader understands chapter 6 to begin the second half of the "christological structure" of chapters 1-12. *The Christology of the Fourth Gospel*, Beiträge zur biblischen Exegese und Theologie 23 (Frankfurt am Main: Verlag Peter Lang, 1989), pp. 45-53. I have suggested that it is a pivotal point in the first twelve chapters at which the extent of Jesus' opposition emerges. *John, the Maverick Gospel*, rev. ed. (Louisville: Westminster John Knox Press, 1993), pp. 14-18. See also Kysar, *John's Story of Jesus* (Minneapolis: Fortress Press, 1984), pp. 39-44.

[5] In this way the goal of this paper is similar to that of Gary A. Phillips, "'This is a Hard Saying. Who Can Listen to It?' Creating a Reader in John 6," *Narrative and Discourse in Structural Exegesis. John 6 and I Thessalonians*, Semeia 26, Daniel Patte, ed. (Chico, CA: Scholars Press, 1983), pp. 23-56. There Phillips attends to the question of "The Text's Work" (pp. 51-53). However, Phillips' expressed method is structuralist, while mine is more akin to some forms of reader response. For a review of the most current methods in the study of the

In particular I seek here a greater self-consciousness in the reading of this text. Consequently, the witness to the reading is intentionally and intensely personal. In this passage I was struck by the way in which Jesus persistently and gradually dismantles the inquiry and the pretense of faith exhibited by his dialogue partners and demolishes the beginnings of some kinds of faith. I experienced this passage as a challenge to one understanding of faith or of the beginnings of faith.[6] To anticipate my conclusion, the text may have the effect of questioning the notion of faith that assumes belief is rooted in personal decision in response to Jesus, a theme that is sometimes attributed to Fourth Gospel.[7]

Of course, a description of the way in which this reader experiences the text is but one among many possibilities, and I make no claim for its being a "true" reading of the text (whatever that might be). It is a witness, if you will, to what the text did to this particular reader at one particular time.[8] One purpose of the paper is to discover what value, if any, there might be in this sort of experiment.

The essay will move through three stages. The first is a summary of a reading experience of the passage. The second stage will reflect on the

---

Fourth Gospel, see Michel Gourgues, "Cinquante ans de recherche johannique: De Bultmann a la narratologie," *De Bien des manières: La recherche biblique aux abords du xxie siecle*, Lectio Divina 163 ACEBAC (Montreal/Paris: Éditions Fides/Éditions du Cerf, 1995), pp. 230-306.

[6] In this sense mine is a self-conscious "resistant reading"—one that resists the implications of the passage for faith. Robert M. Fowler suggests the possibility of becoming "more self-conscious about our acts of assent and our acts of resistance" in reading ("Reader-Response Criticism: Figuring Mark's Reader," *Mark and Method: New Approaches in Biblical Studies*, Janice Capel Anderson and Stephen D. Moore, eds. [Minneapolis: Fortress Press, 1992], pp. 73-81, quotation, p. 81). Furthermore, by attending to my own response to the reading, I am following Anderson's and Moore's injunction: "We are members of the critical guild, in other words, overtrained readers who need to unlearn as well as to learn" (*Mark and Method*, p. 21). But in my method self-consciousness takes the form of autobiographical experience. The autobiographical turn in reader response criticism is found in its fullest and most honest form in Jeffrey L. Staley, *Reading with a Passion: Rhetoric, Autobiography, and the American West in the Gospel of John* (New York: Continuum, 1995). The considerable dangers of such a turn are discussed in *The Postmodern Bible*, George Aichele, et al. eds. (New Haven and London: Yale University Press, 1995), pp. 20-69.

[7] An instance of this view is J. Terence Forestell, *The Word of the Cross*, Analecta Biblica 57 (Rome: Biblical Institute Press, 1974), pp. 103-13.

[8] This reader is an affluent, empowered Caucasian Lutheran Christian male who works within an academic setting and interprets scripture on behalf of the church and its ministry. Furthermore, I do not come as an innocent reader without presuppositions about the text but with an interest in the theme of the "origin of faith" already evident in several redactional critical analyses. Examples include *John, the Maverick Gospel*, pp. 70-74 and "Pursuing the Paradoxes of Johannine Thought: Conceptual Tensions in John 6. A Redaction-Critical Proposal," *The Living Text: Essays in Honor of Ernest W. Saunders*, Dennis E. Groh and Robert Jewett, eds. (Landam, MD: University Press of America, 1985), pp. 189-206.

performance of the text in the reading experience. Finally, the study will offer some theological and hermeneutical conclusions.[9]

A. A READING OF 6:25-71[10]

The general context for the passage includes a number of encounters with previous portions of the Gospel. Most important for our interests is the fact that the reader has seen certain characters engaged in significant discussion with Jesus on at least two occasions—one as remarkably unsuccessful as the other was fruitful. In chapter 3 Nicodemus comes to Jesus with what appears to be an interest in learning from him (i.e., he calls Jesus "teacher," 3:2). But the reader watches as Nicodemus fails to understand Jesus—fails even to be able to ask significant questions—with the result that he is gradually brought to silence and disappears entirely from the discussion. In chapter 4 the reading experience is very different. Here a Samaritan woman engages Jesus in vital issues of tradition and theology. By the conclusion of this dialogue the woman is brought to some degree of faith and shares her new faith with members of her village with the result that they confess Jesus to be "Savior of the World" (4:42).[11] The impression is that discussion with Jesus is possible but not always realized.

The immediate context of the passage under consideration is the experience of reading two wondrous stories. First, Jesus has successfully fed the crowd in 6:1-15, then walked across the chaotic waters to come to his distressed disciples and brought them safely to shore (6:16-21). The reader is filled with a sense of awe as a result of these two episodes and anticipates the popular reception of Jesus, even as 6:15 suggests. So, I enter the discussion that ensues after verse 24 with anticipation of the hero's glorious acclamation by the people. The anticipation is qualified, however, by the fact that 6:15 implies that the crowd's enthusiasm had been wrongly motivated. But by this time in the reading of the Gospel the reader is prepared to be surprised by developments in the plot.

---

[9] A summary of an earlier draft of portions of this paper was published in my article, "Is Faith Possible? A Reading of John 6:25-71 with Homiletical Considerations," in the collection of papers for the Work Groups of the 1995 annual meeting of the Academy of Homiletics.

[10] I will refer to the reader here in the first person singular and the second person masculine singular only because I wish to witness to my own reading experience. In this case, the reference to the reader as male does not imply gender exclusivity. This summary of my reading experience was first written without footnotes. The notes in the section were added later for the sake of the readers of this paper.

[11] Sandra M. Schneiders describes the Samaritan woman as "a genuine theological dialogue partner" (*The Revelatory Text: Interpreting the New Testament as Sacred Literature* [San Francisco: HarperSanFrancisco, 1991], p. 191).

In the light of the two previous attempts to hold discussion with Jesus the reader wonders what success the "crowd" will have in engaging Jesus in dialogue. (The antecedent of "they" in verse 25 appears to be the ὄχλος of verse 24.) Will it be a profitable discussion, like the one with the Samaritan woman, or a futile one as witnessed in 3:1ff? Like the discussion with Nicodemus, this conversation is initiated by the crowd, not by Jesus; and, like Nicodemus (3:2), they call Jesus "Rabbi" (v. 25). The failed effort of the Pharisee to engage Jesus in discussion looms large in the reader's mind. Their initial question is enigmatic,[12] but Jesus' response challenging. Rather than answering their inquiry, he seems to chastise them for their motives in seeking him (v. 26)[13] and then commands them to labor for "food that endures to eternal life" (v. 27). The reader is not sure what that food might be but remembers the "living water" that wells "up to eternal life" (4:10-14). The inference is to compare the feeding story earlier in the chapter with some other form of nourishment still to be discovered.

The crowd responds to Jesus' exhortation to "labor" (ἐργάζεσθε) for food that "endures for eternal life" with a very rational question: "What must we do to be doing the works (ἔργα) of God?" An honest inquiry that has occurred to the perceptive reader. To their question, however, Jesus answers that the work of God is to believe in the one sent by God (v. 29). But what is meant by "the work of God"? Is this an invitation to believe?

His remark evokes a second question in verse 30: "What sign do you do, that we may see, and believe you?" The crowd wants to believe. I remember that experiencing a "sign" occasions faith (2:11) and like this reader, the crowd wants some grounds for believing in Jesus (although one may wonder why the marvelous feeding is not sign enough). They support the legitimacy of their question with appeal to their tradition. God had fed their ancestors in the wilderness. Jesus' reply shocks this reader with its polemic tone and his attack on the crowd's sacred tradition.[14] It was not Moses who fed them but the Father, who gives the true bread for "life." God's bread comes down from heaven (vv. 32-33). So, the food that "remains for eternal life" (v. 27) is not to be identified with God's feeding of Israel.

---

[12] Most commentators find the crowd's question a combined effort to ask how long Jesus had been there and when he had come to this place. See, for example, Raymond E. Brown, *The Gospel According to John (i-xii)*, Anchor Bible, vol. 29 (Garden City, NY: Doubleday and Company, 1966), p. 261, and C. K. Barrett, *The Gospel According to St. John*, 2nd ed. (Philadelphia: Westminster Press, 1978), p. 286. Rudolf Schnackenburg suggests that their question reminds the reader of Jesus' sea-walk (*The Gospel According to St. John*, vol 2 [New York: Seabury Press, 1980], p. 35).

[13] Beasley-Murray calls Jesus' response "brusque" (*John*, p. 90).

[14] In his provocative study of the Fourth Gospel, Norman Peterson argues that this polemic quality is a part of the Johannine Jesus' "anti-language" (*The Gospel of John and the Sociology of Light: Language and Characterization in the Fourth Gospel* [Valley Forge, PA: Trinity International Press, 1993], pp. 89-109).

Even though Jesus has assaulted their religious heritage, the crowd responds with a request for such bread, and the conversation begins to sound as if it will be a productive encounter (compare the Samaritan woman's request in 4:15). Jesus' dialogue partners in this case express an authentic quest and an openness to receive that of which Jesus speaks.[15] The crowd has won this reader's sympathy and even admiration.

Jesus then proceeds to say that he is the bread of life and that those who come to him and believe will never hunger or thirst again (v. 35). But the people have not believed even though they have followed him some distance to this locale. Those who are given (δίδωσιν) to him by the Father come to him, Jesus says (v. 37). Verses 38-40 go on to make claims for the special relationship Jesus has with the Father, followed by God's will that nothing should lost, that those who believe should have "eternal life," and that believers will be "raised up at the last day." Belief becomes vitally important, since it entails eternal life. The conversation has now moved to the crucial matter of faith, life, and the "last day."

While the reader acknowledges that Jesus is offering himself as the bread of life, his words appear harsh and obscure (not unlike the words spoken to Nicodemus), especially given the fact that the people have demonstrated what seems to this reader to be a genuine receptivity. On the other hand, the reader hears echoes of Jesus' conversation with the Samaritan woman. There Jesus claims that he is the source of "living water" (4:10); here he claims to be "bread of life" (v. 35). As he told the Samaritan woman that whoever drinks of the water he gives "will never thirst" (4:14a), he now says to the crowd that those coming to him "shall not hunger" and "shall never thirst" (v. 35). The dialogue has promising possibilities.

But the reader is puzzled when the "crowd" of verses 25-40 suddenly disappears, and at verse 41 another group—"the Jews"—enters the conversation. More important is that the reader has felt some sympathy for the crowd to this point and experienced their questions and requests as genuine inquiry. Whatever promise their exchange with Jesus might have had is unfulfilled. This new group "complained (ἐγόγγυζον) about him" (v. 41). Inquiry has shifted to skepticism: "Is not this Jesus, the son of Joseph?" (v. 42) This reader finds himself an observer, distanced from the new dialogue partners, when earlier he had some sense of participation with the crowd. These "Jews" discern a conflict between what they know about Jesus and what he is now claiming for himself. The reader cannot entirely share that conflict, since he has read 1:1-18 and knows Jesus' true identity.

---

15 John Painter proposes that 6:1-40 is written in the genre of "quest story" (*The Quest for the Messiah: The History, Literature and Theology of the Johannine Community*, 2nd ed. [Nashville: Abingdon Press, 1993], pp. 267-76).

Jesus' response to "the Jews'" complaint is the assertion that they cannot
believe unless they are drawn by the Father (οὐδεὶς δύναται ἐλθεῖν πρός
με ἐὰν μὴ ὁ πατὴρ ὁ πέμψας με ἑλκύσῃ αὐτόν), accompanied by the
repetition of the promise that the believer will be raised up (v. 44). Those
who are taught by God come to him, Jesus says (vv. 45-46). The bread he
offers is contrasted with the manna from heaven known in the tradition, for
this bread provides a life freed from death (vv. 47-51a).

I am caught in a dilemma. Faith is clearly of utmost importance. Yet
faith seems contingent on matters beyond human will. The Father "gives"
believers to Jesus and "draws" them. What role then does the reader have in
responding to Jesus? The disturbing words, "the bread that I shall give for
the life of the world is my flesh" (v. 51b), intensify my dilemma. This
seems an even more drastic claim than those made to the crowd. Strangely,
this reader begins to feel some identification with "the Jews'" complaint, for
I too ask, "How is he able to give his flesh to be eaten?" (v. 52). Jesus'
answer to what "the Jews" ask, and this reader is thinking, doesn't help. His
speech heightens the confusion of the identification of his flesh with the
life-giving bread. One must eat (ἐσθίω) his flesh (v. 53), even "feed on"
(τρώγω) it (v. 54), and drink his blood. Those who do not do so "have no
life," and those who do have "eternal life" and resurrection (vv. 53-54), for
his flesh and blood are "true" (ἀληθής) food and drink (v. 55). They are
promised that they will "abide in" Jesus and he in them (v. 56). And the
speech ends reiterating again the benefit of such a feeding—eternal life (vv.
57-58).

This reader wonders. How am I to eat this flesh and drink this blood?
Faith is the vital link and is invited. But, on the other hand, it seems to
transcend the reader's own volition. Believers are "given" and "drawn" by
God, so what am I left to do in order to believe and hence eat and drink as
Jesus commands? I am left feeling powerless to act in the face of the radical
words I have read.

Struggling with those radical words and the feeling of helplessness given
what has been said about God's role in believing, I am surprised—yet in
another sense reassured—when the identity of the discussion partners shifts
again in verse 60. I am surprised by unbelief among the disciples, since I
had been led to think that they were the ones who believed in Jesus (e.g.,
2:11). Yet I am reassured, because now it is even the disciples who
"complain" about their master's words. With me, they ask who can accept
(ἀκούω) such words (v. 60)? In Jesus' response in verses 61-62 he says in
effect: "You haven't seen anything yet! If this offends you, how will you
respond to the son of man's ascension to where he originated?" But his next
words are the cause of more reflection than offense. He claims that the
"spirit gives life; the flesh is useless" and that his words are spirit (v. 63).
What can this mean in the light of what has just been said about the

importance of eating his own flesh? The shift to spirit suggests that the previous speech is not to be taken literally; but that leaves unresolved what sense it makes if one looks for the "spirit" in it.

The last segment of the speech begins with what should be obvious but is striking: "among you are some who do not believe" (v. 64a). The story-teller explains that Jesus knew "from the first" (ἐξ ἀρχῆς) who believed and who would betray him (v. 64b). Jesus seems to elaborate the narrator's words by reiterating that those who come to him do so only because it is "granted (ἦ δεδομένον) by the Father" (v. 65). Again, this reader must ask what it means to believe, given the fact that some disciples do not believe, that Jesus knew it all along, and that one is able to come to him only because of the Father's "granting" (i.e., "giving") it. The discussion moves toward a tragic conclusion with many of the disciples leaving Jesus (v. 66). The reader is threatened by their abandonment of Jesus, since the whole narrative to this point had nurtured his identification with this group. The discussion has failed, it seems, as did the one with Nicodemus. My sense of any power to contribute to my believing is weakened by the fact that not all disciples believe, that Jesus has foreknowledge of who the believers are, and (again) that faith must be given. I recall 1:11 and wonder if my own uncertainty about my faith takes me with the departing disciples. There is no security in counting oneself among the disciples. I see myself, along with Nicodemus and the disciples, walking back out into the darkness (1:5).

But there is one more installment in the passage. This time Jesus takes the initiative and addresses the "twelve"—the first time in the discussion that Jesus has initiated a conversation with a group. Without extratextual information this reader would have no idea who the "twelve" are, since this is the gospel's first use of that designation. But Jesus asks if they will also leave (v. 67), suggesting that the twelve are not identical with the disciples who have joined "the Jews" in being offended by Jesus' words. Peter makes his bold statement of faith on behalf of the others (vv. 68-69). Faith is possible! One can will (exercise volition) to believe in the face of the difficulties of the words of this puzzling Jesus.

Or, so I may think, until I read Jesus' response to Peter's words. Jesus has "chosen" (ἐξελεξάμην) the twelve, not they him. And yet one of them is a devil (v. 70)! The narrator eases this reader's discomfort a bit by explaining that the "devil" is Judas who will betray Jesus (v. 71). The first the reader hears of betrayal is verse 64, and now the betrayer is named. He is among the intimate faithful circle of disciples, but with some knowledge of the story of Jesus told elsewhere I am inclined to put this Judas in a special category among the group. Still, the believers are the chosen, and even then there may be "devils" among those who are chosen.

With some such uncertainty and discomfort the reader comes to the conclusion of the conversation. I am left still pondering the words about

Jesus' identity as the bread of life and about eating his flesh and drinking his blood. But equally disturbing is how one comes to this banquet at all. Coming to Jesus and believing in him is required for such "eating." Yet the only believers in this discussion are those selected by Jesus and even then there is the possibility of devils among the selected ones!

But what is faith? How am I to understand the origin of this all-important believing? Can one ever know with any confidence that they believe?

B. REFLECTIONS ON THE PERFORMANCE OF THE TEXT

This sketch of my witness to the experience of reading 6:25-71 provides a basis on which to reflect on what the text does—at least to this reader. Even if my own reading experience is alien to others, perhaps these reflections help to understand the performance of the text. Several different kinds of reflections are important for elucidating the way the language of the text works.

First in importance is *the movement of the passage* as it is experienced in the reading. It is comprised of eight discrete movements, with four distinct groups engaging Jesus in dialogue.

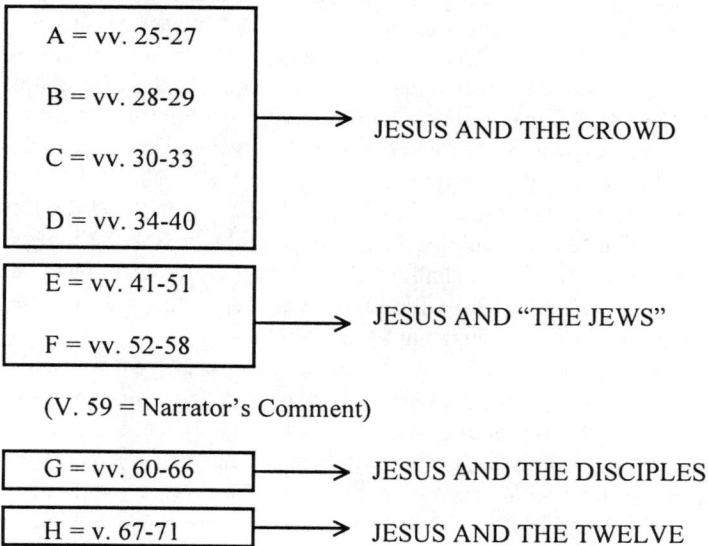

A = vv. 25-27

B = vv. 28-29

C = vv. 30-33 → JESUS AND THE CROWD

D = vv. 34-40

E = vv. 41-51

F = vv. 52-58 → JESUS AND "THE JEWS"

(V. 59 = Narrator's Comment)

G = vv. 60-66 → JESUS AND THE DISCIPLES

H = v. 67-71 → JESUS AND THE TWELVE

With the exception of the last unit, each segment begins with a statement or question by a dialogue partner to which Jesus then responds. In H Jesus takes the initiative to begin a conversation with the twelve.

The groups designated as dialogue partners shift in the process of the development of the passage. The conversation begins with those who are represented as sincere, receptive inquirers and continues through D. They have sought Jesus out, an act associated with the beginnings of discipleship. (The verb, ζητέω, is used of discipleship in 1:38 and 20:15 but elsewhere of those who desire to persecute Jesus, e.g., 71; so, the word is ambiguous of itself and apart from its context). To be sure, their motives for pursuing Jesus are mixed (v. 26). They ask how Jesus got to this side of the lake (A), ask what they are to do to do God's works (B), and request a sign as a basis for the faith (C). In D they are portrayed as making a pious appeal for the bread Jesus has mentioned.[16]

However, in E and F the discussion partners are clearly hostile. Jesus' words in D (not least of all the ἐγώ εἰμι in v. 35) evoke the complaint of "the Jews." They appear in the discussion as those who cannot accept Jesus' claims for himself and as clearly distinguished from the ὄχλος of the previous units. In both E and F they are represented as skeptical of Jesus' words, and Jesus' response to them in E only intensifies their grumbling. In F it is their understanding of Jesus' identity that evokes his radical words about eating his flesh and drinking his blood.[17]

The dialogue partners change to the disciples in G, and they are implicitly identified with "the Jews" in that they too complain (v. 61). The reading effect of having the hostile opponents suddenly become disciples (v. 60) powerfully suggests that unbelief is not limited to Jesus' opponents. The introduction of the phenomenon of unbelieving disciples blurs the distinction between "the Jews" and "the disciples."

---

16 My reading of the crowd is considerably different than that found in many commentaries. Alfred Plummer calls the crowd, "wrongheaded" (*The Gospel According to St. John*, Thornapple Commentaries [Grand Rapids, MI: Baker Book House, 1981, first published 1882], p. 152). More contemporary commentators tend to agree. D. A. Carson, for instance, uses adjectives such as "confused" and "uncertain" to describe the crowd and says of them, "they acknowledge [Jesus] as teacher though they are about to dispute his teaching, they clamour for him as king (v. 15) though they understand little of the nature of his reign" (*The Gospel According to John* [Grand Rapids, MI: William B. Eerdmans Publishing Co., 1991], p. 283). My own sense is that they are genuine seekers, even if they are confused by Jesus' words (as this reader was) and motivated by less than the ideal (as this reader most often is)!

17 My concerns are synchronic, so I leave aside the question of the text's history of composition. Whether or not verses 51b-58 were a later addition to the discourse by either a "friendly" or "unfriendly redactor," the passage exhibits unity as it stands. For my view of the redactional history of the passage see *John*, Augsburg Commentary on the New Testament (Minneapolis: Augsburg Publishing House, 1986), pp. 108-10 and *John, the Maverick Gospel*, pp. 122-26.

Finally Jesus opens a conversation with the twelve in H, in which they are portrayed as a faithful group among the larger circle of the disciples, in spite of the scandalous quality of their master's words. The pattern of movement betrays an increasingly hostile role attributed to the discussion partners in segments E through G, suddenly reversed in H.

The narrator plays an increasingly important role as the passage moves toward a conclusion. That voice first sets the stage for the dialogue and moves the text from narrative to discourse in verse 25a. After that, the narrator introduces the speakers in each of the sections. But the story-teller's role becomes more frequent and more important in sections E through H. The guiding voice identifies the reaction of "the Jews" in verse 41 and describes their response in verse 52. When the discussion shifts to the disciples, that voice gives the reader insight into Jesus' unspoken knowledge: Jesus knows the disciples are murmuring (v. 61) and who among them did not believe (v. 64b). Finally, in section G the narrator tells the reader that "many of the disciples" disown their association with Jesus. In the final segment of the discussion the narrator explains Jesus' comment in verse 70 and names Judas as the betrayer (v. 71).

The information about locale in verse 59 is the most puzzling of the narrator's words.[18] In terms of the reader experience, this intrusion serves as a buffer between "the Jews'" grumbling and that of the disciples. Functionally the verse separates disciples (even unbelieving ones) from the religious institution, the synagogue. Does it then suggest boundaries between disciples, on the one hand, and the crowd and "the Jews" on the other? Yet verse 59 hardly breaks the flow of the whole passage, since the

---

[18] Some commentators take the narrator's statement of the locale as a division in the passage. C. K. Barrett, for instance, proposes that verse 59 ends the first discourse, "Bread from Heaven," and provides a transition to a second discourse comprised of verses 60-71, which he entitles, "Reaction and Confession" (*The Gospel According to St. John*, pp. 300-01). A similar division is used by Barnabas Lindars (*The Gospel of John*, New Century Bible [London: Oliphants, 1972], pp. 249-70). Mark W. G. Stibbe has more recently proposed two different major movements in the passage. After what he understands to be an introduction of the theme of "the true bread from heaven" in verses 25-34a, he speaks of a first section having to do with "Coming to Jesus" (vv. 34b-40 and 41-51) and then a second, "Staying with Jesus" (vv. 52-59 and 60-71). The narrator's comment at verse 59 serves no more than to divide the two halves of the second section (*John*, Readings: A New Biblical Commentary [Sheffield: Sheffield Academic Press, 1993], pp. 87-88). Painter's analysis finds a "quest story" from the first edition of the Gospel in verses 1-40 and "rejection stories" added in later editions in verses 41-71 with verses 36-40 redacted to make the transition. He says of verse 59 only that it moves the locale to an unspecified place. But it clearly delineates the conversation with "the Jews" from that with the disciples (*The Quest of the Messiah*, pp. 267-84). On the basis of a contemporary reading, I doubt that the whole dialogue should be fragmented and hold that the dialogical pattern that continues through the final verses unifies the whole passage. Painter and Stibbe endorse my contention that verse 59 need not be taken as a major division in the text.

passage continues with grumbling and rejection. Location does not, it seems to me, figure prominently in the performance of the text.

The sections move steadily toward more and more extreme claims for Jesus' identity, reaching their climax in F. The movement of the discussion is essentially tragic in structure. It begins with genuine inquirers (if not believers), but Jesus becomes more and more offensive in each of the dialogue units until his words result in the loss of many of his disciples at the conclusion of G (v. 66). The discussion is, then, similar to the one with Nicodemus in which Jesus' dialogue partner fades away, in that case more because of incomprehension than unbelief.[19] The totally tragic quality of the structure of the discussion is qualified with Peter's confession in H. But the final unit too has a still more tragic tone, insofar as it ends with the mention of Judas as one among the "faithful group."[20]

The *style* of the whole tragic passage is repetitious dialogue. The passage is genuine dialogue, as has been shown in the reflections on the movement of the passage. It is important to note, too, that the discussion partners frequently introduce the theme of a section. The crowd first raises the theme of the bread from heaven (v. 31), and Jesus' words about his identity in section F are occasioned by "the Jews'" assertion that they know who Jesus is (v. 52).

But more significant is the fact that the passage is filled with repetition while still progressing in thought.[21] Indeed, those who argue that the Johannine discourse style is spiral find evidence for their view here.[22] The major motif of the discussion is hunger and food as they are related to life. That theme moves toward a transformation in verse 63. Food is immediately introduced in verses 26-27 as is the theme of a nourishment that yields "eternal life." Certain words and phrases are repeated almost tiresomely through the sections of the dialogue. "Eternal life" (ζωὴ αἰώνιος) appears in verses 27, 40, 47, 51, 54, 58, and 68 and "life" (ζωή)

---

[19] Phillips is correct in saying that John 6 demonstrates "how one can engage or not engage Jesus in discourse, indeed the very possibility of having discourse with Jesus at all" (*Narrative and Discourse in Structural Exegesis. John 6 and I Thessalonians*, p. 53).

[20] Stibbe speaks of the "tragic irony" of the discourse but in terms of the elusiveness of Jesus (*John*, pp. 87-88).

[21] John Dominic Crossan describes the style of John 6 as "formulaic, hypnotic, and almost rhapsodic repetition" ("It is Written: A Structuralist Analysis of John 6," *Narrative and Discourse in Structural Exegesis. John 6 and I Thessalonians*, p. 15).

[22] Rudolf Schnackenburg writes that Johannine "thought 'circles', repeating and insisting, and at the same time moving forward, explaining and going on to a higher level" (*The Gospel According to St. John*, vol. I [New York: Seabury Press, 1968], p. 117). This may be a microstylistic feature of what Jeffrey Lloyd Staley argues is the "concentric structure" of the plot of the Gospel of John in its entirety (*The Print's First Kiss: A Rhetorical Investigation of the Implied Reader in the Fourth Gospel*, SBL Dissertation Series 82 [Atlanta: Scholars Press, 1988], pp. 58-71).

in verses 33, 53, 57, and 63. "Bread from heaven" (ἄρτος ἐκ οὐρανοῦ) or "bread of life" (τῆς ζωῆς) is introduced in verse 31 and reoccurs in verses 35, 41, 48, 50, 51, and 58. Since belief is connected with the relationship between bread and eternal life, the verb, "to believe" (πιστεύω) debuts early (v. 29) and is then used at least seven more times—verses 35, 36, 40, 47, 64 (twice), and 69. The bread that has eternal consequences is from heaven, hence it "descends" (καταβαίνω, e.g., v. 33), even as Jesus claims he has descended (e.g., v. 38).[23] The combination of the descending bread and Jesus is found in verse 51. (The verb is also used in vv. 38, 42, 50, and 58.)

Subtle connections between Jesus' identification with the nourishment that provides eternal life are present. The emphasis on the descent of Jesus and the bread climaxes with Jesus' reference to his own ascension (ἀναβαίνω, v. 62). The crowd is urged to seek the food that "remains" (μένω) in verse 27, and in verse 56 Jesus promises that those who feed on his flesh and drink his blood "abide (μένω) in me, and I in them." In the climax of the discussion belief and eternal life are found together (vv. 68-69).

Other expressions are emphasized through repetition. Jesus speaks of himself as sent from God five times (vv. 29, 38, 39, 44, 57). The promise of the eschatological resurrection (ἀναστήσω αὐτὸ ἐν τῇ ἐσχάτῃ ἡμέρα and its variations) appears four times (vv. 39, 40, 44, and 54). The solemn ἀμὴν, ἀμὴν λέγω ὑμῖν is used four times (vv. 26, 32, 47, and 53), and the ἐγώ εἰμι expression three times (vv. 35, 48, and 51).

All of this documents what the reader experiences as a continuous use of key expressions in the conversation—hammering away at the passage's themes. But these repetitions also suggest the way in which terms are nuanced in slight ways to further the progression of the themes of the passage. For example, the verb "eat" (ἐσθίω) is used consistently through the discussion (e.g., vv. 26, 31, 50, 53), but then is replaced by "feed on" (τρώγω, vv. 54-58). Eating is supplemented by references to thirst (e.g., v. 35) and drinking (vv. 53 and 56). The discussion spirals up from the food the son of man gives (v. 27) to the Father's giving the bread from heaven (e.g., v. 32) to Jesus' identity as the bread of life from heaven (v. 51). There is clear progression, therefore, even amid the repetitious style of the passage.

---

[23] The substance of the dialogue is bracketed with descending and ascending. Verse 33 speaks of the bread's coming down (καταβαίνω). After identifying himself as the "bread from heaven," Jesus speaks of the "son of man ascending (ἀναβαίνω) where he was before" (v. 62). See the classic study by Godfrey C. Nicholson, *Death as Departure: The Johannine Descent-Ascent Schema*, SBL Dissertation Series 63 (Chico, CA: Scholars Press, 1983).

The role of reader identification is complex, for the reader's identification with the various groups changes even within their respective sections. The reader gradually became identified with the crowd in their quest and was sympathetic toward their queries. At first distanced from "the Jews," I was brought closer to them by the time of verse 52. This was in part due to the reader's own uneasiness with Jesus' statements and to his discovery of himself in some of the reactions of "the Jews." There was mixed attraction and repulsion toward the disciples. At first I was surprised, since the reading had never revealed unbelief in the characterization of this group. Still, this reader felt reassured by the fact that they too were offended by Jesus' words. The disciples, however, also posed a certain threat to this reader, because of the possibility of my being one of these unbelieving disciples. The twelve elicited immediate identification. The reader wants to think of himself as the faithful believer modeled in Peter's confession. But then the twelve become threatening when Jesus says that they are chosen and that there is a devil among them.

This tracing of the reader's shifting identification is a witness to the power of the text, as well as to the reader's vulnerability to the text. At times I experienced the text almost toying with me—enticing, teasing, pulling me close then pushing me away. The strategy of the text is to keep the reader's response off guard and in a state of flux. While it is dangerously subjective to speak of emotional responses to a text, it seems to me obvious that the work of the text entails such response, especially in a religious document. If the text intends to evoke the response of the whole person, as I believe 20:31 implies, then it will influence the reader at an emotional as well as cognitive and volitional level. At least in the Fourth Gospel, that influence is most often found in the text's characterizations. The reader is invited to struggle with the characters in the plot to discover at a deeper level what has been read in the prologue concerning Jesus' identity. That struggle goes on through the process of identification with and distancing from the persons portrayed in the narrative. In the case of the passage under consideration, the process entails the pulsation between the reader's finding him or herself in each of the four groups with whom Jesus converses and disavowing association with those groups. John 6:25-71 is a prime example of both Johannine characterization and its impact on the careful reader.[24]

The function of metaphor in the passage is also obvious as a result of the reading. The bread that results in eternal life is the central metaphor, and the

---

[24] See Staley, *The Print's First Kiss*, especially pp. 95-118 and "Stumbling in the Dark, Reaching for the Light: Reading Character in John 5 and 9," *The Fourth Gospel from a Literary Perspective*, Semeia 53, R. Alan Culpepper and Fernando F. Segovia, eds. (Atlanta: Scholars Press, 1991), pp. 55-80. In a "Postscript" to the latter, Staley responds to some of the criticisms of a reader response method (pp. 69-70).

passage's performance is largely due to the comparative language around that theme. The metaphor is steadily expanded and its intensity strengthened as the passage progresses. Finally the exaggeration of the metaphor renders the language of the passage offensive to the discussion partners, as well as puzzling to this reader.

The metaphoric language begins in verse 27 with a simple comparison of perishable food that satisfies hunger and "the food that endures to eternal life" (τὴν βρῶσιν τὴν μένουσαν εἰς ζωὴν αἰώνιον)—a comparison not entirely impossible to imagine. Then that potent food is spoken of as God's "bread from heaven" (v. 32) and identified with that which gives life to the world (v. 33). With the mention of life, the comparison begins to threaten the reader's world view. Next the bread is equated with Jesus himself for the first time in verse 35 and contrasted with manna from heaven in verses 49-50. The metaphor is further exaggerated with the identification of the bread from heaven with Jesus' own flesh (v. 51b). It is extended first in verse 53 with the insistence that one must eat (ἐσθίω), then feed on (τρώγω) the flesh of Jesus (vv. 54-58). Second, the metaphor is extended to its final extreme with the inclusion of "drinking my blood" in verses 53-56 and the conclusion that "my flesh is food indeed (ἀληθής ἐστιν βρῶσις) and my blood is drink indeed (ἀληθής ἐστιν πόσις)" in verse 55.

"Feeding on" the food that is Jesus' own flesh and "drinking" his blood is the climactic offense of the passage for the dialogue partners (even the disciples). A simple metaphor has been pursued beyond its ordinary limits. In doing so the passage violates a common sense view of metaphor, namely, that any comparative language has intrinsic limitations. The comparison of one commonly known reality to illumine a lesser known (or unknown) reality works, but only within certain boundaries of similarities. (E.g., to say that he ran like a frightened rabbit is illuminating, but we do not then normally speak of the way the person hopped with his hind legs!)[25]

But this is no simple metaphor (i.e., simile), even though one could say that it begins as such. The language births new meaning through its

---

[25] Crossan asserts that verses 53-56 make "it clear that something more beyond metaphor is happening . . . The language of 6:49-58 is explicable only in terms of eucharistic formulae known from outside the chapter" ("It is Written: A Structuralist Analysis of John 6," p. 15). To my mind his view illustrates one danger in the Eucharistic interpretations of the metaphor in verses 51b-58, namely, that they sometimes tend to domesticate the Gospel's language and thereby lose something of its subversive qualities. While I believe that the text subtly alludes to the Lord's Supper in some way and for some purpose, simply to close the metaphor by saying that the Eucharist is its reference does not take its ambiguity seriously enough. If the interpreter reads the metaphor in terms of the Eucharist, it is necessary then, I believe, to transfer to the sacrament itself something of the ambiguity and mystery intrinsic to the metaphor itself.

radicality.[26] The very absurdity of its eventual form in the passage entices human imagination into new possibilities for construing reality. In Paul Ricoeur's terms, the metaphor of the passage exploits the sense in which such language uses *dissimilarity* rather than *similarity*.[27] In this passage the literal sense of Jesus' words compels the reader to imagine a possible meaning in which Jesus' body is bread, struggling with the obviously ridiculous sense of the equation. The result of the dissimilarity in the metaphor questions the literal meaning while inviting the construction of another meaning. Consequently, the metaphor challenges the reader's construction of reality and implies a new construction, without ever describing that new understanding of reality. The function of the metaphor in sum is to endanger the reader's security in the truth and ignite the pursuit of some new world, yet only insinuated. Its functional nature, then, might be called, "root metaphor," in the sense that the tension between the two terms of the language (bread and flesh) is never resolved and is inexhaustible. The tension is felt most immediately in the fact that the metaphor can never be reduced to a simple propositional statement. That very tension energizes the quest for a new construction of meaning.[28]

So, the heart of the scandal of Jesus' words is a metaphorical language that violates its own limitations. The offense results from the metaphor's questioning of the boundaries of human knowledge. Radical metaphor entices and teases the human imagination to conceive beyond the limits of ordinary language, i.e., language which is supposed to name reality. This sort of absurd metaphor is language pushed beyond the outer limits of that which can be spoken and signifies the unknown and mysterious, promising the possibility of new knowing. Metaphor as it is found here may be part of what others have called Johannine "overlexicalizing" which I take to be the density of reference structured into language.[29] In just such a way the language of our text tests the reader's capacity for imagination and—more fundamentally—calls   into   question   the   adequacy   of   language's

---

[26] Sallie McFague's describes the category, "radical metaphor" in *Speaking in Parables: A Study in Metaphor and Theology* (Philadelphia: Fortress Press, 1975), pp. 50-56.

[27] Paul Ricoeur, *Paul Ricoeur on Biblical Hermeneutics*, Semeia 4, John Dominic Crossan, ed. (Missoula, MT: Scholars Press, 1975), p. 77. Sandra Schneiders' words are helpful: "[Real metaphors] exist in and even as linguistic tension involving a simultaneous affirmation and negation of the likeness between the two terms of the metaphor. The metaphor contains an 'is' and an 'is not' held in irresolvable tension" (*The Revelatory Text*, p. 29).

[28] See Paul Ricoeur, *Interpretation Theory: Discourse and the Surplus of Meaning* (Fort Worth, TX: Texas Christian University, 1976), p. 64.

[29] Bruce J. Malina, "The Gospel of John in Sociolinguistic Perspective," Center for Hermeneutical Studies, Colloquy 48 (Berkeley: Center for Hermeneutical Studies, 1985). Norman Petersen points out that such a use of language is part of the Fourth Gospel's anti-language (*The Gospel of John and the Sociology of Light*, p. 141).

signification. Thereby it challenges the adequacy of the reader's conception of reality, since that conception is constructed and expressed in language.[30]

This raises the final and crucial reflection on this reader's experience of the text. The central metaphor challenges the readers' construction of reality and invites new structures of meaning. Adjunct to this challenge is another: *The demolition of human confidence in decisional faith.* The total impact of the passage is gained through its movement, the use of repetitious dialogue, identification with its characters, and the performance of the central metaphor. For this reader the text works to call into question the human capacity for faith and undermines of any confidence that one can of their own volitional powers will belief. I acknowledge that this is not the sole function of the passage, nor the one that is most often expressed as the "meaning" of the text. Certainly, the heart of the passage is christological, and no careful reading of the text can avoid that conclusion. But, nonetheless, one possible result of a close reading of this christological text for at least some readers is a serious questioning of the assumption that faith is solely a human responsibility.

To understand how the text performs this demolition of decisional faith it is necessary, first, to observe how believing is treated throughout the passage. Belief is among the first themes to be introduced in the passage. In section B Jesus declares, "This is the work of God, that you believe in him whom he has sent" (v. 29). Following that announcement, the value and importance of believing is scattered throughout the passage. In verse 35 it is equated with coming to Jesus and never hungering or thirsting. Faith is crucial for it entails eternal life (e.g., v. 40). Believers even "have eternal life" (ὁ πιστεύων ἔχει ζωὴν αἰώνιον, v. 47). Hence, to feed on Jesus' flesh and drink his blood is the nature of faith which gives life (v. 53).

But, second, we must ask what the passage suggests with regard to the origin of faith. This all-important belief appears at times in the course of the discussion to be the result of the human will—the individual's response to Jesus. In verses 28-29 the crowd asks what they must do, and Jesus responds that belief is the work of God. When taken as a statement of what God demands, this is an invitation to obey through believing. "Coming" and "believing" seem to be human acts (e.g., v. 35). God wills "that everyone (πᾶς) who sees the Son and believes in him should have eternal life . . ." (v. 40). And the climax of the passage has Jesus asking the twelve if they too will leave, implying that it is their decision. What it means to believe seems clearly to entail understanding who Jesus is and accepting his claims.

However, the language of the text also works to challenge the assumption that human will alone is the origin of faith in response to Jesus,

---

[30] See Kysar, "Johannine Metaphor—Meaning and Function: A Literary Case Study of John 10:1-18," *The Fourth Gospel from a Literary Perspective*, pp. 81-111.

or at the very least, to question any human confidence in the will to believe. The challenge begins in verse 29 with the ambiguous phrase, τὸ ἔργον τοῦ θεοῦ,[31] and that ambiguity immediately teases the reader's assumptions about the origin of faith.[32] Do I do God's work when I believe, or is God's work the creation of faith in me?

The questioning of willful belief continues, then, in a number of the passage's recurring themes. The first is in that enigmatic expression regarding the Father's "giving" the Son those who believe. This is spoken of first in verse 37: "Everything that the Father gives me (πᾶν ὃ δίδωσίν μοι) will come to me." In verse 39 the theme is repeated in connection with the God's will: "that I should lose nothing of all that he has given me (πᾶν ὃ δέδωκέν μοι), but raise it up on the last day." However this divine giving remains ambiguous throughout the passage.

Verse 44 is equally ambiguous. There faith is made dependent on a divine "drawing" (ἐλκύσῃ). In response to the unbelief of "the Jews" Jesus seems here to acknowledge that belief is possible only as a result of God's magnetic attraction of humans. That mysterious "drawing" is perhaps

---

[31] The Fourth Gospel uses the word ἔργον and its plural in essentially four different ways: (1) In reference to the deeds done by humans (e.g., 3:19-21; 14:12). (2) In reference to Jesus' deeds (e.g., 7:3; 10:25; 15:24) and (3) the work(s) God has given Jesus to do (e.g., 5:36; 10:37; 17:4). (4) In reference to God's activity (e.g., 4:34; 5:20; 9:3). The ambiguity of τὸ ἔργον τοῦ θεοῦ in verse 29 is intrinsic to the evangelist's use of this language, especially since God's work is enacted in human form in Jesus' deeds. If the association of the dialogues in 6:25-71 and 4:7-42 is as important as the role it assumes in this reading of the former, it may be significant that 4:34 refers to God's ἔργον. See also Brown, *The Gospel According to John (i-xii)*, pp. 526-27.

[32] This contradicts my own easy statement that the expression constitutes an "invitation to believe" in John (p. 98). Commentators generally use verse 29 as an occasion to discuss the relationship between faith and works and/or the difference between Pauline and Johannine thought. Some claim simply that "the work of God" (what God demands) refers to the human faith response to Jesus. Examples include Beasley-Murray, *John*, p. 91 and Ernst Haenchen, *John 1*, Hermeneia (Philadelphia: Fortress Press, 1984), p. 290. Others recognize that human activity is the essential meaning of the expression but that what humans do is evoked by what God does in Christ. Examples include Brown (*The Gospel According to John [i-xii]*, who acknowledges that the expression can mean either "the work that God requires of [humans]" or "the work that God accomplishes in [people]" (p. 262). He writes, "this believing is not so much a work done by [humans] as it is submission to God's work in Jesus" (p. 265). See also Barrett, *The Gospel According to St. John*, p. 227 and Schnackenburg, *The Gospel According to St. John*, 2:39. Rudolf Bultmann's qualification of the human ἔργον of faith is stronger: humans find their "true being not in what [they themselves achieve], but in submission to what God works; [they find] it, that is to say, in what, by faith, [they allow] to happen to [them]" (*The Gospel of John* [Oxford: Basil Blackwell, 1971], p. 222). Adolf Schlatter makes the strongest statement of sense of the text strictly in terms of what God does in human life to implant faith. "Gottes Werk ist auch hier das Werk, das Gott wirkt, nicht das, das er nur verlangt" (*Der Evangelist Johannes: Ein Kommentar zum vierten Evangelium* [Stuttgart: Calwer Verlag, 1960], p. 171).

explicated in the next verse. In what appears to be a free citation of Isaiah 54:13,[33] Jesus speaks of those who are "taught by God." Then he declares, "Everyone who has heard and learned from the Father comes to me." Those who are drawn by God are those who have been taught by God. But how is one taught by God?

The ambiguity of these expressions of the origin of faith is only enhanced by the final segments of the discussion. First, as a result of the narrative the reader has come to think of those who follow Jesus as examples of the faith response to his words and deeds (e.g., 2:11). But verses 60-66 declare that there are disciples who do not believe. That declaration implicitly undermines this reader's confidence in his own supposedly believing response to Jesus. Verses 60-66 also announce that only those to whom it is "granted" (ᾖ δεδομένον—again, "given") are able (δύναται) to come to Jesus (v. 65). That Jesus knows who will not believe (v. 64b) suggests his foreknowledge. But the haunting phrase "from the first" (ἐξ ἀρχῆς) may suggest something more. In 1:1 ἐν ἀρχῇ implies that "the first" is the mysterious beginnings of reality. And the possibilities of some divine determination rooted in eternity menace the reader.[34]

This reader's confidence in any faith decision has at best been shaken by this language—even with its ambiguity. But the concluding segment seems to promise the reconstruction of confidence that decisional faith is possible. The twelve are free to choose, and Peter models the faith response (v. 69). But Jesus has chosen the twelve, not they him, and there is a "devil" among the chosen faithful (v. 70).

When the whole of the passage is in view, one sees that in the discussions with each of the four groups Jesus utters ambiguous statements that can be construed as qualifications of the volitional act of faith. To *the crowd* he speaks of the "work of God" (v. 29) and insists that believers are "given" to him by the Father (vv. 37 and 39). He tells *"the Jews"* that no one can believe unless they are first "drawn" by God (v. 44). *The disciples* are unbelieving, and Jesus knew ἐξ ἀρχῆς who were believers (v. 64). Jesus also repeats to the disciples the claim that believers are given to him by the Father (v. 65). He reminds *the twelve* that he had chosen them. The theme of God's role in originating the faith response runs through the whole discussion and is represented in the dialogue with each group of participants.

---

[33] Brown, *The Gospel According to John (i-xii)*, p. 271.

[34] Among the many discussions of Johannine determinism these are especially worthy of attention: Schnackenburg, *The Gospel According to St. John*, 1:573-75; D. A. Carson, *Divine Sovereignty and Human Responsibility: Biblical Perspectives in Tension* (Atlanta, GA: John Knox, 1981); Roland Bergmeier, *Glauben als Gabe nach Johannes*, Beitrage zur Wissenschaft vom Alten und Neuen Testament (Stuttgart: Kohlhammer, 1980), and C. H. Dodd, *New Testament Essays*, esp. pp. 54-55, 62-68.

The text works to nurture the importance of believing. The issue at stake is nothing less than life, eternal life, and resurrection. But then it works subtly to chip away at the foundation of confidence that faith is possible, at least through human will alone. Is it within human ability alone to respond to Jesus in faith? Does this divine work, giving, drawing, and teaching refer alone to God's initial act in Christ, or to some other activity in the human spirit? Is it enough that one wills faith? Faith may be as ill-motivated as that of the crowd that seeks Jesus out, not because they saw signs but because they had eaten their fill earlier as a result of his wondrous feeding. Faith may be as fragile as that of the disciples who followed Jesus until they hear him expand this metaphor of bread to his own flesh and blood, and then they find their faith demolished by his words. Faith may even be genuine and steady, but there are "devils" among the believers. *The passage performs the demolition of any confidence in faith conceived as human decision.*[35]

C. CONCLUSIONS

The effort has been only to witness to a single reading of John 6:25-71 without any claim to the universal value of my experience of the text's work. But this witness has uncovered a haunting and muffled sub-text within the passage that may perform the dismantling of human confidence and the construction of uncertainty. A few theological and hermeneutical observations are appropriate in conclusion.

First, an essentially christological passage has impact on the issue of faith. Christology cannot stand in isolation from the human response to claims made for Christ's identity. Not accidentally our passage weaves the thread of faith into the fabric of Jesus' identity, for explication of that identity is whole cloth only with the inclusion of belief in that which transcends human experience. This is to say both that Christology evokes human response (belief or unbelief) and that Christology is in itself faith language—the assertion of faith.

But, second, to speak of faith is always to speak of a response to divine presence. The Fourth Gospel is clear about that. The prologue speaks of response, both the rejection of the Word and his acceptance and belief in his

---

[35] A case could be made, I believe, for understanding these ambiguous expressions concerning faith as mini-metaphors. "The work of God," the Father's "giving" and "drawing," and even Jesus' knowing ἐξ ἀρχῆς and "choosing" are themselves radical metaphorical expressions. Their subversive effect on the reader is similar to the disorienting result of the passage's central metaphor—Jesus' flesh is bread and his blood drink. Therefore the challenge of the metaphorical nature of the expressions used of faith is of a piece with that of the central metaphor. Such an argument, however, requires an additional essay beyond the scope of the present one.

name (1:11-12). Faith is always the result of what God does. The issue at stake in this essay is how much God does in evoking faith. That "the Word became flesh and lived among us" (1:14) is designed to evoke faith. But the faith response remains mysterious, insofar as something more in terms of God's activity seems at stake. There is a mysterious "drawing" by some power beyond human will that plays a role in the faith response. That something more, for this reader at least, intrudes itself into the text of 6:25-71. Whether the text performs this function of itself or only as a result of the reader's location and condition or as some strange combination of both is beyond the scope of this inquiry. In its historical context the gospel may have sought among other things to account for why it is some believe while others do not. But this much is certain: The work of the text for this reader has undermined any confidence and certainty in the human will alone to believe. In the place where that confidence and certainty in human will had grown, there is confidence and certainty only in the Word that still lives among us.[36]

Third, this reading of the passage solicits a hermeneutical observation. The readers' presuppositions about faith shape the way they experience the performance of the text. Readers predisposed to conceive of faith as individual decision in response to God's presence will in all likelihood not interpret the text as I did. Perhaps only those of us who have had the certainty of our faith challenged and who have experienced something of what might be called the "mystery of believing" will read the text in ways similar to this discussion of the passage. One is forced, I believe, to acknowledge that any such effort to elucidate the performance of the text's language has to take into account the reader's precondition. The reader's "social location" needs also to include matters such as religious tradition and faith experience, as well as gender, ethnicity, and class.[37]

---

[36] D. A. Carson summarizes the view of the Gospel on this issue with these words: "John holds men and women responsible for believing; unbelief is morally culpable ... But in the last analysis, faith turns on sovereign election by the Son (15:16), on being part of the gift from the Father to the Son (6:37-44). And this, it must be insisted, drums at the heart of a book that is persistently evangelical. God's will is not finally breached, even in the hardness of human hearts (12:37ff)" (*The Gospel According to John*, pp. 99-100). Bultmann's comments are even more interesting. "[F]aith becomes possible when one abandons hold on one's own security, and to abandon one's security is nothing else than to let oneself be drawn by the Father ... It occurs when [one] abandons his [or her] own judgement and 'hears' and 'learns' from the Father, when he [or she] allows God to speak to him [or her]." He goes on to characterize the faith of the disciples who are offended by Jesus' words and leave him as "only a provisional, unauthentic faith" (*The Gospel of John*, pp. 231-32 and 443).

[37] See the two-volume collection of essays edited by Fernando F. Segovia and Mary Ann Tolbert, *Reading from This Place*, Vol. I: *Social Location and Biblical Interpretation in the United States and Reading from This Place*. Vol. II: *Social Location and Biblical Interpretation in Global Perspective* (Minneapolis: Fortress Press, 1994 and 1995). Segovia's

Finally, then, the reader of 6:25-71 has still to experience those provocative words of 12:32: "I, when I am lifted up from the earth, will draw all people to myself." As disabling as 6:15-71 may seem to the human desire to believe, 12:32 suggests the hope that the cross in some enigmatic way is the Father's "drawing" (ἕλκω) referred to in 6:44.[38] If our passage functions to dismantle all human pretense to the capacity for faith, the reader may gain hope that, in the Gospel of John, the cross makes faith possible. John 6:25-71 points beyond itself to the conclusion of the narrative of which it is only one part.

---

article, "The Significance of Social Location in Reading John's Story," is a useful summary of "reader constructs" (*Interpretation* 49 [1995]: 370-78).

[38] Carson warns against allowing 12:32 "to dilute the force" of 6:44 (*The Gospel According to John*, p. 293). I agree that the sense of 6:44 should not be weakened but am convinced that the cross informs us how Johannine thought understands the divine "drawing."

JOHN 6:51c-58: EUCHARIST OR CHRISTOLOGY?[*]

Maarten J. J. Menken

John 6:51c-58,[1] the final part of the discourse on the bread of life (John 6:22-59), faces the exegete with various problems.[2] Interpreters often consider the passage to be about the sacrament of the Eucharist:[3] in their

---

[*] Revised version of a paper presented to the Seminar on the Johannine Writings at the SNTS Meeting in Madrid, July 1992.

[1] I take as John 6:51c the words: "and the bread which I shall give is my flesh for the life of the world."

[2] A useful survey of the history of the exegesis of John 6:22-59 in our century can be found in M. Roberge, "Le discours sur le pain de vie, Jean 6,22-59. Problèmes d'interprétation," *LTP* 38 (1982), 265-99. For the period until 1900, see C. H. Lindijer, *De sacramenten in het vierde evangelie*, Verhandelingen Teylers Godgeleerd Genootschap NS 29 (Haarlem 1964), pp. 9-37. See also C. R. Koester, "John Six and the Lord's Supper," *LQ* 4 (1990), 419-37, esp. 420-26. At the Council of Trent, there was a strong controversy about the two interpretations (christological or eucharistic) of John 6; the Council finally intentionally left the question open, see F. Cavallera, "L'interprétation du chapitre VI de saint Jean. Une controverse exégétique au Concile de Trente," *RHE* 10 (1909), 687-709.

[3] So the scholars listed by Roberge, "Discours," pp. 275-98, and more recently: J. Becker, *Das Evangelium des Johannes* I, ÖTKNT 4/1 (Gütersloh - Würzburg 1979), pp. 199, 219-21; K. Matsunaga, "Is John's Gospel Anti-Sacramental? — A New Solution in the Light of the Evangelist's Milieu," *NTS* 27 (1980-81), 516-24; M. Gourgues, "Section christologique et section eucharistique en Jean VI. Une proposition," *RB* 88 (1981), 515-31, who restricts the eucharistic part to vv. 51c-56 (+ v. 27); S. Légasse, "Le pain de la vie," *BLE* 83 (1982), 243-61, esp. 251-61; J. D. Crossan, "It is Written: A Structuralist Analysis of John 6," *Semeia* 26 (1983), 3-21, esp. 15-16: who considers vv. 49-58 as eucharistic; J. Gnilka, *Johannesevangelium*, Die neue Echter Bibel (Würzburg 1983), pp. 53-54; U. C. von Wahlde, "*Wiederaufnahme* as a Marker of Redaction in Jn 6:51-58," *Bib* 64 (1983), 542-49 (vv. 51-58 are the eucharistic passage); S. Dockx, "Jean 6:51b-58," id., *Chronologies néotestamentaires et Vie de l'Église primitive: Recherches exégétiques* (Leuven 1984), pp. 267-70; S. A. Panimolle, "Fede e sacramento nel discorso di Cafarnao (Gv 6:26-58)," *Fede e sacramenti negli scritti giovannei*, ed. P.-R. Tragan, Studia Anselmiana 90, Sacramentum 8 (Rome 1985), pp. 121-33; L. Schenke, "Die literarische Vorgeschichte von Joh 6:26-58," *BZ* NF 29 (1985), 68-89; H. Weder, "Die Menschwerdung Gottes: Überlegungen zur Auslegungsproblematik des Johannesevangeliums am Beispiel von Joh 6," *ZTK* 82 (1985), 325-60, esp. 328-29, 347-51; D. G. Meade, *Pseudonymity and Canon: An Investigation into the Relationship of Authorship and Authority in Jewish and Earliest Christian Literature*, WUNT 39 (Tübingen 1986), pp. 110-14; C. Burchard, "The Importance of Joseph and Aseneth for the Study of the New Testament: A General Survey and a Fresh Look at the Lord's Supper," *NTS* 33 (1987), 102-34, esp. 119-20; U. Schnelle, *Antidoketische Christologie im Johannesevangelium: Eine Untersuchung zur Stellung des vierten Evangeliums in der johanneischen Schule*, FRLANT 144 (Göttingen 1987), pp. 214-28; P. Stuhlmacher, "Das neutestamentliche Zeugnis vom Herrenmahl," *ZTK* 84 (1987) 1-35, esp. 24-32; L. Wehr, *Arznei der Unsterblichkeit: Die Eucharistie bei Ignatius von Antiochien und im Johannesevangelium*, NTAbh NF 18 (Münster 1987), pp. 182-277; J. Kügler, *Der Jünger, den Jesus liebte: Literarische, theologische und historische Untersuchungen zu einer Schlüsselgestalt johanneischer Theologie und Geschichte. Mit einem Exkurs über die Brotrede in Joh 6*, SBB 16 (Stuttgart 1988), pp. 180-232 (vv. 48-58 constitute the eucharistic passage); C. H. Cosgrove, "The Place where Jesus is: Allusions to Baptism and the Eucharist

view, Jesus' flesh to be eaten and his blood to be drunk indicate, at least primarily, the elements to be consumed by the participant in the Eucharist. "Bread" is here supposed to be a eucharistic term: it denotes the bread used in the sacramental celebration and identified with Jesus. Whoever eats this bread, has eternal life (cf. vv. 53-54, 58). When the closing passage of the discourse is read in this way, it seems to differ from what precedes. In the part of the discourse up to and including v. 51b, the identification of Jesus with the bread of life (explicit in vv. 35, 48, 51) means that Jesus in person, with his words and deeds, is the bread of life that has come down from heaven. To obtain life, one has to come to him, to believe in him (v. 35). "To eat of the bread" (vv. 50, 51) has here a metaphorical sense; it is equivalent to believing in Jesus.[4] This part of the discourse may have faint eucharistic undertones, but its primary intention is to make christological statements.

For some scholars, the supposed difference between the two parts of the discourse has been a reason to consider vv. 51c-58 as an addition by a redactor.[5] They consider the difference to be so strong that it is impossible that the two parts come from the same pen. Others solve the presumed tension by supposing that vv. 51c-58 are traditional material, incorporated by the evangelist,[6] or, conversely, by ascribing vv. 51c-58, and sometimes other parts of the discourse as well, to the evangelist and the rest of the discourse to a source used by him.[7] For others again, the differences are not so great that the two parts of the discourse should be ascribed to different literary levels, but great enough to think that the evangelist wrote them at different times and with different aims.[8]

However, beside the eucharistic interpretation of John 6:51c-58, there has always been another approach to this passage. Many interpreters have read it as a logical continuation of the preceding christological part of the

---

in the Fourth Gospel," *NTS* 35 (1989), 522-539; P. Dschulnigg, "Überlegungen zum Hintergrund der Mahlformel in JosAs. Ein Versuch," *ZNW* 80 (1989), 272-75, esp. 275; J.-M. Sevrin, "L'écriture du IVe évangile comme phénomène de réception: L'exemple de Jn 6," *The New Testament in Early Christianity*, ed. J.-M. Sevrin, BETL 86 (Leuven 1989), pp. 69-83; Ph. Roulet - U. Ruegg, "Étude de Jean 6: la narration et l'histoire de la rédaction," *La communauté johannique et son histoire: La trajectoire de l'évangile de Jean aux deux premiers siècles*, ed. J.-D. Kaestli et al., MDB (Geneva 1990), pp. 231-47, esp. 238, 246-47; J. Beutler, "Zur Struktur von Johannes 6," SNTU 16 (1991), 89-104, esp. 89, 102.

[4] A few scholars take it here in the literal sense and, consequently, have the eucharistic part of the discourse start with v. 48 or 49; see n. 3.

[5] So the authors listed by Roberge, "Discours," pp. 278-89, and also Becker, Gnilka, von Wahlde, Dockx, Weder, Wehr as mentioned in n. 3.

[6] So those mentioned by Roberge, "Discours," pp. 289-92.

[7] So Schenke, Schnelle, Kügler, Sevrin, Roulet and Ruegg as mentioned in n. 3.

[8] So the scholars enumerated by Roberge, "Discours," pp. 293-98, and also Légasse, Cosgrove as mentioned in n. 3.

discourse, a continuation which also contains a christological message. In this approach, the terms "bread," "flesh" and "blood" in vv. 51c-58 refer, primarily at least, to the person of Jesus, and not to the eucharistic elements. It finds support in the "I am"-saying of 6:35: "I am the bread of life. Whoever comes to me, shall not hunger, and whoever believes in me, shall never thirst." This saying suggests that "to eat" and "to drink" metaphorically indicate belief in Jesus. Another keystone is found in vv. 57-58, where Jesus' flesh and blood, mentioned in vv. 53-56, are replaced first by "me" in v. 57, and then by "the bread which came down from heaven" in v. 58, which brings us back to vv. 35-51b. It is true that the exegetes who read vv. 51c-58 in this way differ in the degree to which they are willing to accept secondary eucharistic undertones in the passage, but they agree in considering it as first and foremost making christological statements.[9] An intermediate position is that 6:51c should be understood as christological, being about Jesus' death, and 6:53-58 as eucharistic,[10] but this position is not tenable, since v. 51c is consistent with what follows.[11]

---

[9] Roberge, "Discours," pp. 266-72, distinguishes in the period since the end of the 19th century between three types: a) "interprétation sapientielle excluant toute référence à l'eucharistie" (F. Godet, H. Cremer, B. F. W. Bugge, B. Weiss, J. Kreyenbühl, P. W. Schmiedel, K. Bornhäuser, H. Odeberg, A. Schlatter, H. H. Huber, M. Barth, M. Blanchard, F. J. Moore, W. Cadman, M. Rissi); b) "interprétation sapientielle avec terminologie eucharistique" (H. Strathmann, J. D. G. Dunn, F. Schnider, and W. Stenger); c) "interprétation sapientielle avec enseignement indirect sur l'eucharistie" (B. F. Westcott, R. H. Strachan, J.H. Bernard, P. Borgen, L. Morris, B. Lindars, F. J. Moloney, L. Goppelt). For the period until 1900, see Lindijer, *Sacramenten*, pp. 9-37. Recently, the christological interpretation has also been defended by J. Willemse, *Het vierde evangelie: Een onderzoek naar zijn structuur* (Hilversum - Antwerpen 1965), pp. 187-207 (type c); M. de Jonge, *Jesus: Stranger from Heaven and Son of God: Jesus Christ and the Christians in Johannine Perspective*, SBLSBS 1 (Missoula, MT 1977), p. 208 (type b); F. F. Bruce, *The Gospel of John* (Grand Rapids 1983), pp. 158-62 (type a); W. Kirchschläger, "Beobachtungen zur Struktur von Joh 6:48-58," *Für Kirche und Heimat*, FS. F. Loidl; ed. J. Bauer et al. (Vienna 1985), pp. 105-21 (type c, as it seems); W. Weren, "Structuur en samenhang in Johannes 6," in W. Beuken et al., *Brood uit de hemel: Lijnen van Exodus 16 naar Johannes 6 tegen de achtergrond van de rabbijnse literatuur* (Kampen 1985), pp. 44-61, esp. p. 47 (type a); G. R. Beasley-Murray, *John*, WBC 36 (Waco, TX 1987), pp. 93-96, 98-99 (type c); H. N. Ridderbos, *Het evangelie naar Johannes: Proeve van een theologische exegese I* (Kampen 1987), pp. 274-84 (type a); M. M. Thompson, *The Humanity of Jesus in the Fourth Gospel* (Philadelphia 1988), pp. 44-48 (type b); J. Painter, "Tradition and Interpretation in John 6," *NTS* 35 (1989), 421-50, esp. 442, n. 2, 444-45 (type b; see now also id., *The Quest for the Messiah: Studies of the History, Literature and Theology of the Johannine Community* [Edinburgh 1991], p. 236 n. 79, p. 239); D. A. Carson, *The Gospel according to John* (Grand Rapids 1990), pp. 276-80, 295-99 (type b); Koester, "John Six," pp. 419-37 (type a).

[10] Represented by H. Schürmann, "Joh 6:51c—ein Schlüssel zur großen johanneischen Brotrede," *BZ* NF 2 (1958), 244-262; id., "Die Eucharistie als Repräsentation und Applikation des Heilsgeschehens nach Joh 6:53-58," *TTZ* 58 (1959), 30-45, 108-118.

[11] So rightly J. D. G. Dunn, "John VI—A Eucharistic Discourse?" *NTS* 17 (1970-71), 328-38, esp. 329-30, 334-35. Many of Schürmann's arguments for a christological understanding of 6:51c return in my own reasoning below, but then applied to 6:51c-58.

After some preliminary remarks on the Johannine character of 6:51c-58 and on the use of traditional materials in this passage, I shall in this paper re-examine the arguments usually advanced for the eucharistic interpretation of these verses. It is often more presupposed than proven that John 6:51c-58 is about the Eucharist. It seems to me that the changes as regards content, which U. Schnelle, who may be considered in this respect as representative of many scholars, discerns in vv. 51c-58 when compared with what precedes,[12] are actually the arguments for a eucharistic interpretation:

a. In the part of the discourse on the bread of life up to and including v. 51b, Jesus himself is the bread that came down from heaven, whereas in the part which starts with v. 51c, Jesus' flesh and blood are the bread from heaven.

b. In John 6:32, the Father gives (δίδωσιν) the bread from heaven; in 6:51c, Jesus will give (δώσω) the bread.

c. In the first part of the discourse, the eating of the bread (φαγεῖν) can only be understood in a symbolic way; in vv. 51c-58, however, φαγεῖν and τρώγειν, "to eat," have to be understood literally.

d. In the first part, the issue is Jesus' heavenly provenance, but from v. 51c onwards, it is his corporality and humanity.[13]

In what follows, I shall discuss these four presumed changes. I shall closely consider the terminology of 6:51c-58 and the literary and theological structures of the discourse on the bread of life, and compare these structures with similar structures elsewhere in John. The connection, in v. 51, between vv. 51c-58 and the preceding part of the discourse, deserves special attention. It will appear then that the former two of the presumed changes do not really support a eucharistic interpretation of vv. 51c-58, and that the latter two are no real changes. The thrust of 6:51c-58 will appear to be primarily christological and not eucharistic. That is not to deny that eucharistic undertones can be heard in 6:51c-58 (and in ch. 6 as a whole), or that, conversely, the sacrament of the Eucharist implies a christological statement. The alternative put in the title of this paper amounts to the question whether or not the fourth evangelist explicitly deals with the Eucharist in 6:51c-58. Point d. will confront us with the question of the setting of the passage in Johannine Christianity: does it belong in a discussion with Jews (as v. 52 suggests) or with Docetists, i.e., Christians

---

[12] Schnelle, *Antidoketische Christologie*, pp. 221-22.

[13] Schnelle adds a fifth change: in vv. 51c-58, human activity is of importance (vv. 54, 56), which is not, in his view, the case in what precedes. This change has, however, no independent weight. The human activity in question is to eat Jesus' flesh and to drink his blood; whether the verbs "to eat" and "to drink" in vv. 51c-58 should be understood as indicating human activity in Schnelle's sense, depends upon whether they are interpreted literally or metaphorically, i.e., upon c.

who deny that the heavenly Son of God is fully identical with the man Jesus?

A. PRELIMINARY REMARKS

As we observed above, some scholars have serious doubts about the compatibility of the christological and—supposedly—sacramental parts of the discourse. They evidently presuppose that John 6:51c-58 has indeed a eucharistic meaning, and this view of the theological contents of the passage is then used as an argument for ascribing the two parts of the discourse to two different literary strata. Such a way of arguing runs a double risk: it is easily based on a superficial or even an incorrect view of the content of the text, and it does not sufficiently account for the possibility that the evangelist's logic does not simply coincide with the logic of the modern interpreter. Even if the presupposition about the eucharistic tenor of John 6:51c-58 is right—*quod est demonstrandum*—, there is still the probability that for the fourth evangelist (and not only for him) belief in Jesus and participation in the Eucharist are not mutually exclusive.[14]

To prove that vv. 51c-58 do not belong together with the rest of the discourse on the bread of life, objective literary arguments concerning vocabulary and style are required in the first place, and such arguments cannot be found. I refer here to the recently published work of E. Ruckstuhl and P. Dschulnigg on Johannine style, in which Ruckstuhl's earlier research is enlarged and improved.[15] On the basis of their criteria, John 6:51c-58 can be considered as an average Johannine pericope, just as the preceding part of the discourse.

Of course, this state of affairs leaves open the possibility that the fourth evangelist used sources or traditions in composing his narration; it means that whatever materials he used, he incorporated them in a thorough fashion and put his own stamp on them. It seems probable that in the passage under discussion here, the evangelist used a version of the words spoken by Jesus at the Last Supper; this conclusion can be drawn from a comparison with the other known versions (Mark 14:22-24 // Matt. 26:26-28 on the one

---

[14] The same is valid for the combination of present and future eschatology in John.

[15] E. Ruckstuhl and P. Dschulnigg, *Stilkritik und Verfasserfrage im Johannes-evangelium: Die johanneischen Sprachmerkmale auf dem Hintergrund des Neuen Testaments und des zeitgenössischen hellenistischen Schrifttums*, NTOA 17 (Freiburg/Schweiz - Göttingen 1991); for Ruckstuhl's earlier research, see his *Die literarische Einheit des Johannesevangeliums: Der gegenwärtige Stand der einschlägigen Forschungen*, Studia Friburgensia NF 3 (Freiburg/Schweiz 1951; repr. as NTOA 5; Freiburg/Schweiz -Göttingen 1987).

hand, Luke 22:19-20[16] and 1 Cor. 11:24-25 on the other).[17] The words καὶ ὁ ἄρτος δὲ ὃν ἐγὼ δώσω, "and the bread which I shall give" (v. 51c), make one think of καὶ . . . ἄρτον . . . ἔδωκεν, "and he gave bread," in Mark 14:22 // Luke 22:19 (cf. Matt. 26:26). John's ὑπὲρ τῆς τοῦ κόσμου ζωῆς "for the life of the world" (v. 51c), resembles, in combination with the preceding δώσω, the words to; ὑπὲρ ὑμῶν διδόμενον, "given for you," which Jesus said of his body according to Luke 22:19; we can also compare ὑπὲρ ὑμῶν in 1 Cor. 11:24, and what Jesus said of his blood according to all three Synoptists, that it was shed ὑπὲρ (Matt.: περὶ) πολλῶν, "for many" (Mark 14:24; Matt. 26:28; Luke 22:20). That the ὑπὲρ-formula, which in fact qualifies the act of giving, follows ἡ σάρξ μού, "my flesh," could be explained by the influence of an account of the institution of the Eucharist (see the parallels just adduced).[18] The pair ἡ σάρξ μού/ τὸ αἷμά μου, "my flesh / my blood" in John 6:53-56, parallels the pair τὸ σῶμά μου/ τὸ αἷμά μου, "my body / my blood," in the NT accounts of the institution of the Eucharist (and in Justin, *Apol.* 1.66.3). The terms σάρξ and αἷμα are used by other early Christian authors, notably Ignatius, to indicate the eucharistic elements (Ignatius, *Rom.* 7.3; *Philad.* 4; Justin, *Apol.* 1.66.2; σάρξ alone Ignatius, *Smyrn.* 7.1; cf. αἷμα alone 1 John 5:8). As Ignatius is probably not directly dependent upon John,[19] it is best to explain John's use of σάρξ and αἷμα as use of already extant terminology, not as his own creation.[20]

So it seems reasonable to suppose that eucharistic language, and especially a version of the institution of the Eucharist, have influenced John 6:51c-58. This influence explains why the expressions "to eat someone's flesh" and "to drink someone's blood" do not have here the hostile meaning they have elsewhere (see, e.g., Ezek. 39:17), and why drinking Jesus' blood is not considered as an unlawful practice (see, e.g., Lev. 17:10-14).[21] In the preceding part of the discourse, such clear eucharistic language is not found. There is no need to consider Jesus' words in 6:27 about "the food . . . that

---

[16] The longer text of Luke 22:17-20 should be considered as the original one, see B. M. Metzger, *A Textual Commentary on the Greek New Testament* (London - New York 1971; 1975), pp. 173-77.

[17] An extensive comparison can be found in Schürmann, "Joh 6:51c," pp. 245-49.

[18] Cf. P. Borgen, *Bread from Heaven: An Exegetical Study of the Concept of Manna in the Gospel of John and the Writings of Philo*, NovTSup 10 (Leiden 1965; 1981), pp. 93-94. The variant readings in v. 51c in which the words ὑπὲρ τῆς τοῦ κόσμου ζωῆς are immediately connected with δώσω, are efforts at creating a smoother text.

[19] See, e.g., C. K. Barrett, *The Gospel according to St John*, 2nd ed. (London 1978; orig. 1955), pp. 110-11.

[20] So also W. Bauer, *Das Johannesevangelium*, HNT 6, 3rd ed. (Tübingen 1933), p. 99; R. Bultmann, *Das Evangelium des Johannes*, MeyerK (Göttingen 1941), p. 175, n. 4; Wehr, *Arznei*, pp. 135, 242-45.

[21] Cf. Légasse, "Pain de vie," p. 259, n. 58.

lasts for eternal life, which the Son of Man will give you" as directly referring to the Eucharist; just as the saying in 4:14, they have to be understood on the metaphorical level.[22] John's use of eucharistic language in 6:51c-58 does not mean, however, that the passage is about the Eucharist. Language derived from the celebration of the Eucharist can be used to make statements about subjects that have some relationship to the Eucharist, but are not identical with it. Ignatius for instance, speaks about his approaching and longed for martyrdom in obviously eucharistic terms: "I desire the bread of God, which is the flesh of Jesus Christ, who is from David's seed, and for drink I desire his blood, which is imperishable love" (*Rom.* 7.3).[23] The communion with Christ, which the martyr expects after his death, is here described in terms of the eucharistic communion, but it is not the same as the eucharistic communion. We have to reckon with the possibility that in a comparable way the fourth evangelist makes use of eucharistic language to make christological statements; that is at least what most of the scholars mentioned in n. 9 above think. The question whether they are right or not, can only be answered by a careful study of John 6:51c-58 in its present, Johannine context. We are apparently legitimized to consider the passage as part of the Johannine discourse on the bread of life, and the literary unity of the discourse suggests at least that it constitutes a unity on the level of contents as well.

B. THE TERMS "FLESH" AND "BLOOD"

There is indeed a change in John 6:51c: the bread is now said to be Jesus' σάρξ, from v. 53 onwards combined with his αἷμα, whereas earlier in the discourse it was Jesus himself (vv. 35, 48, 51). Now this change can only be a fairly relative one, as there is again a change at vv. 56/57: σάρξ and αἷμα are in turn replaced by the 1st person singular, and this "I" is then again identified in v. 58, to close the circle of the discourse, with "the bread that came down from heaven." This double shift suggests that σάρξ and αἷμα do not indicate the eucharistic elements, but qualify Jesus' person. We observed above that σάρξ and αἷμα can refer to the eucharistic elements, but this is by no means the usual way of using these words in Early Christianity. From a careful examination of all passages in John where σάρξ is used (apart from 6:51c-58: 1:13, 14; 3:6; 6:63; 8:15; 17:2), M. M. Thompson concludes that the word "refers to the human realm in contrast to the divine and natural existence in contrast to the life given by the spirit,"

---

[22] See R. Schnackenburg, *Das Johannesevangelium* II, HTKNT 4/2 (Freiburg 1971), pp. 48-49.

[23] See on this passage Wehr, *Arznei*, pp. 130-43.

and that "it also connotes what is material or bodily";[24] the same meaning can be found elsewhere in Judaism and Early Christianity.[25] The circumstance that the word denotes man in his frailty and mortality makes it applicable to the dying Jesus: his death is the moment when he proves to be σάρξ (cf., e.g., 1 Pet. 3:18; 4:1; *Barn.* 6.7; 7.5; Ignatius, *Smyrn.* 1.2). Incarnation (John 1:14) entails death (John 6:51c). The suspicion that σάρξ in v. 51c indeed refers to the crucified Jesus, receives support from what follows: ὑπὲρ τῆς τοῦ κόσμου ζωῆς. The preposition ὑπέρ is often used in John and in other early Christian literature, together with a following genitive, to indicate "for" whom or what Jesus' death has a salvific effect;[26] frequently, ὑπέρ is connected, just as in John 6:51c, with the verb (παρα)διδόναι referring to Jesus giving himself.[27] That John has Jesus here speak of "for the life of the world" instead of "for many" or some such formula, is easily explained by the context, in which Jesus identifies himself with the bread which is said to "give life to the world" (6:33).[28] So it is probable that ἡ σάρξ μου in v. 51c refers to Jesus himself as a dying human being.

In vv. 53-56: σάρξ is combined with αἷμα, "blood," a combination that is still out of place in v. 51c, where "bread" and "flesh" are identified, but that was already suggested in v. 35, where Jesus as the bread of life was said to satisfy hunger *and* thirst.[29] When we rightly surmise that αἷμα as well here qualifies Jesus' person, it can only refer to his person as suffering a violent death. "Jesus' blood" often amounts, in early Christian language, to "Jesus' shed blood." Within the Fourth Gospel, this is the case in 19:34, where blood and water are said to flow from the pierced side of Jesus. In Rom. 5:8-10, Jesus' death is mentioned in v. 8, then taken up in v. 9 in the words "in his blood," which are in turn in v. 10 taken up in another reference to Jesus' death. In Ignatius, *Smyrn.* 1.1, "the cross of our Lord Jesus Christ" is in parallel with "the blood of Christ."[30]

A few times, Jesus' σάρξ and αἷμα are mentioned together and refer to his violent death, just as we surmise it to be the case in John 6:53-56. In

[24] Thompson, *Humanity*, pp. 49, 50.

[25] See E. Schweizer, "σάρξ κτλ.," *TWNT* 7:98-151; A. Sand, "σάρξ," *EWNT* 3:549-57.

[26] See John 10:11, 15; 11:50-52; 15:13; 17:19; 18:14, and elsewhere in the NT e.g. Mark 14:24 par.; Rom. 5:6-8; 1 Cor. 11:24; 15:3; 2 Cor. 5:14-15; Heb. 6:20; 1 Pet. 2:21; 1 John 3:16.

[27] See Luke 22:19; Gal. 1:4; 2:20; Eph. 5:2, 25; 1 Tim. 2:6; Tit. 2:14. According to Rom. 8:32, God gave up his own Son "for us all."

[28] Cf. recently Wehr, *Arznei*, pp. 247-48, who however considers the wording in v. 51c as imitation by the redactor.

[29] Beasley-Murray, *John*, p. 94, considers v. 53 "as a development of v 35 in the light of v 51."

[30] See further, e.g., Matt. 27:24-25; Acts 20:28; Rom. 3:25; Eph. 1:7; Heb. 13:12; 1 John 1:7; 5:6; Rev. 5:9; *1 Clem.* 7.4.

Eph. 2:13-14, it is said that the separation between Jew and Gentile has been removed, first ἐν τῷ αἵματι τοῦ Χριστοῦ, "in the blood of Christ" (v. 13), and then ἐν τῇ σαρκὶ αὐτοῦ, "in his flesh" (v. 14); in v. 16: these two references to Jesus' death on the cross are taken up in διὰ τοῦ σταυροῦ, "through the cross." In Col. 1:20-22, we find a comparable parallelism: reconciliation has been brought about διὰ τοῦ αἵματος τοῦ σταυροῦ αὐτοῦ, "by the blood of his cross" (v. 20), and ἐν τῷ σώματι τῆς σαρκὸς αὐτοῦ διὰ τοῦ θανάτου, "in the body of his flesh by his death" (v. 22).[31] This way of speaking, in which "flesh" and "blood" refer to a human being who suffers a violent death, is also found in the OT and in the Jewish environment of Early Christianity.[32] It should be distinguished from the standard expression "flesh and blood" used to indicate man as an earthly being.[33]

So from v. 51c onward Jesus' flesh and blood are identified with the bread from heaven. That is not, however, a change over against what precedes but an intensification of it: Jesus is the bread from heaven, not just as a human being, but as a human being who dies on the cross.[34]

There is one major difference between John 6:51c and Jesus' eucharistic words at the Last Supper as reported by the Synoptists and by Paul, which constitutes, to my mind, a very effective argument against the eucharistic interpretation of "flesh" and "blood" in John 6:51c-58. It is the circumstance that ὁ ἄρτος in v. 51c has already been qualified in what precedes as Jesus himself,[35] whereas in Mark 14:22 parr.; 1 Cor. 11:24; Justin, *Apol.* 1.66.3, the word τοῦτο in the clause τοῦτό ἐστιν τὸ σῶμά μου (or μου τὸ σῶμα), "this is my body," refers to the piece of bread Jesus has just taken in his hands. In the accounts of the Last Supper Jesus identifies a piece of bread with his body, but in John 6:51c he identifies the bread with which he already identified himself in a metaphorical way (6:35, 48, 51), with his dead self. There is, in the discourse on the bread of life in John 6, a movement of increasing unambiguity. In the conversation between Jesus and the crowd in vv. 22-34, the identification of Jesus with the bread of life remains implicit (vv. 27, 29, 32-33). In vv. 35-51b, Jesus explicitly identifies himself with the bread from heaven (vv. 35, 48, 51). In v. 51c, the expression καὶ . . . δὲ marks what follows in vv. 51c-58 as an addition, in

---

[31] See also *1 Clem.* 49.6; Ignatius, *Trall.* 8.1; *Smyrn.* 12.2; *Barn.* 5.1.

[32] See, e.g., Ps. 79:2-3, quoted in 1 Macc. 7:17; Ezek. 32:5-6; 4 Macc. 6:6.

[33] E.g., Sir. 14:18; Matt. 16:17; Gal. 1:16; cf. G. Richter, "Zur Formgeschichte und literarischen Einheit von Joh 6:31-58," in id., *Studien zum Johannesevangelium*, ed. J. Hainz, BU 13 (Regensburg 1977), pp. 88-119, esp. 109-10 (orig. in *ZNW* 60 [1969], 21-55).

[34] So also, e.g., Dunn, "John VI," p. 331.

[35] See Schürmann, "Joh 6:51c," p. 252, and the clarifying outline in Kügler, *Jünger*, p. 207 (K. does not, however, draw the necessary consequences from his observation). Cf. also Carson, *John*, p. 295.

this case a specification, in comparison to what has been said before: the bread of life is Jesus crucified.[36] A eucharistic interpretation of "flesh" and "blood" in vv. 51c-58 fails to appreciate both the connecting function of v. 51c and the structure of the entire discourse.

Other discourses of Jesus in John exhibit a comparable movement: they also end in a reference to Jesus' death and its salvific meaning. Jesus' dialogue with Nicodemus on the birth from above (3:1ff.) turns into Jesus' word on the "lifting up" of the Son of Man, so that the believer may have eternal life (vv. 14-15; cf. 12:32-33; 18:32). The discourse on the shepherd in John 10:1-18 starts with a παροιμία on the shepherd and his sheep (vv. 1-6), which is followed by a section in which Jesus identifies himself with "the door" (vv. 7-10). Then Jesus presents himself in vv. 11-18 as "the good shepherd," and here we find a series of increasingly clear indications of his death: the first in v. 11, that "the good shepherd gives his life for the sheep," in the third person; these words are repeated in the first person in v. 15, and finally Jesus speaks quite overtly and without any image, of giving his life and taking it back in vv. 17-18. Another example of the same movement may be found in 4:1-42, the dialogue of Jesus and the Samaritan woman; at the end of this passage, Jesus speaks to his disciples of accomplishing his Father's work (v. 34), which can only mean his death (cf. 19:28-30).[37] We can observe this movement also in John's account of Jesus' public ministry (chs. 2-12) as a whole: Jesus' final words (apart from the summary of his preaching in 12:44-50, which lacks a setting) are those in 12:23-36: which deal entirely with the signification of his death. Of course, the gospel as a whole also displays this structure, as it ends in Jesus' death and resurrection (chs. 18-21), preceded by the account of Jesus washing the disciples' feet and his farewell discourses, which reveal the signification of these events (chs. 13-17). We can conclude that the development of the discourse on the bread of life sketched above fits in very well with the development of several other discourses in John and of this gospel as a whole.

C. JESUS AS THE FUTURE GIVER OF THE BREAD

It may seem at first sight that the above is contradicted by the fact that Jesus is depicted in John 6:51c as the one who will give the bread, whereas in the

---

[36] On this tripartite structure of the discourse on the bread of life, see M. J. J. Menken, *Numerical Literary Techniques in John: The Fourth Evangelist's Use of Numbers of Words and Syllables*, NovTSup 55 (Leiden 1985), pp. 158-73.

[37] Cf. also 7:14-36: a series of dialogues which is situated on one day (see vv. 14, 37) and ends in Jesus' enigmatic saying about his return to the one who sent him (vv. 33-36); 7:37-8:30, a series of connected dialogues as well, containing allusions to Jesus' death and its meaning which become increasingly more overt (7:39; 8:14, 21) and end, just as was the case in ch. 3, with the "lifting up" of the Son of Man (8:28).

preceding part it was the Father who gave the bread (which is Jesus): should not "the bread which I shall give" refer to the eucharistic bread?

Such an interpretation is made impossible first of all by the observation made above, that ὁ ἄρτος in v. 51c has already been qualified as Jesus himself. The words ὃν ἐγὼ δώσω have to refer then, not to Jesus distributing bread at the Last Supper (which is not narrated in John) or, as the risen Lord, in the celebration of the Eucharist, but to Jesus giving himself in his death. The same has to be valid for the food, to be given by the Son of Man, in 6:27. These words announce in a veiled way what will be said more overtly in the final part of the discourse.

It can be shown in addition, that this understanding of v. 51c, necessary because of its context, is quite in line with a basic structure of Johannine christology. In the Fourth Gospel, the Father sends or gives the Son, Jesus, and this action reaches its goal not just in Jesus' incarnation, but in his death. God's giving of Jesus reaches its goal in Jesus' giving of himself. Outside of ch. 6: the Father is said to give Jesus in 3:16: "For God so loved the world, that he gave his only Son, that everyone who believes in him should not perish but have eternal life." Here, ἔδωκεν, "he gave," is parallel to ἀπέστειλεν, "he sent," in 3:17: "For God did not send his Son into the world that he should condemn the world, but that the world should be saved through him." Both the words "God gave his only Son" and "God sent his Son" are parallel to "the Son of Man must be lifted up" in 3:14, an evident reference to his death (note also the causal conjunction γάρ at the beginning of vv. 16, 17). That Jesus' salvific death is the goal of the Father giving or sending him because of his love for the world is also clearly stated in 1 John 4:9-10.[38]

According to John 4:34, Jesus says: "My food is that I do the will of the one who sent me, and accomplish his work." The accomplishment of the Father's work consists in Jesus' death (see 19:28-30), which is then the realization of the will of his sender (see also 17:4).

In 10:36: Jesus says that the Father has sanctified him and sent him into the world; in 17:19, he says that he sanctifies himself for his disciples, which must refer to his imminent death.[39] In 17:18-19, it is suggested that the Father's sending of Jesus is continued in Jesus' act of sanctifying himself, his death. John's use of ἁγιάζειν, "to sanctify," in 10:36; 17:19 exactly parallels his use of διδόναι in 6:32, 51: the Father gives or sanctifies Jesus in sending him; Jesus gives or sanctifies himself by fulfilling his Father's will in his death.

---

[38] See E. Schweizer, "Was meinen wir eigentlich, wenn wir sagen 'Gott sandte seinen Sohn. . .'?" NTS 37 (1991), 204-24, esp. 212-16.

[39] See Menken, Numerical Literary Techniques, p. 265.

The same structure can be discerned in John in passages about the love of the Father and the Son. As the Father has loved the Son, so the Son has loved his disciples (15:9-10), and this love of the Son manifests itself in that he gives his life for his own (15:12-13; cf. 17:23, 26). According to 3:16, the love of the Father reaches its climax in the death of the Son (see above). The love of the Father for the Son is on the one hand prior to creation (17:24; cf. 3:35; 5:20); on the other hand, the Father loves the Son because the Son gives his life and takes it again (10:17-18). The love of the Son for his own realizes itself during his earthly ministry (see, e.g., 11:5; 13:23), but it culminates in his death (13:1; 15:12-13).

We touch here on a peculiar feature of the Fourth Gospel: both Jesus' incarnation and his death are considered as salvific events (cf., e.g., 5:21 and 10:28 with 3:14-17 and 14:19, or 5:22 and 9:39 with 12:31 and 16:8, 11). This feature can be explained by the circumstance that for the evangelist Jesus' death is the moment when the incarnation reaches its goal. Such a view is consistent with the situation of the (believing) readers or hearers of the gospel: they are no eyewitnesses of Jesus' ministry, but they look back after the event on the whole of Jesus' work, from the incarnation up to and including his cross and resurrection. They only know the earthly Jesus as the one who has also been crucified.

The structure of John's christology just sketched makes it clear that Jesus' act of giving himself as bread (6:51c) constitutes the climax of the Father's act of giving Jesus as bread (6:32). Jesus *gives* what he *is*: the bread of life. This idea, that Jesus gives what he is, can also be shown to be thoroughly Johannine. Several qualifications, which John attributes to Jesus' person, especially in "I am"-sayings, are at the same time qualifications of the gift that he brings. Jesus is life (11:25; 14:6),[40] and he gives life (5:21; 6:33; 10:28; 17:2). He is the resurrection (11:25), and raises believers (6:39, 40, 44, 54). That he is the resurrection and the life is demonstrated in his act of raising Lazarus (11:1-44; cf. 12:1, 9, 17), and also in other signs (4:46-54; 5:1-9). He is light (1:9; 8:12; 9:5),[41] and he gives light (1:5, 9), which is demonstrated in the healing of the man born blind (ch. 9). Jesus is the truth (14:6),[42] and he speaks the truth (8:40, 45, 46; 16:7). He is God's word (1:1, 14), and speaks God's word or words (3:34; 14:10, 24; 17:8, 14).[43] The evangelist may have found a model for this way of presenting Jesus as both bread and giver of bread in Jewish ideas about Wisdom. In Sir. 24:19-21, Wisdom is portrayed both as the

---

[40] Cf. also 1:4; 5:26; 6:35, 48, 51, 57, 63, 68.
[41] Cf. also 1:4, 8; 3:19-21; 12:35-36, 46.
[42] Cf. also 1:14, 17.
[43] Cf. also 12:48-50; 17:6.

giver of food and drink, and as food and drink themselves.[44] In *Det.* 115-118, Philo identifies Wisdom with the rock from Deut. 32:13, which gives honey and oil, and then identifies the rock with the manna, the divine word, from which two cakes are made, one of honey, the other of oil (cf. Exod. 16:31; Num. 11:8), so that here as well, Wisdom is food and gives food.[45] All these parallels to John 6:51 make clear that the transition from Jesus as bread to Jesus as the giver of bread remains within a christological framework.

D. METAPHORICAL OR LITERAL EATING AND DRINKING?

It is evident that in John 6:50, 51, "to eat of the bread of life" can only be understood in a metaphorical way: it stands for belief in Jesus (cf. 6:35). According to the eucharistic interpretation of 6:51c-58, "to eat" and "to drink" in vv. 52-58 have however to be understood literally. The usual argument is that τρώγειν has a more realistic meaning than simply "to eat"; it should mean "to chew." A secondary argument is that there is a difference between φαγεῖν ἐκ in vv. 50-51b and simple φαγεῖν or τρώγειν in vv. 51c-58.[46]

A literal understanding of "to eat" and "to drink" in vv. 53-58 (for the moment, I leave aside the misunderstanding in v. 52; see below, under E.) is possible only when "flesh" and "blood" indicate the eucharistic elements; when these terms here refer to the crucified Jesus, as has been demonstrated above, the verbs have to be understood in the same metaphorical way as "to eat" in vv. 50, 51ab. "To eat Jesus' flesh and to drink his blood" then means: to believe in him as the one who dies for the life of the world. Or, in slightly different words: to believe that in Jesus' violent death God is acting for the life of the world. In vv. 48, 50-51b both the verb "to eat" and its object "bread" are used metaphorically; in vv. 53-58 the verbs "to eat" and "to drink" are used metaphorically, but the objects "flesh" and "blood," or "me" (v. 57), are not. The metaphor is in part blown up by reality.[47] Something similar already happened in 6:35. There, at the beginning of the central part of the discourse, we find a similar combination of metaphorical

---

[44] For Wisdom as giving food and drink, see also Prov. 9:2-5; Sir. 15:3. Wisdom is compared to water in *1 Enoch* 49.1.

[45] See K.-G. Sandelin, "The Johannine Writings within the Setting of Their Cultural History," *Aspects on the Johannine Literature*, ed. L. Hartman and B. Olsson, ConNT 18 (Uppsala 1987), pp. 9-26, esp. 19-20.

[46] Given by Schürmann, "Joh 6:51c," pp. 253-54; J. J. O'Rourke, "Two Notes on St. John's Gospel," *CBQ* 25 (1963), 124-28, esp. 126-28; Schnackenburg, *Johannesevangelium*, 2:92.

[47] So also F. Schnider and W. Stenger, *Johannes und die Synoptiker: Vergleich ihrer Parellelen*, Biblische Handbibliothek 9 (Munich 1971), p. 163.

and literal language: "to come to me" and "to believe in me" are put together with the imagery of the satisfaction of hunger and thirst. I recall here an observation made above (under B.) on John 10:1-18, the discourse on the shepherd: in its final part, we found a series of increasingly clear references to Jesus' death (vv. 11, 15, 17-18). There as well, there is a gradual decrease of metaphorical language and increase of literal language.

Another point is of importance here: in the case that literal eating and drinking were meant in 6:51c-58, one would expect in v. 56 the sequence: "I remain in him, and he in me."[48] The fact that the sequence is inverted (as elsewhere in John: 14:20; 15:4, 5, 7)[49] suggests, to my mind, that eating and drinking have to be understood here metaphorically.

That τρώγειν has a stronger sense than φαγεῖν is in itself not untrue, but not relevant in the present instance. For John, the two verbs are interchangeable. He simply uses τρώγειν as the present tense that corresponds to the aorist φαγεῖν,[50] as it was quite common in later Greek.[51] The interchangeability of the two verbs is evident from the antithetic parallelism in 6:53-54, in which φάγητε and τρώγων are parallel, and from the quotation from Ps. 41:10 in 13:18, where we find τρώγων where the LXX has ἐσθίων.[52]

There is of course a slight difference between φαγεῖν + acc. and φαγεῖν ἐκ + gen., "to eat" and "to eat of."[53] However, the difference is not very essential, and it cannot be made a criterion for distinguishing between a eucharistic and a non-eucharistic meaning. In the eucharistic passage in 1 Cor. 11, for instance, Paul speaks in vv. 26, 27 of ἐσθίειν τὸν ἄρτον and πίνειν τὸ ποτήριον, and then in v. 28, without a discernible change of meaning, of ἐκ τοῦ ἄρτου ἐσθίειν and ἐκ τοῦ ποτηρίου πίνειν. Similarly in Mark 14:25 // Matt. 26:28, in the account of the Last Supper: πίνειν ἐκ τοῦ γενήματος τῆς ἀμπέλου, "to drink of the fruit of the vine," is taken up in αὐτὸ πίνειν, "to drink it."[54]

---

[48] See X. Léon-Dufour, *Lecture de l'Évangile selon Jean* II, Parole de Dieu (Paris 1990), pp. 170-72; cf. M.-J. Lagrange, *Évangile selon saint Jean*, EB, 6th ed. (Paris 1936; orig. 1925), pp. 184-85.

[49] Considered as an argument for a Johannine incorporation of tradition in 6:51c-58 by E. Schweizer, "Joh 6:51c-58—vom Evangelisten übernommene Tradition?" *ZNW* 82 (1991), 274.

[50] In a comparable way, his use of ἀποστέλλειν or πέμπειν is governed by the desired verbal form.

[51] See LSJ, s.v. τρώγω III, and also L. Goppelt, "τρώγω," *TWNT*, 8:236-37, who then, however, wrongly remarks that the change of verbal form can clarify the intention of the section 6:51c-58: the passage deals, in his view, with real, corporeal eating in the Eucharist.

[52] See M. J. J. Menken, "The Translation of Psalm 41.10 in John 13.18," *JSNT* 40 (1990), 61-79, esp. 65.

[53] Both expressions are used in John 6 (vv. 23, 26, 31*bis*, 49, 50, 51, 52, 53).

[54] See also, e.g., Luke 22:16 with *v.l.*; 1 Cor. 9:7, and Exod. 12 and Lev. 22 LXX.

In v. 55, Jesus' flesh is said to be ἀληθής βρῶσις, "true food," and his blood ἀληθής πόσις, "true drink." The adjective does not mean that Jesus' flesh and blood are food and drink in the literal sense of the word, but that they achieve what food and drink ought to achieve. Just as food and drink procure life, so Jesus' flesh and blood procure eternal life (cf. v. 54).[55] One could almost translate ἀληθής with "trustworthy," just as in John 3:33; 5:31-32 for example. So the "food" and "drink" of v. 55 should be interpreted on the same metaphorical level as "eating" and "drinking."

E. JOHN 6:51C-58 AS A DISCUSSION WITH JEWS

It is often supposed that the eucharistic statements of John 6:51c-58 are statements which imply an anti-docetic christology: the real consumption of Jesus' flesh and blood implies his real humanity. Because he is a real human being, his flesh and blood can be consumed in the eucharistic celebration. Ignatius, *Smyrn.* 7.1 is often referred to in this context; according to this passage, the Docetists stay away from the celebration of the Eucharist and from the communal prayer, "because they do not confess that the Eucharist is the flesh of our saviour Jesus Christ, that has suffered for our sins." Here, a link between a docetic christology and avoidance of the Eucharist is indeed evident.[56]

The christology of the preceding part of the discourse differs from this supposed anti-Docetism. In that part, the evangelist wants to demonstrate that the man Jesus is the bread from heaven. The murmuring of "the Jews" about the claim of Jesus, the son of Joseph, whose parents they know, to be the bread from heaven (6:41) exactly formulates the issue under discussion. The same point of discussion is at stake, in various terms, in other disputes between Jesus and the Jews in John (see, e.g., 5:17-18; 7:25-31; 10:22-39). We may surmise that these disputes in John's Gospel reflect disputes between Johannine Christians and their Jewish environment. John 6:51c-58, when interpreted as an anti-docetic passage, is different, because in that case the issue here is that Jesus, the bread from heaven, is really human. The views of Jesus held by the Johannine Jews and the Docetists are poles apart: the Jews know that Jesus is a fully human being, and therefore he

---

[55] The *v.l.* ἀληθῶς probably arose because "superficially the adjective ἀληθής appears to be inappropriate," so Metzger, *Textual Commentary*, p. 214. See further the discussion in F. Neirynck et al., *Jean et les synoptiques: Examen critique de l'exégèse de M.-É. Boismard*, BETL 49 (Leuven 1979), pp. 211-13, and Léon-Dufour, *Jean*, 2:166.

[56] A positive relationship between "orthodox" christology and the Eucharist may be discerned in Ignatius, *Eph.* 20.2 and *Rom.* 7.3, see Wehr, *Arznei*, pp. 164-65. See also Justin, *Apol.* 1.66.2.

cannot be the Son of God; the Docetists know that he is the Son of God, and therefore he cannot be a fully human being.

In the anti-docetic interpretation of John 6:51c-58, which is not strictly bound to the eucharistic interpretation,[57] the objection of the Jews in v. 52 becomes problematic, because it seems that it does not represent here the Jewish point of view but the docetic one:[58] it seems to express doubt about Jesus' capacity to give his flesh to be eaten, i.e., doubt about Jesus' real humanity. V. 59 ("Jesus said these things in the synagogue, teaching, at Capernaum") seems also to be out of place, when an anti-docetic passage has immediately preceded it. The questions that arise are then: when we interpret John 6:51c-58 as a primarily christological text on the necessity of accepting Jesus' death, what then remains of its presumed anti-docetic character, and is it then possible to understand v. 52 as a Jewish objection, just as it presents itself?

On the basis of what we observed above (under B. and C.), we can say that the tenor of John 6:53-58 is that belief in Jesus as the one in whose death God is acting is necessary to obtain eternal life. Jesus not only came down from heaven; his descent is brought to completion in his death, and he has to be accepted as come down from heaven "unto death, even death on a cross," to use the words of Phil. 2:8. In this connection, it is of importance that John has Jesus speak in v. 53 not of *his* flesh and blood, but of the flesh and blood *of the Son of Man*. In John, the title "Son of Man" characterizes Jesus as the one who came from God and has returned to God by way of his exaltation / glorification (see 3:13-14; 6:62; 8:28; 12:23, 34; 13:31). Earlier in the discourse on the bread of life, the Son of Man has been said to be the one on whom "the Father, God, has set his seal" (6:27). So it is stated in v. 53 that in order to obtain life, one has to accept Jesus' death as the death of the Son of Man who came from heaven and returned there.[59] When we hear

---

[57] As is proved by authors who interpret John 6:51c-58 as anti-docetic but not eucharistic, such as Borgen, *Bread from Heaven*, pp. 147-92 (who interprets John 6:31-58 in its entirety as anti-docetic) and Dunn, "John VI," pp. 335-38, and by authors who interpret the passage as eucharistic but not anti-docetic, such as Becker, *Johannes* 1:222-23 and Kügler, *Jünger*, pp. 221-26.

[58] Cosgrove, "Place," pp. 527-30, is aware of the problem "that the ostensible audience does not seem to match up with the implied audience of Jesus' words" (527), but does not solve it by considering "secret believers" as the implied audience. U. Wilckens, "Der eucharistische Abschnitt der johanneischen Rede vom Lebensbrot (Joh 6:51c-58)," *Neues Testament und Kirche,* FS. R. Schnackenburg, ed. J. Gnilka (Freiburg 1974), pp. 220-48, esp. 236-43, also sees the problem, and solves it by considering the Jews in 6:41, 52 as "paradigmatische Repräsentanten des Unglaubens" (236); this solution is too general.

[59] Cf. C. K. Barrett, "Das Fleisch des Menschensohnes (Joh 6:53)," *Jesus und der Menschensohn*, FS. A. Vögtle; ed. R. Pesch and R. Schnackenburg (Freiburg 1975), pp. 342-54, esp. 352-53. That the title "Son of Man" was especially at home in the Eucharist (see e.g. Barrett, "Fleisch," pp. 350-52; Becker, *Johannes*, 1:222; Wehr, *Arznei*, pp. 252-54), is

then in v. 54, the positive half of the parallelism 6:53-54, about "eating *my* flesh" and "drinking *my* blood," we should keep in mind that Jesus has just presented himself as the Son of Man.

The above means that 6:53-58 is at least as much directed against a Jewish point of view as against a docetic one. As said above, the Jews are presented in John as people who know Jesus as a fully human being, who therefore cannot be the Son of God. It is only to be expected that they certainly cannot accept that God acts in Jesus' death, which pre-eminently makes him into a fully human being.[60] I here refer once more to the end of the discourse on the shepherd: there, Jesus speaks overtly of his death as the execution of God's commandment, whereupon part of the Jewish audience reacts with the words: "He has a demon and is mad; why do you listen to him?" (10:17-20). One could also think of Paul's words in 1 Cor. 1:23, that "Christ crucified" is "a stumbling block to Jews" (cf. Gal. 5:11; John 6:61).

The point is that in understanding such christological statements as: "My flesh and blood are the bread from heaven," or: "The bread from heaven is my flesh and blood," the decision about what is the subject and what is the predicate depends upon the knowledge the reader or hearer already has about the issue in question. A Jewish reader, and a Christian reader who is sensitive to Jewish propaganda, know that Jesus is a human being, who died on a cross, and they can either accept or reject the new information offered to them, that Jesus is "the bread from heaven." A docetic reader, however, already knows about the Son of God who is "the bread from heaven," and for him or her the new information to be accepted or rejected is, that this bread is fully identical with the crucified human being, Jesus.[61]

So the basic christological content of John 6:51c-58, that the crucified Jesus is the bread from heaven, can in itself be directed against both a Jewish and a docetic point of view. Which of the two was originally aimed at can only be decided by a look at John's Gospel as a whole. It is evident then that the dispute with the Jewish point of view has an important place in it, whereas a clear anti-Docetism is hardly discernible. Passages such as John 1:14 and 19:34-35 (a text which is notoriously difficult to interpret) are by no means certain witnesses of anti-docetic polemics. In the Johannine

---

difficult to prove. Ignatius, *Eph.* 20.2, uses it in a eucharistic context, but interprets it as referring to Jesus' humanity.

[60] Similarly H. Strathmann, *Das Evangelium nach Johannes*, NTD 4 (Göttingen 1951), p. 123; Schnider and Stenger, *Johannes und die Synoptiker*, pp. 163-64; Painter, "Tradition," pp. 444-45 (= *Quest*, p. 239).

[61] Borgen, *Bread from Heaven*, pp. 183-92, rightly stresses that "the Jews" of John 6:41, 52 sharply distinguish between the spiritual bread from heaven and the man Jesus, but his identification of these Jews with Docetists does not seem to be justified: the Johannine Jews deny Jesus' heavenly provenance, the Docetists deny his humanity that culminates in his death.

Epistles, such polemics are perceptible (see 1 John 4:2; 5:6; 2 John 7),[62] which suggests that some people in the Johannine community (or communities) interpreted John's Gospel in a docetic way.[63] The struggle of the Johannine Christians with the Docetists postdates their conflict with the Jews.

We now have to test the presumption that the misunderstanding in v. 52 can be understood as a Jewish misunderstanding, comparable with other misunderstandings on the part of the Jews in John. There is here, first of all, a textual problem: should we read τὴν σάρκα or τὴν σάρκα αὐτοῦ? There are three good reasons to prefer the shorter reading: the longer text is easily understood as an explanation of the shorter one, it can be explained as an accommodation to ἡ σάρξ μου in the preceding verse (cf. also vv. 53-56), and the shorter text makes better sense in the context. In v. 51c, Jesus says that he will give *his* flesh, the Jews misquote him in v. 52 by omitting the possessive, and Jesus corrects the omission in v. 53: they have to eat the flesh *of the Son of Man*.[64]

As far as its wording is concerned, the misunderstanding in 6:52 resembles other misunderstandings in John: it starts with πῶς, "how" (cf., e.g., 3:4, 9; 6:42; 8:33; 12:34), followed by δύναται, "can he" (cf. 3:4, 9), and contains a slightly disdaining οὗτός "that fellow" (cf. 6:42; 7:35; 12:34).

As regards its contents: it occurs frequently in the Fourth Gospel that the Jews misunderstand sayings of Jesus about his imminent death, and that Jesus does not try to remove their incomprehension. In 2:20, they understand Jesus' saying: "Destroy this temple, and in three days I shall raise it up" (2:19), to be about the Jerusalem temple instead of about Jesus'

---

[62] It seems that for the opponents of 1 John it was not so much Jesus' humanity in general as his *death* that caused problems, see esp. 1 John 5:6. Σάρξ in 1 John 4:2 and 2 John 7 refers then to Jesus' death, as we presumed it to be the case in John 6:51c-58; see M. C. de Boer, "The Death of Jesus Christ and His Coming in the Flesh (1 John 4:2)," *NT* 33 (1991), 326-46. In a different way L. Schenke, "Das johanneische Schisma und die 'Zwölf' (Johannes 6.60-71)," *NTS* 38 (1992), 105-21, problematically identifies the opponents in 1 John with the many disciples who leave Jesus in John 6:60-71; in their christology, Jesus would have been the Christ and Son of God only after his resurrection. Of course, 1 John 5:6 constitutes for him an insurmountable problem (see his p. 107).

[63] See M. J. J. Menken, "De christologie van het vierde evangelie: Een overzicht van resultaten van recent onderzoek," *NedTTs* 45 (1991), 16-33, esp. 25-27 (in discussion with Schnelle, *Antidoketische Christologie*, and Thompson, *Humanity*; expanded English version: "The Christology of the Fourth Gospel: A Survey of Recent Research," *From Jesus to John: Essays on Jesus and New Testament Christology*, FS. M. de Jonge, ed. M. C. de Boer, JSNTSS 84 [Sheffield 1993], pp. 292-320, esp. 307-09).

[64] See further Menken, *Numerical Literary Techniques*, pp. 139-40, and for instances of "misunderstanding by omission" in John: id., "Some Remarks on the Course of the Dialogue: John 6:25-34," *Bijdragen* 48 (1987), 139-49, esp. 142-44, on John 3:4; 6:28, 41-42, 52; 16:30.

body (cf. 2:21). In 7:33-34, Jesus says to the Jews: "For a little longer I am with you, and I go to him who sent me. You will seek me and you will not find me, and where I am, you cannot come." The Jews do not understand these words; they only wonder whether he aims at the Diaspora with the place to where he will go and where they cannot find him (7:35-36). Something similar happens in 8:21-22, where Jesus says: "I go away and you will seek me, and you will die in your sin; where I am going, you cannot come" (v. 21); the Jews interpret his words as a plan to kill himself (v. 22). In 12:34, Jesus' saying that "the Son of Man must be lifted up" (12:32), is not understood by the Jews; they suppose it to contradict what they heard from the Law, that "the Christ remains for ever."

In all these misunderstandings, the Jews attribute only a superficial meaning to what Jesus says about his imminent death and its significance. This also happens in 6:52: when Jesus says that the bread of life, which he will give, is his mortal flesh (6:51c), the Jews wonder "how this fellow can give the flesh to eat." A saying of Jesus in which he points, in more or less veiled terms, to his death is ridiculed by interpreting it in a grossly literal way.[65] The flesh of the one who came down from heaven is made into "the flesh"; as noted above, the omission is corrected in the next verse, when Jesus speaks of "the flesh of the Son of Man."

I conclude that it is by no means necessary to consider John 6:51c-58 as an anti-docetic passage, and the misunderstanding of the Jews in 6:52 as a docetic misunderstanding; the entire passage 6:51c-58 has to be read primarily, in agreement with its context, both in ch. 6 and in John as a whole, as a discussion with a Jewish point of view concerning Jesus' death.[66]

F. CONCLUDING REMARKS

John 6:51c-58 should be considered as an integral part of John 6. It is quite probable that the evangelist made use here of eucharistic terminology, especially of a version known to him of the words on the bread and the wine, spoken by Jesus at the Last Supper. However, that does not mean that the passage is primarily about the Eucharist. Jesus' "flesh" and his "blood" indicate here the crucified Jesus, and "the bread" mentioned in v. 51c is not the eucharistic bread, but the bread of life with which Jesus already identified himself. There is a logical transition, in v. 51c, from the Father's present gift of Jesus to Jesus' future gift of himself. Eating Jesus' flesh and drinking his blood in vv. 53-56 stand for belief in him as the one who dies

---

[65] Cf. R. A. Culpepper, *Anatomy of the Fourth Gospel: A Study in Literary Design*, Foundations and Facets: New Testament (Philadelphia 1983), pp. 156-57, 162-63.

[66] Cf. Meade, *Pseudonymity*, p. 113.

for the life of the world. The entire passage, including the misunderstanding in v. 52, can be understood as a discussion with a Jewish point of view concerning Jesus' death. Numerous parallels, elsewhere in John, to the various aspects of John 6:51c-58 just mentioned, support this christological interpretation.

There is no reason to doubt that the Johannine Christians celebrated the Eucharist;[67] the fact that John makes use of the words of institution in 6:51c, testifies to this practice. It is quite probable that a reader or hearer of this gospel, when hearing the passage discussed in this paper, also thought of the Eucharist as the occasion when he or she experienced in a tangible way his or her belief in the crucified Jesus. However, John puts the Eucharist in its proper place by focusing on that which gives meaning to this sacrament: Jesus' salvific death. John betrays no interest in church practices or structures in themselves; he tacitly presupposes them and concentrates on the person of Christ as their basis. The discourse in which Jesus identifies himself with the bread from heaven was an apt place for the evangelist to make use of eucharistic material in a christological perspective.

Finally, a few words have to be said about John 6:60-71, the passage that follows the discourse on the bread of life. As a consequence of the above, the division among the disciples related here should be considered as reflecting a schism in the Johannine community or communities between those who accepted the crucified Jesus as the bread from heaven and those who returned to the Jewish point of view. John 6:60-71 has often been considered as lacking connections with 6:51c-58: the cause of the disciples' offence in 6:60-65 is said to be Jesus' claim to have come down from heaven (cf. 6:41-42), to which the remark on his ascension (v. 62) points back, and the use of "flesh" in v. 63 is said to be different from that in 6:51c-58.[68] However, that vv. 60-71 have no connections with vv. 51c-58, is not correct, not only because of v. 58, where we hear about "the bread come down from heaven," but also for other reasons.

The λόγος at which the disciples take offence (v. 60), is the entire preceding discourse. Jesus answers their offence with the anacoluthon: "Then what if you see the Son of Man ascend to where he was before?" (v. 62). Jesus' ascension to his Father is, in John, the inward significance which the believer perceives in the outward event of Jesus' death (see, e.g., 13:1; 16:28; 20:17).[69] Jesus' saying in v. 62 indicates the moment at which his

---

[67] That they were not familiar with the Eucharist is suggested by Koester, "John Six," pp. 432-33.

[68] See esp. G. Bornkamm, "Die eucharistische Rede im Johannes-Evangelium," *ZNW* 47 (1956), 161-69, esp. 166-68 (repr. in id., *Geschichte und Glaube* I, Ges. Aufsätze 3; BEVT 48 [Munich 1968], pp. 60-67).

[69] In 20:17, the evangelist considers Jesus' death, resurrection and exaltation as one event; for the outsider, only the death is discernible.

preceding discourse will be verified, so that the suppressed words of the anacoluthon should be something like: "Will you then accept my words?" For those who, just as the Jews in vv. 41-42, 52, cannot accept that in his life *and* death, Jesus is the bread that came down from heaven, his death will be the confirmation of his failure, and for them the scandal will be enhanced; for those who believe, his ascension to the Father will be the verification of his claim to be, in his life *and* death, the bread that came down from heaven, and for them the scandal will be removed.[70]

In Jesus' saying: "It is the spirit that gives life, the flesh is of no avail" (v. 63), πνεῦμα and σάρξ are apparently used as anthropological, not christological concepts. John's usage here makes the reader think of 3:6 and of Pauline passages such as Rom. 8:4-17; Gal. 5:16-26.[71] It seems we should distinguish, in the Fourth Gospel, between σάρξ applied to Christ, and a more general, anthropological usage of the word. The latter occurs several times (1:13; 3:6; 6:63; 8:15),[72] and the two usages are of course related, because God's Son assumes *the* flesh (cf. 1:14), so that it becomes *his* flesh. In their misunderstanding in v. 52, the Jews try precisely to make *Jesus'* flesh into *the* flesh (see above). V. 63 continues the question of belief and unbelief that has been brought up in vv. 61-62. Jesus' discourse is "spirit and life" for the believer, but for the one who remains at the level of "the flesh" and who therefore cannot see in Jesus' flesh the flesh of the Son of Man, come down from and ascended to heaven, they are meaningless.[73]

Belief and unbelief as the answers to what Jesus said in his discourse continue to be the theme until the end of the chapter. Judas exemplifies the latter, Simon Peter, as the spokesman of the Twelve, the former. The mention of Judas' betrayal (vv. 64, 71) brings Jesus' death once more to the fore. The title ὁ ἅγιος τοῦ θεοῦ, "the Holy One of God," which Peter attributes to Jesus in his confession in v. 69, may do the same. As we saw above (under C.), John uses ἁγιάζειν, "to sanctify," in 10:36 and 17:19 to indicate the Father's sanctification of the Son in sending him unto death and the Son's continuation of this act in sanctifying himself by his death. So a possible explanation for the use of the singular title "the Holy One of God" in 6:69 could be that it characterizes Jesus as consecrated to death.[74]

---

[70] Cf., e.g., Léon-Dufour, *Jean*, 2:180-81.

[71] V. 63a might well be a traditional saying, so, e.g., Kügler, *Jünger*, pp. 192-93, 213-14.

[72] In 17:2, we meet the semitism πᾶσα σάρξ, "all flesh," indicating mankind.

[73] I now think that the purely christological interpretation of 6:63a, which I gave, following many others, in *Numerical Literary Techniques*, p. 141, needs to be corrected. H. Van den Bussche, *Het Boek der Werken. Verklaring van Johannes 5-12*, Het vierde evangelie 2 (Tielt - Den Haag 1960), p. 148; Wilckens, "Der eucharistische Abschnitt," pp. 243-45; Ridderbos, *Johannes*, 1:286-88, and Koester, "John Six," p. 431, who consider ch. 6 in its entirety as Johannine, also distinguish σάρξ in v. 63 from σάρξ in vv. 51c-58.

[74] Similarly Schürmann, "Joh 6:51c," p. 260; Beasley-Murray, *John*, p. 97.

I conclude that John 6:60-71 fits in well with 6:51c-58, the closing passage of the preceding discourse, when we interpret this passage in the way proposed in this paper.[75]

---

[75] I thank Mrs. K. M. Court for correcting my English text.

THE JOHANNINE SCHISM AND THE "TWELVE"
(JOHN 6:60-71)*

Ludger Schenke

In 1 John 2:18f.; 4:1-6 we read of a christological schism in the "Johannine" community. The schismatics are called "antichrists" and "pseudo-prophets." There are many of them. They are, however, "Christ-believers" (2:19), who apparently claim to represent the "correct" christology. They sought adherents to this christology among the members of the community, which the author of 1 John calls "seduction" (2:26; cf. 4:5f.).

The central features of their christology are explicitly mentioned in 1 John 2:22 and 4:2f. Whether 5:6f. may be adduced in establishing the position of the schismatics, is questionable, however. According to 2:22 they say: "Jesus is not the Christ." Since the schismatics claimed to be "Christians," not every christological confession can have been rejected, but evidently only the specific confession propounded by the author and his readers. These acknowledge "Jesus as the Christ come in the flesh" (4:2). Whoever does not assent to this sentence, does not acknowledge τὸν Ἰησοῦν—or "makes τὸν Ἰησοῦν of no effect," if the reading λύει is original—and is not "of God" (4:3). So the dispute is about the "human Jesus" and about his worthiness of being the Christ or the "Son of God" (cf. 4:15; 5:1, 5). Clearly the schismatics contradicted the christological view according to which the "human Jesus" was the "Messiah" or the "Son of God" from the beginning of his existence. In so doing they necessarily denied the notion of the incarnation of a preexistent "heavenly Christ" or of the "Son of God" in the "human Jesus" (4:2; cf. 2 John. 7). The author of 1 John calls this a denial "of the Father and of the Son" (2:22). The schismatics appear, then, to have rejected an intra-divine differentiation between "Father and Son" and thereby to have disputed also the preconditions for the incarnation as a tenet of faith.

The christological position of the schismatics cannot, however, be unambiguously discerned.[1] According to whether one's starting point in the

---

* This article first appeared in German in *NTS* 38 (1992), 105-21: The translation into English is by David E. Orton.

[1] For discussion cf. H. Thyen, art. "Johannesbriefe," *TRE* 17 (Berlin, 1988), pp. 186-200; K. Wengst & J. Beutler, *ANRW* II.25:5 (Berlin & New York, 1988), pp. 3753-90. In recent literature cf. J. Blank, "Die Irrlehrer des ersten Johannesbriefes," *Kairos* 26 (1984), 166-93; R. E. Brown, *Ringen um die Gemeinde* (Salzburg, 1982), pp. 73-112; N. Brox, "'Doketismus'—eine Problemanzeige," *ZKG* 95 (1984), 301-14; H.J. Klauck, "Gegner von innen: Der Umgang mit den Sezessionisten im ersten Johannesbrief," *Conc* 24 (1988), 467-73; idem, "Der Antichrist und das johanneische Schisma," *Christus Bezeugen*, ed. K. Kertelge et al. (Leipzig, 1989), pp. 237-48; idem, "Bekenntnis zu Jesus und Zeugnis Gottes. Die christologische Linienführung im ersten Johannesbrief," *Anfänge der Christologie*, ed. C.

interpretation of the texts is the hellenistic/dualistic model of transcendence or the Jewish/Jewish-Christian view of God, different positions arise. According to the hellenistic/dualistic (gnostic) model the schismatics did one of two things. Either they denied the real "humanity" of Jesus alongside the notion of incarnation, in which case the question arises why it can be said of them that they do not acknowledge τὸν Ἰησοῦν or make him "of no account" (4:3) and deny "the Father and the Son" (2:22). Or did the schismatics deny only the *incarnational* connection between the "heavenly Christ" or "Son of God" with the "human Jesus" and think of the connection as "spirit-investment" or "indwelling"? They would then, however, if the accusations had any foundation, have had to reckon with this connection being dissolved at the time of the passion of Jesus. But where is there any indication that this is the case?

If, on the other hand, the texts are interpreted on the basis of the Jewish idea of God, which is my own suggestion, then another picture emerges. For the schismatics there would then be no question of Jesus' having been a "real human being"; rather they would dispute that the "Christ" or "Son of God" (or Logos) appeared in the "human Jesus" *since his birth*. The dispute would then centre on the salvific relevance of the "human Jesus" in his earthly existence. Perhaps the Christian schismatics assumed that Jesus was elevated to "Messiah" and "Son of God" only by the resurrection/exaltation, thereby linking up with an early, Jewish-Christian christology (cf. Rom. 1:3f.; 1 Pet. 3:18; 1 Tim. 3:16). They were indeed Jewish-Christians, then, who presumably rejected any christological speculation about pre-existence and any statement about incarnation out of a concern for a pure monotheism, but still venerated the "exalted" one as "Messiah" or "Son of God." What significance they attached to the "human Jesus" is not clear from 1 John 2:22; 4:1-6: What does seem clear, however, is that they regarded him as a real human being ("flesh").[2]

Breytenbach & H. Paulsen (Göttingen, 1991), pp. 239-306; idem, *Der erste Johannesbrief*; J. Kügler, "In Tat und Wahrheit. Zur Problemlage des Ersten Johannesbriefes," *BN* 48 (1989), 61-88; U. B. Müller, *Die Geschichte der Christologie in der johanneischen Gemeinde*, SBS 77 (Stuttgart, 1975), pp. 65ff.; idem, *Die Menschwerdung des Gottessohnes*, SBS 140 (Stuttgart, 1990), pp. 84-101; J. Painter, "The 'Opponents' in I John," *NTS* 32 (1986), 72-93; G. Strecker, *Die Johannesbriefe* (Göttingen, 1989); M. Theobald, *Die Fleischwerdung des Logos*, NTS NF 20 (Münster, 1988), pp. 400-37; idem, "Geist- und Inkarnationschristologie," *ZKT* 112 (1990), 129-49; H.-J. Venetz, *"Durch Wasser und Blut gekommen,"* FS E. Schweizer (Göttingen, 1983), pp. 345-61; F. Vouga, "The Johannine School: A Gnostic Tradition in Primitive Christianity?" *Bib* 69 (1988), 371-85; idem, *Die Johannesbriefe* (Tübingen, 1990); K. Weiss, "Orthodoxie und Heterodoxie im 1: Johannesbrief," *ZNW* 58 (1967), 247-55; idem, "Die 'Gnosis' im Hintergrund und im Spiegel der Johannesbriefe," *Gnosis und Neues Testament*, ed. K.W. Tröger (Gütersloh, 1973), pp. 341-56; K. Wengst, *Häresie und Orthodoxie im Spiegel des ersten Johannesbriefes* (Gütersloh, 1976).

[2] Their christology cannot therefore be called docetic; correctly so, Wengst, *Häresie und Orthodoxie*, pp. 37f.; P. Hofrichter, *Nicht aus Blut sondern monogen aus Gott geboren* (Würzburg, 1978), pp. 157ff.; H. Thyen, "Aus der Literatur zum Johannesevangelium," *TRu*

The matter becomes more complicated if the schismatics' position can also be discerned in 1 John 5:6f.: "This is he who came through water and blood, Jesus Christ. Not in water only, but in water and blood." Unlike in 2:22f. and 4:2f., however, the author gives no hint here that he is repeating and refuting the views of the schismatics. The statement stands in clear parallel to 4:2 and like that passage intends to give expression to the fully real incarnation of the pre-existent "Son of God" (5:5).[3] But what does the opposing position look like? Does it consist in the statement that "Jesus Christ is come (only) in water," and is there an allusion to the baptism of Jesus here? Did the schismatics then take the view that the "human Jesus" had become "Messiah" or "Son of God" in the water baptism, through the gift of the Pneuma? This would be compatible with what we have said about the christological position of the schismatics. But one would have to ask why the author of 1 John can say of this position that it does not confess τὸν Ἰησοῦν (4:3). For we would then have a statement about the elevated position of the "human Jesus" even if he were not also seen as the incarnation of the pre-existent "Son of God." But this is precisely what has to be proclaimed about the "human Jesus" (4:3). Whoever does not make this confession about him denies "the Father and the Son" (2:22).

In what follows we aim to shed light on the christological dispute in 1 John from a passage in the Gospel of John. The passage John 6:60-71 has, in my view, to be interpreted in the light of and as a reflection of the "Johannine" schism. This will be shown here. If the attempt can claim plausibility, the textual basis for the reconstruction of the intra-community schism which the Johannine letters speak of will be extended and further clarification of the christology of the schismatics will be gained.

I

At 6:60 a new scene begins. The actors are only Jesus and the disciples. The people (6:22, 24) or "the Jews" (6:41, 52) have disappeared from view. Conversely, the preceding dialogue in 6:26-58 presupposes the disciples as hearers, but not as discussion partners. The concluding verse 6:59 has a clear dividing function.

Despite dialogical elements 6:60-71 has, in contrast to 6:26-58, a narrative character. The narrative concerns the disciples' reaction to Jesus' discourse. "Many" of them take offence at it and separate from Jesus (6:60,

---

44 (1979), 121ff. Doubt is also expressed by Brox, "'Doketismus'," pp. 313f.; cf. P. Weigandt, "Der Doketismus im Urchristentum und in der theologischen Entwicklung des zweiten Jahrhunderts" (Diss. Heidelberg, 1961), pp. 103ff.; U. Schnelle, *Antidoketische Christologie im Johannesevangelium* (Göttingen, 1987), pp. 80f.

[3] "Blood" here is a cipher for the process by which "Jesus Christ" comes into being in the womb, and for his birth: so, Hofrichter, *Nicht aus Blut, passim*; Wengst, *Häresie und Orthodoxie*, pp. 18ff.

66). Others, including the "Twelve" with Simon Peter, accept it and stay
with Jesus. But even among the "Twelve" there is one who will fall away
from Jesus (6:64b, 70f.). The narrator shows extraordinary commitment in
the matter. It is striking how he piles up comments which challenge the
alertness of the reader and are intended to direct the reader's understanding
(6:61, 64b, 71).

Although 6:60-71 is clearly set apart from the dialogue 6:26-58, as a
new scene, it still remains closely associated with the preceding context. At
several points it refers to it directly.

—The "disciples" mentioned in 6:60, 66 are of course such people as those
who "follow" him in 6:2 and acknowledge him as "prophet" and "king"
(6:14f.). Unlike the "Jews" they expect real gifts of salvation (6:24, 35). But
what they expect is described by Jesus as earthly and ephemeral (6:15, 26,
35). The true gift of salvation is Jesus himself.

—The objection of the "disciples" in 6:60 is directed against the preceding
revelatory discourse of Jesus. Both Jesus (6:63) and Peter (6:68) refer to
this.[4]

—Jesus' counter-question in 6:62 arises from the statements concerning the
"descent" of the "Son of Man" (6:3, 38, 41, 46, 50, 51, 58). It is these
statements, not just the ones about the "flesh" and "blood" of the Son of
Man as meat and drink, that evidently arouse the "indignation" of the
disciples.

—The exalted "Son of Man" was already in view in 6:27, 53, and the
announcement of an "ascent" to "where he was beforehand" (6:62), picks
up on 6:46.

---

[4] 6:60, 63, 68 could, it is true, be placed next to any passage in John. But this is no reason
to separate 6:60-71 away from the present context (against R. Bultmann, *Das Evangelium des
Johannes*, 20th edn. [Göttingen, 1985], pp. 214f.). I have shown elsewhere that the bread-of-
life discourse 6:26-58 is a well-planned compositional unit which derives from the final
redactor of John's Gospel. With H. Thyen I call him the "evangelist" (cf. *BZ* 24 [1980], 21-
41; 29 [1985], 68-89). If the matter is viewed in this way, all explanations, however
ingenious, of the way 6:60-71 belongs with the rest of the bread-of-life discourse, on the other
side of 6:53-58, are superfluous. In effect what they claim is that the final redactor of 6:26-58
is a "dope" who in his "blind zeal" against the docetistic deniers of the eucharist does not
notice that 6:63 at least contradicts him and is grist for the mill of the docetists (against G.
Bornkamm, *Geschichte und Glaube. Gesammelte Aufsätze III* [München, 1968], pp. 63f.; G.
Richter, *Studien zum Johannesevangelium* [Regensburg, 1977], pp. 115f., 175; H.
Schürmann, "Joh 6,51c - ein Schlüssel zur großen johanneischen Brotrede," *BZ* 2 [1958],
258f.; idem, "Die Eucharistie als Repräsentation und Applikation des Heilsgeschehens nach
Joh 6, 53-58," *TTZ* 68 [1959], 30-45, 18-118; S. Schulz, *Das Evangelium nach Johannes*, 5th
edn. [Göttingen, 1987], p. 110; W. Wilckens, *Der eucharistische Abschnitt der johanneischen
Rede vom Lebensbrot [Joh 6,51c-58]*, FS R. Schnackenburg [Freiburg, 1974], p. 245). But if
6:26-58 is a literary compositional unit of the final redactor, then the latter has related 6:60-
71 to the whole bread-of-life discourse. Our task is to find out what his intentions were in so
doing.

—The σάρξ of 6:63 cannot differ greatly from that of 6:51, 53ff., even it is only here that σάρξ is placed in antithetical contrast to πνεῦμα. This antithesis is still comparable to that of 6:27a.

—6:64a corresponds with 6:36, particularly if it is read together with 6:62. Finally, 6:65, with which Jesus recalls 6:37, 44, is a direct backward reference. It is also notable that in 6:64, 65 we find the same train of thought as in 6:36, 37.

If these connections between 6:60-71 and the preceding context are taken into account, then greater significance can be attached to the fact that in 6:60-65 many *disciples* behave just as the "Jews" did previously. They are angry about Jesus' speech and want to hear no more of it. They separate from Jesus and return to the ranks of the "Jews."

These observations show that the narrative section 6:60-71 relates to the dialogue of 6:26-58 in a similar way to the preceding narrative, 6:1-25. There, however, the *semeion* of the feeding of the multitude who "follow" Jesus (6:2, 24) is positively received but fundamentally misunderstood. They look to Jesus for earthly food that will satisfy their hunger (6:26). They also acknowledge him as a wonder-working prophet and earthly Messiah-king (6:14f.). But they do not understand the true meaning of the *semeion*, or they would not look to Jesus for "perishable" food but food "which remains to eternal life" (6:27). What this consists in is elaborated in the dialogue of 6:26-58. In 6:60-71 it is finally made clear that these "disciples" stick to their misunderstanding. They think of it as something fleshly and earthly, as something of "no use" (6:63), for they do not believe that Jesus is the envoy of God who has come from heaven (6:64a; cf. 6:29, 33, 51, 58). Their "following" of Jesus was therefore not a true discipleship, because it was not "given them by the Father" (6:65). Only few real "disciples" stand with Jesus, among whom are the "Twelve."

At this point we examine further the function of the "Twelve" and of Simon Peter. In John, except for 20:24, the "Twelve" are mentioned only in 6:67, 70f. Even in places where one would expect a reference to the "Twelve," they are not mentioned (cf. 12:4 despite 6:71; 13:1; 21:2). One must conclude that for the "evangelist," unlike for Mark, the "Twelve" are not identical with the disciples of Jesus.[5] In John the circle of disciples consists of more people, and different people, than just the "Twelve" (cf. 3:26; 4:1; 10:41f.; 21:2). Nathanael should be mentioned in this connection (1:45f.; 21:2) and especially the "beloved disciple" (1:36f.; 13:23; 19:26f.; 20:2ff.; 21:7, 20). It is fairly obvious that these two are also among the disciples who stay with Jesus after the bread-of-life discourse. One cannot tell unequivocally from 6:60, 66 that it is just the "Twelve" who stay with Jesus or whether the formerly more numerous circle of disciples has shrunk

---

[5] Against Bultmann, *Das Evangelium*, p. 80, n. 4; J. Becker, *Das Evangelium nach Johannes* I (Gütersloh, 1979), p. 214.

in size.[6] Many disciples do fall away from Jesus, but not all apart from the "Twelve." These are only one group among the disciples who have stayed with Jesus. If this is the view of the "evangelist," the question arises why he mentions the "Twelve" precisely at this point.

Simon Peter functions here as the speaker of the "Twelve" (6:68f.). It may be presumed that this function also plays a part in the later mentions of him in John (cf. 13:24; 20:2; 21:7, 15ff.). Alongside Peter, in John's Gospel the "beloved disciple" appears time and again (1:35-42; 13:2ff.; 18:15ff.; 20:2ff.; 21:7, 15-23). He too appears as the representative of a group of disciples, particularly as the representative of the "Johannine" fraternity (19:35; 21:24).[7] The mutual relationship between these two figures representing the disciples is not free from an element of competition. Peter is regarded as "the first" disciple (1:42), but the beloved disciple is called before Peter (1:35ff.). He is closer to Jesus (13:23; 19:26f.), is quicker than Peter to believe in Jesus' resurrection (20:8) and to recognize the resurrected one (21:7). However, Peter is undisputedly regarded as the "shepherd" of Jesus' "sheep" (21:15ff.). Despite his failure during Jesus' passion, his leading role is unquestioned (cf. 18:15-18, 25-27; 21:15ff.) and his martyrdom for Jesus is emphasized (13:36f.; 21:18f.).[8] Equally, the "beloved disciple" is venerated by the group of Christians in which the Gospel of John emerged as the "true witness" (19:35; 21:24), whose particular claim and commission has substance next to Peter's leadership commission (21:22). The significance of the "beloved disciple" is in no way diminished by Peter. The two figures stand next to one another, each in his own right. The question arises whether we may not trace the relationship between Peter and the "beloved disciple" back to the post-Easter communities of disciples which they represent. Could it be that in the two representative disciple figures the relationship between two Christian communities is intended to be presented and explained: the relationship between the "Johannine" fraternity and "Petrine" Christianity?

II

The premise for our continuing consideration of 6:60-65 has to be the fact that those who call Jesus' words "hard" are described as disciples. Their

[6] So Bultmann, *Das Evangelium*, pp. 214, 340; Becker, *Das Evangelium*, p. 214; J. Wellhausen, *Das Evangelium Johannis* (Berlin, 1908), p. 33.

[7] Cf. most recently, K. Quast, *Peter and the Beloved Disciple: Figures for a Community in Crisis*, JSNTSup 32 (Sheffield, 1989).

[8] Correctly, R. Schnackenburg, "Zur Herkunft des Johannesevangeliums," *BZ* 14 (1970), 19f.; H. Thyen, "Aus der Literatur zum Johannesevangelium," *TRu* 42 (1977), 254; H.-J. Klauck, "Gemeinde ohne Amt?" *BZ* 29 (1985), 215f.; there are problems with the contrary view of T. Lorenzen, *Der Lieblingsjünger im Johannesevangelium* (Stuttgart, 1971), pp. 89-96.

status only changes after Jesus' reply in 6:62ff.: they separate from Jesus and—one has to fill in the picture here—become "Jews."[9] But up to that point they have followed Jesus and have recognized him on the basis of his semeia, at least as a prophet sent from God (6:14f.). The reversal in their attitude to Jesus is emphasized by the revelation discourse, 6:26-58, which they cannot accept.

The thing that causes them "offence" is not directly expressed in 6:60 and has to be extracted from Jesus' reply in 6:61-64a. The reply aims to counteract the object of offence by reducing it to the decisive heart of the question. It constructs a self-contained counter-argument with a clear rhetorical line. In 6:62 Jesus points the "disciples" in question to the fact of his "ascent." Will they interpret this fact correctly? 6:63a should offer the key to this, an antithetical sentence which the "disciples" would surely assent to,[10] and 6:63b turns this sentence to the revelation discourse of 6:26-58: the words of Jesus do not belong to the realm of the "flesh" but are "spirit" and "life." 6:64a establishes the futility of Jesus" response. The "disciples" have committed themselves to their unbelief. The verse does, however, also make it clear that Jesus' answer—correctly understood—could provide a way out of the offence.

Before we take a closer look at this counter-argument of Jesus' in 6:62f., it should be pointed out once again that 6:60-65, 66 is to be interpreted with reference to 1 John 2:18f. (cf. 4:1-6). The passage is a narrative way of overcoming the schism in the "Johannine" community, the beginnings of which are here placed back into the life of Jesus.[11] 6:64f. shows that for the reader the schism is no longer something in the future,

---

[9] Analogous situations can be frequently observed in John. In 2:23 people arrive who believe in Jesus because of the signs, but their faith is evidently inadequate (2:23f.). In 3:2 Nicodemus too recognizes Jesus as the "teacher come from God." In the course of the conversation by night the inadequacy of his confession becomes especially clear. In the middle of the great controversy in chs. 7–8 various people appear who believe in Jesus (8:30; cf. 7:12, 31, 40) but then do not "stay" with his word, but return to the ranks of the "Jews" (8:31ff.; cf. 7:13).

[10] The meaning of this sentence is determined by 6:62: it must have a christological reference; so correctly R. Schnackenburg, *Das Johannesevangelium* II, 4th edn. (Freiburg, 1985), pp. 106f.; Bultmann, *Das Evangelium*, pp. 341f.; Schürmann, "Joh 6,51c," p. 258 n. 43; against Bornkamm, *Geschichte und Glaube*, p. 65; Wilckens, *Der eucharistische Abschnitt*, p. 245.

[11] As far as I am aware, this insight was put forward by F. Neugebauer, *Die Entstehung des Johannes-evangeliums* (Stuttgart, 1968), p. 20, and taken up by H. Thyen, "Aus der Literatur zum Johanneseveanglium," *TRu* 43 (1978), 341; idem, "Entwicklungen innerhalb der johanneischen Theologie und Kirche im Spiegel von Joh 21 und der Lieblingsjüngertexte des Evangeliums," *L'Evangile de Jean*, ed. M. de Jonge (Louvain, 1977), p. 277; W. Langbrandtner, *Weltferner Gott oder Gott der Liebe* (Frankfurt, 1977), pp. 9f.; and has rightly become standard; cf. B. Lindars, *The Gospel of John* (London, 1972), p. 271; K. Wengst, *Bedrängte Gemeinde und verherrlichter Christus* (Neukirchen, 1981), pp. 72f.; Schnelle, *Antidoketische Christologie*, p. 227. Schnackenburg, *Das Johannesevangelium*, 2:102f., also expounds 6:60-65, 66 from the "present intention of the Evangelist," who sees his readers "threatened by obstacles to faith." But this is much too general.

but something which has already occurred. Our text aims to explain it theologically, not to give a warning of it. So it has no paraenetic function.[12]

The schismatic "disciples" of 6:60, 66 are placed on the same level as the "Jews." But they were "disciples" and therefore Jewish Christians, and previously members of the "Johannine" community (1 John 2:19). At least they must have shared basic christological convictions with that community. These could be what is being referred to in 6:62.

The meaning of Jesus' question here is disputed. R. Bultmann supplements as follows: ". . . then the annoyance will *really* be great"; the annoyance is being increased.[13] But can the "ascent of the Son of Man into heaven," which is spoken of only here (cf. 3:13; 13:1; 14:2f.; 16:5, 7, 28; 20:17), be an annoyance for Christians—of any persuasion?[14] Rather, the schismatic "disciples" are spoken to in this way because they too have seen Jesus' "ascent." They too hold to the resurrection/"exaltation" of the crucified one. That should really move them on and allow them to overcome the offence.[15]

6:62 also sheds light on the heart of the offence. The "ascent" leads the "Son of Man" to "where he was before." This seems to be the decisive counter-argument against the schismatic "disciples." The latter clearly, like the "Jews" before them (6:41f.), rejected the statement that Jesus had "come down from heaven" (6:33, 38, 50, 58). However, they will probably have accepted that as the "exalted one" he "went up to heaven." They attached significance for salvation to the "exalted one," but not to the "human Jesus." 6:62 says, by contrast, that at his "exaltation," Jesus as "Son of

---

[12] Against Schnackenburg, *Das Johannesevangelium*, 2:103, 108; Wengst, *Bedrängte Gemeinde*, p. 73. Our text must, therefore, has come about later than 1 John 2:18f.; 4:1-6, where the schism is clearly regarded as a developing event; so, too, Kügler, "In Tat und Wahrheit," p. 84.

[13] *Das Evangelium*, p. 341; so too Bornkamm, *Geschichte und Glaube*, p. 64; W. Wilkens, *Die Entstehungsgeschichte des vierten Evangeliums* (Zollikon, 1958), pp. 140f.; Schulz, *Das Evangelium*, p. 110; Becker, *Das Evangelium*, p. 202; Wilckens, *Der eucharistische Abschnitt*, p. 244; E. Schweizer, *Neotestamentica* (Zürich, 1963), p. 389.

[14] One must not read the paradoxical idea of the "exaltation of Jesus on the cross" (3:14; 8:28; 12:32) into this text, even if it would not be at all out of place. But it is not there, and so Bultmann's exposition is not permissible (*Das Evangelium*, pp. 341f.: "The hearer of Jesus' words should be clear about the meaning of this; if he is already offended by Jesus' words now, he will be all the more offended by the cross"). The whole character of 6:62 argues against this view (cf. also W. Thüsing, *Die Erhöhung und Verherrlichung Jesu im Johannesevangelium*, 2nd edn. [Münster, 1970], pp. 261f.). Why does Jesus here direct a question to the "disciples" and not simply make a statement? Why is it accepted that the "disciples" will "see" the "ascent" of Jesus? All this surely indicates that 6:62 aims to be a convincing argument. Only at 6:64 is there an indication that the schismatic "disciples" are not prepared to be convinced by it.

[15] Schürmann ("Joh 6,51c," pp. 258f.) takes no account of 6:62-64a and thus comes to an untenable interpretation: it is not the one who has "come down from heaven" who gives life and salvation, but only the "exalted one." The bread-of-life discourse takes the whole Jesus event as a unity, so that Schürmann's sharpening of the focus is wrong. By this means he also misses the point of concern between the "evangelist" and the schismatic "disciples" in 6:62ff.

Man" went to "where he was before." So he was "from above" (3:31), was previously "with the Father" (6:46), and "came down from heaven" (6:33, 38, 51, 58). All these statements have to be made already by the "human Jesus," whose father and mother are known (6:42).

As early as 3:6, 13, the "evangelist" had explained that whoever ascends to the heavenly sphere must have come from there. This is also true of the believer. He or she has to be born "from above" in order to gain admission to the Basileia of God (3:3, 5). By means of "birth from above," "of water and the spirit," he/she becomes a pneuma-being (3:8), without ceasing to be a carnal human being. He/she becomes a "child of God" and is still at the same time an earthly human being. One's carnal heritage does not determine one's true nature or one's pneumatic origin (cf. 1:12f.).

If this is true of the believer, it is much more so of the "human Jesus." If he comes "from above," he is pneumatic (3:31, 34). If he ascends into the heavenly sphere, he must have come "from above" (3:13). In this sense 6:63 follows on logically from 6:62. It was not only at the "exaltation" that the "human Jesus" first became a pneumatic being.[16] If this were so, then the "human Jesus" would as such be a "mere human being" and nothing else, "flesh, which is good for nothing." His words would not be able to bring "pneuma and life." But the "human Jesus" is "life-giving pneuma," which can bring "pneuma and life" (6:63). Jesus' humanity does not exclude his pneumatic origin "from above." He is both "carnal" and pneumatic at the same time (cf. Ign. *Eph.* 7.2; 18.2). As long as the schismatic "disciples" see in him nothing more than a "teacher sent from God" (3:2), wonder-working prophet (6:14f.) or earthly, political "messiah" (1:41; 4:25; 6:15; 7:40f.), they assess him as "flesh, which is good for nothing." Thereby they rank on the same level as the "Jews," who judge the "human Jesus" κάτα σάρκα (8:15).[17] The "ascent" of Jesus ought, however, to show them that Jesus, as "flesh," is at the same time "pneuma," namely the Logos (1:1f., 14), the "Son of God" (3:34; 10:30, 36; 20:28, 31).[18]

The schismatic "disciples" must, on the other hand, have credited the "exalted one" with a pneumatic form of existence in the first place. Even if

---

[16] L. Schottroff, *Der Glaubende und die feindliche Welt* (Neukirchen, 1970), p. 272, presumes that 6:62f. supersedes the christological tradition in Rom. 1:3f.; 1 Tim. 3:16; 1 Pet. 3:18, in which two forms of existence of Jesus before and after the resurrection occur in succession (κάτα σάρκα/ κάτα πνεῦμα): the author has "both taken recourse to the two-tier, temporal succession of σάρξ and πνεῦμα for Jesus, and to the designation πνεῦμα for giving the existence of the exalted one ... Jesus' heavenly existence is not to be situated after the σάρξ existence in the Johannine sense, but simultaneously with the σάρξ existence."

[17] Schweizer, *Neotestamentica*, pp. 389f., interprets correctly at this point.

[18] Schottroff, *Der Glaubende*, pp. 274f., has correctly pointed out that "flesh" and "spirit" are not opposed to one another in 6:63 in the same way as in gnostic dualism. "Flesh" in this case means the human person in his/her world, who is unable to attain divine salvation through his/her own efforts (cf. Matt. 16:17; 1 Cor. 15:45-47).

they did not contest all the worthiness of the "human Jesus," but regarded him as a "teacher sent from God" (3:2) and the "eschatological prophet" (6:14), through whom the pneuma or the divine Logos spoke, still for them he was not the incarnation of the divine Logos himself. They rejected the incarnational statement in 1:14, because in their thinking the divine pneuma sphere and the earthly "flesh" sphere remained strictly separate. They took offence at the suggestion that in the "human Jesus," according to the confession of the evangelist, the eternal Logos of God was supposed to have entered into an incarnational relationship with the "flesh" sphere. Probably for them the "exalted one" no longer had "flesh and blood" anyway, but had become a purely pneumatic being. So they rejected the eucharistic statements in 6:51-58 along with the whole bread-of-life discourse. They contradicted the christological view of the "evangelist," according to which the divine Logos had become "flesh," had become "human" (1:14) and had ascended back to heaven "as a bodily human being," though not in an earthly bodily form, but in a form changed by the pneuma (cf. 20:19-29).

It is self-evident that these christological views of the schismatic "disciples" cannot be called docetism.[19] They did not deny the true humanity of Jesus. The "evangelist" does not need to defend this at any point. But the sentence "the word became flesh" (1:14) is presumably aimed at them. They did take offence at the identification between the earthly/exalted Jesus and the divine Logos because this mixed the divine-pneumatic sphere with the earthly/fleshly sphere. The sincerity of their objection should not be doubted.

In 6:62f. the schismatic "disciples" are confronted with the unavoidable consequence of their denial of the incarnation. Jesus, whom they too venerate as the "teacher" sent by God and as a charismatic prophet, they degrade by calling him a "mere human being." But "the flesh is good for nothing"! As a mere human being he cannot give "life." If his work in word and deed really brings salvation, if his words are "pneuma and life," then this must be true of him also. No one can pass on what he does not have, what is not available to him, or make anyone anything that he is not himself (cf. 1:12, 16; 3:34; 5:26; 6:45f., 51 etc.). "Salvation can only come from the sphere of the spirit (= of God), not from the sphere of the flesh (= the earthly, the human). If Jesus were of human origin, he would not be able to

---

[19] As was said above (n. 2), the schismatics in John and the Johannine Epistles should not be described as "docetists" and their christology should not be described as ("naive") "docetism." Strictly speaking, these terms could in any case only be used analogously and could at best indicate that the schismatics already subscribed to a christology which was "similar" to that of the later early-church heretics. But even the "similarity" rests on a mistaken view. The decisive difference probably consists in the fact that the later docetists contested the incarnation from the point of view of a gnostic dualism, while the schismatic Johannine Christians did so from the point of view of their genuinely Jewish heritage. In it they saw a danger to the transcendence of the biblical God and to monotheism.

create life (= salvation). But in fact he comes from the sphere of the spirit, the divine."[20] If the schismatic "disciples" stand by their denial of the incarnation, then they must necessarily contest any ability of the historical person Jesus to bring salvation. Jesus is then no more and no less than Moses or John the Baptist, who are also regarded as having "not seen God" (6:46), not "ascended to heaven" (3:13), not able to give "life" (6:32, 49), not the "light" (1:8). His word cannot then have been the unsurpassable word of God, the definitive self-revelation of God. The saving significance of the death of Jesus can no longer be supported (6:51c) and the celebration of the eucharist hangs in the air (6:53-58).[21]

6:64a concludes the reply of Jesus in resignation (cf. 6:36). Jesus' "argumentation" is not honoured. The schismatic "disciples" stand by their objection. Here and in the narrative commentary in 6:64b it is clear that the dispute with the schismatics is at an end. The separation is complete. The backdating of the "Johannine" schism to the days of Jesus—not without its problems—and its situation in the knowledge of Jesus "from the beginning" could indicate that the "evangelist" can look back on a lengthy controversial christological dispute, dating back as far as the post-Easter beginnings of the "Johannine" communities.[22] Looking back from the point of view of the occurrence of the christological schism he can say that the track towards the schismatic "disciples'" false belief in Christ was laid at an early stage, indeed right "from the beginning." The strongly deterministic saying of Jesus in 6:65, which picks up on 6:37, 44, brands the whole history of the controversy as the result of an internal inability to believe, right from the beginning. 6:45f. has to be read in this context. The schismatic "disciples" have never really allowed themselves to be taught by Jesus, the only one who has seen the Father. That is why it is never "given" them by the Father to come to Jesus along the only true way of discipleship (cf. 1 John 2:19).

In summary, it can be said that the Jewish-Christian profile of the "Johannine" schismatic, which was mooted at the beginning of this article, is confirmed by John 6:60-65. Their offence at the christological confession

---

[20] Richter, *Studien*, p. 115; cf. also p. 175.

[21] That the "sacramental doctrine" of 6:53-58 is sharply rejected in 6:62f. (E. Haenchen, *Johannesevangelium* [Tübingen, 1980], p. 338), is of course as false as the verdict that v. 63 cannot possibly "come from the man who wrote vv. 51b-58" (Richter, *Studien*, p. 116). Both statements are found in one and the same text and must at least have been thought of together by the author. There is no difficulty here either. Just as Jesus was not only "merely human," but Logos and "flesh" at the same time, so too the eucharistic gift is not mere "flesh and blood," but the "flesh and blood of the Son of Man," of the pneumatic Jesus, that is. In fact the Johannine Christians too do not eat and drink human flesh and blood during their eucharistic rites (as in the misunderstanding of the Jews in 6:52), but "bread" and "wine."

[22] On this see also my attempted reconstruction in *NTS* 34 (1988), 573-60; the attempt to understand the history of "Johannine" Christianity as the history of a christological controversy has been taken furthest by G. Richter; cf. his *Studien*, e.g. pp. 120-42, 149-98, 266-80, 281-87, 288-314.

of the "evangelist" is understandable from the point of view of Jewish presuppositions.[23] They see a danger for monotheism and the transcendence of God. Their christological position is, if anything, "conservative." For them, Jesus was a "mere" human being, who like the prophets and John the Baptist was an instrument of the spirit of God. He was not the incarnation of the Logos, or the "heavenly Christ," but became "Christ" or "Son of God" through the resurrection/exaltation. Jesus Christ's pre-existence and equality with God were therefore ruled out, and the "human Jesus" was devalued. They rejected the christology of the "evangelist" as blasphemy, because it threatened monotheism and the transcendence of God, and they parted company from him and his group.

III

6:66-71 must also be interpreted from the perspective of the already complete "Johannine" schism. The reader understands the event in the days of Jesus from the point of view of his/her own situation. The schismatic "disciples" are described as those who have fallen away from Jesus and have returned to the circle of the "Jews." They have "turned back" and no longer walk in the "tracks" of Jesus. They are in the majority by comparison with those who stay with Jesus (πολλοί, 6:60, 66). Here the minority situation of the "true believing" Johannine group comes to expression. This is confirmed by John's further point: the Johannine Christians form a fraternity (21:23), grouped around the "beloved disciple," living together in a concrete community of love (13:14f.; 15:12). They are "friends" of Jesus (15:14f.), "chosen" by him out of the cosmos (15:16, 19). The "world" hates them (15:18) and persecutes them (16:2). The world is the "Jews." They have excluded the Johannine Christians from the synagogue (16:2).

Among those who stay with Jesus are also the "Twelve," but not only the Twelve (see above). The "Twelve" have a supporting role alongside the "true believers," the Johannine community. Peter, as their spokesman, expressly acknowledges Jesus' bread-of-life discourse (6:26-58), as well as Jesus' reply to the schismatic "disciples" (6:62f.), as "words of eternal life." In a way he thereby confirms the "Johannine" kerygma in the name of the "Twelve" (6:68).

Like the "Johannine" Christians, the "Twelve" also—the καί in 6:69 probably bears this connotation—have "believed and acknowledged" (cf. 8:31) that Jesus is "the Holy One of God." This christological title has clearly been very deliberately chosen. It far surpasses the belief in the messiah to which Peter has already attained (cf. 1:41f.). Although it occurs only once in John's Gospel, it fully corresponds with the christological

---

[23] So also Richter, *Studien*, p. 108.

confession of the "Johannine" kerygma (cf. 10:36; 1 John 2:20). What the Johannine kerygma expresses by the title Logos, or the "Son," by the "descent/ascent" scheme and by the statements about the unity of the Father and the Son (10:30; 14:10f.; 17:21), is also encapsulated in the title "the Holy One of God." Jesus confronts "the world as the altogether Other"[24] and shares "in God's innermost and most intimate being."[25] The christological confession of Peter and the "Twelve" thus coincides with the confession of the "Johannine" community.

This view was evidently especially important in the concrete situation of the "Johannine" group. The group probably consciously made the connection to the "great Church" which traced its authority to Peter and the "Twelve," but stood firm on its specific kerygma and its tradition.[26] It placed itself under the authority of the office of Peter (21:15ff.), which in 6:68f. recognizes the "Johannine" tradition almost "officially,"[27] but maintained the spiritual superiority of the "beloved disciple." It based itself on his spirit-inspired witness to Christ.[28]

In a sort of counter-operation the credentials of the "Twelve" as true disciples of Jesus are produced in 6:70. They too have been "chosen" by him, like the "Johannine" remnant community (cf. 15:16, 19). But they are not spared apostasy either. One of them is a "devil." In 6:64b the "evangelist" had already mentioned the "betrayer" in the same breath as the schismatic "disciples." In 6:71 a narrative commentary is resumed, in which the name of the traitor is given. The "evangelist" closes emphatically with the exclamation "one of the 'Twelve'." As surely as the passion of Jesus, caused in part by the treachery of one of the "Twelve," is foreshadowed in this passage, just as certainly other intentions too have a part to play in this committed commentary. Perhaps the "evangelist" wanted to comfort his group with the indication that even the "Petrine" church was and is not free from apostasy, and perhaps he also wanted to warn the "great church" not

---

[24] Bultmann, *Das Evangelium*, p. 344.

[25] Schnackenburg, *Das Johannesevangelium*, 2:112. On this, cf. Klauck, "Gemeinde ohne Amt?" pp. 215f.

[26] So also R. Schnackenburg, "Zur Herkunft des Johannesevangeliums," *BZ* 14 (1970), 1-23; cf. Quast, *Peter and the Beloved Disciple*, pp. 48, 52f.

[27] Cf. Thyen, "Aus der Literatur zum Johannesevangelium," *TRu* 42 (1977), 254.

[28] The occasional assimilation of the Johannine representation of the ministry of Jesus to that of the Synoptics also belongs in this context. The intention of this assimilation is probably to demonstrate agreement; cf. L. Schenke, "Das Szenarium von Joh 6,1-25," *TTZ* 92 (1983), 191-203, idem, "Die literarische Vorgeschichte von Joh 1,19-51," *BN* 46 (1989), 24-57; H. Thyen, "Aus der Literatur zum Johannesevangelium," *TRu* 39 (1974), 293; 43 (1978), 332; Langbrandtner, *Weltferner Gott oder Gott der Liebe*, pp. 77f.; R. Baum-Bodenbender, *Hoheit in Niedrigkeit* (Würzburg, 1984), pp. 191-203; K.-Th. Kleinknecht, "Johannes 13, die Synoptiker und die 'Methode' der johanneischen Evangelien-überlieferung," *ZTK* 82 (1985), 361-88; J. Kügler, *Der Jünger, den Jesus liebte* (Stuttgart, 1988), pp. 175ff., 229ff., 346ff., 415ff.

to look back too judgmentally on the small crowd of "true-believing" Johannine Christians who had gone through a schism.

IV

Some considerations concerning the pre-history and composition of the passage discussed in this paper should be appended at this point. In my view its present form derives from the author to whom we owe the Gospel of John as a whole in its present version. I call this person the "evangelist" and see him as the editor who formed the present Gospel of John from already fixed written sources and orally transmitted material.[29] He will have found Jesus' reply in 6:62f. already in the original form of the bread-of-life discourse, which I have tried to show to be part of a more comprehensive "dialogue between Jesus and the Jews."[30] Originally it may have followed 6:45f. The "evangelist"/editor now turns it against the schismatics who have adopted the Jewish objections to the christology of the "Johannine" group. Out of the tragic experience of the internal church schism he reforms the whole section 6:60-65 within the framework of the composition of John 6. He has certainly not only made particular additions to an already existing textual whole (e.g. 6:64b, 65).[31]

This is true also of 6:66-71. Here the beginnings of the schism (6:66) and the reaction of the "Twelve" and of Peter (6:68f.) are reported. The old dispute over whether a church tradition independent of the synoptic tradition of the Petrine confession (cf. Mark 8:27-30 par.) has been taken up here[32] or whether the narrative is intentionally linked to the synoptic account,[33] can then be decided with some certainty in favour of the latter option, even if scarcely any verbal agreements are to be found. In general terms it may be regarded as certain that the "evangelist"/editor has taken upon himself the formation of the Fourth Gospel in full awareness of the synoptics, and has assimilated it to them, or balanced it with them, again and again.[34] In 6:66-71 the structural similarities to the synoptic presentations of the confession of Peter are unmistakable. Jesus challenges the "Twelve" to establish their position in respect of his person and his ministry (6:67; cf. Mark 8:29a par.). "Simon Peter" answers the challenge as the spokesman for all the disciples with a christological confession: σὺ εἶ (6:68f.; cf. Mark 8:29b par.). In Mark 8:31 par. the confession of Peter is

[29] On this cf. my essays in *NTS* 34 (1988), 573, esp. pp. 598ff., and *BN* 46 (1989), 24-57.
[30] Cf. *NTS* 34 (1988), 573-603, esp. p. 591, and *BZ* 29 (1985), 68-89.
[31] So Becker, *Das Evangelium*, p. 216.
[32] So C.H. Dodd, *Historical Tradition in the Fourth Gospel* (Cambridge, 1963), pp. 221f.; R.E. Brown, *The Gospel according to John I-XII* (New York, 1966), p. 301; Becker, *Das Evangelium*, p. 217.
[33] So H. Thyen, "Aus der Literatur zum Johannesevangelium," *TRu* 44 (1979), 98.
[34] Cf. note 28 above.

followed by Jesus' first passion prediction. 6:70f. must also be understood as a reference to the passion. It is important to note that this thematic sequence in Mark, in my view, can only be explained as coming from the redactional work of the evangelist.[35] The deviations from the synoptic account in 6:66-71 should be explicable as an intentional reworking by the "evangelist"/editor.

Above we have already presented some considerations as to why the "evangelist"/editor has Peter appear at this point as spokesman for the "Twelve." Peter confirms the christological confession of the "Johannine" group given in 6:26-58, 62f. as "words of eternal life" and confesses Jesus, like the "Johannine" Christians, as the "Holy One of God." The "evangelist"/editor's intention will have been to integrate the "Johannine" remnant community, which has gone through the schism, into the union of Christian communities represented by Peter and the "Twelve," while preserving its particular character and tradition. The adoption of elements of the synoptic presentation in the Fourth Gospel points in the same direction. The "evangelist"/editor thus shows that the tradition of the "Johannine" remnant community, which goes back to the witness of the "beloved disciple," is in agreement with that of the "great church" in which the synoptics have their validity. By this means he seeks, in the arena of the "great church," acknowledgement of the "Johannine" tradition fixed in the Fourth Gospel.[36]

---

[35] Becker, *Das Evangelium*, p. 217, points out that the Mark 8 sequence of feeding narrative (Mark 8:1-10), demand for signs (Mark 8:11-13), Peter's confession (8:27-30) and passion prediction (Mark 8:31) is also evident in John 6 (6:1-14, 30f., 67-69, 70f.). He regards this sequence as a traditional scheme, however, which continued to have influence in the Johannine community tradition. I would like to interpret this observation conversely as a further indication that the "evangelist"/editor of the present Gospel of John has produced this sequence in conscious assimilation to the Markan composition. In this context I refer the reader also to my observations on the "Szenarium von Joh 6,1-25," *TTZ* 92 (1983), 191-203.

[36] Similarly, Schnackenburg, "Zur Herkunft," p. 20.

THINKING ABOUT GOD:
WISDOM AND THEOLOGY IN JOHN 6

Marianne Meye Thompson

After the Prologue, perhaps no single chapter of John has generated as much scholarly output as its sixth chapter. The essays in this book bear witness to its perennial capacity to fascinate interpreters of the Fourth Gospel.[1] That John 6 continues to pique scholarly interest ought not to be surprising, for it contains within it numerous typically Johannine features: a sign of Jesus; the subsequent misunderstanding of Jesus' acts and words; and a revelatory "I am" discourse that corrects the misunderstanding and focuses on the central Johannine theme of life. Indeed, one so naturally characterizes the chapter's structure—sign, misunderstanding, "I am" saying, and explanatory discourse—as "typically Johannine" that one forgets how few chapters of John actually manifest this pattern! Even so, the chapter virtually summarizes the Gospel's major theme (God's gift of life through the Son) and digests its plot (the revelation and rejection of the Word). But it also raises puzzling questions of a literary, historical, and theological nature. In short, it is hard to think of a chapter that provides a greater variety of grist for the interpretative mill or that better represents the range of questions that arise in interpretation of this Gospel.[2]

There is, however, one feature of this chapter that remains substantially unexplored, and that is its theology—not its "theological viewpoints" on such issues as eschatology or eucharist, which have well-worn pedigrees, but rather the explicit affirmations and implicit assumptions about God central to the chapter's argument, imagery, and themes. Hence the subtitle of this essay, "Wisdom and Theology in John 6," intends theology proper— thinking about *God*, in part because this topic has been largely ignored. With good warrant, one can argue that this state of affairs holds true for New Testament studies generally. A number of years ago, in an essay now frequently cited, Nils A. Dahl called attention to "The Neglected Factor in New Testament Theology."[3] That neglected factor, according to Dahl, is God. A decade later Leander Keck asserted that Dahl's assessment was indeed correct. "The understanding of God has been the neglected factor in the study of New Testament theology as a whole. This is particularly true of the study of New Testament christology, even though every statement about

---

[1] Jürgen Becker makes this same observation ("Aus der Literatur zum Johannesevangelium (1978-1980)," *TRu* 47 [1982], 323).

[2] Hartwig Thyen speaks of the text as a *locus classicus* for addressing the question of the composition of the Gospel, and further comments that in John 6 the specifically johannine problems are gathered in an uncommonly dense fashion ("Aus der Literatur zum Johannesevangelium," *TRu* 43 [1978], 328).

[3] *Reflections* 75 (1975), 5-8.

Christ implicates God, beginning with the designation of Jesus as the Anointed."[4]

Not only has theology been ignored as a central factor in New Testament theology, but it has been ignored at the peril of misconstruing Christology. Echoing Keck's sentiments, J. D. G. Dunn urges us, "to realize once again that in the New Testament Christology functions within theology."[5] Moreover, with respect to the Gospels themselves, neglect of the theological factor severs these narratives from the very moorings which anchor them historically and literarily. In terms of the historical setting of the Gospel of John, without attention to theology the Gospel's origins and *Sitz-im-Leben* will be misunderstood. The Gospel's roots are in an emphatically monotheistic faith,[6] and studies of the last several decades have time and again proposed that one of the basic issues debated between the Johannine community and its adversaries was the appropriate way of conceiving of Jesus' relationship to God. As literary products, the Gospel narratives—although obviously accounts which focus on Jesus of Nazareth —seek to make arguments for who God is and how God relates to the world through the narration of the story of Jesus. As Paul Minear notes, "Gospel writers thought about God by telling stories about Jesus."[7]

The Fourth Gospel has been a prime exemplar in recent scholarship of the neglect of the theological question, having been routinely read as a narrowly christological and sometimes even more acutely as a "christocentric" Gospel. Hence, the necessary placement of christological reflection within its proper theological framework has been lost. By contrast, noted Johannine scholar C. K. Barrett argued that "John is writing about, and directing our attention to, God."[8] In fact, while 20:30-31 has often been taken as the purpose statement of the entire Gospel, Barrett suggests that the clause of 4:23, "the Father seeks true worshippers," has perhaps "as much claim as 20:30f. to be regarded as expressing the purpose

---

[4] "Toward the Renewal of New Testament Christology," *NTS* 32 (1986), 362-77.

[5] "Christology as an Aspect of Theology," *The Future of Christology: Essays in Honor of Leander E. Keck*, ed. Abraham J. Malherbe and Wayne A. Meeks (Minneapolis: Fortress, 1993), pp. 202-03.

[6] Whether or at what point Judaism can properly be called "monotheistic" has been the subject of considerable debate, and the bibliography here on both sides is extensive. But Jewish and Christian texts prior to and contemporaneous with the Gospel of John—with the exception of certain Gnostic texts—do not easily lend themselves to other than a monotheistic interpretation. See J. D. G. Dunn, "Was Christianity a Monotheistic Faith from the Beginning?" *SJT* 35 (1982), 303-36; Paul Rainbow, "Jewish Monotheism as the Matrix for New Testament Christology: A Review Article," *NovT* 33 (1991), 78-91; Peter Hayman, "Monotheism—A Misused Word in Jewish Studies?" *JJS* 42 (1991), 1-15; Margaret Barker, *The Great Angel: A Study of Israel's Second God* (London: SPCK, 1992).

[7] Paul S. Minear, *The God of the Gospels* (Atlanta: John Knox, 1988), p. 12.

[8] "Christocentric or Theocentric? Observations on the Theological Method of the Fourth Gospel," *La Notion biblique de Dieu*, ed. J. Coppens; BETL 41 (Leuven: University Press, 1976), p. 363.

of the gospel."[9] In other words, God is both the *subject* (who sends the Son, seeks true worshippers, draws people to faith, and gives life) and *object* (of worship and faith) of the primary action of the Gospel. Jesus is *God's* agent for the salvation of the world, the revealer of *God*, the way to *God*, and the life from *God*.

It is precisely the depiction of Jesus as God's agent that directs our attention to God, and further demands that we set the multiple *christ*-ological affirmations of this chapter within their *theo*-logical framework. John's "agency christology" not only naturally suggests but, even more pointedly, requires reflection on the character of God and of God's activity and presence in the world. For if in the work of the agent one sees the work of God, and if in the words of that same agent one hears the words of God, then we have good reason to ask how that God is understood. The purpose of this essay, then, is to read the sixth chapter of the Gospel with ears attuned to its *theo*-logical dimensions, where by "theological" we mean thinking about *theos*, about God.

To carry out this agenda, it will be useful, first, to review briefly the primary categories of agency suggested for explaining the christology of John 6. These categories include the *shaliach* figure, Jewish wisdom speculation, the Word in the OT, and *Logos* speculation (as represented by Philo). The point of this survey is to be neither exhaustive nor innovative, but rather to demonstrate that the agency figures which prove most illuminating in interpreting this chapter are those which unite agent (Jesus) and sender (God) most closely. Moreover, I will argue that while the *shaliach* figure does much to explain the character of Jesus' "agency," in the end it does not explain enough; in particular, it does not explain the language and imagery of John 6. For this task, the category of wisdom proves essential. Finally, having argued that John 6 uses categories of agency to establish the unity Jesus and God and the unity of their work in the world, we are led quite naturally to inquire about the character of that work and of God's presence in the world. Indeed, to neglect this question is to stop the inquiry short of the goal towards which the Gospel itself draws us.

A. THE JOHANNINE CHRISTOLOGY OF AGENCY

The designations for Jesus, including prophet (6:14), king (6:15), and Son of Man (6:27), all fall within the broad category of "agent of God." But while these designations identify Jesus as God's agent, they neither exhaust the categories in which the Gospel portrays the agency of Jesus nor provide the fundamental conceptual framework in which these titles properly

---

[9] C. K. Barrett, *The Gospel According to St. John*, 2nd rev. ed. (Philadelphia: Westminster, 1978), p. 238.

belong. That is to say, there are other categories of agency, often explored with relationship to John and particularly with reference to John 6, that furnish the materials for understanding how these other titles do and do not apply to Jesus. These other categories include the concept of the *shaliach* figure, the *Logos* of God, and the *wisdom* of God, although wisdom and word are so closely connected that we shall discuss them together.[10]

What these figures share in common is that each of them points to the closest possible relationship between the agent figure and the one whom that agent represents. With respect to the *shaliach* figure of Judaism, we read in rabbinic sources that, "A man's shaliach is like the one who sent him."[11] Because the *shaliach* represents "the one who sent him" not just informally but in a legally binding relationship, he is to be received and respected as the one who sent him. In the presence of the *shaliach*, one is in the presence of the one who sent him. The Fourth Evangelist's use of the *shaliach* figure as a type for explaining the relationship of Jesus to the Father would go a long way towards explaining the following features of Johannine christology: the unity of the work of the Father and Son (5:17-18; 10:29-30); the obedience, and even "subordination" of the agent to the sender, or of the Son to the Father; the call to honor the Son as one would the Father (5:23); the experience of the presence of the Father in the presence of Jesus (14:8-11); and the language of sending (6:29, 38, 44, 57).

So striking are the parallels between Johannine christology and halakhic principles of agency that A. E. Harvey has concluded that "much of the language used of Jesus in the Fourth Gospel [is] drawn from juridical practice." The Jewish conception of "agency" explains even the designation "son of God," when it is recognized that a principal's son could be considered his supreme and natural agent.[12] A recognition of the influence of the *shaliach* figure on Johannine christology implies that the Evangelist conceived of the work of Jesus as God's own work. One could then expect a fairly fluid interchange between the work of Jesus and the work of God: what Jesus does is God's work; God works through Jesus. When the *shaliach* figure provides the primary type for Jesus' mission, the resulting emphasis falls naturally on the unity of the will and work of Jesus and God. Hence, scrutiny of Jesus' actions and words in the Gospel would help to uncover the character of the God who stands behind them. But Harvey's phrase "much of the language" is telling, for while the category of agency helps to account for much of the specific idiom of the Gospel's christology,

---

[10] "Agent" will be used as a broad and open-ended designation to refer to any figure who represents another, is commissioned, authorized, or sent by another, or who carries on the work of another in their absence. For the more technical usage familiar from Jewish sources, I shall use *shaliach*.

[11] A common saying in the rabbis was "the one who is sent like the one who sent him" (*m. Ber.* 5:5; *b. B. Mes.* 96a; *b. Hag.* 10b; *b. Menah* 93b; *b. Nazir* 12b; *b. Qidd.* 42b, 43a).

[12] A. E. Harvey, "Christ as Agent," *The Glory of Christ in the New Testament: Studies in Christology*, ed. L. D. Hurst and N. T. Wright (Oxford: Clarendon Press, 1987), p. 241.

it does not explain adequately the themes of John 6, such as the descent of the Son from above, and the language of "eating" and "drinking" that permeates that chapter. In trying to establish the *shaliach* as the primary agent figure behind John's christology, Harvey is arguing against the views of Peder Borgen and others that a combination of *halakhic* and mystical thought, such as one finds in the early stages of merkabah mysticism, provides the necessary and missing link to explain Johannine christology. More specifically, Borgen contends that the *shaliach* figure does not explain "the fact that Jesus according to John is not just a human and earthly agent but a divine and heavenly agent who has come down among men."[13] Similarly, J.-A. Bühner proposed that John's distinctive christology is to be located in the fusion of prophet and angel or, more specifically, the apocalyptic-prophetic seer with the son of man understood as a divine angelic being.[14]

In other words, both Borgen and Bühner deem it imperative to appeal to some heavenly figure to clarify the total shape of John's "agency" christology. Dunn agrees with the assessment that the *shaliach* figure, on its own, cannot provide an adequate hold on the distinctive and central features of Johannine christology, such as pre-existence and the intimate union between Father and Son. Indeed, these are precisely the points that John desires to underscore: "The Fourth Evangelist wants to persuade his readers of a *heavenly origin* for Jesus the Messiah which goes back to the beginning of time, and of a *closeness of continuity* between Father and Son which is more than simply identity of will or function."[15] Dunn stands in the stream of scholarship which argues that in order to portray Jesus as the pre-existent, heavenly visitant, the Evangelist utilized the figure of Wisdom and the imagery and speculation associated with it. By depicting Jesus as the incarnation of divine wisdom, the Evangelist drew upon an agent figure to which can be ascribed heavenly origin and cosmic pre-existence.

To be sure, many others have explored the so-called "wisdom christology" of the Gospel of John, and not all agree on the extent to which

---

[13] "God's Agent in the Fourth Gospel" (reprinted in *The Interpretation of John*, ed. John Ashton (Philadelphia: Fortress; London: SPCK, 1986), p. 72.

[14] *Der Gesandte und sein Weg im 4. Evangelium*, WUNT 1; 2. Reihe (Tübingen: Mohr-Siebeck, 1977). More recently, John Ashton has suggested that John's christology is "an angel christology *tout court*" (*Studying John: Approaches to the Fourth Gospel* [Oxford: Clarendon Press, 1994], p. 75).

[15] James D. G. Dunn, "Let John be John: A Gospel for Its Time," *Das Evangelium und die Evangelien*, WUNT 28 (Tübingen: Mohr-Siebeck, 1983), p. 330. See also Mark Appold, *The Oneness Motif in the Fourth Gospel*, WUNT 2; 2d. Reihe (Tübingen: Mohr-Siebeck, 1976), pp. 20-22, 282-83, who argues that the motif of "sending" and the "sent one" cannot be construed as the central theme of the Gospel's christology, precisely because the Jewish *shaliach* assumes a secondary and deputy-like role which the Johannine Jesus, one with the Father in love, does not take on.

wisdom has shaped John's portrait of Jesus.[16] While wisdom influence on
the Prologue has long been acknowledged, the degree to which such
speculation has colored other facets or narratives of the Gospel remains
open to discussion. In a recent detailed discussion of wisdom and the
Gospel of John, Martin Scott suggests that to speak of "wisdom influence"
on the Gospel comes up short, for "John presents a thoroughgoing sophia
christology."[17] He then proceeds to argue that nearly every important feature
of the Gospel has significant parallels in wisdom speculation. In John 6 the
question becomes acute due to the dictional and thematic coherence
between the words of Jesus in this chapter and the descriptions and words of
wisdom in biblical and post-biblical texts. By contrast, D. A. Carson writes,
"The so-called sapiential interpretation of John 6 is not so much wrong as
peripheral."[18] Although Carson allows possible allusions to Proverbs 8:5 and
9:5, he suggests that the more likely intertextual links are to be found with
Isaiah 55, which has both an invitation to all who are thirsty to come eat and
drink (vv. 1-2), as well as an affirmation of the efficacy of God's word (vv.
10-11)—and both of these, moreover, in the context of eschatological
salvation and the new covenant.[19]

But one does not need to choose between the influence on the Gospel of
John of "wisdom" and "word" (or Torah) theologies, for these are already
inextricably joined in Jewish thought prior to John's day.[20] The beginning
of speculation on personified wisdom can be found in Proverbs 1-9. In this
context one finds multiple admonitions to hear and learn from wisdom, and
wisdom invites people to eat her bread (9:5), a metaphor for learning to
"walk in the way of insight." In the wisdom tradition, instruction and
learning are dominant themes, making an eventual identification of law with
wisdom an easy and natural step. So it is that Sirach 24 notes that God
commands wisdom to dwell in Israel (vv. 8, 12), and designates this

---

[16] J. Rendel Harris, *The Origin of the Prologue to St. John's Gospel* (Cambridge: Cambridge University Press, 1917); Raymond E. Brown, *The Gospel according to John*, 2 vols. (New York: Doubleday, 1966, 1968), *passim*; J. D. G. Dunn, "Let John be John"; idem, *Christology in the Making: An Inquiry into the Origins of the Doctrine of the Incarnation*, 2nd ed. (London: SCM Press, 1989 [1980]), pp. 163-212; Martin A. Scott, *Sophia and the Johannine Jesus*, JSNTSupp 71 (Sheffield: Sheffield Academic Press, 1992); Craig A. Evans, *Word and Glory: On the Exegetical and Theological Background of John's Prologue*, JSNTSup 89 (Sheffield: Sheffield Academic Press, 1993); and Ben Witherington, *Jesus the Sage* (Philadelphia: Fortress, 1994).

[17] Scott, *Sophia*, p. 29.

[18] D. A. Carson, *The Gospel According to John* (Grand Rapids: Eerdmans; Leicester: InterVarsity, 1991), p. 289.

[19] That Isaiah 55 formed the background for John's bread of life discourse was earlier suggested by Brown, *John*, 1:521, who nevertheless also acknowledged the influence of wisdom terminology and thought on the chapter.

[20] See especially the parallels adduced by Eldon Jay Epp, "Wisdom, Torah, Word: The Johannine Prologue and the Purpose of the Fourth Gospel," *Current Issues in Biblical and Patristic Interpretation*, ed. G. F. Hawthorne (Grand Rapids: Eerdmans, 1975), pp. 128-46; Severino Pancaro, *The Law in the Fourth Gospel*, NovTSupp 52 (Leiden: Brill, 1975), pp. 455-58.

wisdom as "the law which Moses commanded us" (v. 23; cf. 15:1, "whoever holds to the law will obtain wisdom"). Similarly, in Baruch 4:1 wisdom is called "the book of the commandments of God, and the law that endures forever," and the book of Wisdom equates God's word and God's wisdom (Wis. 18:15). Philo assumed this equation in speculating about the Logos, a concept in which he is arguably far more interested than in wisdom.[21]

Of further interest in the present context is the fact that the law was sometimes symbolized by manna.[22] Bread itself was already a standing symbol for the nourishment provided by the law, and therefore the bread sent from heaven, the manna, served aptly as a symbol for the law. It is then but a short step to conceiving of wisdom, sometimes equated with Torah or viewed as embodied in it, as providing nourishment or inviting people to her feast.[23] The midrash on Exodus 16:4 combines God's promise of the "bread from heaven" with the invitation of wisdom to "Come, eat of my bread," found in Prov. 9:5, thus at least insinuating the identification of manna and wisdom. In more than one place, Philo allegorizes the manna as the divine gift of wisdom.[24] It seems likely that the Fourth Evangelist was aware of the use of bread and particularly the heavenly manna as a symbol for Torah and/or wisdom, and that he used this identification to argue for the surpassing wisdom and revelation to be found in the true bread of life which came not through the mediation of Moses, but directly from God.[25]

---

[21] See, e.g., this striking passage in *Fug.* 18 §97, urges the able to press forward "to the highest word of God, which is the fountain of wisdom, in order that by drinking of that stream he may find everlasting life instead of death."

[22] *Mek.* on Exod. 13:17; see especially Bruce J. Malina, *The Palestinian Manna Tradition* (Leiden: Brill, 1968).

[23] Deut 8:3; Isa. 55:10-11; Sir. 15:3; Wis. 16:20, 26; *Gen. Rab.* 70:5 [on Gen 28:20], which quotes Prov. 9:5.

[24] Thus in commenting on Exodus 16:4, Philo (*Mut.* 44 §§259-260), as Peder Borgen [*Bread from Heaven*, pp. 111-12] points out, simply replaces the word for manna with the word for wisdom (*sophia*), yielding the following comment: "Can you find any more trustworthy than Moses, who says that while other men receive their food from earth, the nation of vision alone has it from heaven? The earthly food is produced with the co-operation of husbandmen, but the heavenly is sent like the snow by God the solely self-acting, with none to share his work. And indeed it says 'Behold I rain upon you bread from heaven' (Ex. xvi.4). Of what food can he rightly say that it is rained from heaven, save of heavenly wisdom which is sent from above on souls which yearn for virtue by Him who sheds the gift of prudence in rich abundance, whose grace waters the universe, and chiefly so in the holy seventh (year) which he calls the Sabbath?" See also *Her.* 39 §191, where Philo, again commenting on the distribution of manna in Exodus 16, notes "The heavenly food of the soul, wisdom, which Moses calls 'manna,' is distributed to all who will use it in equal portions by the divine Word, careful above all things to maintain equality."

[25] See C. H. Dodd, *The Interpretation of the Fourth Gospel* (Cambridge: Cambridge University Press, 1953), pp. 336-37; Epp, "Wisdom, Torah, Word," 136-37; Brevard S. Childs, *The New Testament as Canon: An Introduction* (Philadelphia: Fortress, 1984), p. 137: "In a conscious polemic against the synagogue the claim is being made by the evangelist that the

Further parallels with wisdom thought may help to account for other motifs of John 6. The explicit invitation to "eat" and "drink" (6:35; cf. 7:37) certainly echoes those of wisdom in Proverbs 9:5 ("Come, eat of the my bread and drink of the wine I have mixed.") and Sirach 24:19 ("Come to me, you who desire me, and eat your fill of my fruits. . . . Those who eat of me will hunger for more, and those who drink of me will thirst for more."). These invitations are, of course, metaphorical. In Proverbs, wisdom invites the simple and immature to learn the ways of insight. In Sirach 24, the invitation to eat and drink is construed as an invitation to obey Torah.

Whoever obeys me will not be put to shame,
and those who work with my help will not sin (24:22).

[The law] overflows, like the Pishon, with wisdom . . .
It runs over, like the Euphrates, with understanding . . .
It pours forth instruction like the Nile . . .
(vv. 25, 26, 27)

Earlier, Sirach tells us that wisdom nourishes those who fear the Lord with "the bread of learning, and [gives them] the water of wisdom to drink." Indeed, following the path of wisdom, learning the lessons of wisdom, is the way to attain to life (Prov. 8:35; Wis. 8:13; Sir. 9:18). The invitations to eat and drink, understood as symbolic expressions for learning from God's wisdom, provide more than casual correspondences with John 6, where the invitation to eat and drink (6:35) is glossed as a call to believe (6:36) in the one sent from heaven (6:38), belief which is possible for those who are "taught by God" and who have "heard and learned from the Father" (6:45). Eating of this bread, hearing and learning from God, leads to eternal life (6:27, 33, 35, 39-40, 44, 47-48, 50-51, 53-58).

In sum, wisdom is a figure which combines in itself a heavenly origin and dwelling (Prov. 8; Sir. 24:1, 4; Wis. 18:15); a subsequent descent to earth (Wis. 9; Sir. 24:3-17);[26] emphasis on learning and hearing the

---

hermeneutical key to the divine will is not to be found merely in an identity of wisdom and torah, but in the incarnation of Jesus Christ in whom both the wisdom and the law of God is united."

[26] While wisdom pre-exists the created order and comes to earth at God's command, it is not clear that the wisdom narrative can account fully for the descent/ascent schema of the Gospel, as Martin Scott acknowledges (*Sophia*, p. 137). Indeed, it is the lack of a parallel to this key element of Johannine christology that leads Bühner to reject the influence of wisdom tradition on the Fourth Gospel (*Der Gesandte und sein Weg*, 87-103). Yet Borgen's contention ("God's Agent," p. 71) that the return to the Father can be explained by the halakhic agent's "return and report to the sender upon completing his mission" runs aground on the very text which he himself cites, namely, *P. Hag.* 76d: "Behold we send you to a great man as our shaliach, and *he is equivalent to us until such time as he return to us*" (emphasis added). But that Jesus ceases to be one with God upon his return to God would be a hard point to defend from the Fourth Gospel. Scott argues that John presents not so much a descent/ascent schema as he does a descent/going-away schema (*Sophia*, pp. 137-39). This accords more closely with the theme of wisdom's hiddenness or

instruction of God; (4) a unique embodiment in the shape of the Torah, given exclusively to Israel (Sir. 24:7-12; Bar. 3:36-37; Wis. 9:10; 4Q185 1:4, 10);[27] and the promise of life. One of the items missing from this list associated with wisdom in the wisdom tradition, is its role as the "master worker" alongside God in creation (Prov. 8:30; Wis. 9:9). While wisdom's role as God's agent in creation likely influences the thought of the Prologue (1:3-4), this theme is not developed in John 6. Instead, John 6 develops another strand of wisdom speculation, namely, that wisdom accompanied and guided the Israelites all along its pilgrimage towards the promised Land (Wis. 10-11). One of the great saving events of Israel's history—the Exodus, with its miraculous feedings in the wilderness culminating in the Sinai theophany and the giving of the law through Moses—prefigures God's actions through Jesus in John 6. However, even granting the influence of wisdom traditions on John and, in particular, on John 6, further

---

withdrawal in judgment (Prov. 1:18; Sir. 4:19; 4 Ezra 5:9-10). John shapes this descent-withdrawal schema by introducing a beneficial aspect of the withdrawal for those who have faith. Witherington argues that the V-shaped plot of the Gospel (descent/ascent) is modelled after the sapiential path as found particularly in *1 Enoch* 42, where wisdom descends to earth, but is rejected and returns to heaven (*Jesus the Sage*, pp. 371-73, 379). But Ashton contends that John's view "takes a stand against the pessimistic view of *1 Enoch* 42 that it was only iniquity that found a dwelling-place on earth" (*Studying John,* pp. 16-17). The Gospel, like Sirach, testifies that God's wisdom did indeed find a dwelling place on earth (John 1:14; Sir. 24:8, 12; contrast *1 Enoch* 42:1-2). Clearly there is no unified or single "wisdom mythology" which our Gospel draws upon, but it is doubtful that *1 Enoch* 42 provides a sufficient parallel to Jesus' path in the Gospel. Indeed, the whole tenor of John's presentation of Jesus as incarnate wisdom is to stress the manifestation of God's presence which, though hidden, nevertheless remains accessible to those who have eyes to see and ears to hear. There is a striking parallel between Wis 7:29-30 ("Compared with the light she is found to be superior, for it is succeeded by the night, but against wisdom evil does not prevail.") and John 1:5, "The light shines in the darkness, and the darkness did not overcome it."). In other words, the descent of the word has positive revelatory effects, for which the myth in *1 Enoch* 42 cannot account.

27 It has often been pointed that John uses the term *logos* (word) rather than *sophia* (wisdom), raising the question whether John has a "wisdom christology." While it is true that John uses *logos*, not *sophia*, the term *logos* does not appear outside the prologue (1:1; 1:14), and both in the prologue and the rest of the Gospel the imagery and language used to portray Jesus has at least as many, if not more, affinities with the biblical wisdom tradition as with speculation about the Word. A typical suggestion for John's preference for *logos* to *sophia* is that *logos*, like Jesus, is male. But Paul had no hesitation in calling Jesus "the wisdom of God" (1 Cor. 1:24). A more likely explanation is to be found in some combination of the following factors: First, wisdom and word had already coalesced and overlapped in the tradition, making their interchange natural. Second, John's interest is particularly in the relationship of Jesus and *Torah* which, however much it embodies wisdom, is nevertheless better described by "word." It is telling that in two instances where Jesus is contrasted with the law or argues from the scriptures (chs. 1 and 6), "wisdom" imagery comes into play, suggesting that John always has in the mind wisdom as embodied in the law. As Torah became even more dominant in the self-definition of the Jewish people, particularly in conflict with Christians, it became more important to identify Jesus as "word." Finally, John may be located historically along a trajectory in which *logos* becomes a more important concept in interpreting the faith. Philo, for example, identifies wisdom with word, but greatly prefers the concept *logos* when speculating about the manner of God's manifestation to the world. *Logos* would certainly allow a better point of contact with the pagan world.

questions remain. At what point does John dip into the stream of wisdom speculation? In its early stages as found in Proverbs 8, or in its somewhat more philosophically and finely developed stages as crystallized in the book of Wisdom? The answer to this question might shed light on understanding the author's context, audience, and purpose(s). This issue also leads directly to a question which is, for the purposes of this essay, still more germane. How, exactly, does John conceive of "wisdom?" If the Jesus of John and of John 6 is portrayed as wisdom incarnate, then what exactly does the Evangelist wish to assert about Jesus? What conception of the person or significance of Jesus arises from the recognition of his portrayal as God's wisdom incarnate? What—or who—is this wisdom?

We go back to the observation of James Dunn that "The Fourth Evangelist wants to persuade his readers . . . of a *closeness of continuity* between Father and Son which is more than simply identity of will or function."[28] It is wisdom, more than any other agent figure, which can provide the pattern for portraying this "closeness." For while with other agent figures (such as prophet, shaliach, or angel) we speak of the "relationship" between these figures and God, in the case of "logos" and "wisdom" it is arguable whether "relationship" is even the proper characterization of the situation. It is not so much that word and wisdom are "related" to God, for the Word that God speaks is an expression of God, and wisdom is an expression of God's mind or thought. Wisdom and word both refer to something which belongs to and comes from God, something inward or peculiar to God which is externally expressed.[29] To speak of Jesus as God's wisdom incarnate is to say that he is God's self-expression, God's thought or mind, God's interior word spoken aloud. And because and insofar as these are externally expressed, they can be known by human beings. They are manifestations of God's activity in the world.[30] Although wisdom can be personified as having independent reality and existence apart from God, and depicted as inviting people to eat, offering them life, and searching for a place to dwell in Israel, this wisdom is not, in the end, separable from God, but is rather the concrete manifestation of God's own ways with and in the world. Wisdom's unique status can be thrown into relief when compared with God's other agents, whether heavenly or human, in the world. Whereas a prophet or angel has a separate existence and even a distinct will from God, and could be said to obey or disobey God, such

---

[28] "Let John be John," p. 330.

[29] This is perhaps most explicit in the refined wisdom speculation in Wisdom 7, where wisdom is said to be "a breath of the power of God, a pure emanation of the glory of the Almighty . . . a reflection of eternal light, a spotless mirror of the working of God, and an image of his goodness" (7:25-26).

[30] A point made repeatedly by Dunn of both wisdom and the word. In *Christology in the Making* Dunn writes that Spirit, wisdom and word "are simply alternative ways of speaking about the effective power of God in his active relationship with his world and its inhabitants" (p. 219); cf. "Let John be John," pp. 322-23.

predications are not possible of wisdom. Wisdom does not exist unless God thinks it. Wisdom is a category of agency that allows for the closest possible unity between the agent and God. One may speak truly of inseparability.

Thus wisdom is not a force immanent and operative in the world apart from God, but the power or activity of God manifest in a particular way: namely, as instruction or guidance of the people of God in order to bring them to life.[31] To speak of God's activity, guidance, or plan, can leave the impression that we are dealing only with the results or effects of God's actions, but not with God's own presence. This is precisely the tension and mystery that wisdom presents to us, for while wisdom is the very manifestation of God's thought, God's plan, it can too easily be objectified into a thing apart from God.[32] But as the very expression of God's thought, wisdom cannot be cut off from its origin in God. Wisdom provides us, then, not with materials for thinking abstractly about God, but rather for thinking very concretely about the presence of God in and with the world. It is this "activity" of God which is manifested or concretized through the true wisdom of God, the "true bread that gives life to the world," in the person of Jesus. To be sure, Jesus is more than simply the projection of God's thoughts onto the canvas of the world, but what comes to fruition in and through him is no less than God's divine plan for the salvation of the world. The designation of Jesus as God's wisdom incarnate thus forces us to think about the God whom Jesus represents and manifests as present in and with the world. And chapter 6 affords an excellent avenue for such consideration.

B. GOD'S WORD AND WORK ACCORDING TO JOHN 6

Although God's activity is rather fully described, nowhere in this chapter— or in the Gospel—are God's actions dramatized. There is less "showing" what God does than there is "telling" about God and God's work: God is "the Father," who has "set his seal" on the Son of man (6:27), "sent" this Son of man (6:29, 57), gives the true bread of life (6:32-34); gives believers to Jesus (6:37, 39); teaches (6:45) and "draws" people to Jesus (6:44, 65), and who is alone the source of life (6:33, 57). Although some of the verbs refer to past action and some to future, many refer to present action, and almost all have Jesus either as the object (God loves, knows, sends, gives Jesus or the Son) or else the agent with the believer as the object (draws,

---

[31] Dodd speaks of wisdom as "the hypostatized thought of God projected into creation, and remaining as an immanent power within the world and in man" (*Interpretation*, p. 275). See also John Painter, "Theology, Eschatology and the Prologue of John," *SJT* 46 (1993), 27-42.

[32] For the insistence that wisdom should be construed as God's cosmic plan, see especially C. H. Dodd, *Interpretation*, p. 277; also cf. Ashton, *Studying John*, pp. 19-23, 31, who calls attention to the striking parallel between 1QS 11:11 and John 1:3: "All things came to pass by his knowledge, He establishes all things by his design, And without Him nothing is done."

teaches, gives). All of the statements about God are sentences with active verbs ("God has set his seal"; "my Father gives you the true bread from heaven") rather than affirmations of God's virtue ("God is faithful"), character ("God is gracious") or essence ("God is all-seeing"). This state of affairs, in which God is both the active subject behind Jesus' ministry and yet never portrayed directly as the actor, is the natural outgrowth of the christology of agency which has provided the framework for the chapter. Rather than offer a series of assertions about God, the chapter narrates God's action through Jesus so that Jesus' deeds embody God's character. The actions and words of Jesus, God's agent and God's wisdom, are therefore a characterization of God. As Alan Culpepper notes,

> God is characterized not by what He says or does but by what Jesus, His fully authorized emissary, says about him. Even to describe the situation in these terms, however, is to risk distortion. It might be better, therefore, to say that God is characterized by Jesus and that having understood the gospel's characterization of Jesus one has grasped its characterization of God.[33]

How, then, does John 6 characterize God's presence and activity in the world? The chapter gives evidence of a number of assumptions and beliefs about God common in first-century Judaism which come to light not through direct predications about God but through the narration of particular deeds of Jesus and his interpretative discourse. These shared assumptions include the following items, also evident in this narrative: First, God is the source of all life. Second, God, whose sovereignty governs the world, desires and effects human flourishing and reveals the pathway to attaining it (6:27-29, 33, 39-40, 45). Third, as Father, God calls forth children, a people, and provides and cares for them, as God's faithfulness to Israel throughout its history makes evident (6:1-13, 31-33). Fourth, the transcendent God is accessible to that people, not directly (6:46), but rather through multiple means and agents: Scripture (6:31, 45), the Spirit (6:63), human beings like Moses (6:14, 31-32), the provision of manna (6:31-33, 48-50). By revelation through various means, God seeks a response of obedience and faith, and judges those who are disobedient and unfaithful. Finally, God will bring the faithful to their promised destiny of salvation and life (6:33, 39-40, 44, 47-51, 54, 58).

It is difficult to keep these points distinct from one another, for each one implies or depends on one or more of the others. For example, although one may distinguish God's work in creating from that of governing the world,

---

[33] R. Alan Culpepper, *Anatomy of the Fourth Gospel: A Study in Literary Design* (Philadelphia: Fortress, 1983), p. 113.

God's creative work is regularly understood in first-century Jewish and Christian texts to imply and even demand the constant superintendence of the world. God governs the world because God created it. God's sovereignty cannot be construed abstractly in terms of some vague governance over the events of the world, but rather has its focus in the election and care of a specific people. This governance and care is expressed and revealed through a variety of means, including angelic announcement, prophets, the revelation of Scripture, and so on. The point is not that John makes lists of the attributes or actions of God and then applies these things to Jesus, but that the kinds of actions ascribed, explicitly and implicitly, to Jesus are actions typically predicated of God—and uniquely so. Thus we shall examine each of the five affirmations listed above, to discover not only what is said about God but also how Jesus' deeds and words in this chapter portray him as God's agent and, even more, depict his presence as the manifestation of God's presence in the world.

1. The living God. Once in this chapter (6:57) we have the epithet "the living Father," reflecting the common biblical phrase "the living God."[34] The epithet "living God" contrasts God with "dead idols," and so also refers to God as creator and source of life.[35] These descriptions of God are basic assumptions of Judaism, and countless examples could be given. Philo, for example, writes often of God as Creator, and stresses the importance of the creating role with a wide range of titles for God in that capacity, including Creator and Maker (*Spec.* I.30; *Somn.* I.76; *Mut.* 29); planter of the world (*Conf.* 196); Father (*Spec.* II.197; *Opif.* 74; *Mut.* 29; "Father of all things, for he begat them," *Cher.* 49); Parent (*Spec.* II.197); "Cause of all things" (*Somn.* I.67); Fountain of life (*Fug.* 198);[36] and Light (*Somn.* I.75). Josephus assumes that the God of Israel is "The God who made heaven and earth and sea" (*Ag. Ap.* 2.121, 190f).[37] It is also assumed, by both Philo and Josephus, that God, unlike other beings, is uncreated, and thereby necessarily the source of the life of the world.[38] Instructive also is the LXX translation of "I am who I am" (Exod. 3:14) as "I am the one who is" (ἐγώ εἰμι ὁ ὤν). Philo echoes the LXX at this point, repeatedly referring to God either as ὁ ὤν or,

---

[34] For examples of the phrase "living God," see Deut. 5:26; Josh. 3:10; 1 Sam. 17:26, 36; 2 Kgs. 19:4; Ps. 84:2; Isa. 37:4, 17; Jer. 10:10; Dan. 6:20, 26; Hos. 1:10; Bel. 5, 24; Add. Esth. 16:16; Matt. 16:16; 26:63; Acts 14:15; 2 Cor. 3:3; 6:16; 1 Thess. 1:9; Heb. 3:12; 9:14; 10:31; 12:22; Rev. 7:2; *Jub.* 1:25.

[35] Note the contrast between idols, made by human hands, and the Lord who creates in Isa. 44:9-20, 24; 45:16-22. Jer. 10:8-10 adds, "[Idols] are the work of the artisan and of the hands of the goldsmith. . . . they are all the product of skilled workers. But the Lord is the true God; he is the living God and the everlasting King."

[36] "God is the most ancient of all fountains. . . . God alone is the cause of animation and of that life which is in union with prudence; for the matter is dead. But God is something more than life; he is, as he himself has said, the everlasting fountain of living."

[37] See also Jdt. 9:12; *Jub.* 2:31-32; 12:19; 16:26-27; 22:5, 66-67; 2 Macc. 1:24; 7:28.

[38] Josephus, *Ag.Ap.* 2:167, 190, 239; Philo, *Her.* 42:206.

more frequently, τὸ ὄν, "that which is." Indeed, Philo's emphasis at this
point has led one writer to comment that for Philo "God is just existence."[39]
The conception of God as the living God and hence the creator of the world
and all that is in it can be found in the documents at Qumran, throughout the
Pseudepigrapha, and in rabbinic sources.[40]

That God is the creator and source of life are also important themes in
the wisdom literature (Prov. 8:27-30; 3:19; Wis. 7:21; 8:4-6; 9:1-2, 9),
which also speak of wisdom's mediating role in the creation of the world
(cf. Jer. 10:12; 1QH 9:7, 14, 19; 11QPs^a 26:14). Elsewhere, God is said to
have created the world by his word (Ps. 33:6) or by the Torah (*Tanhuma,
Bereshit*, § 1 [6b]; *Gen.Rab.* 1:1; *m. Abot* 3:15). Not only is God the creator
of the world and source of its life, but God created the world through an
agent—usually wisdom or Torah. The prologue of John is an example of
such thought, when it affirms the creation of the world through the agency
of the Logos. Although the sixth chapter of John does not directly state that
God created the world, its emphasis on God's gift of life through the agency
of Jesus—wisdom incarnate—shows the unity of the life-giving work of
God and Jesus, creator and incarnate wisdom. The conception of Jesus as
wisdom incarnate further facilitates the testimony to the unity of the life-
giving work of Jesus and God inasmuch as wisdom was understood to be
the pathway to life (see below).

We might venture to say that the thesis of the chapter is that God wills
and desires to give people life through the words and deeds of Jesus the Son
(6:40). Not only does Jesus promise to give eternal life, the life that God
gives, but he works a sign which itself manifests God's life-giving work and
presence in the world. Jesus feeds the multitudes, and interprets his action
as representative of a ministry that brings the bread of life to the world. The
analogy between the physical feeding of the miracle and the spiritual
feeding which Jesus promises depends on seeing both these works as the
work of God and on interpreting them against the story of the first Exodus,
when God gave the people bread in order to sustain life.[41]

The continuity of Jesus' work with that of the God of Israel is one of the
assumptions upon which John's argument is based, as the exegetical

---

[39] Ephraim Uhrbach, *The Sages: Their Concepts and Beliefs* (ET Cambridge: Harvard, 1987),
p. 40. Some examples of Philo's emphasis on the existence of God can be found in *Det.* 160;
Mut. 10-12, 17; *Somn.* I.230-31.

[40] For example, 1QS 3:15, 25; 9:25; 11:11; 11QPs^a 19:3-4; *T. Abr.* 9:6; 16:1; 17:11; *Jos. As.*
8:4; 12:1; 3 Macc. 2:2-3; Pr. Man. 2f; *2 Bar.* 21:4-11; *1 Enoch* 84:2-4; *Jub.* 12:19; in *b. Ber.* 28b
Johanan ben Zakkai is quoted as describing God as "the Holy One, who lives and endures
forever." See also the chapter on "God and the World," in G. F. Moore, *Judaism* (New York:
Schocken, 1927), 1:357-85.

[41] According to *Tg. Eccles.* 12:11, the halakoth and midrashim were given through Moses, the
prophet, "who alone fed the people of the house of Israel in the desert with manna and desirable
things." See Malina, *Manna Traditions*, pp. 86-88, for issues of dating the traditions in this
Targum.

discussion over the interpretation of the biblical texts will show. This debate has to do with the proper understanding of certain biblical texts, most notably "He gave them bread from heaven to eat" (6:31), probably a paraphrase of one or more OT texts (Exod. 16:4, 15; Neh. 9:15; Ps. 78:24).[42] The citation of this text may well be intended to recall the entire narrative of the Exodus 16, with the surprising gift of manna in response to the complaints of the wandering Israelites (bread: Exod. 16:4, 15; John 6:31, 32, 33, 51; and murmuring, Exod. 16:2; John 6:41, 43).[43] Jesus, however, tells the people how to understand and read the text—not with the past tense "gave" but with a present tense "gives," with God as the subject of the present activity of giving life-giving bread. Here there is both continuity and contrast with the provision of God in the wilderness, for although the people ate "bread from heaven," they died. Yet their death was not due to a failure of God's provision, but rather to their lack of faithfulness, as the regular biblical emphasis on the murmuring and disobedience of the wandering Israelites makes clear.

Consequently, in the recital of God's saving deeds to Israel found in Psalms 78, a number of themes also found in John 6 coalesce. Thus, according to v. 11, "They forgot what he had done, and the miracles that he had shown them," quite like the request of the people to Jesus to "Show us a sign" (6:30), in spite of the sign of the feeding which he had already worked in their sight. Psalm 78 also combines the generous provision of water and drink (vv. 15-16, 20) and bread (vv. 19, 23-25) and notes repeatedly that in spite of God's wonders and signs, the people did not believe in or trust God (vv. 11, 17-19, 22, 32, 36-37, 40-43, 56-57). The same themes are found in Nehemiah 9:15. Similarly, other accounts of the Exodus and wilderness wanderings refer regularly to the "murmurings" of the Israelites against God (e.g., Num. 11:4-6; 21:5-6; Ps. 106:7, 13). According to these different

---

[42] John 6:31 echoes various OT passages, including: Exod. 16:4, "I am going to rain bread from heaven for you" and Exod. 16:15, "It is bread, which the Lord has given you to eat;" Neh. 9:15, "For their hunger you gave them bread from heaven, and for their thirst you brought water for them out of the rock;" and Ps. 78:24, "He rained down on them manna to eat, and gave them the grain of heaven."

[43] Borgen, *Bread from Heaven*, pp. 40-43. Borgen compares the citations in John with the MT, LXX and Philo. All the relevant Targums render the figurative "rain" with either "send" or "come down;" thus, "send down" (*Tg.Onq.* Exod. 16:4); "come down" (*Tg. Neof.* Exod. 16:4); "send down" (*Tg.* Ps. 78:24). Targum Pseudo-Jonathan at Exodus 16:15 reads, "And Moses said to them, 'This is the bread which has been preserved for you *from the beginning* in the *high heavens* and is now given [literally: they give you] to you to eat," thus emphasizing both the pre-existence and heavenly origins of the manna. Geza Vermes argues that Targum Neofiti at Exodus 16:15 should be translated as follows, 'The children of Israel saw and said to one another, 'What is he?' [or: 'Who is he?'], for they did not know Moses. And Moses said, 'He is the bread which the Lord has given you to eat.'" If this translation were to be adopted, the heavenly bread would symbolize Moses. However, not only is this reading questionable, but the late date of the emendations of the Targum renders it useless for the present study ("'He is the Bread' [Targum Neofiti Exodus 16:15]," *Neotestamentica et Semitica: Studies in Honour of Matthew Black*, ed. E. Earle Ellis and Max Wilcox [Edinburgh: T. & T. Clark, 1969], pp. 256-63).

accounts of the Exodus, God's provision for the Israelites did not lead to thankfulness or obedience.[44] Thus while the verbal correspondences are perhaps closest to the text of Exodus, there are thematic links to the traditions found in other passages of the people's lack of faith despite God's provisions for them.

John 6 presupposes the story of Israel's Exodus and wanderings, the role of Moses and the gift of manna, for it presupposes the activity of the one God in nourishing and leading the people of God. This link implies that the revelation through Jesus builds upon, rather than supplants, what has preceded. The historical narrative, rather than being rejected, is validated, but it must be heard through the grid of the christological interpretation of the passage. John sees a continuity with what has occurred before, but which cannot be reduced to a recurring pattern of similar events. What God has done through Jesus is "to bring to its climax . . . the whole history of Israel."[45] But the climax of a story does not erase what has come before. Rather, the climax everywhere depends upon what has gone before. Thus it is not only Scripture but the history of God's dealings with Israel (to which the Scriptures) testify which serve to attest Jesus' witness to God—again, not in the abstract, but in terms of God's provision, guidance, nurture, and care. This is also a God who continually works to gather a people to live in faithful obedience in spite of their continual murmuring, disobedience, and unbelief.

Here too the OT provides the crucial backdrop for understanding John. In Deuteronomy Moses says to the people of Israel, "You have seen all that the Lord did before your eyes in the land of Egypt, to Pharaoh and to all his servants and to all his land, the great trials which your eyes saw, the signs, and those great wonders, but to this day the Lord has not given you a mind to understand, or eyes to see, or ears to hear" (Deut. 29:2-4). Even those who were witnesses to and beneficiaries of God's acts of deliverance did not understand their implications or hear their call to obedience. Similarly, Jeremiah laments that the signs and wonders which God had done did not lead the people to repentance or obedience (32:20-23). It will be necessary

---

[44] Philo gives us an illuminating parallel when he writes of God's abundant provision for the people of Israel in their wilderness wanderings and their positive and grateful response: "We . . . do not ascribe our preservation to any corruptible thing, but to God the Parent and Father and Savior of the world and all that is therein, Who has the power and the right to nourish and sustain us by means of these or without these. See, for example, how the many thousands of our forefathers . . . [were] nourished by Him . . . how He opened fountains unknown before to give them abundance of drink for their use; how He rained food from heaven, neither more nor less than what sufficed for each day, that they . . . taking little thought of the bounties received [might] rather reverence and worship the bountiful Giver and honour Him with the hymns and benedictions that are His due" (*Spec.* II.32 §§198-99). Borgen (*Bread from Heaven*, pp. 7-10) discusses six texts from the Palestinian midrash and Philo which state that God reversed the natural order in making bread come down from heaven, rather than up from the earth.

[45] N. T. Wright, *The New Testament and the People of God*, Vol. 1: *Christian Origins and the Question of God* (Minneapolis: Fortress, 1992), p. 402.

for God to establish a new covenant, written on the hearts of the people (31:33; cf. John 6:46). Clearly, signs were to elicit obedience and faithfulness. But they evoke faith because they are God's redemptive acts on behalf of his people. They are not magnificent displays designed to coerce faith, but tokens of God's gracious and redeeming love on behalf of the people.

David Hill's apt summary of the biblical understanding of life illuminates the Fourth Gospel's view as well:

> We may reiterate what is perhaps the most significant aspect of the Hebrew understanding of 'life,' namely, its dependence on God. Wherever there is life, it is God's gift. . . . That life in all its aspects should be so dependent on God need not surprise us, for the God of the Old Testament is himself the Living God, active and creative. He is the 'Living One.' . . . Life here and now, life after death, are given and sustained by him.[46]

The miracle of the feeding of the 5000 and the imagery of "eating" and "drinking" express exactly the relationship of dependence upon God which corresponds to the view of God as "the living God," the source of life. In such dependence there is life. As Philo put it, "Is it not life eternal to take refuge with Him that is, and death to flee away from Him?"[47] Or as the Johannine Jesus puts it, "Very truly, I tell you, unless you eat the flesh of the Son of Man and drink his blood, you have no life in you" (6:53).

2. The sovereign God. God, who created and governs the world, desires human flourishing and reveals the path to it (6:27-29, 33, 39-40, 45). Because God seeks human well-being, God has made known the pathway to attaining it. This pathway is, as numerous passages from the OT show, the pathway to life, a pathway which entails obedience to the one who made the world, whose will governs the world, and who calls for obedience. Because the way of obedience, the way of life, has been made known, there is no excuse for those who fail to walk in it, and those who are disobedient or unfaithful are judged. Thus life and judgment are opposed to each other. Even as the prerogative of bestowing life belongs to the sovereign God who created all things, so also does the power to judge. That there are two paths with the different ends of life and death is a recurrent theme of the wisdom literature, in which the way of life is the way of wisdom, and the rejection of wisdom leads to judgment and death. A sampling of texts illustrates the point:

---

[46] David Hill, *Greek Words and Hebrew Meanings* (Cambridge: University Press, 1967), p. 168.

[47] Philo, *Fug.* 15 §78.

Whoever finds me finds life
    and obtains favor from the Lord;
but those who miss me injure themselves;
    all who hate me love death (Prov. 8:35; 3:16-18, 22).

Learn where there is wisdom,
    where there is strength,
    where there is understanding . . .
    where there is length of days,
        and life,
    where there is light for the eyes,
        and peace (Bar. 3:14).

The paths of those on earth were set right,
And people were taught what pleases you,
and were saved by wisdom (Wis. 9:18; cf. 7:10, 26-29;
8:13, 17; 10:17).

The same sentiments can be multiplied with respect to Torah.[48]

I will never forget your precepts,
    for by them you have given me life.
Through your precepts I get understanding;
    therefore I hate every false way.
Your word is a lamp to my feet and a light to my path
(Ps. 119:93, 104-105).

For the commandment is a lamp
and the teaching is a light,
and the reproofs of discipline are the way of life
(Prov. 6:23).

She is the book of the commandments of God,
    the law that endures forever.
All who hold her fast will live,
and those who forsake her will die (Bar. 4:1).

These two paths of life and death, of salvation and judgment, are well
known from the Fourth Gospel. Thus, for example, in chapter 5, Jesus says
"he who hears my word and believes him who sent me, has eternal life; he
does not come into judgment, but has passed from death to life" (5:24; cf.

---

[48] On this point, and for extensive references, see Epp, "Wisdom, Torah, Word," p. 134; and Borgen, *Bread from Heaven*, p. 148.

5:22, 27-29, 30). In chapter 6, the word "judgment" does not appear, but the contrast between death and life, and specifically eternal life, runs throughout the chapter. Since death serves as a figure for judgment (cf. 5:24), the contrast is also between those who are judged or condemned and those who are saved (3:16-18).

The Gospel's conception of these two actions of God, judging and saving, taking and giving life, are surely related to the theories of Philo and the rabbis of the "two powers of God" (sometimes the two "attributes" or "measures" of God), usually deemed to be the power of mercy and the power of justice.[49] Philo assigns the creative power (identified with goodness) to the term *theos*, and the royal or authoritative power to *kyrios*.[50] As "God" and "Lord," the "Existent One" exercises the powers of creation and sovereignty in the world. In the end it is the peculiar property of God to act with goodness as well as authority, with graciousness as well as punishment. The Rabbis similarly discussed "the two powers of God" as the powers of justice and mercy, and assigned mercy to God as *kyrios* (Yahweh) and justice to *theos* (Elohim).[51] The attribution to Jesus of the powers to give life and to pass judgment reflects the discussions of the divine prerogatives such as one finds in Philo and the Rabbis, and shows how the Evangelist uses contemporary conceptions of God's power to argue for Jesus as the agent and mediator of God's work and presence. Moreover, wisdom itself is envisioned as the agent of giving life and passing judgment, as we saw above, where the book of Proverbs states that to find wisdom is to find life, but to miss it or to hate it is to find death (8:35). The parallel to John 3:16-17 is arresting, for there God determines to save the world, but the response of the individual to God's sending of the Son leads either to life or death. As wisdom incarnate, Jesus brings life to those who come to him. And this is none other than the work of the life-giving God.

3. God as Father. The most common designation of God in John and in this chapter is "father." In its biblical context and historical setting, the term "father" connotes several ideas. First, "father" refers to the one who is viewed as the source of a family's life, the ancestor who provides an inheritance to his children. Second, "father" suggests providence or care,

---

[49] H. A. Wolfson calls attention to the fact that there are a variety of schemas by which Philo tries to enumerate the powers of God, sometimes counting four (creative, regal, propitious, and legislative), sometimes two (i.e. merciful and authoritative, *Cherub.* 9 §§27-28; *Sacr.* 15 §59; or beneficent and kingly, *Abr.* 25 §§124-125; *Quaes. in Exod.* 2.68) (*Philo: Foundations of Religious Philosophy in Judaism, Christianity, and Islam*, 2 vols. [Cambridge: Harvard University Press, 1947], 2:135) .

[50] There is a stimulating discussion of these passages and related passages in Philo in Jerome H. Neyrey, S.J., *An Ideology of Revolt: John's Christology in Social-Science Perspective* (Philadelphia: Fortress, 1988), pp. 25-29. See also Alan F. Segal, *Two Powers in Heaven: Early Rabbinic Reports About Christianity and Gnosticism*, SJLA 29 (Leiden: Brill, 1977), pp. 39, 159, 170-217.

[51] See Segal, *Two Powers in Heaven*, pp. 33-155.

inasmuch as the father has the obligation to care for and protect his children.[52] Third, having the power to discipline and govern his household, the father is one to whom honor and obedience are due.[53] All these characteristics of the human father are ascribed to God as Father.[54] Thus Israel is styled as God's firstborn, and so also as God's heir (Jer. 3:19; 31:9; Isa. 61:7-10; Zech.9:12). As a child, an heir, Israel owes God obedience (Deut. 32:4-6, 18; Jer. 3:19; Mal. 2:10). The paternal care of God for Israel becomes the grounds for the prophets' censure of Israel's unfaithfulness: God has protected and cared for Israel, but Israel has not remained faithful to God (Hos. 11:1, 3, 4; Jer. 31:9; 31:18, 20; Prov. 3:11-12). And even as honor and obedience are due to one's earthly parents (Exod. 20:2; Deut. 5:16), so are they due to God. "Father" connotes a social relationship, based on a hierarchy, in which the "father" and "children" are not peers. Fathers exercise their rights of discipline, require obedience, instruct, and provide, and these roles cannot be simply reversed. Yet the ideal father is one who "has compassion for his children" and who "knows how we were made; he remembers that we are dust" (Ps. 103:13, 14).

John's usage reflects all these facets of God's fatherhood. The idea of kinship and inheritance are important, perhaps more so in other chapters (e.g., chapter 8) than here. But it is notable that in this chapter only Jesus calls God "Father." It is Jesus' prerogative to identify God as his Father ("my Father," 6:32, 40; "the Father who sent me," 44, 57), for he is the Son, the heir. In all cases in this chapter in which "Father" is used of God, there is in view the relationship of God to Jesus, or something that God does for or to Jesus (6:27, 37, 40, 44, 45, 46, 57). The crowds do not refer to God as Father, even in contexts where Jesus does so (see 6:27-28) or as a counterpoint to Jesus' claims. The only mention of Jesus' father refers to Joseph. The implication is clear: apart from faith in Jesus, God is not recognized as Father, for the heir of the inheritance has not been acknowledged. Jesus can mediate relationship to God, because he is the Son, the heir, who knows the Father (v. 46), so that those who reject the heir

---

[52] For the use of Father with respect to protection and care see Tob. 13:4; Wis. 11:10; Sir. 23:1, 4; 51:10; 3 Macc. 6:3, 8; 7:6; *Jub.* 1:25, 28. For Father with the sense of progenitor or source of life, see Jer. 31:9; 3 Macc. 2:21; Philo *Opif.* 2. §7, §10; *Cher.* 14 §49, "Father of all things for he begat them"; *Mut.* 4 §29; *De. fug.* 20 §109. In *Ant.* 12.11.2 §22 Josephus states that the correct view of God is based on the etymology of the name as meaning one who "gives life." In the NT, compare 1 Cor. 8:6, "One God, the Father, from whom are all things and unto whom we exist;" Eph. 2:18; 3:14-19; 4:6, "One God, father of the universe"; 5:20; 6:23.

[53] See Mary Rose D'Angelo, "'*Abba*' and 'Father': Imperial Theology and the Jesus Traditions," *JBL* 111 (1992), 611-30; Bruce Chilton, "God as 'Father' in the Targumim, Non-canonical Literatures of Early Judaism and Primitive Christianity, and in Matthew," *Judaic Approaches to the Gospels* (Atlanta: Scholars Press, 1994), pp. 39-73.

[54] Josephus (*Ag. Ap.* 2 §§239-42) criticizes Greek conceptions of Zeus because "the father of gods is in reality a tyrant and a despot," who cannot even save his own offspring. Josephus shows that the content of "father" should rather be of one who, because he has power, uses it for the protection of his own children.

reject the Father as well and do not honor him as they ought (cf. 8:49). Even as the true heir alone knows and acknowledges the father, so the father recognizes and knows the heir (cf. 8:31-44). The heir is designated as the one on whom "God has set his seal" (6:27), the one whose authority and truth have been attested by God.[55]

The care of the Father for his children is amply demonstrated through the generous provision of the feeding of the 5000 and the promise of continued nourishment through the true bread of life, especially as these betoken the faithfulness and guidance of God in the Exodus. Moreover, the Father's providence governs the world, as the sending of Jesus for its salvation demonstrates. Nothing escapes God's providence, as the use of *panta* and other similar concepts suggests ("Everything that the Father gives me will come to me," 6:37; "This is the will of him who sent me, that I should lose nothing of all that he has given me," 6:39; "Everyone who has heard and learned from the Father comes to me," 6:45, etc.).

4. The transcendent God. God is accessible to and knowable by people through the agency of the Son. God gives the bread from heaven—but does so through the agency of the Son. God draws and teaches people, namely, those who hear and respond to the words of Jesus by coming to faith. God sustains people—now as then, but there are manifold means and agents by which God accomplishes these actions.

The chapter contains the statement that no one has seen the Father (6:46; 1:18). Throughout the Bible, there are divine manifestations in the forms of visions (Isaiah's throne vision, for example) or theophanies (Moses' burning bush) or angelic visitants (as to Abraham). But none of these is found in the Fourth Gospel. In fact the Gospel contains explicit denials that anyone has seen God. "No one has ever seen God" (1:18; 6:46), "God's form you have never seen" (5:37), and Philip's request, "Show us the Father" (14:8), point not so much in an ontological direction towards the "invisibility" or the "spirituality" of God, but towards the limitation of the vision to Jesus alone, since it is implied that God can be seen.[56] Indeed, the Son has "seen" him (1:18; 6:46). In John, God is not so much invisible or inaccessible as unrecognized.[57] Here the Gospel may well be alluding to a commonly received interpretation of Israel as meaning "the one who sees God." Israel, in other words, is the people who have "seen God," although perhaps in the person of Moses at Sinai, rather than as a whole. But if it is

---

[55] Barrett, *John*, p. 287.

[56] The literature of the Johannine circles echoes the tradition that one can see God (1 John 3:2; Rev. 4-5). In other traditions (Jewish, Christian, and philosophic), God is invisible and hence cannot be seen (*T. Abr.* 16:3, 4; Josephus, *Ag. Ap.* 2.22 §§ 190-91; *Sib. Or.* 3:11, 17; 4:12; 1 Tim. 6:16).

[57] Mark W. G. Stibbe, *John as Storyteller: Narrative Criticism and the Fourth Gospel*, SNTSMS 73 (Cambridge: Cambridge University Press, 1992), pp. 132-33; Ashton, *Studying John*, pp. 7-10.

only Jesus who has "seen God," then it would seem to imply that neither
Israel nor Moses has. Indeed this is blatantly asserted in 5:37 (cf. 1:17-18).

Because this entire chapter reverberates with echoes of the Exodus, it is
surely also likely that in view is Moses' own encounter with God on Sinai.
According to Exod. 24:10, Moses and others "saw the God of Israel." But
according to Exod. 33:20, God said to Moses, "You cannot see my face, for
no one shall see me and live." The rabbis reconciled these two traditions by
noting that Moses and others saw the glory of the Lord (1:14; 12:42).[58]
According to Philo, Moses saw God (*Mos.* 1.28 §158). Genesis 17:1 ("he
Lord was seen of Abraham") is explained by Philo not as an appearance of
"the Existent One," but as "the manifestation of one of the Potencies which
attend him" (*Mut.* 3 §§15-17). Like Philo, John limits the vision of God to a
mediator. For Philo, it is Moses; for John, it is Jesus. Apart from the
mediating role of Jesus, Israel cannot "see God," in spite of the suggestive
etymology of its name. Jesus does not take God's place or serve as God's
surrogate; rather, Jesus manifests the presence of God in such a way that to
see, with insight, what Jesus brings and accomplishes, is to enjoy a vision of
God. One does not "see God" simply by looking at Jesus; one sees God by
understanding how it is that Jesus is God's commissioned agent, the
incarnation of God's wisdom and word for the life of the world.

It is in this context that the walking on the water is probably to be
understood. This is a somewhat unusual sign in John, since no one is the
recipient of Jesus' gifts of healing or life. The theme of life, so prominent in
connection with other healings, is nowhere evident here. Indeed, there is no
interpretation of the significance of this event at all, leading some
commentators to suspect that it has found its way into the narrative simply
because of its traditional linking with the feeding of the 5000. But a few
simple items in the narrative call for attention and point to the meaning of
this event in its narrative context. First, whereas it is the crowd (6:2, 5) or
the people (6:10, 14-15) who are fed and try to make Jesus king (vv. 14-15),
it is the disciples (6:16; Andrew and Philip, vv. 5, 7, 8) who are probably to
be understood as those who are in the boat when Jesus appears to them
while they are struggling against the storm on the sea. Second, Jesus'
withdrawal from the crowds when they wished to force him to become king
(6:15) shows that the crowd has in fact misunderstood the nature of Jesus'
deed: it is not a bid for power, and Jesus' withdrawal judges their
misunderstanding. The bread of life discourse will correct their

---

[58] Segal, *Two Powers*, pp. 40, 168. In retelling the story of the giving of the law at Sinai,
Pseudo-Philo glosses Exod. 20:19f ("And they said to Moses, 'You speak to us, but do not let
God speak to us lest perhaps we die") with the following statement, "For behold today we know
that God speaks to a man face to face that many may live," thus contrasting what might happen to
them if they were to see God with what would happen to Moses (*Bib. Ant.* 11:14; cf. *Bib. Ant.*
42:10). Chilton, "God as Father," holds that the vision of God's fatherhood in the first century
was connected with his cosmological grandeur and power over creation, availability through and
response to prayer, and the peculiar relationship between God and his people.

misunderstanding, if they will hear. Finally, Jesus, having withdrawn from the crowds, "comes near" the disciples in the boat, and even appears to them using the revelatory formula *ego eimi*.

Hence, the entire scene is framed as the disciples' theophanic encounter with the Son of God.[59] That they have experienced just such an encounter will be confirmed when, after others have turned away (6:66), Peter and the twelve refuse to abandon him: "Lord, to whom can we go? You have the words of eternal life" (6:68). Even so, Jesus will later need to interpret to Philip and the others the meaning of their encounters with him: "Have I been with you all this time, Philip, and you still do not know me? Whoever has seen me has seen the Father. How can you say, 'Show us the Father?' Do you not believe that I am in the Father and the Father is in me?" (14:9-10). Not even the disciples elude the absolute Johannine statements that "No one has ever seen God" (1:18; 5:37; 6:46). But because of the unity of Father and Son, sender and agent, of God and God's wisdom/word, the one who has seen Jesus has been brought into God's own presence. The Son now gathers up into himself the roles of Torah and wisdom in mediating the presence of the transcendent God.

The insistence that Jesus embodies God's wisdom, already understood as God's law, implies that Jesus serves as the full manifestation of what the Torah intended. Thus it is Jesus—not Torah alone—who shows the way to God. It is Jesus—not bread or manna—who feeds God's people. And it is Jesus—not wisdom alone—who gives guidance for life. I have phrased the argument in this way because I believe that the author's argument does not so much intend to show that Jesus has replaced or supplanted God's wisdom and Torah, but that Jesus has fully embodied that wisdom and that Torah. To recognize in Jesus God's life-giving wisdom, one must not reject Torah and Moses, but rather understand the gifts to which they pointed and so come to see the way in which these same realities are now manifested in Jesus. One must see the same life-giving God, graciously manifested through the revelation of Torah, now also fully embodied in the person of Jesus, the "true bread."

But that God's presence is mediated through the Son does not imply that God is either absent or distant, for God actively "draws" and "teaches" (6:44-45). Crucial to the whole discourse is the quotation of Isaiah 54:13, "All your children shall be taught by the Lord." The community of Qumran viewed itself as taught by God, sometimes through the Teacher of Righteousness and its study of Torah, but other at times God was thought to instruct the heart of the individual directly (CD 20:4; 1QH 6:8-11; 7:14; 8:36; 1QS 2:3; 4:22; 10:12; 17). And there is a rabbinic text which implies that Torah scholars were taught by God (*Ber.* 64a). In John 6 the point is

---

[59] Borgen, *Bread From Heaven*, p. 180, n. 1, and "John 6," p. 270; Craig R. Koester, *Symbolism in the Fourth Gospel: Meaning, Mystery, Community* (Minneapolis: Fortress, 1995), pp. 92-94.

that God directly teaches those who hear and respond to Jesus' words. But while God teaches, God does so through the means of Jesus' word—and not through direct or mystical encounter, as the caveat of 6:46 makes clear: "Not that any one has seen the Father!"

5. The faithful God. God will bring the faithful to their promised destiny of salvation and life (6:33, 39-40, 44, 47-51, 54, 58). The extravagant provision for the 5000 calls to mind promises of the messianic age, and the feeding itself suggests the return of the treasury of manna from on high in the age to come.[60] 2 Baruch 29:6-30:1 states that at the end of time the Messiah comes, manna is restored, and the righteous rise in the resurrection and eat of it. These hopes point to the expectation of the continuity in the work of God as well as a consummation or completion of the work of God. The "omega" fits the "alpha"; the end fits the beginning.

Thus Jesus promises believers that they will have eternal life, and that he will raise them to that life "at the last day." The fulfillment of these hopes turns upon what happens in the death of Jesus: he gives his flesh as the "life for the world" (6:51). We may call attention to the following series of statements: "This is the will of him who sent me, that I should lose nothing of all that he has given me, and I will raise it up on the last day" (6:39-40); "This is indeed the will of my Father, that all who see the Son and believe in him may have eternal life, and I will raise them up on the last day" (6:40); "No one can come to me unless drawn by the Father who sent me; and I will raise them up on the last day" (6:44); "Whoever believes has eternal life" (6:47); "Those who eat my flesh and drink my blood have eternal life, and I will raise them up on the last day" (6:54); "Whoever eats me will live because of me . . . The one who eats this bread will live forever" (6:58-59). The future fulfillment of God's promises is not alien but rather integral to the entire context of chapter 6. This should scarcely surprise the reader who comes to the text with the biblical view that God is "the everlasting God" or "the living God." Eschatology, realized or future, is an aspect of John's theology, not merely his christology.

Moreover, God's actions through Jesus have as their goal the gathering together of a people, a community. In the exilic prophets, there are hopes for the restoration of the people (Isa. 43:1-8, 15; 44:6; 45:18-25; 52:7; Jer. 31-33; Ezek. 34, 37:15-18; Mic. 2:12-13; Zeph. 3:15; Obad. 21). These hopes continue to be found also in the post-exilic prophets (Isa. 59:9-21; Zech. 14:9, 16-19), as well as in several apocryphal and pseudepigraphical writings (Tob. 13; Sir. 36:1-17; 48:10; *Pss. Sol.* 8:28-34; 11:2-3; 17-18). Jesus' life and death effect this "gathering together of the children of God scattered abroad" (11:52; cf. 10:16; 12:24). This note of "gathering in" recurs in John 6 in the passages which stress that Jesus will "lose nothing of

---

[60] See Gärtner, *John 6*, pp. 14-20; Brown, *John*, 1:265; Malina, *Manna Traditions*, pp. 91-93.

all the [God] has given [him]" (6:39; cf. vv. 37, 45, 64-65). All will be
drawn and taught; none will be lost. This theme is in itself prefigured by the
climax of the story of the feeding of the 5000, in which Jesus commands his
disciples, "Gather up the fragments left over, so that nothing may be lost.
So they gathered them up, and from the fragments of the five barley loaves,
left by those who had eaten, they filled twelve baskets" (6:13-14). The
gathering of the twelve baskets, with nothing "lost," symbolizes Jesus'
unfailing faithfulness in gathering together his own, of which none are lost
(6:39; cf. 18:9; 10:28). Moreover, while the manna could be gathered only
daily, and could not be stored up lest it rot, the bread that Jesus gives
endures. Indeed it is not "food that perishes," but rather that "endures for
eternal life" (6:27). Those who are gathered by Jesus are gathered for
eternal life. Whereas those who ate the manna died (6:49), those who eat the
true and living bread "will live forever" (v. 51).

C. AN ARGUMENT FOR GOD

The author of this chapter hopes to persuade his readers to "hear and learn
from God" through and in the gifts which God has given. These gifts are
given to Israel in a particular way, as the Scriptures bear witness. Hence
Israel's history and the Scriptures aid in the human endeavor to discern the
ways of God in the world. Similarly, the sign—the feeding of the 5000—
which the bread of life discourse interprets, points to a generous and life-
giving God, a God known to Israel from its own story of the abundant
provisions in the wilderness wanderings. But God's activities are not limited
to the past, nor to Israel's past. In fact, one of the exegetical points which
the narrative hopes to make is that God is *always* in the business of "giving
life"— as in the past, so now in the present through Jesus, and in the future
as well through resurrection to eternal life. Moreover, God's life-giving
activity has a peculiar manifestation in the form of instruction, which is not
the impartation of dogma, but the creation and maintenance of relationship
between God and humankind. Finally, God's life-giving activity takes a
specific shape as well in the death of Jesus, who gives his flesh "for the life
of the world." All this is the work of God in the world, but it cannot simply
be read off the events of Jesus' ministry. Rather, God's work is to be
spiritually discerned. In the end, it cannot be discerned apart from the one
who accomplishes it. If wisdom does not exist unless God "thinks it," then
neither can wisdom be known by human beings unless God expresses it.
Since wisdom has been expressed by God, human beings are invited to
discern and receive it.

   The author of this narrative hopes to persuade those who read it to
accept these affirmations and so to find life in Jesus, the "true bread." These
affirmations can only be accepted as such by those who accept Jesus as

God's mediator, God's agent. The stress falls on every part of this identification of Jesus: *Jesus* mediates the gift of life, because Jesus is the fullest embodiment of God's divine wisdom. Because Jesus embodies God's wisdom, Jesus *mediates* or becomes the gateway to God's life. Jesus is, finally, the agent of *God*. This final point is particularly important, for the others depend upon it. If Jesus is not the agent of God then, quite clearly, he is not the embodiment of divine wisdom, nor can he mediate God's life in the world. While Jesus argues this case on the basis of his work, in the end the work of salvation itself and of bringing people to the knowledge of God are the work of God alone. The agent of this saving work is the Son, Jesus. But the gift of life is the gift of the God who sent him.

JOHN 6: CURRENT RESEARCH IN RETROSPECT

R. Alan Culpepper

The foregoing essays are a testimony to the artistry and subtlety of the Gospel of John. This remarkable piece of literature has attracted some of the ablest interpreters, who have probed every facet of its historical context, its literary texture, and its theological nuances. Working with a wide variety of methods and approaches to interpretation, these essays serve also as a milepost in the history of Johannine scholarship. They allow us to mark the progress in methodology and interpretation, and allowing us to take stock of where there is currently consensus on the interpretation of the John 6 and where differences invite further study.

The exercise of reading these essays in relation to one another is all the more instructive because of the variety of methods they employ. Anderson is eclectic, but makes significant use of rhetorical analysis. Relying on the work of J. Louis Martyn, he relates his interpretation of the chapter to a reconstructed history of the community in four periods. Painter's approach is similar, as he argues for "a developing interpretation of the tradition" (p. 61). In method, his work blends traditional, historical critical concerns for understanding a text's sources and composition history with literary and narrative critical concerns for the genre and plot of the narrative. Beutler offers an analysis of the chiastic structure of the chapter. Borgen employs historical-critical tools for the study of the relation of John 6 to John 5. Moloney and O'Day employ narrative-critical tools. Kysar illustrates the contribution of perspectives drawn from reader-response criticism. Schenke sets the debate in John 6 in relation to the schismatics mentioned in 1 John, and Thompson turns attention to the portrayal of God in John 6.

We may assess the current status of Johannine scholarship in this area by reflecting on the contributions of this collection of essays in five areas: (1) The origin and composition of John 6, (2) the unity of the chapter, (3) its structure, (4) the interpretation of John 6:51-59, and (5) the theology and purpose of the chapter.

A. THE ORIGIN AND COMPOSITION OF JOHN 6

Anderson endorses Lindars' view that John 6 is basically a unitive composition that was added to an earlier version of the Gospel as an extension of the reference to Moses' testimony in John 5:46 (p. 8). The original sequence of the chapters was 4, 5, 7, so the debate over the Sabbath in John 7:15-52 followed shortly after 5:16-47. The similarities and differences between John 6 and Mark 6 and 8 argue for common dependence on oral tradition rather than any direct dependence of John on Mark (pp. 8-11).

Painter agrees, subjecting John 6 to a close comparison with the parallel synoptic accounts. The result is that if John is dependent on the synoptics, he must be dependent on all of them, not just Mark alone. It is far more likely, Painter argues, that John is dependent on a synoptic-like source. Although the feeding and sea-crossing stories were originally independent, they had already been linked in the traditions known to Mark and John. While John uses the sea-crossing story to separate Jesus from the crowd and show his rejection of the political role into which they wanted to cast him, John did not develop the story into a theophany (contrast O'Day's reading of this story). In the discourse that follows, Painter points out that there are two references to the crowd in 6:22-35, two references to the Jews in 6:41-59, two references to the disciples in 6:60-66, and two references to the twelve in 6:67-71. A progression of Christological formulations is evident in these sections of the chapter as well. Consequently, Painter identifies 6:1-40 as the quest story in the first edition of the Gospel. Although the original quest story appears to have had a positive ending. It has been reshaped by the transition in verses 36-40 to prepare for the addition of a series of rejection stories in subsequent editions of the Gospel. The Law failed to bring life. The introduction of a new audience in verse 41 (the Jews) signals a new phase in the interpretation of the tradition. Concern shifts from the call to believe in Jesus as the emissary of God to debate over the salvific significance of his death. Similarly, the change of location and audience in verse 60 introduces a new section, which results in the rejection of those who opposed the development of a more exalted Christology and an assurance to those in the Johannine community who embraced the higher Christology of Jesus' death and exaltation. Verses 67-71 contain some conflicting elements, but on the whole Painter concludes that they are a commendation story which functions to reconcile the Johannine community with those who prized the tradition of Peter.

Borgen extends his own earlier work on this chapter by showing how progressively it demonstrates that "Jesus is not just the Prophet-like-Moses, John 6:1-21" (pp. 98-99); that Jesus is "The Son of Man—the Father's Accredited Envoy, John 6:22-27" (pp. 100-102); that he is "The Manna-bread from Heaven, the Sign of the Son of Man, John 6:28-59" (pp. 103-111); and then reports the reaction among the disciples, John 6:60-71 (pp. 112-113). Borgen also shows how John 5:31-47 serves as "the thematic background of ch. 6" (pp. 113-115) in its present sequence.

The essay by Borgen follows Painter's because Borgen extends his own earlier interpretation of this chapter by engaging Painter in debate at four points. First, Borgen takes issue with Painter's treatment of the sea-crossing as an extension of the feeding story, arguing that the sea-crossing shows that while Jesus withdrew from the crowd he came to the disciples. The story describes "an authentic and epiphanic encounter with Jesus" (p. 99). Second, Borgen responds to Painter's challenge, that verse 35 is the pronouncement to which the dialogue in verses 25-35 leads, and hence that the Old Testament quotation in 6:31b does not have the central function that Borgen attributes to it (pp. 80-81, 107). Third, Borgen contends that Painter's attribution of the quest stories in 6:1-35 to the first edition of the Gospel and his assignment of the rejection stories that follow to the second edition breaks down in 6:36-40 (pp. 85-86, 108). Verse 36 already indicates that the crowd did not believe. Fourth, the two differ over the significance of the introduction of the term "the Jews" in verse 41. Painter contends that it signals the introduction of another phase in the interpretation of the tradition; Borgen responds that this change of terminology cannot mean that "the Jews" rejected Jesus while the crowd did not (pp. 86-89, 110).

With the exception of Schenke, the contributors to this volume who raise questions about the composition history of the Gospel favor the view that John 6 is informed by a synoptic-like tradition rather than by dependence on one or more of the synoptics. The relationships between John 6 and the ending of John 5, on the one hand, and between the debates in John 5 and 7, on the other, can both be explained if John 6 was added at a secondary stage to an early edition of the Gospel in which John 7 followed immediately after John 5. If that is the case, however, one encounters the anomaly that the story of the feeding of the 5,000, the only miracle found in all four Gospels, which appears to be the core of the tradition of Jesus' Galilean ministry, is a secondary addition to the Gospel of John. Anderson and Painter, however, have also demonstrated that John 6 itself reflects an extended composition history that reflects various periods of the history of the Johannine community.

B. THE UNITY OF JOHN 6

Challenging long-held assumptions, Anderson contends that John 6 is a unity and that "'aporias' are not necessarily indicative of editorial seams in John 6" (p. 4). John 6 is stylistically, literarily, and theologically a unity. The theme of testing and the presentation of false notions of spiritual reality by each of Jesus' conversation partners and his responses to each serve as the organizing principle. In each case the misunderstanding has a rhetorical function. The four dialogue partners reflect four crises in the life of the Johannine community. In each case, again, something Jesus says or does evokes a response from the dialogue partner that reflects a fundamental misunderstanding, and a clarifying discourse follows.

1. The crowd: The misunderstanding of Jesus' miracle revolves around the failure to distinguish physical and existential nourishment (6:25-40).
2. The Jews: The dialogue with the synagogue juxtaposes the torah and the Bread from heaven (6:29-51).

3. The disciples: The threat of a second schism over the issue of Gentile converts with docetizing tendencies evokes affirmations of the corporeality of Jesus' body (6:51-66).
4. Peter: The portrayal of Peter illustrates Johannine Christianity's dialectical relationship with the mainstream church (6:67-70).

From the progression of these four misunderstandings, Anderson is able to reconstruct the history of Johannine Christianity in four periods:

Phase 1: *Beginning Chapters* (55-70 CE)—The gospel comes to Asia Minor; the evangelist brings with him his own independent gospel tradition.
Phase 2: *Tensions with the Local Synagogue* (70-90)—A reform effort on the part of scripture-based Pharisees following the destruction of the temple succeeds in drawing some Jesus-followers back into Judaism.
Phase 3: *The Onset of Roman Persecution and the Departure of Gentile Christians*—Persecution by Domitian caused some Gentile Christians to renounce their faith. In response, the Johannine leadership emphasized the Lordship of Christ and the importance of his suffering and death in the flesh.
Phase 4: *Tensions with the Mainstream Church*—While the mainstream church established an institutional structure that maintained Christ's connection to the church through the apostles, Johannine Christianity, with its emphasis on Spirit and kinship, responded by compiling and "publishing" the witness of the Beloved Disciple.

The complexity of John 6 is due in part, therefore, to its evolution and development throughout the course of the history of Johannine Christianity. It remains not only as a record of the history but as a testimony to the genius of Johannine Christianity in coping with schism by re-interpreting its theological traditions and re-presenting them in narrative form. In the end, John 6 calls on all its readers to abandon human ploys and rely continually on God, through the revelation in Jesus Christ for that which sustains life.

Beutler finds evidence in the chiastic structure of the chapter for "the internal coherence of the existing discourse on the Bread of Life including its so-called 'eucharistic' section" (p. 130). We will discuss Beutler's proposal in detail in the next section, but it certainly represents the prevailing sentiment that John 6 is a literary unity as it stands, even if it is the product of a complicated composition history as Anderson and Painter contend.

C. THE STRUCTURE OF JOHN 6

Anderson takes issue with Borgen's influential study, arguing that the manna texts seldom served as the primary or Proem text, but often as a rebuttal or "trump card." In this case it is a card played by the crowd in their effort to manipulate Jesus into providing more bread—hence, not unlike the Tempter's use of scripture in the synoptic temptation scenes. The four discussants, or conversation partners, offer four interpretations of the bread (6:25-40, 29-51, 51-66, 67-70). For Anderson, therefore, analysis of the literary structure of the chapter provides an opening for understanding its composition history and the historical setting of each section.

Beutler's contribution is primarily concerned with the structure of John 6 and its implications for interpretation. Beginning with a division of the chapter into scenes identified by changes in time, locale, or characters, Beutler finds a well-developed chiasm in the chapter. Although he focuses on the discourse in 6:22-59, the chapter has two introductions and two conclusions, resulting in the following structure.

A. 6:1-15
    B. 6:16-21
        C. 6:22-27
            D. 6:28-29
                E. 6:30-33
                E'. 6:34-40
            D.' 6:41-51
        C'. 6:52-59
    B'. 6:60-65
A'. 6:66-71

The discourse is built around Jesus' first self-predication, "I am the Bread of Life" in 6:35 and moves toward the climactic confession at its conclusion. Beutler finds confirming correspondences between the matched pairs of exchanges in this dialogue. The significance of such a chiastic structure is that it shows the internal coherence of John 6, including the so-called eucharistic section.

Moloney joins in the argument for the unity of the chapter, though he divides it into a different set of units: (1) 6:1-4, an introduction to the narrative; (2) 6:5-15, the miracle of the loaves; (3) 6:16-21, the sea-crossing; (4) 6:22-24, a second introduction; (5) 6:25-59, the discourse on the bread from heaven; and (6) 6:60-71, the κρίσις created by the word of Jesus, which elicits two responses in 6:60-65 and 6:66-71. Moloney also endorses Borgen's thesis that the discourse is a homiletic midrash based on the text in 6:31. Moloney's own contribution, however, falls in the area of the theology and purpose of John 6 (discussed below).

Close comparison of these proposals regarding the structure of John 6 reveals that while there is a general consensus about some of the major divisions, the readings differ greatly regarding the structure of this chapter. For example, Anderson and Moloney begin a new section with verse 35, while Beutler does not. Beutler and Moloney begin a new section with verse 60, while Anderson does not. Moreover, the relationship between stages of composition and the final literary structure of the chapter still calls for further attention.

D. THE INTERPRETATION OF JOHN 6:51-59

Maarten Menken mounts a carefully considered challenge to the widely held interpretation of John 6:51c-58 as a unit of material that deviates from the christological orientation of the rest of the discourse by virtue of its explicitly eucharistic language. Menken reexamines the basis of this line of interpretation, demonstrating that it does not stand up to rigorous examination. On the contrary, these verses extend the Christological focus of the rest of the discourse. The eucharistic interpretation of John 6:51c-58 is based on the presumption that these verses introduce four changes in the discourse: (1) Earlier in the discourse Jesus himself is the bread, but beginning with v. 51c, "Jesus' flesh and blood are the bread from heaven" (p. 190); (2) Earlier Jesus said that the Father gives the bread from heaven; now he says that he will give the bread; (3) In these verses the eating of bread ceases to be symbolic language and must be understood literally; and (4) In the foregoing part of the discourse the issue was Jesus' heavenly origin; from 51c on it is his "corporality and humanity" (p. 190).

Menken responds that the first two changes do not support a eucharistic interpretation, and the latter two presumed changes are not supported by the text. Beginning at verse 51c the bread is Jesus' flesh, and from verse 53 on it is combined with his blood. Contrary to the usage of flesh and blood in the eucharistic formulations in the other gospels and Paul, however, the preceding discourse has already qualified the bread as Jesus himself. Like other Johannine discourses, John 6 also ends with references to Jesus' death and its salvific significance. The first change beginning at verse 51c does not, therefore, require that the eucharistic interpretation of these verses becomes primary. Likewise, the words, "which I shall give," cannot refer to the distribution of the eucharistic bread but to Jesus giving himself in death: "Jesus *gives* what he *is*: the bread of life" (p. 198). This understanding of Jesus' words is supported by John 3:16, "he gave," and Jesus' allusion in 4:34 to fulfilling the work he was sent to do. Eating the bread of life (6:50, 51), therefore, must also be understood metaphorically as believing in Jesus as the one whose death gives life to the world. Finally, Menken argues, it is unnecessary to regard 6:51c-58 as antidocetic. Like the rest of John 6, these verses respond to the Jewish misunderstanding of the salvific importance of

Jesus' death. There is no reason to doubt that Johannine Christians celebrated the Eucharist, or that John 6:51c-58 uses eucharistic language, but its primary emphasis is Christological. As a result, John 6:51c-58 is an integral part of John 6.

With surprising unanimity, other contributors also support the view that John 6:51c-58 is an integral part of the chapter. Anderson writes pungently: "The 'eucharistic interpolation in John 6" is neither (p. 5). These verses, he contends, interpret Jesus as the bread in relation to the cross and in opposition to the docetizing tendencies. Painter argues that it is unnecessary to view John 6:51c-58 as a redactional addition since these verses merely extend the foregoing concern with "the life-giving function of the giving of Jesus' life for the world" (p. 89). Kysar does not discuss the composition history of the chapter but merely comments that regardless of whether verses 51b-58 were a later addition or not, "the passage exhibits a unity as it stands" (p. 175 n. 17). Agreeing with Painter, Kysar says that verse 59 need not be taken as a major division in the text (p. 176 n. 18). In another passing comment, Kysar warns of the danger of domesticating the Gospel's language and evacuating the ambiguity and mystery of the metaphor in these verses by reading it exclusively in terms of the Eucharist (p. 180 n. 25). Likewise, the sacrament should be allowed to retain some of the ambiguity of the metaphor.

One of the chief contributions of this collection of essays, therefore, is to reverse the long-held view that John 6:51c-58 is a later redactional insertion that jarringly introduces a eucharistic interpretation of the bread of life theme. The continuities of theme and language are much stronger than was previously assumed, meaning that these verses should now be read as an integral part of the discourse.

E. THE THEOLOGY AND PURPOSE OF JOHN 6

Drawing on the narrative-critical work of Girard Genette, Moloney discovers a fascinating literary and theological coherence in the chapter's prolepses, i.e., narrative references that allude to or foreshadow coming events. The first prolepsis occurs in 6:12-13, when Jesus instructs the disciples to gather the κλάσματα so that they may not be lost. The gathering of the κλάσματα opens the possibility that they continue to be available in some way for the disciples. In verse 27 Jesus points to the food "which the Son of Man will give to you." Then Jesus promises bread that will give life to the world (6:32-33). Those who come to him will never hunger or thirst (6:35). The intensified concern with the bread or food that Jesus will give is further clarified by the prolepsis in 6:51c, "The bread which I shall give is my flesh for the life of the world." The clarification, however, introduces a new set of questions: how will Jesus "give his flesh"? Answers begin to emerge in 6:53-54. Jesus' gift will be the gift of his flesh and blood: "Jesus will offer his broken body and his spilt blood, his whole self, as the bread which will give life to the world" (p. 149). This series of prolepses, therefore, draws the reader into a fuller grasp of the significance of Jesus' coming death, much as do the "lifting up" sayings. Although the emphasis is not primarily eucharistic, the language of 6:53-57 certainly carries eucharistic overtones that provide a resolution for the building set of prolepses in this discourse: "It is in the Eucharist where one can encounter the flesh and blood of Jesus the Christ, and the κλάσματα consigned by Jesus to his disciples (vv. 12-13) have lurked behind the story reminding the reader of such celebrations" (p. 151).

Gail O'Day turns her attention to a neglected paragraph in John 6: the story of Jesus walking on the water. Noting that most Johannine scholars have explained the presence of this story in John as evidence of an early linkage in the oral tradition with the story of the feeding of the multitude, O'Day responds, "That Jesus walking on the water is included at all (note its absence in Luke) and in this particular location in John 6 derives from narrative and theological strategy and not simply the requirements of the tradition" (p. 156). The first clue to John's narrative strategy appears in the way in which John alters the easy transition from the feeding story as one sees it in Matthew and Mark by means of Jesus' rejection of the crowd's understanding of his identity and by his abrupt ascent of the mountain. By noting the absence of details from the tradition in Matthew and Mark in the Johannine account, O'Day finds that the focus of the story is not on the disciples' distress but on what the disciples see: "The Johannine story of Jesus walking on water is a story of theophany, not rescue. It is a story of the revelation of the divine in Jesus" (p. 159). Jesus demonstrates God's sovereign dominion over the chaos. Moreover, John omits any reference to the disciples' terror or mistaken identity of Jesus as a phantom. Jesus' language in 6:20 is theophanic; the emphasis is on disclosure, "I am, do not be afraid." Extending Borgen's argument for the integral relationship between John 6 and the latter section of John 5, O'Day shows how the theophany in 6:15-21 buttresses the argument in 5:19-30 that Jesus shares in "the character and identity of God" (p. 163).

Whereas Painter and Borgen contend that the story of the sea crossing serves to separate Jesus from the crowd and to contrast Jesus and the crowd, O'Day argues that the theophany provides an important corollary to the feeding story and serves as an important part of the background for the discourse that follows. Within the larger scope of the Gospel, this story supplies a vivid confirmation of the unity of the Father and the Son that is declared in the prologue, in 5:19-30, and in 10:30. Rather than a scrap of tradition that was included almost by accident in the Gospel, in the light of O'Day's reading of John 6:15-21 one can see that the story is in fact "emblematic of the theological reality in which the entire Gospel is grounded" (p. 165.).

Robert Kysar shares his own critical reading of the text, claiming neither that it should be normative nor that it engages the major Christological themes of the chapter. Instead, he points to the ways in which the discourse progressively and systematically undermines the reader's confidence in decisional faith. While Kysar detects eight discrete movements, with four dialogue partners, he calls attention to the recurring vocabulary and themes that provide continuity for the whole discourse and discourage treating it as an aggregate of discrete units. Departing from other commentators, Kysar perceives the crowd not as "wrongheaded" or "confused" but as "genuine seekers," even if they are confused by Jesus' language and their motives are "less than the ideal" (p. 175 n. 16). Throughout the discourse, the reader encounters metaphorical language that calls the reader to re-conceive and re-image faith and life and the role of Jesus as the sustainer of life. Contrary formulations are juxtaposed. The importance of faith is maintained, but repeatedly Jesus says that one cannot believe unless he or she is "called," "drawn," or "chosen" by the Father. The phrase "the work of God" (6:29) further undermines the reader's assumptions about faith: "Do I do God's work when I believe, or is God's work the creation of faith in me?" (p. 182). As the discourse builds to Peter's confession, it may seem to return to the importance of the individual's response, but again Jesus tells the twelve that they had been chosen (6:70). Even more unsettling, one of them is a devil. Kysar concludes that "the passage performs the demolition of any confidence in faith conceived as human decision" (p. 184). In conclusion, Kysar observes that Christology both evokes human response and is itself the assertion of faith. Second, "to speak of faith is always to speak of a response to divine presence" (p. 185). The discourse, however, has shifted even the possibility of confidence or certainty from the human response through faith to the reality that "the Word still lives among us" (p. 185).

Ludger Schenke's work on John 6:60-71 could just as easily have been treated above in the sections on the composition and origin of John 6 because it has far-reaching implications for one's understanding not only of this chapter but of the history of the Johannine community and the relationship between John and the synoptics. Schenke contends that these verses were written by the evangelist in light of the schism in the Johannine community that is evident from 1 John 2:18f. and 4:1-6. Moreover, Schenke reads the exchange between Jesus and the disciples who remained with him on the basis of the Jewish idea of God rather than against the background of a hellenistic/dualistic docetism. John 6:59, he argues, has "a clear dividing function" (p. 211) and what follows has a narrative character. Those who stay with Jesus are not just the Twelve but other disciples also. In the exchange, Jesus asserts that "The 'ascent' leads the 'Son of Man' to 'where he was before.'" This clarification is pivotal because it responds to a Jewish Christian denial of the incarnation. The Johannine schismatics reflected in the position of the disciples who withdrew from Jesus did not deny the

256   R. ALAN CULPEPPER

humanity of Jesus (and hence they were not docetists). They rejected the
identification of the "earthly/exalted Jesus" with the divine Logos (p. 218).
As a result, the evangelist responds, they make Jesus a "mere human
being."

The conclusion of Schenke's exegesis is that the Johannine schismatics
maintained a Jewish-Christian rather than a docetic orientation. They
sought, conservatively, to protect monotheism and divine transcendence.
Jesus was a mere human being who became the "Christ" and the "Son of
God" through the resurrection/exaltation. The treachery of one of the twelve
shows that the group that favored the Petrine tradition was vulnerable to
defections also. Finally, Schenke contends that these verses reflect not only
the Johannine situation but also the evangelist's knowledge of Mark, as the
evangelist shows that the tradition of the Johannine community is in
agreement with that of the "great church" (p. 223).

Marianne Meye Thompson examines the theological center of John 6.
What does it say specifically about God? The focus of her essay is all the
more important because, as she observes, in this Gospel, "Jesus is *God's*
agent for the salvation of the world, the revealer of *God*, the way to *God*,
and the life from *God*" (p. 227). The Jewish concept of agency sheds some
light on the particular way in which Jesus is depicted in the Gospel of John,
especially the dependence of the Son's work on the Father, the
subordination of the Son to the Father, the declaration that honoring the Son
honors the Father, and the language of sending. On the other hand, the
interpretation of Jesus as a *shaliach* figure does not explain some of the
most distinctive features of John 6: the descent of the Son from above, or
the importance of the language of eating and drinking. For these conceptual
elements the materials of the wisdom tradition are more helpful. Reflection
on "word" and "wisdom" was thoroughly interrelated by the first century,
and the law was at times symbolized by manna.

The view that John develops a wisdom Christology also provides a
useful category for understanding how John presents the "closeness of
continuity" between Jesus and the Father. It is not a close relationship such
as one might find between two separate but closely related figures but rather
one is the expression of the other. Wisdom has its origin in God, manifests
the presence of God, and accomplishes God's life-giving work. Thompson
perceptively analyzes the ways in which the deeds and discourse of Jesus in
John 6 characterize God: (1) God is the source of all life; (2) God's
sovereignty governs the world; (3) as Father, God calls forth and provides
for a people as his children; (4) although transcendent, God is accessible
through multiple means and agents; and (5) God will bring the faithful to
salvation and life. As Thompson shows, each of these facets of Jesus'
characterization of the Father develops motifs that are already present in the
wisdom tradition. The author of John 6, therefore, shows that God is
continually giving life, but that "life-giving activity takes a specific shape"

in the life and death of Jesus. God's work is spiritually discerned, but those who are able to discern find life in Jesus, the "true bread."

It is not the purpose of a collection of essays such as this to furnish final answers or end debate. These essays began as working papers in the ongoing work of the Johannine Seminar of the Society for New Testament Studies. They reflect a diversity of concerns, traditions, methods, and theological perspectives. Each contributor has called attention to facets of the gospel narrative that have been neglected or read differently in the past. Now, as a milestone in the study of John 6, they invite other contributions and responses.

INDEX OF REFERENCES

INDEX OF AUTHORS